ADVERTISING
AND SOCIETY

Second Edition

ADVERTISING
AND SOCIETY
An Introduction

Edited by Carol J. Pardun

WILEY Blackwell

This second edition first published 2014
© 2014 John Wiley & Sons, Inc.

Edition History: Blackwell Publishing Ltd (1e, 2009)

Registered Office
John Wiley & Sons Ltd, The Atrium, Southern Gate, Chichester, West Sussex, PO19 8SQ, UK

Editorial Offices
350 Main Street, Malden, MA 02148-5020, USA
9600 Garsington Road, Oxford, OX4 2DQ, UK
The Atrium, Southern Gate, Chichester, West Sussex, PO19 8SQ, UK

For details of our global editorial offices, for customer services, and for information about how to apply for permission to reuse the copyright material in this book please see our website at www.wiley.com/wiley-blackwell.

The right of Carol J. Pardun to be identified as the author of the editorial material in this work has been asserted in accordance with the UK Copyright, Designs and Patents Act 1988.

Library of Congress Cataloging-in-Publication data is available for this book.

ISBN 9780470673096 (paperback)   1007537320

A catalogue record for this book is available from the British Library.

Cover image (main) © Matthew Ashton/AMA/Corbis; burger © Sukharevskyy Dmytro / Shutterstock
Cover design by Simon Levy

Set in 10/12.5pt ITC Century by Toppan Best-set Premedia Limited
Printed and bound in Malaysia by Vivar Printing Sdn Bhd

3   2016

Contents

Notes on Contributors

Penny Abernethy is the Knight Chair of Journalism and Digital Media Economics at the University of North Carolina at Chapel Hill. She previously held executive positions at several news organizations, including the *Wall Street Journal*, the *New York Times*, and *Harvard Business Review*. Her research has focused on new business models for news organizations.

Saleem Alhabash is an assistant professor at Michigan State University where he has joint appointments in the Department of Telecommunication, Information Studies and Media, and the Department of Advertising and Public Relations. His research focuses on the processes and effects of new and social media.

Beth E. Barnes is director of the School of Journalism and Telecommunications at the University of Kentucky where she also serves as associate dean for undergraduate and international programs for the College of Communication and Information. She has worked with several journalism and mass communication programs in Europe and Africa. Her research has focused on strategic communication campaign development and media audience research.

Charles Bierbauer has been dean and professor in the College of Mass Communications and Information Studies at the University of South Carolina since 2002. He is a former Washington and foreign correspondent with CNN and ABC News. He was president of the White House Correspondents' Association in 1992–3. His teaching and writing focus on the intersection of media, politics, and government.

Michael L. Capella is the associate dean of Graduate and Executive Programs, and an associate professor of Marketing, at the Villanova School of Business at Villanova University. His research focuses on topics related to marketing and public policy issues, including advertising effects, pharmaceutical marketing, and retail pricing strategy. Prior to joining the academy, he spent almost 10 years in professional sales management with a food manufacturer.

Angeline G. Close is an assistant professor in advertising and public relations at the University of Texas at Austin. Her expertise is in event marketing – namely how consumers' experiences at sponsored events influence attitudes and consumer behavior as well as the business aspect of advertising.

Timothy Dewhirst is an associate professor in the Department of Marketing and Consumer Studies at the University of Guelph in Canada. Much of his research has focused on tobacco marketing and public policy, and he has also provided expert testimony in Canadian and US tobacco litigation. He is an associate editor of the *British Medical Journal* publication, *Tobacco Control*. He served as an invited consultant for the World Health Organization, in which he was named an expert for the elaboration of a template for a protocol on cross-border advertising, promotion, and sponsorship (with respect to the Framework Convention on Tobacco Control).

Kathy Roberts Forde is an associate professor in the School of Journalism and Mass Communications at the University of South Carolina. She is a media historian with primary interests in the role of print culture in democratic struggle. She is an associate editor of *American Journalism* and the director of the Media and Civil Rights History Symposium.

Marie Hardin is a professor of journalism and associate dean of the College of Communications at Penn State University. She is also associate director of the John Curley Center for Sports Journalism and director of the Arthur W. Page Center for Integrity in Public Communication. Her research has focused on issues of ethics and diversity in mediated sports.

Joe Bob Hester is an associate professor in the School of Journalism and Mass Communication at the University of North Carolina at Chapel Hill. His research interests include social media, research methodology, and media agenda-setting. He can be followed on Twitter at @joebobhester.

R. Michael Hoefges is an associate professor in the School of Journalism and Mass Communication at the University of North Carolina at Chapel Hill, and teaches media law. He has published numerous articles in mass communication and legal journals, and is a public member of the National Advertising Review Board. He earned his JD and PhD from the University of Florida and was in private law practice for about eight years.

C. Ann Hollifield is the Thomas C. Dowden Professor of Media Research and department head of the Department of Telecommunications at the University of Georgia. She is the former chair of the Elected Standing Committee on Research for the Association of Education in Journalism and Mass Communication and currently serves on the Executive Board of the University of Georgia's Teaching

Academy. Her research focuses on media economics and management and the impact of information industries on economic development.

Adrienne Holz Ivory is an assistant professor in the Department of Communication at Virginia Tech. Her research interests include health communication; media effects; media portrayals of gender, race, and sexuality; and the social impact of new communication technology.

James D. Ivory is an associate professor in the Department of Communication at Virginia Tech. His primary research interests are in the social and psychological dimensions of new media and communication technologies, particularly the content and effects of interactive communication technologies such as video games, virtual environments, and simulations. He is the current chair of the International Communication Association's Game Studies Interest Group.

Anne Johnston is a professor in the School of Journalism and Mass Communication at the University of North Carolina, Chapel Hill. Her research interests include political communication, diversity issues in the media, and media coverage of sex trafficking. She has taught courses in research methods and gender and communication.

Wan Seop Jung is an assistant professor of Marketing Communications at the American University in Dubai with expertise in designing and teaching marketing communication courses. His research interests include advertising effects, with emphasis on dual mediation modeling and direct-to-consumer drug advertising.

Peggy Kreshel is an associate professor of advertising at the Grady College of Journalism and Mass Communication and an affiliate faculty member of the Institute for Women's Studies at the University of Georgia. She is a member of the American Academy of Advertising and the Association for Educators in Journalism and Mass Communication. Her research interests are feminist media studies; media culture and diversity; and advertising history, professional culture, and ethics.

Jane Marcellus is a professor at Middle Tennessee State University where her research focuses on gender representation and women in early twentieth-century journalism. A former head of the AEJMC Cultural and Critical Studies Division, she has been published in *Journalism & Mass Communication Quarterly*, *American Journalism*, and *Feminist Media Studies* and is the author of *Business Girls and Two-Job Wives: Emerging Media Stereotypes of Employed Women* (Hampton Press, 2011).

Debra Merskin is an associate professor of media studies in the School of Journalism and Communication at the University of Oregon. She is the author of *Media, Minorities, and Meaning: A Critical Introduction*. Her research focuses on the ethics of representation of women and people of color in media.

Margaret Morrison is a professor and director of the School of Advertising and Public Relations at the University of Tennessee, Knoxville. She is the former vice president and treasurer of the American Academy of Advertising. Her research focuses on issues related to brand planning. She teaches courses in qualitative research, advertising campaigns, account planning, and advertising and society.

Jon P. Nelson is professor emeritus of economics at Penn State University, University Park. He is the author of three books and over 100 articles. He has been a reviewer and consultant for the National Institute on Alcohol Abuse and Alcoholism, Robert Wood Johnson Foundation, American Civil Liberties Union, and the International Center for Alcohol Policies. His current research is focused on meta-analysis in economics, especially advertising and pricing of alcohol.

Dan Panici is an associate professor of communication and media studies at the University of Southern Maine. He is currently serving on the editorial board for Journalism and Communication Monographs and manuscript reviewer for the *Journal of Broadcasting & Electronic Media*. His research interests include children and media, media ecology, and media framing and sports.

Carol J. Pardun is a professor of advertising and director of the School of Journalism and Mass Communications at the University of South Carolina. She was president of the Association for Education in Journalism and Mass Communication from 2009 to 2010. She is currently a member of the Accrediting Council on Education in Journalism and Mass Communication. Her research has focused on the impact of the media on early adolescents' sexual health.

Charles Pearce is emeritus professor of advertising at Kansas State University where he was the associate director of the School of Journalism and Mass Communications. He previously taught at Southern Illinois University in Carbondale, the University of Nebraska in Lincoln, and Middle Tennessee State University.

Geah Pressgrove is an assistant professor of public relations at the Perley Isaac Reed School of Journalism at West Virginia University. Her research has focused on public relations, emergent technologies, and nonprofits, while her teaching interests encompass areas of strategic communication.

Tom Reichert is a professor of advertising and department head of Advertising and Public Relations in the Henry W. Grady College of Journalism and Mass Communication at the University of Georgia. He teaches advertising and mass communication courses, and his primary research examines the prevalence, nature, and effects of sexual information in persuasive communication.

Kathy Brittain Richardson is a professor of communication and provost at Berry College in Rome, Georgia. She has served as editor of Journalism & Communication Monographs and is the author *of Applied Public Relations* and coauthor of *Media Ethics: Cases in Moral Reasoning*. Her research has focused on product placement, media ethics, and music video imagery.

J. Walker Smith is executive chairman of the Futures Company. *Fortune* described Walker as "one of America's leading analysts on consumer trends." He is coauthor of four books, a columnist for *Marketing Management*, a blogger for Branding Strategy Insider, a former public radio commentator, and a frequent keynote speaker, including the opening presentation at TEDxPeachtree 2012. He is a member of the N.C. Advertising Hall of Fame.

Charles R. Taylor is the John A. Murphy Professor of Marketing. He is a past president of the American Academy of Advertising and has received the Ivan L. Preston Award for Outstanding Contribution to Research. Taylor currently serves as editor-in-chief of *International Journal of Advertising*. His research interests include public policy issues in advertising, international advertising, and consumer behavior.

Esther Thorson is professor, associate dean for graduate studies, and director of research for the Reynolds Journalism Institute at the School of Journalism, University of Missouri–Columbia. Thorson has published extensively on the news industry, advertising, news effects, and health communication. Her scholarly work has won many research and writing awards and she has been adviser on more than 40 doctoral dissertations. She applies research, both hers and that of her colleagues, in newsrooms and advertising agencies across the United States and abroad.

Albert R. Tims is director of the School of Journalism and Mass Communication at the University of Minnesota. He is president of the board of directors of the National Scholastic Press Association and the Associated Collegiate Press. His research on public opinion formation, social cognition, and political advertising has appeared in *Communication Research, Journal of Advertising, International Journal of Public Opinion Research, Human Communication Research*, and *Journalism Quarterly*.

Debbie Treise is a professor in advertising and senior associate dean of Research and Graduate Studies at the University of Florida's College of Journalism and Communications. She was president of the American Academy of Advertising in 2012. Her research is centered around health and science communications.

Tom Weir is an associate professor in the School of Journalism and Mass Communications at the University of South Carolina. His research focuses on media effects, assessment, and information-gathering. He has twice received the Golden Torch Award for excellence and has been recognized as the Advertising Educator of the Year by the tenth district of the American Advertising Federation.

Erin Whiteside is an assistant professor of Journalism and Electronic Media at the University of Tennessee. Her research explores the relationship between social issues and sports media, and her work has recently appeared in *Communication, Culture & Critique, Journal of Sports Media*, and *International*

Review for the Sociology of Sport, among others. She is an active member of the Association for Education in Journalism and Mass Communication, serving as the chair of the Sports Communication Interest Group, from 2013 to 2014.

Kevin Wise is an associate professor of strategic communication and codirector of the Psychological Research on Information and Media Effects (PRIME) Lab at the University of Missouri School of Journalism. His research explores how different features of online media affect cognition and emotion.

1

Introduction

Why Does Everyone Have an Opinion about Advertising?

Carol J. Pardun

University of South Carolina, USA

Will Rogers once said, "Advertising is the art of convincing people to spend money they don't have for something they don't need." On the other hand, at the beginning of his address to the Advertising Federation of America at the Hotel Pennsylvania in New York City on June 15, 1931, Franklin D. Roosevelt had this to say about advertising:

> If I were starting life over again, I am inclined to think that I would go into the advertising business in preference to almost any other. The general raising of the standards of modern civilization among all groups of people during the past half century would have been impossible without the spreading of the knowledge of higher standards by means of advertising.

So, which is it? A noble method for improving modern civilization? Or a questionable process to wrestle money out of the hands of people who can't afford to let it go? The reality is, it's a bit of both. And, that's what this book is about. Both sides of controversial issues about advertising.

The pros and cons of advertising have been debated ever since advertising emerged as the means to support our growing mass media consumption habits. A few years ago, I went sailing along the Amalfi Coast of Italy. We stopped along the way to visit Pompeii, a place that had intrigued me since I was a kid and first saw pictures of people encased in lava ash casts from the great volcano. Experiencing the ancient city of Pompeii for myself was breathtaking. But what surprised me even more than the former citizens forever frozen in screams of terror was seeing some frescoes on some buildings' remains. They were faint

---

Advertising and Society: An Introduction, Second Edition. Edited by Carol J. Pardun.
© 2014 John Wiley & Sons, Inc. Published 2014 by John Wiley & Sons, Inc.

(the volcano erupted in 79 AD, so it's not a surprise that these paintings had faded over time!) but clear enough to see that these pictures were a kind of early outdoor advertising displaying what customers could expect if they entered the store.

Clearly, business people of modern civilization understood very early that it is important to convey some kind of message to people that you hope would eventually buy what you're selling. In the hundreds of years since, advertising has only become more important.

It's no coincidence that advertising as an industry grew alongside businesses in the United States during the industrial revolution. Before technology allowed products to be mass produced far away from their point of sale, consumers had to rely on their home-town merchant to decide what products to provide. They would most likely visit the country store where the manager would sell whatever goods he had available. You most likely bought a pound of flour. You didn't get to choose between Gold Medal and King Arthur. But, once mass production took off, all sorts of products flooded the market and advertising was needed to make sense of the choices – and also to help create the needs for the different choices.

While the slogans might be different today, the basic premise is the same. Advertising is still helping us to understand the differences between products – even if they are only perceived differences. (Really, there's no discernible difference between Coca-Cola and Pepsi-Cola, but don't try telling the die-hards that!)

To consider the roles and responsibilities that advertising can have in a society, it's helpful to think about the specific role that advertising has played in the growth of some companies. One of my favorites to look at is General Electric. My dad was a lifelong GE executive. I had the privilege (and challenge!) of moving all over the country during my childhood as my father oversaw the growth of GE's appliance parks. One of the happy side effects of being a GE family was being early adopters of some of the electric gadgets that the company would develop. The first iteration of electric curlers was interesting – and painful! The early electric potato peeler was another curiosity. (As far as I could tell, it looked like a regular peeler. You still had to make the peeling motion. It just came with a little motor.)

Inventor Thomas Edison was the mastermind behind General Electric. Begun in the late 1800s, GE has consistently been a leader in innovation, both in its products and in its advertising. Its current advertising slogan "Imagination at Work" seems to embody the mission of GE. Much of its advertising through the years has been trying to explain new products to the potential consumer. From the light bulb, to electric irons, to refrigerators, when GE started advertising these products – consumers didn't know they needed them. But who today would say that the light bulb is a luxury?

So, at the very least, advertising can provide important information about products. The controversy tends to be when the advertising moves beyond information. As historian Michael Schudson (1984) has said, advertising lets us know how things ought to be. Of course, it's the advertisers' opinion on how this is conveyed – and that's often when the conversations get heated.

A Mirror of Society, or an Agent of Change?

Over 20 years ago, Richard Pollay (1986) wrote a scholarly article laying out the argument about the role of advertising. It's a seminal paper and has been quoted by many advertising scholars through the years. Whenever I teach an advertising class, I ask my students those two questions on the first day of class. Is advertising a mirror of society? Or is it an agent of change? The basic premise is something like this: If advertising were a mirror of society, then the advertising industry is not really to blame for all the problems associated with bad advertising. *We're* to blame. If we don't like the ads, we should stop watching the shows that they're on, or stop buying the products, or tell the advertising agencies that we hate their ads. But if we respond (as we might to sexy ads), then that shows advertising is only going in that direction because it's what we want. It's a reflection of our culture. We look in the mirror and we see (and have no one to blame but) ourselves.

On the other hand, could advertising be an agent of change? This means that advertising can change our views about a particular product and eventually contribute significantly to what we purchase. *If that's true, then it's advertising's fault we're the way we are.*

I'll admit that I am a huge fan of reality television. I love any cooking contest show (*Master Chef* is a favorite), and I love *Property Brothers, House Hunters International, Shark Tank, American Idol, The Sing-Off, The Voice,* and those are just the top-of-mind shows. I do not watch *Here Comes Honey Boo Boo.* But about 2.5 million of us do. (For a cable show, that's a highly respectable number.) No one claims this show elevates our society. But *Honey Boo Boo* is clearly a vehicle that can attract advertising because the audience is solid. Without exception, the show exploits people. So why should we be surprised if the advertising on that show is also low-brow? Shows like *Here Comes Honey Boo Boo* are classic examples that provide evidence that advertising is a mirror of society.

But how about agents of change? The above discussion of General Electric's advertising is a good example here. People didn't know that they needed light bulbs. The *advertising* told them that they did. Consumers responded and welcomed electricity into their homes. If ever there was an agent of change, this was it. With electricity, people could stay indoors longer, which changed the amount of time they sat on their front porches, which changed the amount of time they communicated with their neighbors, and so on. Sure, advertising wasn't the only reason this happened – but it certainly played a part.

What about Apple's now iconic Macintosh *1984* Super Bowl commercial? That one commercial ushered in a whole new way of thinking about computers. It was most definitely an agent of change. (Okay, some would also argue it was a mirror of society in that we were ready for the change. See how complicated this is?)

While these are only a couple of examples, they demonstrate how many people through the years have argued that all sorts of ads have impacted people and persuaded them to change their buying behaviors – and ultimately their lives. Some people claim they have friends who drink vodka now simply because of those funky, art-inspired ads. Of course, they never think advertising has impacted them personally. Only others. (This is called third-person effect and there are whole books written on this very interesting media theory.) Many people have argued that advertising is to blame for why so many young kids smoke. You'll read more about that in Chapter 5. So there is a lot of evidence that advertising is, indeed, an agent of change.

Now, at this point, you're probably thinking the answer's clear: it's both – advertising must be both a mirror of society *and* an agent of change. That's right, of course. But it's way more interesting – and instructive – to stick to one side or the other. That's what I make my students do. When I ask the "agent of change"/"mirror of society" question on the first day of class, they typically start out answering the expected "both." I ask them to explain. The answers are not very interesting. After a few minutes of trying to give an "on the one hand/on the other hand" answer, they give up, shrug their shoulders and say, "Well, it just is. I don't know why."

Then I tell them they have to choose a side. Each student must vote one way or the other. I have the "mirror of society" people move to one side of the class-room and the "agent of change" people move to the other side. Then I'll ask them to tell me why they are on the left (or right) side of the room. Finally, the answers start getting interesting. My students really start to think. They start to get passionate about the issues. They're starting to form an opinion. They're learning.

That's what this book is about. It's about examining the controversies, thinking about the consequences of perspectives, and then choosing a side. Intuitively we already know that both sides have merits, but we end up learning more about *both* sides if we're willing to argue *one* side. Even if we argue a side we don't actually believe, we can come to appreciate the other side of the argument and learn more about our own convictions.

There are a number of fine books on the market that deal with the impact of advertising on society. What is different about this book is that it is organized by "controversies and consequences." I've asked a number of advertising experts to write essays about a controversial topic – but to write the essay primarily from one perspective. I found that as I read the essays I would be persuaded by the first argument – and then persuaded by the second argument. With the essays side by side, it becomes easier to see that these topics are complex and not to be dismissed easily.

The idea for this book came out of a class I taught when I was an advertising faculty member at the University of North Carolina at Chapel Hill. I had my students conduct research and debates about many of these very topics. I put them into teams without considering what their personal views were about a particular topic. In fact, if I knew they felt one way, I would try to put them on the opposite team. After researching the topic and trying to develop a strong argument, they would begin to see that the other side also had a point. Over the course of the semester, they came to understand that there is more than one way to look at just about everything that has to do with advertising – and many other socially oriented subjects.

That class – in 2005 – was the last class I taught at UNC – and the students wholeheartedly embraced the notion of thinking more deeply about controversial issues. Of all the classes I taught during my tenure there, that was by far my favorite class. In their quest to find answers, these students helped me become a student again. Every one of those 40 students helped me to think more critically about advertising. I will be forever grateful to each of them.

What's Different about the Second Edition?

The first edition of *Advertising and society: Controversies and consequences* was published in 2009. Some things have changed since then – and some have not. Therefore, for this second edition, I've divided the books into two parts: "Enduring Issues" and "Emerging Issues." The enduring issues have been around for years – and most likely will continue to be important to examine. Sex in advertising, tobacco advertising, and the use of stereotypes in advertising are examples of enduring issues.

But there are some new issues that are tackled in this second edition. Advertisements in journalistic environments (Chapter 12) is a good example. In recent years, we've seen more and more advertisements in places that would have been off-limits just a few years ago. That's the financial reality in which our media now reside. But is it right?

Advertising in the world of social media (Chapter 10) is another example of an emerging issue. As ads permeate Facebook and other social media outlets, are there new privacy issues that should make us rethink our approach to advertising?

Some of the original essays have been updated for this edition. But some of the essays (even in the "Enduring Issues" section) are completely new. I've also updated and expanded the questions at the end of each chapter as well as provided some ideas for other debates you could have that are related to these topics.

But what hasn't changed is looking at controversial issues from more than one perspective. How convincing are the essays in this edition? *You decide.*

Ideas to Get You Thinking . . .

1   Think about all the great ads you've seen recently and not so recently. What do they have in common? Why do you think you can remember them?

2   Make a list of everything you would change about advertising if you could. How different would the world look if you had the power to adopt every change you wrote down? Would it be a better world? Why or why not?
3   If you could create *one* law about advertising, what would it be? Why?
4   Can you think of an example of an ad that might have changed your behavior (or attitude) about a product? If not yourself, what about a friend? What did the ad do that was so effective?
5   Do you and your friends have a favorite cola? If so, try a blind taste test. (For example, you might compare Diet Coke and Diet Pepsi.) How many could tell the difference? What did you learn from this?

If You'd Like to Know More . . .

Berger, A. (2007). *Ads, fads, and consumer culture: Advertising's impact on American character and society*. Lanham, MD: Rowman & Littlefield.

Bronstein, C. (2012). Advertising and the corporate conscience. *Journal of Mass Media Ethics* 27(2): 152–154. doi:10.1080/08900523.2012.684597

Burt, E. V. (2012). From "true woman" to "new woman." *Journalism History* 37(4), 207–217.

Cushman, D. P. and Sanderson, S. (2003). *Communication best practices at Dell, General Electric, Microsoft, and Monsanto*. Albany: SUNY Press.

Gandy, O. H., Jr. (2012). Advertising, society, and consumer culture. *Journalism & Mass Communication Quarterly* 89(2): 322–324. doi:10.1177/1077699012442837

Reich, L. S. (1992). Lighting the path to profit: GE's control of the electric lamp industry, 1892–1941. *Business History Review* 66(2): 305–334.

Rotzoll, K. B. and Haefner, J. E. (1996). *Advertising in contemporary society: Perspectives toward understanding*. Urbana: University of Illinois Press.

Schneider, T. and Woolgar, S. (2012). Technologies of ironic revelation: Enacting consumers in neuromarkets. *Consumption Markets & Culture* 15(2): 169–189. doi:10.1080/10253866.2012.654959

Sheehan, K. B. (2003). *Controversies in contemporary advertising*. Thousand Oaks, CA: Sage.

Zlatevska, N. and Spence, M. T. (2012). Do violent social cause advertisements promote social change? An examination of implicit associations. *Psychology & Marketing* 29(5): 322–333. doi:10.1002/mar.20524

References

Pollay, R. W. (1986). The distorted mirror: Reflections on the unintended consequences of advertising. *Journal of Marketing* 50(Apr.): 18–36.

Schudson, M. (1984). *Advertising, the uneasy persuasion: Its dubious impact on American society*. New York: Basic Books.

Part I

Enduring Issues

2

The Economic Impact
of Advertising

> *Mass demand has been created
> almost entirely through the
> development of advertising.*
>
> Calvin Coolidge

Some topics in advertising are just plain more interesting than others – or so it might seem. Should cigarette advertising be regulated? To what level do we manipulate children with advertising? How far can we stretch the truth in our advertising claims? But – economics in advertising? Who wants to talk about money anyway? And what's the controversy?

In reality, the topic of the economic impact of advertising is critical – and fascinating! Have you ever thought about what the world would look like without advertising? Sure, the highways might be more natural without billboards, but it's a lot more convenient (and safe!) to learn about what exit to take for the next Cracker Barrel when we're hungry than it is to check our smartphones. Without advertising, would we have as many food choices in the grocery store? Perhaps we would end up with only store brands as choices. If I walked down the aisles and saw 10 choices of laundry detergents, but couldn't recall any advertising images, would I be equipped to figure out which brand I wanted?

Advertising and Society: An Introduction, Second Edition. Edited by Carol J. Pardun.
© 2014 John Wiley & Sons, Inc. Published 2014 by John Wiley & Sons, Inc.

What would happen to our favorite television programs without the commercials in them? Without advertising, would we still have magazines to read? What about the newspaper? We don't often think about the role that advertising plays in letting us consume the different kinds of media we have come to rely on. Things that we get for free – or nearly free – like newspapers, magazines, radio, primetime television, are all supported by advertising. Then there are the people who work in advertising, creating the ads, buying and selling the ads, and so on. How much does advertising contribute to our economy anyway? What kind of money are we talking about?

You have probably heard about the outrageous costs of a 30-second Super Bowl commercial ($3.5 million on average for 2012, give or take a few hundred thousand dollars!). Any way you look at it, there is a lot of money involved in advertising.

Why Is the Economic Impact of Advertising an Ethical Issue? What's the Controversy?

This chapter attempts to answer the question of whether advertising ultimately increases or decreases the price of products. Why should we care anyway? Think of it this way: If advertising actually lowers the price of products, it means that people who may not be able to afford a product without advertising can do so *with* advertising. It might not be so important whether or not we can buy luxury items, but if a mother can afford to buy healthy food for her children because the prices are held in check thanks to advertising, it's not too much of a stretch to see how this can become an ethical – and controversial – issue. However, what if the above were true, but in the process the advertising creates false needs for a mother who can't really afford the particular food? Like pomegranate juice, for example. Some research indicates the antioxidant value of drinking pomegranate juice, but it's expensive compared to other juices.

Or, what if the price of the product the mother wanted were, indeed, lower, but a cheaper brand (perhaps the store brand) with the same ingredients is also available? (Tropicana 100 percent orange juice versus Kroger 100 percent orange juice, for example.) The price for the Tropicana orange juice might be lower than it would be without advertising, but the mother would actually be spending more money because she chooses Tropicana when she should pick the Kroger brand because the advertising made her think that Tropicana was healthier for her children. Would it be a controversial decision then?

And who says we need all these choices, anyway? When I walk down the grocery store aisle, it's a little stressful to try to figure out exactly what kind of peanut butter I need. The one with honey? The natural one? The one that Choosy Mothers Choose Most?

But I also like choice. I would hate to walk through the grocery aisles and only have "Value Packs" to choose from. I like to ponder the differences between my rainforest-friendly whole-bean coffee and my naturally brewed ground Kona. Besides, the last time I checked, this was a free market economy. People are free to buy – or not.

The authors of these essays, C. Ann Hollifield and Penny Abernethy, have written many articles about the business side of advertising. Here they take nuanced opposite approaches and each makes compelling arguments for their particular side. Hollifield argues that, generally speaking, advertising lowers the price of products. Abernethy, however, disagrees – but with a twist. Her argument is that there is an add-on cost to advertising (a tax, if you will), but it is a small price to pay for the benefit that it brings us – benefits like a free press, information, and a robust democracy. Does advertising make products cheaper (by increasing competition) or more expensive (passing the ad expense on to the customer)? *You decide.*

Ideas to Get You Thinking . . .

1   Make a list of all the advertising you encounter in a given day. Besides television, think of billboards you pass on your way to work or school, commercials that pop up on the radio, Internet ads that pop out at you without warning. Make a list of all the kinds of people who you imagine might be involved in these ads. Go beyond the obvious. How long is your list? Are you surprised?

2   How much would you be willing to pay for your media use without advertising? Would that be enough to cover the cost of the medium? Do some research and see if you can figure out how much it costs to produce. What would happen to the media without advertising?

3   Think about your use of social media. Have you noticed an increase in the advertising on social media sites? What do you think about that? See if you can compare some non-advertising-supported with ad-supported social media. What are the advantages and disadvantages of each? For example, if you have a smartphone, look at some apps that are free. Do they have an advertising option? Is the only way you can have the more complex apps to pay for them? Which do you prefer?

Other Topics to Debate

1   Advertising costs have gotten out of control. Therefore, the government needs to limit the amount that advertisers can charge networks for Super Bowl advertising.

2   There should be stronger advertising regulations on the benefits of products so that consumers can tell whether a more expensive product is worth the price.

3   Consumers have a right to know how much advertising is spent on products
they consume. Therefore, this information needs to be readily accessible to
everyone.

If You'd Like to Know More . . .

Ekelund, R. B. and Saurman, D. S. (1988). *Advertising and the market process: A modern economic view*. San Francisco: Pacific Research Institute.

Goldfarb, A. (2006). State dependence at internet portals. *Journal of Economics & Management Strategy* 15(2): 317–352.

Kirkpatrick, J. (2007). *In defense of advertising: Arguments from reason, ethical egoism, and laissez-faire capitalism*. Claremont, CA: TLJ Books.

Liu, Y., Yang, Y. K., and Hsieh, C. (2012). Regulation and competition in the Taiwanese pharmaceutical market under national health insurance. *Journal of Health Economics* 31(3): 471–483. doi:http://dx.doi.org/10.1016/j.jhealeco.2012.03.003

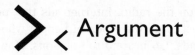

Argument

Advertising lowers prices for consumers

C. Ann Hollifield

University of Georgia, USA

When the economy slows – as it did during the severe recession that affected the United States and much of the world beginning in 2008 – experts look for ways to boost economic activity. Advertising is supposed to increase sales of advertised products, so you would expect businesses to advertise more during hard times. In fact, however, the opposite usually happens. Advertising is often one of the first budget items most businesses cut as sales drop during hard times.

Given that's the case, experts ask whether advertising *really* boosts sales and, if so, why? What effect does advertising have that causes sales to rise? Research shows that advertising does increase current and future earnings at the industry level for most products (Graham and Frankenberger, 2011). Additionally, for consumer and industrial products, the positive effects of advertising on sales are stronger during recessions than they are when times are better, although the same is not true for service industries. Finally, the positive effects on sales were found to last for up to three years after the advertising campaign. But the question that was not answered by recent research was the question of *why* advertising increases sales, particularly during recessions.

There are several possible explanations. One is that advertising may help consumers remember specific products and increase the perception that the product has value, even if the consumer can't buy the item right away.

Another possible explanation is that advertising increases sales by lowering the prices of products through increased consumer demand and competition between products. This second explanation leads us straight into another controversy, however. Experts have long debated whether advertising helps lower product prices or, conversely, causes prices to rise by adding marketing costs to the costs of production. It's an important question and one that is worth exploring.

Advertising Increases Demand

Without question, the relationship between advertising and prices is complicated. There is evidence to support both sides of the argument. Research suggests that advertising has different effects on prices depending on (1) what part of the manufacturing and distribution process you look at and (2) on what type of product is being sold.

So how does advertising act to lower prices? There are several ways. First, advertising increases demand (Steiner 1973; Leach and Reekie 1996; Erdem et al. 2008). In a study of the toy industry, Steiner demonstrated that after the Mattel Company began advertising on *The Mickey Mouse Club* in 1955, demand for toys, in general, and for heavily advertised toys, in particular, rose sharply in the United States. During the same period, demand for toys remained unchanged in countries where toys were not heavily advertised.

As demand rises, manufacturers gain what are known as "economies of scale." This means that it costs the manufacturer less to produce each unit of a product as the total number of units it makes of that product rises. The cost savings come about because the manufacturer is able to spread overhead costs such as the costs of raw materials, labor, and manufacturing equipment over more units, thereby lowering the cost of each individual unit. As production costs per unit fall, the manufacturer can cut the price charged for each unit sold and still maintain the same level of profit. In industries where there are many manufacturers and, thus, a lot of competition, manufacturers may pass along some of the gains from economies of scales to consumers by lowering prices.

But as those who argue that advertising raises prices point out, manufacturers don't always pass on the savings. Instead, they sometimes keep them as increased profits. Even then, however, the increased demand created by advertising can still lower prices. As consumer demand for a product rises, retail stores sell more of the product and the products move off of stores' shelves faster. Steiner (1973) found that as the sales of advertised products increased, retailers cut prices by reducing *retail* profit margins on the products. The retailers were willing to take less of a markup on each item because they made more money overall as the result of higher sales volumes. This idea of selling more for less is the basic business model for discount retailers, but it requires high consumer demand for the products sold.

Critics argue that when advertising focuses consumer demand on a particular brand of a product, the price of that brand may rise as the manufacturer and retailers try to maximize profits from consumers' brand loyalty. However, even if the prices of the most popular brands increase, if advertising increases overall consumer demand for a product category, the number of manufacturers producing versions of that product will grow. Retailers often offer both brand-name and private-label versions. As the number of brands battling for market share increases, consumers will have more product choices. Usually, the average price for the product category then falls, even if the price of certain name brands remain high (Steiner 1973; Albion and Farris, 1981).

An example of this would be the rapid decrease in the price of flat screen HD TVs. Between 2006 and 2011, the average price of flat screen HD TVs fell dramatically – more than 60 percent for some models. While it is not possible to attribute the lower prices for such products to advertising directly, it is clear that as demand for these products increased, prices fell.

Advertising Is Information

Another way advertising lowers prices is by providing consumers with product information. Advertising informs consumers about the range of products available and, sometimes, the prices at which those products are being sold. As consumers become more aware of their choices, the level of competition at both the manufacturing and retail levels goes up, which causes the prices for the advertised products to come down. Research has shown that when a producer or retailer advertises a product on the basis of price, competitors often cut their prices in response.

Advertising is particularly effective in helping lower the prices of "convenience" goods as compared to "non-convenience" goods (Reekie 1977; Albion and Farris 1981). Convenience goods are products such as soap, soft drinks, toothpaste, and so on, where the price is low, the product is quickly consumed and frequently replaced, and there is little risk to the consumer in making a "wrong" choice.

Advertising puts downward pressure on the price of convenience goods in several ways. First, the prices of convenience goods are so low to begin with that the risk in buying the wrong product is minimal. As a result, consumers don't invest much time in researching convenience products, and advertising is the primary source of information about product choices. Thus, advertising materially affects consumers' purchase decisions. Second, advertising may make some brands of convenience goods so well known that retailers are almost forced to stock them (Steiner 1973). When that happens, retailers often cut prices on the brand-name products, using them as "loss leaders" to attract customers away from competing retailers.

Finally, the information function of advertising can help lower the price of even unadvertised products. As individual brands in a product category are advertised, consumers develop a general idea of what products in that product category should cost. This has the effect of creating an invisible "price cap" on most, if not all, products in the category. Manufacturers and retailers hesitate to raise prices above that perceived cap out of fear that consumers will start thinking those manufacturers or retailers are overpriced on everything they sell (Steiner 1973).

Research suggests that advertising has less effect on the prices of more expensive, "non-convenience" goods such as cars, expensive clothing, or high-end electronics. Non-convenience goods cost more and consumers tend to own them and use them for longer periods of time. Thus, buying decisions for non-convenience goods are riskier for consumers. While advertising may make consumers aware that a particular non-convenience product is available, consumers are unlikely to actually buy the product without doing additional research and talking with the sales staff at the retailer (Reekie 1977).

Advertising Improves Operating Efficiencies

A third way advertising may help keep prices low is by improving retailers' operating efficiency. Advertising informs consumers about the product choices available and the specific characteristics of individual brands. Customers who feel able to make buying decisions based on the information they've gained from advertising don't need as much customer assistance from the retailer. That allows retailers to cut back on customer-service costs by replacing sales clerks and customer-service representatives with searchable inventory computers and self-service checkout devices. The result has been a move toward a self-service economy, but some of the cost savings are passed on to consumers through lower prices.

A final way advertising keeps consumer prices low is by helping new competitors gain a foothold in the market. One of the biggest challenges facing new manufacturers and retailers is making potential customers aware that they exist. Advertising helps create that awareness. As competition in a market increases, prices fall as the competitors vie for market share.

Conclusion

Despite the arguments and evidence that advertising helps keep consumer prices low, the debate on the issue is unlikely to be settled any time soon. For one thing, it is almost impossible to directly test the effects of advertising on prices. The problem is that it is difficult, if not impossible, to find consumer products that are *not* advertised in some way. That makes it hard to study the relationship between advertising and price (Albion and Farris 1981). Similarly, slight differences in products make it hard to judge whether price variations are caused by differences in advertising or by differences in product quality, product size, or even packaging (Telser 1964; Reekie 1974).

Another complicating factor is that research shows that higher-quality and, by extension, higher-priced products are more likely to be advertised than lower-quality and lower-priced products (Telser 1964; Reekie 1974; Albion and Farris 1981). But it's not clear why that's the case. Are higher-priced products more likely to be advertised in order to increase the likelihood that they will sell? Or does increased advertising create the need for higher prices?

Because of questions like these, we can expect the debate over the effects of advertising on prices to continue. It is likely that the truth lies somewhere between the extremes of the argument: the relationship between advertising and prices probably varies depending upon the type of product being advertised and the amount of competition between manufacturers and retailers.

What is clear is that the long-standing argument that advertising *raises* prices can no longer go unchallenged. There is substantial evidence that advertising has played an important role in the development of discount retailing and low-cost private-label brands. We can conclude, therefore, that consumers benefit – in some cases, at least – from advertising because advertising *lowers* prices for some of the most commonly used products. Thus, during difficult economic times advertising provides benefits to both businesses and consumers.

References

Albion, M. S. and Farris, P. W. (1981). *The advertising controversy: Evidence on the economic effects of advertising*. Boston: Auburn House.

Erdem, T., Keane, M. P., and Sun, B. (2008). The impact of advertising on consumer price sensitivity in experience goods markets. *Quantitative Marketing and Economics* 6: 139–176.

Graham, R. C. and Frankenberger, K. D. (2011). The earnings effects of marketing communication expenditures during recessions. *Journal of Advertising* 40(2): 5–24.

Leach, D. F. and Reekie, W. D. (1996). A natural experiment on the effect of advertising on sales: The SASOL case. *Applied Economics* 28: 1081–1091.

Reekie, W. D. (1974). *Advertising: Its place in political and managerial economics*. London: Macmillan.

Reekie, W. D. (1977). The market in advertising. In I. R. C. Hirst and W. D. Reekie (eds.), *The consumer society*. London: Tavistock Publications, pp. 65–89.

Steiner, R. L. (1973). Does advertising lower consumer prices? *Journal of Marketing* 37 (Oct.): 19–26.

Telser, L. G. (1964). Advertising and competition. *Journal of Political Economy* 72: 537–562.

Counterargument > <

Advertising makes products more expensive

Penny Abernethy

University of North Carolina, USA

As consumers, we witness it all the time. A new technology is unveiled with great fanfare – the iPhone, for example. "Early adopters," who can afford the hefty price tag, race to purchase it and pronounce it a must-have. Noticing the demand for the new product, other manufacturers develop their own versions of a smartphone. Over time, the price we pay comes down substantially.

Economics 101 teaches us that the price of the goods and services we purchase is determined by the intersection of supply and demand. The more demand for a product, the more incentive producers – both the original manufacturer, as well as "imitators" – have to increase supply and, over time, this increase in supply usually brings down the price.

In the twenty-first century, advertising and marketing are essential to creating demand – whether it involves introducing a product in a cluttered global marketplace, inducing consumers to try a new item, or reinforcing their loyalty once they have switched. But marketing comes at a cost that must be taken into account when a manufacturer decides what price he or she will charge for a product.

Accounting 101 teaches us that in order to make a profit, a producer needs to recoup all his or her costs – the fixed costs of developing and manufacturing the very first product, plus all the direct and indirect costs associated with each item he or she then offers to the consumers.

Marketing costs can be direct – such as the amount of advertising a manufacturer spends on television or magazine commercials to promote the product. Or it can be indirect – such as the salary paid to an employee to tweet about the new product or to befriend users on the company's Facebook page.

Therefore, as consumers, we should acknowledge *both* classic economic theory and pragmatic accounting principles and assume that a savvy producer has priced the product to cover the cost of marketing. This means that the price we pay may come down over time, as advertising and marketing increase demand. But regardless of what we pay, the price is still higher than it would be if the producer did not have to pay to market the product.

Unfair Tax or Public Good?

If, using this logic, we conclude that advertising or marketing ultimately makes products more expensive – if only marginally – we are then confronted with a secondary economic policy issue: Is advertising an unfair excise tax on consumers? Or could it be construed as a public good? (National defense is an example of a public good, since our collective taxes ensure the safety of all US citizens.)

Classical economists tend to focus on the symbiotic interdependency of the industrial revolution, which enabled mass production of products, and the growth of advertising, which allowed manufacturers to introduce their products to the masses directly (spread over 3,000 miles in the continental United States) without an intermediary – a wholesale distributor.

But advertising has also provided the financial underpinnings that fueled the growth of the mass media in the United States – from print in the nineteenth century to broadcast in the twentieth century to digital in the twenty-first century. With the introduction of each new medium has come a new method for advertisers to reach consumers – from display and classified advertising in newspapers and magazines to commercials over radio and television airwaves to search advertising in the digital world.

In the early nineteenth century, newspapers, pamphlets, and magazines depended on the fees they charged consumers – either through subscriptions or street sales – to cover the cost of both producing and distributing their publications. This business model constrained the size and profitability of media entities since it was limited by the amount consumers were able and willing to pay. The arrival of mass market advertising changed everything.

Today, between 80 and 90 percent of the revenues – and all of the profits – booked at a typical consumer media company comes from advertising. This is true whether it's Google, or the large television networks, or the small community newspaper in your hometown. (Consider this: In most cases, the cost of an annual subscription for a popular monthly magazine barely defrays even a small portion of the cost of distributing that magazine to your doorstep, to say nothing of the cost of producing the content that goes into the magazine.)

Advertising has become such a big business in the United States that it accounts for roughly 2 percent of the US gross domestic product (GDP) in any given year – and has for a century. Recent research at the University of North Carolina (UNC) suggests that if the definition of advertising is broadened to include new forms of nontraditional marketing nurtured by the digital world – such as search or mobile couponing, or sponsorship of online events and content – advertising may actually account for upwards of 5 percent of GDP.

In other words, advertising is a major US industry that employs a substantial number of people, and, in the process, aids the growth of its national economy. (In terms of dollars spent, the United States is by far the largest advertising market in the world. It is almost triple the size of the next largest national market, Japan.)

But advertising has done more than provide paychecks for a sizable portion of the population (including those employed in manufacturing, who benefit indirectly as a result of increased demand for certain products). It has also fueled the explosion and profitability of mass media in the United States. And that may be the strongest argument in support of the notion that advertising in the United States is a public good – or an indirect "tax" that benefits us all.

As a result of the advertising revenues that flow into newspapers such as the *New York Times* or your small hometown newspaper, we have access to timely and credible news and information that help us elect public officials wisely and, in turn, help them (from the mayor to the president) make better decisions about issues that affect the quality of our daily lives and the state of our democracy.

Similarly, advertising revenues at the *Wall Street Journal* or at regional business magazines give us insights into the workings and future profitability of companies, both public and private. This information provides needed transparency for our capitalist economy and gives potential investors credible information about current strategies and business practices. This, in turn, further promotes the growth of our national economy.

So, as the founders of our country intended, thanks to advertising and the dependable profitable business models that evolved over the last century, news media have grown into their intended role of public watchdog – of both government and industry. We depend on them to be the Fourth Estate or the fourth public arm of government.

But the benefits do not stop there. We depend on the marketing dollars of industry to fund the production and/or distribution of much of our quality entertainment – from the *CBS Playhouse* series in the 1950s to the PBS imports on public television stations today.

So, when making both private and public decisions – from listening to a radio program or electing a county commissioner – we have available to us a multitude of inexpensive, quality sources of news and information, as well as entertainment. The production and distribution of that inexpensive quality news and entertainment is made possible in the United States by the small indirect "tax" we all pay on each item we purchase (which, in turn, covers the manufacturer's cost of advertising that product.)

Creative Destruction and the Future of Advertising and Mass Media

As just illustrated, the vibrancy and financial health of our mass media – and by extension the advertising industry that supports it – have historically been good for our democracy and our capitalist economy.

But we are living through a period of immense economic disruption in the media and advertising landscape. As they say in the financial world, past performance is no indication of future returns – especially in a digital age.

The economist Joseph Schumpeter coined the term "creative destruction" to describe just such a disruption of business models. Ultimately, all media and advertising companies will have to transform themselves if they are to survive and thrive in the twenty-first century. But the transformation will not be easy – nor will it occur overnight. At the moment, our oldest mass medium – newspapers – is most at peril. You should care about the survival of newspapers for two reasons.

First, they have, historically, set the agenda for public debate – determining which public policy issues we focus on. Research done at the University of North Carolina in the late 1960s and 1970s concluded that newspapers – both large and small – accomplish this by choosing which stories consistently get front-page treatment. The broadcasting outlets follow suit, by giving these stories more air time.

Newspapers evolved as agenda setters in the twentieth century because editors and publishers established standards for objective and fair reporting while simultaneously erecting a "wall" between advertising and editorial departments to prevent advertisers from exercising influence over editorial matters. This wall led to consumer credibility. In an age of product placement and digital sponsorships of online content, this wall between advertising and other editorial content is breaking down – in news, as well as entertainment – with unknown consequences.

Second, and equally important, by some estimates, as much as 80 percent of the public policy reporting that makes it into the general news "food chain" (such as the local television or radio show, or online search engine) originates with newspapers. Research at Duke University has shown that news consumers do not typically seek out this type of content. In the online world, for example, consumers most consistently search for news and information about sporting events, how-to articles or gossip on celebrities and public figures. There is little consumer demand for objective or investigative news articles about public policy issues.

Newspapers were the original aggregators of all sorts of news and information – including gossip, sports, and how-to articles, along with investigative pieces and breaking news. They funded those front-page public policy stories through the fees they charged advertisers who paid to be part of the daily bundling of news and advertising called the newspaper. In the process of skimming over the headlines, consumers often came across a public policy issue they previously didn't know they should care about.

In a disaggregated age, who funds public policy reporting? And how will the vast majority of us know what is happening in our own backyards if we able to search for and read only articles that interest us?

In the early 1970s, then UNC Professor Maxwell McCombs set out to prove a statement made in the mid-1960s by Charles Scripps, chairman of Scripps-Howard Newspapers, who observed that – despite the introduction of two new media (radio and television) in the first half of the twentieth century – the amount of money spent on advertising had remained "relatively constant" – roughly 2 percent of GDP.

This is called the *principle of relative constancy* and it has very dismal economic implications for traditional media – such as newspapers, magazines, and broadcasting – in the twenty-first century. It basically suggests that existing media are destined to accept a smaller and smaller piece of the advertising revenue pie as new media enter the market and siphon away existing advertising dollars from traditional media. Economists call this a "zero sum game." Taken to its logical conclusion, it means that newspapers – and public policy reporting – will be greatly diminished in this digital age as the Internet and mobility gain traction, and advertisers move dollars out of print into online venues.

But recent research conducted at UNC pegs the amount of money spent on all types of marketing – not just traditional advertising – at 5 percent (instead of 2 percent). This offers the potential for a different outcome – especially for savvy, forward-thinking newspaper publishers who take advantage of the new forms of interactive marketing and advertising made possible by the digital age, and previously unavailable to advertisers in the twentieth century.

Even traditional advertising – a one-way message designed to increase demand for a product – has historically performed numerous functions, from introducing a new one to reinforcing loyalty on an old one. The digital age, with its interactivity, opens up a panoply of other options for all traditional media that embrace it. As the digital age matures, smart and creative media owners will learn to accurately assess the value of the marketing opportunities they can offer advertisers and to price according to the value delivered.

This is called *value-based pricing* – as distinct from cost-based or demand-based pricing. There are numerous examples already in the marketplace – from the subscription prices offered to students versus adults on newspapers to lower pricing of long-distance phone calls in off-peak business hours. The digital age requires a whole new way of thinking about the value delivered by a print advertisement versus a television commercial versus a digital banner ad. Pricing based on click-throughs of online advertising is but the first step in the evolution to a new form of digital value-based pricing of advertising.

Those who can't imagine a new way of doing things are victims of "cultural lock-in," according to Richard Foster, a senior fellow at Yale University's School of Management and author of *Creative destruction: Why companies that are built to last underperform the market*. These companies are doomed to a slow corporate death – they will either be subsumed by other more vibrant corporations or slowly slip into bankruptcy. The technology landscape is littered with such companies. The question is whether a decade from now the advertising and media landscape will also be in this position.

In a lecture at Indiana University, entitled "The rise and fall of American mass media: Roles of technology and leadership," UNC professor Donald Shaw (1991) looked at the life cycle of three mass media in the United States – newspapers, magazines, and broadcasting. He examined specifically how magazines had adjusted to the rise of radio and television. The successful magazines focused on profitable niches, which in turn attracted advertisers intent on reaching certain target audiences.

His lecture, delivered in a pre-Internet age, nevertheless offers very relevant conclusions about today's situation: "While media rise and fall, and audience interests shift, there has been a constant need for (news) and advertising information . . . The means changed; the needs did not." What's most needed during a time of disruption and change, he concluded, are "leaders (who) creatively use technology and content to hold or reach unique audiences" (Shaw 1991).

This seems a fitting coda for this essay, as well as a challenge for advertisers – and for the media companies they have nurtured over the past two centuries in the United States. Historically, we consumers have paid an indirect tax on the goods and services we ultimately purchase – a tax that has defrayed the marketing costs that promoted those products. But that tax has also created an economic public good – making high-quality entertainment and credible news and information inexpensively available to all in the United States.

The digital age disrupts that business model. The question is whether it can be beneficially recreated in the twenty-first century so that the end result is the creation of a public good for the digital age – continued, inexpensive access to quality information and entertainment.

If so, it will be a small price to pay.

References

Bergemann, D. and Bonatti, A. (2011). Targeting in advertising markets: Implications for offline versus online media. *RAND Journal of Economics* 42(3): 417–443.

Erdem, T., Kean, M. B., and Sun, B. (2008). The impact of advertising on consumer price sensitivity in experience goods markets. *Quantitative Marketing and Economics* 6: 139–176.

Farris, P. W. and Albion, M. S. (1980). The impact of advertising on the price of consumer products. *Journal of Marketing* 44: 17–35.

Gaerig, A. (2010). The new economics of advertising: The theory of relative constancy reconsidered. Paper presented at the Association for Education in Journalism and Mass Communication (AEJMC), Aug.

Hoskins, C., McFadyen, S., and Finn, A. (2004a). Government intervention. In *Media economics: Applying economics to new and traditional media*. Thousand Oaks: Sage, pp. 287–309.

Hoskins, C., McFadyen, S., and Finn, A. (2004b). Pricing and market segmentation. In *Media economics: Applying economics to new and traditional media*. Thousand Oaks: Sage, pp. 215–246.

McCombs, M. E. (1972). Mass media in the market place. *Journalism Mongraphs* 24: 1–105.

McCombs, M. E. and Shaw, D. L. (1993). The evolution of agenda-setting research: Twenty-five years in the marketplace of ideas. *Journal of Communication* 43: 58–67.

Olmstead, K., Mitchell, A., and Rosenstile, T. (2011). Online: Key questions facing digital news. *The State of the News Media 2011: An Annual Report on American Journalism*. At http://stateofthemedia.org/2011/online-essay/, accessed Mar. 19, 2013.

Pergelova, A., Prior, D., and Rialp, J. (2010). Assessing advertising efficiency: Does the Internet play a role? *Journal of Advertising* 39(3): 39–54.

Shaw, D. L. (1991). The rise and fall of American mass media: Roles of technology and leadership. The Second Annual Roy W. Howard Lecture, presented at Indiana University, Apr.

Wanta, W. and Ghanem, S. (2007). Effects of agenda setting. In R. W. Priess et al. (eds.), *Mass media effects research: Advances through meta-analysis*. Mahwah, NJ: Lawrence Erlbaum, pp. 37–51.

Wright, M. (2009). A new theorem for optimizing the advertising budget. *Journal of Advertising Research* 49(2): 164–169.

3

Advertising to Children

> *In general, my children
> refused to eat anything that
> hadn't danced on TV.*
>
> Erma Bombeck

Advertising to children is a topic that creates strong emotions in people. Parent groups want to protect their kids from questionable media and advertisers. Advocacy groups want to protect a vulnerable group they (and the law, for the most part) have decided can't protect itself. And, in the era of doing more with less money, educators find themselves torn between accepting help from media conglomerates willing to fund educational programs, all the while assuring parents that schools are still protected turf.

What's a grown-up to do? If we take a "big effects" approach to the media – and especially to advertising – it's a short leap to imploring the government to impose stricter guidelines on advertisers. But as you've already seen in this book, nothing is as easy as it might seem at first.

What are the issues? First, it's easy to blame advertising for all the communication ills of the world – and particularly for children who may have run amok.

Advertising and Society: An Introduction, Second Edition. Edited by Carol J. Pardun.
© 2014 John Wiley & Sons, Inc. Published 2014 by John Wiley & Sons, Inc.

Business Library — Issue Receipt

Customer name: Jindal, Suruchi

Title: Advertising and society : an introduction / edited by Carol J. Pardun.
ID: 1007537320
Due: 30/09/2017 23:59

Total items: 1
16/08/2017 17:51

All items must be returned before the due date and time.
The Loan period may be shortened if the item is requested.

www.nottingham.ac.uk/library

Portland Building
B- Floor.

For one thing, it takes the responsibility away from bad parenting. Yes, it may be nasty to have questionable material imprinted on a second grader's lunch box, but the parent doesn't have to buy the lunch box, the argument goes. Blaming advertisers without looking at the media as a whole is short-sighted at best – and dangerous at worst. As long as grown-ups are willing to digest hundreds of hours of every gruesome episode of *NCIS* and *Criminal Minds*, it seems a little hollow to get upset because someone slipped a picture of a Coke can in a Disney movie, doesn't it? Besides, as Walker Smith's Argument points out, kids are consumers too. In some sense, they have earned the right to be treated as a target market.

Or have they? As Dan Panici points out in his Counterargument, children are vulnerable and don't understand the heavy-hitting tactics that come raining down on them day after day as advertisers try to convince them that they need a certain cereal, a certain brand of jeans, a certain back-to-school notepad. And it's not just about cereals, jeans, and school supplies. The American Psychological Association has called for an outright ban on advertising to children under eight. The recent national concern about obesity in children – and the role of advertising in making kids fat – is fuel for the fire. Lots of laws in the United States have been created for the sole purpose of protecting children. No one debates this. Yet just curtailing advertising to children may be easier said than done.

First, hardly anyone would expect children to watch only children-appropriate programming on television. Wildly popular shows like *American Idol* appeal to entire families. It would be impossible (even if everyone agreed this were a good idea) to keep *American Idol* fans under eight from watching the commercials during the show. Second, if there were no commercials on television programs specifically geared toward children, it wouldn't take long before there were no shows for them at all. Like it or not, commercial television is a conduit for advertisers. Demographically segmented shows deliver important consumer segments to the companies that pay for the right to advertise. It is impossible to filter out the "media waste" – audience members that the advertisers are not targeting.

Third, it's not always easy to differentiate between children's and adults' entertainment. The 2012 movie *The Lorax*, for example, is based on a Dr. Seuss book. It's an animated movie, so it must be for kids. But, reportedly, over 70 advertisers were involved in the movie including very grown-up products like Mazda and Whole Foods. What about *Harry Potter and the Deathly Hallows, Part 2*, which was released in 2011 and earned over $90 million on its opening day? Clearly, movies and many other forms of children's entertainment are big, big business.

Fourth, there is an additional economic issue. While parents may deride the idea of advertising in the classroom, given the lack of adequate funding for public education, who can blame educators who "sell out" for books, audiovisual equipment, and other necessary materials to run a school adequately? As you can see, the issue is rarely as simple as it might seem on the surface.

And what about programs like the Siemens Competition in Math, Science and Technology, which gives out millions in scholarship money to budding scientists? The corporate name is closely tied to the program. Or the Scripps National Spelling Bee? Are these any different than kids being exposed to ads on television? If so, how?

What do we know about the impact of advertising on children? Some researchers have argued that there is a fundamental difference in strategy between advertising to adults and advertising to children. Hudson and colleagues (2008) argue that ads geared toward adults tend to focus on brand loyalty while ads geared toward kids focus on merchandizing tie-ins. (An example of this would be an ad campaign that encourages kids to go to McDonald's to get their Happy Meal toy based on a current blockbuster movie.)

With the recent interest in the role that advertising plays in childhood obesity, there is renewed discussion on who is to blame. Is it the ads (true, there is lots and lots of non-nutritional advertising aimed straight at kids), or is it the inactivity of children (and poor eating habits) that are largely to blame? Richard Berman, writing in *Advertising Age* (2005), comments that 25 percent of children today get no exercise whatsoever! This is a classic example of trying to figure out which came first. Do the ads cause obesity? Or do obese children simply watch more television? In research lingo, we call this the debate between causality and association.

Even if the food industry wanted to be helpful, efforts can backfire. As Berman points out, "voluntarily limiting food advertising to children looks like an implicit admission of guilt." What's an advertiser to do? It looks like there are plenty of people on both sides of the issue who have some ideas.

It's about protecting a vulnerable group that can't protect itself. It's about preserving a free market society. It's about recognizing that a free market comes with responsibility. It's about allowing parents to decide how they want their children to behave. It's about kids being rewarded – and, some would argue, respected – for having opinions. As you can see, this is a complicated issue.

So, what's the right side of the argument? *You decide.*

Ideas to Get You Thinking . . .

1   Watch an hour of television for a program that you think is geared toward children. (Try any program on the Disney Channel for starters.) Describe all the ads that you see in one show. Now watch an hour of "grown-up" prime-time TV. Describe those ads. What kinds of similarities and differences do you see? Do you think any of the commercials you saw in the children's program were inappropriate?

2   Talk to some young children about the advertisements they see. What kinds of conclusions could you make based on these conversations?

3   Some researchers say that children eight and under have more positive attitudes toward advertising (and, as a result, are probably more willing to be persuaded by the ad) than children older than eight. Test this idea. Talk to some young kids and ask them about ads. Then ask the older kids about the same ads. What have you discovered?

4   Take a trip to the grocery store and walk around until you find a parent or babysitter with a young child in tow. Without being obnoxious, try to observe the child's behavior as the shopper walks down the aisle. Is the child asking for particular brands? How is the adult responding?

Other Topics to Debate

1   Television programs geared toward children under the age of 12 should not include any advertising at all.

2   Children's movies should include only merchandizing tie-ins that are child-appropriate.

3   Food advertisements on television programs geared toward children should include only healthy foods.

If You'd Like to Know More . . .

Calvert, S. L. (2008). Children as consumers: Advertising and marketing. *Future of Children* 18(1), 205–234.

Calvert, S. L. and Wilson, B. J. (eds.) (2011). *The handbook of children, media, and development*. Oxford: Wiley-Blackwell.

Clark, E. (2007). *The real toy story: Inside the ruthless battle for America's youngest consumers*. New York: Free Press.

Gunter, B., Oates, C., and Blades, M. (2005). *Advertising to children on TV: Content, impact and regulation*. Mahwah, NJ: Lawrence Erlbaum.

Thomas, S. G. (2007). *Buy, buy baby: How consumer culture manipulates parents and harms young minds*. Boston: Houghton Mifflin.

References

Berman, R. (2005). Sloth, not ads, is responsible for fat kids; "food police" loath to recognize real science linking sedentary lifestyles with rise in obesity. *Advertising Age* (Midwest region edn) 76(16): 30.

Hudson, S., Hudson, D., and Peloza, J. (2008). Meet the parents: A parents' perspective on product placement in children's films. *Journal of Business Ethics* 80(2): 289–304. doi:10.1007/s10551-007-9421-5

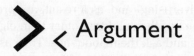

Children are smarter than we think. Let's respect them as the consumers they are!

J. Walker Smith

Excecutive Chairman, Futures Company, USA

Marketers care about only one kind of person: consumers of their products. Admittedly, they care more about purchasers than mere users, but a person who is neither is of no interest to them. This is the only reason marketers are interested in children – that's where the demand for their products is found. Like it or not, kids are consumers.

Marketers didn't invent this fact. This is the reality within which they operate. Perhaps it could be argued that marketers should not care so much or in certain ways about particular sorts of consumers. But if so, that's for policy-makers to decide. Setting the rules is not the same thing as playing the game. Marketers can hardly be blamed for competing within the rules.

Vilifying marketers as con artists who prey on children is nothing but attacking a straw man in a discussion that should center on the social and economic roles we are willing to let different people play as well as the corollary consequences we are willing to accept. Kids are consumers because, by and large, we're okay with it. After all, parents are not shy about entrusting their children with central roles in household shopping decisions.

The 2005 Yankelovich Youth Monitor survey questioned 1,458 teens and preteens six to 17 years of age, along with a parent or guardian of each of the children interviewed. The results are a reminder of what everyone knows to be true – kids have a very big say in the decisions that shape the consumer marketplace:

- Eighty-five percent of kids reported that they had helped their parents pick out the sneakers they wear, while 90 percent of parents said that their children's preferences for sneakers are very or somewhat important in their decisions about what to buy.
- Figures are comparable for all kids' categories (respective percentages show the percentage of kids who said they helped and the percentage of parents who think children's preferences are very or somewhat important). Kids'

clothes: 84/96 percent. School supplies: 83/92 percent. Snack foods: 78/88
percent.

- Figures are only slightly lower for family dining decisions. Fast food restaurants: 76/84 percent. Breakfast foods: 70/88 percent. Dinner foods: 64/86
percent.
- Figures for the choice of family products show sizable participation by children, even if not the majority in some cases. Place to go for vacation: 50/79
percent. Family car: 26/38 percent. Hotel to stay at when traveling: 20/37
percent.

There is nothing unexpected in these findings. For years (maybe forever!)
parents have accommodated their children's preferences by including them in
household decisions, thereby making their kids into exactly the kinds of people
who affect the bottom lines of businesses. Directly and indirectly, kids influence
the spending of roughly $400 billion each year. No wonder marketers target kids.
Influencing the decisions of those who buy and use their products is what marketers do, and, indeed, what marketers must be allowed to do if the marketing
process is to work.

Yet, much as parents want their children to learn by getting hands-on experience as consumers – and not infrequently, by taking complete control of many
household buying decisions – they don't want marketers overwhelming their
kids with ads. In the Yankelovich Youth Monitor Survey, 77 percent of parents
agree that their children are bombarded with too much advertising. But as long
as marketers don't subvert their authority, parents are okay with what their kids
watch – 68 percent agree that television has the potential to reinforce the family's values.

Parents are following through on their determination to teach their children
how to use media and to be smart consumers. From 2001 to 2005, the proportion
of parents reporting that they discuss TV commercials with their children went
up from one-third to just over half, while 70 to 80 percent of parents talk to their
children about TV shows and news stories.

In spite of the growing time and resource pressures of contemporary life,
more and more parents are trying to be a buffer between their children and
marketers. Parents are enforcing limits by using ads as a teaching moment. Of
course, this may not be enough. Children are said to be so much more vulnerable
to the importuning of marketers that they need special protections beyond what
parents are able to provide.

The vulnerability and special needs of children are not in question. Marketers
don't dispute any of the definitive and extensive body of academic research
demonstrating this. Indeed, children are afforded special consideration and
treatment in a wide variety of realms, not the least of which are the workplace
and the criminal justice system. But when it comes to marketing, the case for
special protections is less clear.

Regulating the access of marketers to consumers based on the cognitive
abilities of consumers is a knotty challenge. It has never been the case that a

particular type of cognition is required in order to be allowed to shop. There is no prescreening for rational over emotional thinking or for the ability to differentiate reality from fantasy or for holistic versus materialistic responses to ads, or, indeed, for anything. Different consumers think and process information and advertising in different ways. Except for outright fraud, marketers are free to engage consumers in whatever way might boost sales.

When it comes to the machinations of advertisers, adults are no less cognitively challenged than children. The literature on the cognitive incapacities of adults is just as extensive and definitive as that about children. (There are just as many critics of advertising to adults as there are critics of advertising to children. Advertising is an easy and convenient fall guy for many social ills.) Princeton University social psychologist Daniel Kahneman was awarded the 2002 Nobel Prize in Economics for a lifetime of research (much of which was completed with his late collaborator Amos Tversky) into the innate cognitive biases that cause people to routinely reach decisions and take actions that, technically and even economically speaking, are illogical, irrational, suboptimal, and oftentimes not in their own best interests.

Academic research about bad decision-making periodically makes for bestsellers. Arizona State University Regents' Professor of Psychology Robert Cialdini's (2006) widely read introduction to the principles of persuasion, now in its fifth edition, borrows more examples from advertising than from academic experiments. In fact, his book can be found on the bookshelves of many marketers. Not only does Cialdini dissect the ways in which perceptions can be manipulated, but he counsels readers on how to protect themselves from persuasive appeals that take advantage of their mental habits and biases. In other words, Cialdini cautions adult readers to take special measures to protect themselves from their cognitive incapacities.

Harvard University social psychologist Daniel Gilbert (2006) recently tackled the issue of happiness in his bestselling book. After an exhaustive, book-long review of academic research on the numerous ways in which cognitive processes lead people astray, Gilbert concludes that people mistakenly believe that money brings greater happiness because they are simply no good at all at predicting what will make them happy.

David Myers, the well-known Hope College social psychologist, is the author of two widely used psychology textbooks as well as many bestselling books that address key social issues from the perspective of social psychological research. In his text on social psychology (2005), Myers does more than simply report what's known. He gives students practical suggestions about how to manage their own attitudes and behaviors. In chapter 7 of the latest, eighth edition, Myers includes a section entitled "How can persuasion be resisted?" (which has a subsection called "Inoculating children against the influence of advertising"). Like Cialdini, Myers knows that, because of their innate cognitive biases, adults need as much special coaching and protection as children.

If the cognitive incapacities of children justify more restrictions on marketers, then the same restrictions must be applied to most, if not all, adults too. Adults are not making voluntary decisions to practice poor consumer decision-making any more than children are, nor are adults any more aware of their biases. To keep marketers from advertising to children because children's minds don't work in accordance with some preset criterion is to presume that there is only one kind of mental process that marketers should be permitted to target. If this is true, then it applies as much to adults as to children. Stricter limits on advertising to children that are justified on the basis of cognitive incapacities create a slippery slope that would shut marketing down entirely (and thus the consumer economy too).

One of the more common criticisms of advertising to children is that it makes kids too materialistic and overly infatuated with brands. Whether or not this is true, the notion that this is bad is not a scientific critique; it is a value judgment. It's chancy to base policy on value judgments in a free market system in which the fundamental role of policy should be to safeguard the ability of different people to subscribe to different values. If advertising is required to impart a certain set of values or to induce certain types of responses in order to be permitted, then it becomes little more than an organ of the state. Besides, whatever the merits and failings of materialism – a debate with a long, quarrelsome, and wholly inconclusive intellectual history – in a highly sophisticated consumer-based economy such as America's, it is probably good for children to learn about it early and to be intimately immersed in it and deeply knowledgeable about it.

One of the more extreme recommendations about regulating advertising to children is that marketers not be allowed even to conduct research in support of marketing to kids. This idea is so excessive that it might sound too far-fetched to ever happen, but in fact once the screw begins to tighten on marketing to children everything connected with it becomes fair game, marketing knowledge no less than marketing practice. But if marketing researchers aren't allowed to study what persuades kids, then academic researchers won't be allowed to do so either. It's the knowledge itself that would be taboo, not the source of the research generating such knowledge. Limits on marketing to children will not seem reasonable and benign once they begin their inevitable snowball and start impinging on the very research collected and used by critics to justify such limits. This is the paradox inherent in trying to dictate outcomes by limiting access. Prohibitions on research run counter to basic American ideals about the free exchange of knowledge and opinions.

Of course, there is no need to fret over the difficulties of regulating advertising to children if there is no need to do so to begin with. Maybe kids are naive, but in the 2005 Yankelovich Youth Monitor Survey, 81 percent of the 6- to 17-year-old respondents agreed that more companies should ask kids their opinions of things. Children want a voice with marketers. Just over half feel that companies do not understand the kinds of foods kids like to eat or the kinds of clothes kids like to wear. Kids want their say as consumers.

In fact, the entire consumer marketplace is moving in the direction of greater consumer control, to the point that *Time* magazine's 2006 Person of the Year was "You" (2006–7). What *Time*'s choice recognized was that the marketplace has now crossed a threshold such that marketers can no longer succeed without involving consumers in a collaborative, power-sharing relationship. Kids have dramatically changed the marketing landscape already through Internet sites like YouTube and Facebook. They are now coming of age in a world in which they are expected to be in charge, and as a result, they will be even more assertive tomorrow.

Participation is the essential characteristic of every technology at the disposal of teens and preteens nowadays. Reinvention is the dynamic that their involvement brings to the marketplace. In a very real sense, kids are no longer at the mercy of marketers so much as marketers are at the mercy of kids. Maybe marketers are naive, but this is exactly how they feel these days. A. G. Lafley (Creamer 2006), CEO of Procter & Gamble, the most storied consumer marketing company of all time, now speaks passionately of the modern "let go" world in which marketers can retain control of their brands only by ceding more control to consumers.

Not only has the Internet put new tools into the hands of consumers – with which children are often the most proficient – but it has also opened up information to consumers that they have never had access to before. In particular, the Internet has put people in touch with other people. Peer-to-peer interaction is the true essence (if not the utter genius) of the Internet, giving people unprecedented fingertip access to opinions, feedback, and counsel that provide a ready counter to marketing and advertising. In particular, parents are able to use this information to their advantage in their attempts to buffer their children from marketers. But for kids no less than for their parents, consumer control and empowerment is the future of the marketplace.

The popular culture to which children are exposed nowadays is teaching them new skills and perhaps making them smarter at the same time. Science writer Steven Johnson (2005), a Distinguished Writer in Residence at New York University, contends that contemporary popular culture is far from the mind-numbing wasteland it is often made out to be. Johnson marshals research and personal experience to argue that video games, primetime TV shows, the Internet, and movies are teaching kids new ways of thinking and of processing information that have made today's children measurably smarter than yesterday's children. Marketers face an increasingly sophisticated audience of teens and preteens. The playing field may not be level but it is by no means tilted heavily in favor of marketers any longer.

Kids are not marketing dupes, but they are not marketing resistance masterminds either. Sometimes they need help. But helping kids by regulating marketers opens a Pandora's box of problems and precedents. The best way to help kids is not to impose more regulations on marketers but to change the character of demand in the marketplace. Whatever the angle of the playing field they encounter, that's how marketers play the game.

Ted Levitt (1986), the late, renowned Harvard Business School marketing authority, once wrote that "Consumers don't buy products. They buy solutions to problems." This is business and marketing at its best – solving people's problems in innovative and affordable ways. One way to understand Levitt's observation is to recognize that problems constitute demand. What marketers do is respond to demand. If problems change, demand changes. When demand changes, marketers change.

Regulations are hard to put in place and harder still to enforce. Business lobbies will fight against the imposition of stricter regulations and businesses themselves will push the envelope with ways to operate within the law while still marketing aggressively to children. This is what always happens. Despite the best intentions, regulations continue to come up short in giving kids the help they need. That's why this debate about protecting children from advertising goes on and on . . . and on and on and on. There is too much faith in regulation as a panacea.

While marketers resist the yoke of regulation, they do not fight against demand. Instead, they pursue it – because that's where money is to be made. To enlist the support of marketers in the cause of improving marketing to kids, the focus must be on changing the character of demand, not on imposing more regulations.

Demand can be changed in many ways. Educating kids and parents is the most obvious way. Governmental and nonprofit institutions can offer instruction and alternatives that would cause kids to be different kinds of consumers. There are successes to emulate from programs focused on things like drugs, smoking, and sexual behavior. Myers (2005) cites one notable example in which an educational program proved very effective at giving children a "more realistic understanding" of advertising.

Even greater impact can come from direct incentives, however. If there are foods or toys or activities that are better for children, then the answer is to "pay" children or their parents to consume these things. Marketers will scramble to offer more of anything that people are being "paid" to buy. Probably the best way to do this is to subsidize the preferred offerings so that they are cheaper. But however it's accomplished, the idea is to give kids a compelling reason to consume differently.

Even more important than incentives for children and their parents are incentives for marketers. These kinds of incentives change the character of demand by introducing governmental purchasing or tax policies into the picture. It's known to work. Many of the foods marketed to children are said to be unhealthy because they contain high-fructose corn syrup, a sweetener that is widely used because governmental agricultural subsidies make it the cheapest alternative for food and beverage companies to put into the products they produce and market (Maclean 2002). Changing the ways in which governmental subsidies affect marketers' bottom lines is a much more straightforward way to get marketers to market different foods – and products of all sorts – to children.

In short, the best way to do the right thing by children is to work with marketers, not to do battle with them. More regulation guarantees a fight without guaranteeing anything for children. It's not clear that children need a lot more protection, but the best way to insure that they get what they need is to make it profitable for marketers to provide it. If there is demand for it, marketers will do so willingly and enthusiastically. They aren't so ambitious that they will try to lead demand, but if the demand is there, they will definitely go after it.

Let's stop trying to put marketers off the scent of the consumer demand coming from children. Let's be smarter and put marketers on to the new scent of a different demand coming from children so that they will gladly give children what they ought to have.

References

Cialdini, R. (2006). *Influence: The psychology of persuasion*, rev. edn. New York: Collins Business Essentials.

Creamer, M. (2006). P&G CEO to ANA: Just let go: A. G. Lafley tells marketers to cede control to consumers to be "in touch." *Advertising Age* (Oct. 6). At http://adage.com/article/special-report-ana06/p-g-ceo-ana/112311/, accessed Mar. 19, 2013.

Gilbert, D. (2006). *Stumbling on happiness*. New York: Knopf.

Johnson, S. (2005). *Everything bad is good for you: How today's popular culture is actually making us smarter*. New York: Riverhead Books.

Levitt, T. (1986). *The marketing imagination, expanded edn*. New York: Free Press.

Maclean, M. (2002). When corn is king. *Christian Science Monitor* (Oct. 31).

Myers, D. G. (2005). *Social psychology*, 8th edn. New York: McGraw-Hill.

Counterargument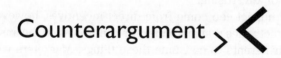

Children need more protection from advertising!

Dan Panici

University of Southern Maine, USA

The government has an independent interest in the well-being of its youth.

Supreme Court of the United States, 1968

Children are bombarded with advertising messages from television, Internet sites, and school hallways and classrooms. Nearly $20 billion is spent by companies advertising to children in the United States, $4 billion alone by the fast food industry. Despite the ample evidence to suggest that children are vulnerable to advertising messages, current Federal Communication Commission (FCC) and Federal Trade Commission regulations offer minimal protection for children. Those opposed to stricter regulation of advertising aimed at children suggest that industry self-regulation and media literacy initiatives are enough protection for children. However, these actions are not mitigating the detrimental effects of advertising on children. Children need more protection from advertising than what is currently afforded to them.

The Commercialization of Childhood

By all accounts, children in the United States live in a media-saturated environment. American children use media almost seven hours a day, not counting media use for school; for older children, the average is closer to eight hours a day. When we consider "media multitasking" (using more than one medium at a time), children manage to expose themselves to a total of 10 hours and 45 minutes' worth of media content into seven and a half hours of media use; an increase of over two hours a day since 2004. Various studies indicate that the amount of time spent with media by children increases from year to year. Of this overall media use, television viewing continues to be the most common media activity for most American children, attracting close to four and a half hours of a child's day. Children most often watch television alone or with their peers, live in a home where television is usually on during meals and left on even if no one is watching, and have a television set in their bedroom (Rideout et al. 2010).

One result of the use of media at the levels we see today is the increasing commercialization of childhood. There are a number of factors that have contributed to an unprecedented growth in both the amount and type of advertising aimed at children (American Psychological Association 2004; Calvert 2008). First, the diffusion of cable television and direct broadcast satellite technologies has escalated the number of television channels one can receive in the home. The consequence of the burgeoning number of television channels has been the growth of niche program services or "narrowcasting," which targets a narrow demographic segment. As a result, audiences comprising children have become very profitable to marketers and advertisers.

There are a number of cable stations devoted to children's programming including Nickelodeon, Nick Jr., Cartoon Network, Disney Channel, ABC Family, The Hub, Disney XD, and Noggin. With the growth in children's niche programming comes the opportunity for advertisers to deliver an astonishing amount of advertising messages aimed at children. These advertising messages include traditional commercial segments and product sponsorships that are linked to programs and program characters, such as branded characters, product placement, and stealth advertising (Calvert 2008). For example, Fisher-Price uses Nicklodeon's *Dora the Explorer* character and Disney's *Winnie the Pooh, Mickey*

Mouse, and *Handy Manny* characters to sell children's toys, clothing, and other related children's products. The expansion of children's programming imposes "much greater exposure to child-oriented advertising than any previous generation of youth has experienced" (American Psychological Association 2004: 3).

The increasing commercialization of childhood has coincided with the growth of the Internet. Home computer access to the Internet has expanded dramatically over the past two decades. The percentage of children with home access to computers has increased from 15 percent in 1984 to more than 90 percent in 2009. Further, the percentage of children who use the Internet at home rose from 22 percent in 1997 to 93 percent in 2009. Youth spend nearly an hour and a half, excluding schoolwork, at a computer each day (Rideout et al. 2004).

Thousands of child-oriented websites have been launched, with nearly all of them supported by advertising. Unlike television advertising regulation, which requires a clear separation between programming and commercial content, the boundaries between commercial and noncommercial content on children's websites are hazy and unregulated. Advertisers are taking advantage of this situation and are developing new advertising techniques such as "advergames" for this new medium (see Chapter 13). Advergames are "online video games with a subtle or overt commercial message where the use of product placement is common" (Calvert 2008: 209). For instance, one of the most popular sites on the Web for children, with over 35 million users worldwide, is MoshiMonsters (www. moshimonsters.com). In this educational social game aimed at young children, children adopt and care for their own pet monsters, create a home for it in Monstro City, and play games. As children play in this virtual world, they are exposed to banner ads for Toys "R" Us where they can purchase MoshiMonsters trading cards and virtual prize codes, plush toys and mini-figurines. Or a child could visit the official MoshiMonsters store (www.store.moshimonsters.com) to purchase Moshling backpack buddies, Moshling collectible figures, or Moshi mashup trading cards. Butcher suggests that advergaming

> is a new direction for brands aimed at kids. In the old world toys might give rise to a game, these days the games are creating real-world toys . . . content is giving rise to new brands and if the idea resonates with kids, a major licensing program can be spun off. (2011: 1)

One of the reasons the founder of MoshiMonsters created the game was to tap into the $22 billion annually spent in the United States on toys.

Finally, the American Psychological Association reports that "as advertising to children has expanded with the diffusion of cable television, the Internet and other new vehicles of communication, its presence has mushroomed in classrooms and other school venues over the past few decades" (2004: 1). Commercial activities most prevalent in schools include: *product sales* ("pouring contracts" for soft drinks like Coke and Pepsi to be sold in vending machines and at school events), *direct advertising* (Channel One, a daily 12-minute news program with two minutes of advertisements broadcast in classroom, and Star Broadcasting which provides music and advertisements to school hallways and lunchrooms), and *indirect advertising* (corporate-sponsored educational materials, teacher training, contests, and promotion programs that provide recognition and rewards for educational achievements). In-school commercialization is of particular concern because children are a captive audience and the effects of advertising are potentially stronger.

Why Children Need More Protection

For the past 70 years, various public policies state that advertising must be "recognized by the target audience as obvious attempts to persuade" (Strasburger et al. 2009: 53). If the target audience of an advertisement is unaware or incapable of recognizing the persuasive attempt of the advertisement, they are more vulnerable to its persuasive intent. In such cases, the advertising message is considered to be inherently unfair and deceptive. In order for children to achieve a mature understanding of an advertising message, they must possess two information-processing skills: the ability to discriminate at a perceptual level commercial from noncommercial content and the ability to attribute persuasive intent to advertising (American Psychological Association 2004).

A consensus among developmental experts has emerged as to the age at which children acquire the capacity to fully understand the intent of advertising. A substantial body of evidence supports the notion that most children below the age of five do not discriminate between television programming and commercial content; children below the age of eight typically lack the cognitive ability to understand and evaluate the persuasive intent of advertising (American Psychological Association 2004; Calvert 2008; Strasburger et al. 2009). Further, studies have shown that children consider all advertising as accurate and fail to comprehend the advertiser's motive to embellish the product (Institute of Medicine 2006). It is certainly safe to assume that the evidence strongly indicates that children under the age of eight may be deceived by an advertising message that would not likely deceive older children or even adults.

Exposure to and the Effects of Advertising

An estimated $15 to $17 billion dollars is spent by companies advertising to children in the United States (Shah 2010). Over $4 billion was spent in 2009 by the fast food industry alone. The most compelling information concerning children's exposure to advertising is found in the American Academy of Pediatrics report *Children, adolescents, and advertising* (2006). Children view more than 40,000 ads per year on television alone and are increasingly being exposed to advertising on the Internet, and in schools.

Children younger than 12 spend approximately $25 billion a year, and influence another $200 billion of their parents' spending per year. Children view more than 3,000 ads per day on television, on the Internet, on billboards, and in magazines; thus, in a typical year a child may view more than one million ads.

Studies show that there are a handful of key products targeted at children in television advertisements: sugar-coated cereals, fast food restaurants, candy, soft drinks, and toys (American Psychological Association 2004; Calvert 2008). These same products also dominate the new commercial terrains of cable television and the Internet. Further, the appeals used in children's advertising emphasize how fun a product is or how good it tastes, rather than offering actual information about it (Strasburger et al. 2009). Consequently, children interpret advertisements as fun and entertaining and as a source of unbiased information (Story and French 2004).

There is ample empirical evidence to suggest that there are many detrimental effects of exposing young children to commercial messages. Both correlational and causal studies report that the negative effects of advertising on children include: parent–child conflict, cynicism, obesity, depression, an increased emphasis on materialism, discontent, diminished self-esteem, and cultivating positive attitudes toward tobacco and alcohol consumption (American Psychological Association 2004; American Academy of Pediatrics 2006; Calvert 2008; and Strasburger et al. 2009).

Although children are bombarded with advertising that is detrimental to their well-being, there are few safeguards to protect them. Through the Children's Television Act, the Federal Communication Commission limits advertising to 10.5 minutes an hour at weekends and 12 minutes an hour on weekdays. However, Calvert reports that "these limits are frequently violated" (2008: 213). During the past 30 years, the Federal Trade Commission has brought a number of cases challenging deceptive performance claims in toy advertisements and nutritional claims for foods that are likely appealing to children. Although it was successful in these cases, the Federal Trade Commission has jurisdiction to regulate advertising that is "unfair or deceptive" only on a case-by-case basis.

Turning a Blind Eye to Stricter Regulation and More Protection

Despite the overwhelming evidence that targeting advertising to children under the age of eight "raises strong concerns about potential negative impacts on the social development and well-being of children" (American Psychological Association 2004: 1), opponents of stricter regulation and safeguards for children rely on a few arguments to ward off such initiatives.

Many suggest that industry self-regulation mitigates the negative effects of advertising aimed at children. The National Advertising Review Council, in a move acknowledging the vulnerability of children to advertising, created the Children's Advertising Review Unit (CARU). CARU's mission is to "ensure that advertising aimed at children younger than twelve is not misleading and takes into consideration children's level of cognitive development" (Mello 2010: 234). Although self-industry regulation is a sound theoretical position to hold, indicators suggest that it is ineffective in tempering the negative effects of children's advertising. The Federal Trade Commission and the Department of Health and Human Services (2006) criticize CARU for: (1) having guidelines that are too broad in scope, rendering them meaningless, (2) allowing inconsistent adherence to the guidelines by advertisers, and (3) lacking a strong enforcement process. The Institute of Medicine (2006) notes that CARU's guidelines and enforcement ignore the impact of both the volume of advertising aimed at children and the broader marketing environment. For example, findings from the Rudd Center (2010) show that although fast food companies pledged to reduce marketing of unhealthy foods to children, they actually increased their marketing efforts aimed at children. Given the mounting evidence that advertising is harmful to the healthy development of children, industry self-regulation has fallen short of the level needed to avoid the negative effects of advertising.

Another argument used to shield advertisers from stricter regulation centers on the notion that if children are taught media literacy skills they will be empowered with the cognitive ability to discern the inherent nature of advertising, thus lessening the negative effects. However, there is no consensus on what the term "media literacy" even means. Potter argues that "the body of literature about media literacy is a large complex patchwork of ideas, and the variety of interpretation of media literacy can be confusing" (2010: 676). Further, there is a lack of findings indicating what type of media literacy interventions work consistently. What is known about media literacy interventions is that they may have a short-term effect on older children, but there is sufficient evidence to indicate that it is difficult to train children below the age of eight to protect themselves from the negative effects of advertising (American Psychological Association 2004).

Many opponents of regulatory efforts also argue that commercial speech is protected under the First Amendment and is immune to government regulation. Indeed, commercial speech does have First Amendment protection, but it is *limited* protection. The Supreme Court ruled in the landmark *Central Hudson Gas* case (*Central Hudson Gas and Electric Corp. v. Public Service Commission of New York*, 477 U.S., 1980) on the conditions in which commercial speech can be restricted. In its ruling the Supreme Court stated that if commercial speech were to receive full First Amendment protection it must be truthful and not misleading. However, the Court did set forth the conditions under which truthful commercial speech could be regulated: the government has a substantial interest in restricting commercial speech, the restriction must advance that interest, and the restriction is no more extensive than necessary to serve the government's interest (Mello 2010; Harris and Graf 2012).

Calls for More Protection

In the face of the overwhelming commercialization of childhood, it is easy to echo those who call for the United States government to offer more safeguards to protect children similar to those offered by a number of European countries and Australia. Sweden bans television and radio advertisements directed at children under the age of 12. Belgium does not allow commercials during children's programming and bans advertisements five minutes before or after a children's program airs. Australia does not allow ads during television programs for preschoolers. Although these full restrictive measures afford more protection to children, there is little political will in the United States to implement a complete ban on children's advertising. Nonetheless, advocacy groups and public policy makers are offering more practical solutions that will protect children from the onslaught of advertising.

In an effort to lessen the negative effects of advertising to children, the American Academy of Pediatrics (2006) is asking Congress and the FCC to cut the amount of advertising allowed on children's programming to no more than five to six minutes an hour. They are also asking that interactive advertising to children on digital television be prohibited.

The American Psychological Association argues that "the existing base of knowledge about young children's limited comprehension of television advertising presents a clear and compelling case in support of a restriction of all advertising primarily directed to audiences of children below the age of seven to eight" (2004: 22). Along with the American Academy of Pediatrics (2011), the American Psychological Association (2010) advocates a restriction on advertising during television programming that is viewed predominately by children under the age of eight. The goal is that this restriction would reduce children's viewing of advertising that is most salient to them.

In perhaps the most focused and practical policy concerning children's advertising, Centers for Disease Control and Prevention, the Federal Drug Administration, the Federal Trade Commission, the US Department of Agriculture, and other advocacy groups are beginning to target nutritional advertising to stem the obesity epidemic plaguing children. The Centers for Disease Control and Prevention (2012) reports that, from 1980 to 2008, the rate of obesity among children aged six to 11 years tripled from 6.5 to 19.6 percent. Among children two to five years old, the rate of obesity has more than doubled (5 to 12.4%).

Almost two-thirds (60%) of overweight children have at least one cardiovascular risk factor, and children who are obese are at risk of becoming obese as adults (Story and French 2004; American Psychological Association 2010). The prevalence of type 2 diabetes is also increasing in youth. Many researchers conclude that one cause of obesity includes the advertising of unhealthy foods and beverages to children. Almost 90 percent of the food advertisements aimed at children are for carbonated beverages, breakfast cereals, fast food restaurants, snack foods, and candy (Centers for Disease Control and Prevention 2012). Children's exposure to ads for unhealthy foods such as high-calorie and low-nutrient snacks, fast foods, and sweetened drinks are a significant risk factor for obesity (Gantz et al. 2007; American Psychological Association 2010). Story and French (2004) report that studies show children exposed to advertising will choose advertised food significantly more often than unadvertised foods.

To combat the marketing of unhealthy foods and beverages to children, many are calling for the government to ban the marketing of unhealthy food to children (American Psychological Association 2010; Mello 2010; American Academy of Pediatrics 2011; Centers for Disease Control and Prevention 2012). Food industry groups assert that the First Amendment prohibits such regulation. However, as outlined above, case law establishes that the First Amendment does not protect "inherently misleading" commercial speech. A mounting body of cognitive research indicates that young children are vulnerable to advertising. Even the US Supreme Court in its ruling in *Ginsberg v. New York* (390 U.S. 629, 1968) argued that children are a vulnerable population and the government has an interest in protecting the well-being of its youth. Because the government can prohibit "inherently misleading" advertising, and children cannot understand the persuasive intent of commercial messages, advertising to children younger than eight should be considered beyond First Amendment protection and, therefore, restricted (Mello 2010; Graff et al. 2012; Harris and Graf 2012).

Conclusion

In recent decades, advertisers have viewed children as a major marketing demographic. As a result, children are aggressively targeted, and are exposed to an unprecedented amount of advertising and commercialization. Although children live in a commercialized media-saturated world, many young children do not understand that advertising is designed to sell products, nor do they have the ability to comprehend or evaluate the advertising that is aimed at them. Given the known detrimental effects of advertising to children, many advocates and regulatory agencies view this situation as exploitive. Children deserve more safeguards and protections from advertising.

References

American Academy of Pediatrics, Committee on Communications (2006). *Children, adolescents, and advertising.* At http://pediatrics.aappublications.org/content/118/6/2563.full.pdf, accessed Mar. 19, 2013.

American Academy of Pediatrics (2011). Policy statement: Children, adolescents, obesity, and the media. *Pediatrics* 128(1): 201–208.

American Psychological Association (2004). *Report of the APA Task Force on Advertising and Children.* At http://www.apa.org/pi/families/resources/advertising-children.pdf, accessed Mar. 19, 2013.

American Psychological Association (2010). *The impact of food advertising on childhood obesity.* At http://www.apa.org/topics/kids-media/food.aspx, accessed Mar. 19, 2013.

Butcher, M. (2011). MoshiMonsters launches first toy range, aims at $22 billion US market. At http://techcrunch.com/2011/01/24/moshimonsters-launches-first-toy-range-aims-at-22-billion-us-market/, accessed Mar. 19, 2013.

Calvert, S. L. (2008). Children as consumers: Advertising and marketing. *Children and Electronic Media* 18(1): 205–234.

Centers for Disease Control and Prevention (2012). Nutrition advertising targeting children. *Centers for Disease Control and Prevention.* At http://www.cdc.gov/phlp/winnable/advertising_children.html, accessed Apr. 2, 2013.

Federal Trade Commission and Department of Health and Human Services (2006). *Perspectives on marketing, self-regulation, & childhood obesity.* Washington, DC: Federal Trade Commission and Department of Health and Human Services.

Gantz, W., Schwartz, N., Angelini, J., and Rideout, V. (2007). *Food for thought: Television food advertising to children in the United States: A Kaiser Family Foundation Report.* At http://www.kff.org/entmedia/upload/7618.pdf, accessed Mar. 19, 2013.

Graff, S., Kunkel, D., and Mermin, S. (2012). Government can regulate food advertising to children because it is inherently misleading. *Health Affairs* 31(2): 392–398. doi:10.1377/hithaff.2011.0609

Harris, J. L. and Graff, S. (2012). Protecting young people from junk food advertising: Implications of psychological research for First Amendment law. *American Journal of Public Health* 102(2): 214–222. doi:10.2105/AJPH

Institute of Medicine (2006). Report: *Food marketing to children and youth: Threat or opportunity?* At http://www.iom.edu/Reports/2005/Food-Marketing-to-Children-and-Youth-Threat-or-Opportunity.aspx, accessed Mar. 19, 2013.

Mello, M. (2010). Federal Trade Commission regulation of food advertising to children: Possibilities for a reinvigorated role. *Journal of Health Politics, Policy, and Law* 35(2): 227–276. doi:10.1215/03616878-2009-051

Potter, J. (2010). The state of media literacy. *Journal of Broadcasting & Electronic Media* 54(4): 675–696. doi:10.1080/08838151.2011.521462

Rideout, V. J., Ulla, F. G., and Roberts, D. F. (2010). *Generation M2: Media in the lives of 8- to 18-year-olds: A Kaiser Family Foundation Study.* At http://www.kff.org/entmedia/upload/8010.pdf, accessed Mar. 19, 2013.

Rudd Center (2010). *Fast food F.A.C.T.S: Evaluating fast food nutrition and marketing to youth.* At http://www.fastfoodmarketing.org/media/FastFoodFACTS_Report.pdf, accessed Mar. 19, 2013.

Shah, A. (2010). Children as consumers. At http://globalissues.org/article/237/children-as-consumers, accessed Mar. 19, 2013.

Story, M. and French, S. (2004). Food advertising and marketing directed at children and adolescents in the US. *International Journal of Behavioral Nutrition and Physical Activity* 1(3): 1–17.

Strasburger, V. C., Wilson, B. J., and Jordan, A. B. (2009). *Children, adolescents, and the media*, 2nd edn. Los Angeles: Sage.

4

Political Advertising

*It is necessary for me to
establish a winner image.
Therefore, I have to beat
somebody.*

Richard M. Nixon

The presidential campaign of 2012 may go down in history as the most expensive political campaign ever. Best estimates are that about $1 billion for advertising was spent by Barack Obama and Mitt Romney in their quests for the presidency. The vast majority of these ads were negative. The whole country breathed a collective sigh of relief when the election was over and these over-the-top ads stopped. It was bad enough to experience the ads in states that were solidly "red" or "blue," but for the handful of swing states, it was almost unbearable.

As we all know by now, the presidential campaign of 2012 focused on the relatively few undecideds, which makes the exorbitantly high expenditures seem all the more questionable. Most political pundits argued that it would be those few undecideds who would end up deciding the outcome of the election, which up until results started pouring in, most people thought would be a close race. (It was not as close as the pollsters predicted; Obama ended up winning 332 electoral votes compared to Romney's 206.)

Advertising and Society: An Introduction, Second Edition. Edited by Carol J. Pardun.
© 2014 John Wiley & Sons, Inc. Published 2014 by John Wiley & Sons, Inc.

Whatever we think about negative advertising in general, much of the research seems to indicate that negative political ads work – even when the fact checkers work overtime and question the claims of these negative ads. By the time the presidential election was over, each presidential candidate had aired about a million ads mostly trying to convince us that the other guy was unfit to hold office. Whether or not the ads were ultimately persuasive is hard to determine – especially when both sides used negative advertising as their main arsenal of choice.

It's easy enough to decide that you are against negative advertising. That seems like the nobler approach. But if you believe in a cause – and you want others to feel as passionate about it as you do – it's easy to see how a "Can't we all just get along?" approach might seem too mild for the issues at stake.

In these two essays, each researcher understands the seedier side of negative advertising. Some of the differences in their arguments are nuanced. For example, you'll have to decide whether all negative advertising is "mudslinging," or if there is a range of acceptability in negative ad messages.

Whatever side we might debate on, we can be sure of one thing: negative political ads are here to stay. Is that good or bad? *You decide.*

Ideas to Get You Thinking . . .

1   Go to YouTube and look up some ads that ran during the 2012 presidential election. If you have a hard time finding ads, try "Eastwooding," "47 percent," or "ObamaCare Ad" to get you started. List what you think are the facts in these ads. Now, do some research and see if the facts bear out. What did you learn?

2   Look up some former presidential advertising campaigns. (You can find books with print ads, as well as websites with campaigns.) Pick some ads from several decades. Has there been a trend toward negative advertising over the years? Or have the campaigns always been negative? What do you think?

3   Find a negative print political advertisement. (Any decade and candidate will do.) Rewrite the copy, turning it into a positive message (for some candidates, this might be fairly difficult!). Now, retype the negative ad. When you have both sets of copy side by side, show them to some classmates or friends. Ask them which they think is the most persuasive ad. Make sure to ask them why. What conclusions can you draw from this exercise?

4   Do you think negative advertising is effective only with political ads? Look for some negative consumer advertising. Do you think it is effective? Why, or why not?

5   Find 10 ads that ran during the last presidential campaign that were approved by the candidate. Now find 10 ads that were created by outside groups. Are there differences between these two kinds of ads? What did you notice?

Other Topics to Debate

1   All negative comments in political advertising should be required by law to include substantiated support.
2   Political advertising should be held to the same First Amendment standard as commercial advertising.
3   Television political advertisements should only be seen on network television (no cable) and only during prime time.

If You'd Like to Know More . . .

Fowler, E. F. and Ridout, T. N. (2010). Advertising trends in 2010. *Forum* 8(4). doi:10.2202/1540–8884.1411

Franz, M. M., Freedman, P., Goldstein, K., and Ridout, T. N. (2008). Understanding the effect of political advertising on voter turnout. *Journal of Politics* 70(1): 262–268. doi:10.1017/S0022381607080188

Krupnikov, Y. (2012). Negative advertising and voter choice: The role of ads in candidate selection. *Political Communication* 29(4): 387–413. doi:10.1080/10584609.2012. 721868

Lovejoy, J., Riffe, D., and Cheng, H. (2012). Campaign interest and issue knowledge: Did the media – and negative political advertising – matter in "battleground Ohio"? *Atlantic Journal of Communication* 20(4): 201–220. doi:10.1080/15456870.2012. 711148

Schemer, C. (2012). Reinforcing spirals of negative affects and selective attention to advertising in a political campaign. *Communication Research* 39(3): 413–434. doi:10.1177/0093650211427141

 Argument

What's so positive about negative advertising?

Anne Johnston

University of North Carolina, USA

There is perhaps no topic during a political campaign that gets more attention and creates more angst than a discussion of the attacks, misinformation, mudslinging that we see during the election season. Why do we see so much negative advertising during an election? One reason is that those using the ads believe they work. But do they work? Do they work at scaring the electorate from voting, that is, do they depress voter turnout? Do they work at making us feel more alienated from the political process? Do they make us think negatively about the candidate who is using the negative ad or about the opponent who is the target of the ad?

To understand negative advertising, we must first understand its role in our political system and why we have negative political advertising. Historically, political advertising has served several important functions for candidates and for campaigns (Sabato 1981; Devlin 1986; Jamieson 1986). Political advertising can serve to rally votes for a candidate, to create enthusiasm for a candidate, and to encourage people to vote in general. Ads can help candidates define and redefine their image for voters and provide a forum for explaining issue positions. Finally, ads have helped candidates speak to the American public without the filter of news media or news coverage and served to counteract any negative or nonexistent coverage the candidate has received in the media. News media sometimes concentrate their coverage on well-known candidates or front-runners (Graber 1993). For some candidates the only way of equalizing that coverage is to use advertising to bring their campaign vision and message to the American public. One reason we see negative ads is because of the advantage that those already in office have over those who are running for that office. Incumbent candidates generally have an advantage in terms of media coverage, so challengers have used their ads to contrast their issue stands and their policies with those of incumbents (Kaid and Johnston 2001).

Negative advertising and slogans have been a part of political campaigns since campaigning began. And certainly television spots (typically traced to first use in the 1952 presidential campaign) have always included opponent-focused ads. A study of presidential ads from 1952 to 1996 found that negative ads represented about 38 percent of all advertising during that time, with a jump during the 1990s when negative advertising represented a little over 60 percent of the ads used (Kaid and Johnston 2001).

Two concerns about negative advertising are that it cost lots of money, and we don't always know who is sponsoring the attacks. This is actually true, but it's also true for many aspects of the communication we see, hear, receive, and read during a modern political campaign. If an ad is run by and sponsored by a political candidate, it must be clear that the candidate approved the ad. But super PACs (political action committees) can provide advertising to promote or attack candidates, and voters sometimes don't know who the super PACs are or whom they support. Lots of money in the 2012 presidential campaign came from super PACs. And here's why: in January 2010, the Supreme Court ruled (*Citizens United v. Federal Election Commission*) that free speech rights meant that the government could not limit corporate and labor union spending for political purposes. This meant that PACs could not be limited in terms of the money they could raise and give to particular candidates.

This Supreme Court ruling (5–4) rejected limits on corporate spending in political campaigns, reflecting the narrow majority's desire to leave all political speech alone. As Justice Kennedy wrote,

> When government seeks to use its full power, including the criminal law, to command where a person may get his or her information or what distrusted source he or she may not hear, it uses censorship to control thought. This is unlawful. The First Amendment confirms the freedom to think for ourselves. (quoted in Liptak 2010)

Although activities between the candidate's campaign organization and the PAC cannot be coordinated, the end result of the ruling was that there was an explosion of super PACs formed to support or attack candidates running for office in congressional elections in 2010 and in the 2012 presidential election. The ads sponsored by the super PACs (with names like "Restore our Future," "Winning Our Future," "Make Us Great Again," "House Majority PAC") both then and now contain some of the most negative attacks, and voters might be confused about who is sponsoring the ads or who is behind them.

Super PACs are spending lots of money on advertising that tells you what's wrong with the other candidate. And there's not much we can do about that. But citizens and voters certainly have the resources and ability to investigate how much money is being spent by the super PACs or candidates. OpenSecrets.org is a website, sponsored by the Center for Responsive Politics, that tracks this spending. One of the things you can find out from the website is that by February 2012 over 56 million dollars had been spent by outside groups (including super PACs, parties, corporations, and unions) to distribute literature, run ads, call voters, and so on for the 2012 election. Over $46 million of that amount came from 318 super PACs (Sunlight Foundation 2013). This fact won't stop the money from coming into our election campaigns, but it's the type of information that helps demystify where the money's coming from and where it's going.

Do negative ads decrease voter turnout and make us feel bad about ourselves, or about the political process? Voters have proved to be more skeptical and cynical about the claims in negative ads than was earlier thought. Although people generally express contempt for campaigns because of negative advertising and find negative advertising less useful, they don't become more apathetic about politics because of negative advertising (Pinkleton et al. 2002). There is also contradictory evidence about the effects of negative advertising on voter turnout, with some studies showing that negative advertising may actually stimulate voter turnout (Goldstein and Freedman 2002) and more recent studies showing that negative advertising neither increases nor decreases turnout (Clinton and Lapinski 2004).

Is negative advertising mainly emotionally driven and focused on the image and character of candidates? Not all negative ads are attacks on a candidate's character. Of the 462 negative ads used in presidential TV advertising from 1952 to 1996, 74 percent were dominated by issue concerns and attacks on issue stands (Kaid and Johnston 2001). During the same period, the main appeals used in negative ads were emotional appeals; but emotional appeals were the main types of appeals in positive ads too. In fact, this early longitudinal study of advertising found that negative ads used more fact- and evidence-based logical appeals than positive ads did and that most of the negative ads were focused on issue stands and the consistency of the opponent (85%). More recent studies have found that negative ads contain attacks on both issue stands and personality characteristics of the opponent and that negative advertising can be effective in persuading voters to think more about certain issues or personal characteristics (Druckman et al. 2009; Ridout and Franz 2008). Political ads are used to help a candidate define or reshape his or her image for voters. Candidates certainly do spend time in their ads talking about their personality characteristics, and have used negative advertising to focus on personal characteristics like performance and success, honesty and integrity, and competency (Kaid and Johnston 2001).

One problem with trying to address the criticisms of negative advertising is that not all negative ads are alike. Some negative ads can be called true mudslinging ads, which denigrate the opponent's character, but there are other negative ads that compare and contrast the issue stands and policy positions of the candidate with those of his or her opponent. These types of negative ads can actually contribute to learning and debate during a political campaign. Negative ads that compare two candidates on specific points can stimulate voters to think of counterarguments to the ads and of facts that contradict the ads (Meirick 2002), and they can be more effective than ads that simply attack the opponent on some issue stand or for some perceived character flaw (Pinkelton 1997; Gaski 2010).

There are also studies that reveal that voters who were more knowledgeable or sophisticated about politics or who already had some basic information about the campaign, the candidates, and the issues, gained lots of information from negative ads (Valentino et al. 2004; Stevens 2005). And there is good evidence that voters are becoming more sophisticated at evaluating the civility and relevance of negative advertising (Fridkin and Kenney 2008). Even more nuanced effects of negative advertising have been found depending upon the gender of the candidate. For example, Fridkin, and colleagues (2009), showed that negative advertising was more effective against male candidates than against female candidates. In addition, certain types of ads that contained "uncivil" attacks and/or were irrelevant, unfair, and unwarranted were not effective in attacks on female candidates and in some cases "backlashed" against the sponsor of the ad.

Because of this backlash or boomerang effect, negative ads are hardly a sure thing, because they don't always work in the way the candidate wants them to work. The backlash on the sponsor, coined the "boomerang effect" (Garramone 1984), continues to be evident in research on the effects of negative advertising. Repeated exposure to ads may actually damage the image of the person sponsoring the ads (King and McConnell 2003). Although these researchers found that exposure to one negative ad helped the sponsor of the ad (no immediate backlash effect), they also found evidence that repeated viewing of negative ads resulted in negative evaluations of the sponsor of the ad (a boomerang effect).

Negative ads, then, have been shown to contribute to learning about the candidates and their issue stands and personal characteristics during a campaign, and sometimes to be more detrimental to the sponsor of the attack than to their target. But do negative ads make us more negative about politics? Some studies have shown that really nasty ads or those that contain uncivil messages can make us feel more negative about politicians or politics (Kahn and Kenney 1999, 2004; Mutz and Reeves 2005; Stevens 2009). But other studies find mixed or no evidence that exposure to lots of negative ads during a campaign leads to more negative evaluations of politics and of Congress or government in general (Brooks and Geer 2007; Jackson et al. 2009). Voters may also have more varied and more critical responses to negative advertising than to positive ads. In one study, negative ads were viewed as being less persuasive and influential than positive ads (Phillips et al. 2008). However this same study did find contradictory evidence that the negative ads had some effect in both changing vote intention and in reinforcing and strengthening the position of voters who were committed to the candidate sponsoring the ads.

Many critics would say that political ads are not the place where a lengthy discussion of issues can occur, and nor should they be. This is true. Political ads were never designed to function as the sole source of political information. In fact, debates, conventions, and news coverage all serve to show the voters what the candidates' issue and political stands are. In the past, news media have not always done a good job of covering and analyzing candidates and their ads during an election. In 2004, local television news in states where the candidates were competing for votes devoted less time to campaign news than to campaign advertising. Almost half of the campaign stories were devoted to strategy or details of the daily horserace and fewer than a third of the stories focused on campaign issues, according to the Lear Center Local News Archive website (www.localnewsarchive.org). Even when news organizations have provided "ad watches" or analyses of the claims and visual images used in ads, they have not always helped voters to understand or become more critical about the ads (Kaid et al. 1996; Gobetz and Chanslor 1999).

One of the reasons we might believe that negative advertising is all around us during an election is that negative ads elicit lots of emotion, and therefore we may remember them more than we remember positive ads (Bradley et al. 2007). But the truth is that the advertising isn't the only negative communication during a political campaign. In a study of 2008 presidential election coverage, researchers found that the news coverage of John McCain had been more negative than positive with "nearly six in ten of the stories studied . . . decidedly negative in nature (57%), while fewer than two in ten were positive" (Pew Research Center 2008).

What we know about negative political ads is that they encourage discussion and debate on issues. They also can set the agenda of what is being talked about in the election, forcing news media to cover those issues. Political ads, positive or negative, were never meant to be the sole source of information about the candidates, or about the issues, for voters. They are source-sponsored communications about a candidate's or a group's vision of a campaign, their stand on an issue, or a comparison with the opponent. They are not substitutes for good news coverage and campaign analysis or for voters' information-seeking.

Uncomfortable and sick of negative advertising as we can get during an election, we have to be willing to allow all types of communication to exist during an election season. Why should we tolerate negative ads during an election? Because allowing all forms of political speech during an election, including negative ads, is a sign of a strong democracy, may promote even more communication about an event, and may force us to decide what we need to investigate, look up, and attend to in terms of information if we are going to be well-informed voters. And in order not to limit political speech, we have to be willing to put up with the negativity that comes with modern day election campaigns. And what's the solution to negative speech in advertising during these elections? Not censorship, but more speech, as advocated by the Supreme Court in 1927: "If there be time to expose through discussion the falsehood and fallacies, to avert the evil by the processes of education, the remedy to be applied is more speech, not enforced silence" (*Whitney v. California*, 274 U.S. 357, 377, 1927).

References

Bradley, S. D., Angelini, J. R., and Lee, S. (2007). Psychophysiological and memory effects of negative political ads: Aversive, arousing, and well remembered. *Journal of Advertising* 36(4): 115–127.

Brooks, D. J. and Geer, J. G. (2007). Beyond negativity: The effects of incivility on the electorate. *American Journal of Political Science* 51: 1–16.

Clinton, J. D. and Lapinski, J. S. (2004). "Targeted" advertising and voter turnout: An experimental study of the 2000 presidential election. *Journal of Politics* 66(1): 69–96.

Devlin, L. P. (1986). An analysis of presidential television commercials, 1952–1984. In L. L. Kaid, D. Nimmo, and K. R. Sanders (eds.), *New perspectives on political advertising. Carbondale: Southern Illinois University Press*, pp. 21–54.

Druckman, J. N., Kifer, M. J., and Parkin, M. (2009). Campaign communications in US congressional elections. *American Political Science Review* 103(3): 343–366.

Fridkin, K. L. and Kenney, P. J. (2008). The dimensions of negative messages. *American Politics Research* 36: 694–723.

Fridkin, K. L., Kenney, P. J., and Woodall, G. S. (2009). Bad for men, better for women: The impact of stereotypes during negative campaigns. *Political Behavior* 31: 53–77.

Garramone, G. M. (1984). Voter responses to negative political ads. *Journalism Quarterly* 61: 250–259.

Gaski, J. F. (2010). Positive effects of negative political ads. *Washington Times* (Nov. 1), section B, commentary, p. 3.

Gobetz, R. H. and Chanslor, M. (1999). A content analysis of CNN "Inside politics" adwatch coverage of high-profile, nonpresidential races. In L. L. Kaid and D. G.

Bystrom (eds.), *The electronic election: Perspectives on the 1996 campaign communication.* Mahwah, NJ: Lawrence Erlbaum, pp. 113–121.

Goldstein, K. and Freedman, P. (2002). Campaign advertising and voter turnout: New evidence for a stimulation effect. *Journal of Politics* 64(3): 721–740.

Graber, D. A. (1993). *Mass media and American politics,* 4th edn. Washington, DC: CQ Press.

Jackson, R. A., Mondak, J. J., and Huckfeldt, R. (2009). Examining the possible corrosive impact of negative advertising on citizens' attitudes toward politics. *Political Research Quarterly* 62(1): 55–69.

Jamieson, K. H. (1986). The evolution of political advertising in America. In L. L. Kaid, D. Nimmo, and K. R. Sanders (eds.), *New perspectives on political advertising. Carbondale: Southern Illinois University Press,* pp. 1–20.

Kahn, K. F. and Kenney, P. J. (1999). Do negative campaigns mobilize or suppress turnout? Clarifying the relationship between negativity and participation. *American Political Science Review* 93: 877–890.

Kahn, K. F. and Kenney, P. J. (2004). *No holds barred: Negativity in U.S. Senate campaigns.* Upper Saddle River, NJ: Pearson Prentice Hall.

Kaid, L. L. and Johnston, A. (2001). *Videostyle in presidential campaigns: Style and content of televised political advertising.* Westport, CT: Praeger.

Kaid, L. L., Tedesco, J. C., and McKinnon, L. M. (1996). Presidential ads as nightly news: A content analysis of 1988 and 1992 televised ad watches. *Journal of Broadcasting & Electronic Media* 40: 297–308.

King, J. D. and McConnell, J. B. (2003). The effect of negative campaign advertising on vote choice: The mediating influence of gender. *Social Science Quarterly* 84: 843–858.

Liptak, A. (2010). Justices, 5–4, reject corporate spending limit. *New York Times* (Jan. 21). At http://www.nytimes.com/2010/01/22/us/politics/22scotus.html?, accessed Mar. 20, 2013.

Meirick, P. (2002). Cognitive responses to negative and comparative political advertising. *Journal of Advertising* 31: 49–62.

Mutz, D. C. and Reeves, B. (2005). The new videomalaise: Effects of televised incivility on political trust. *American Political Science Review* 99: 1–16.

Pew Research Center (2008). Winning the media campaign: How the press reported the 2008 general election. *Pew Research Center's Project for Excellence in Journalism* (Oct. 22). At http://www.journalism.org/node/13307, accessed Mar. 20, 2013.

Phillips, J. M., Urbany, J. E., and Reynolds, T. J. (2008). Confirmation and the effects of valenced political advertising: A field experiment. *Journal of Consumer Research* 34: 794–806.

Pinkleton, B. E. (1997). The effects of negative comparative political advertising on candidate evaluations and advertising evaluations: An exploration. *Journal of Advertising* 26: 19–29.

Pinkleton, B. E., Um, N., and Austin, E. W. (2002). An exploration of the effects of negative political advertising on political decision making. *Journal of Politics* 31: 13–26.

Ridout, T. N. and Franz, M. (2008). Evaluating measures of campaign tone. *Political Communication* 25: 158–179.

Sabato, L. J. (1981). *The rise of political consultants: New ways of winning elections.* New York: Basic Books.

Stevens, D. (2005). Separate and unequal effects: Information, political sophistication and negative advertising in American elections. *Political Research Quarterly* 58: 413–426.

Stevens, D. (2009). Elements of negativity: Volume and proportion in exposure to negative advertising. *Political Behavior* 31: 429–454.

Sunlight Foundation (2013). Super PACs: Totals for 2011–2012 cycle. *Sunlight Foundation Reporting Group* (Apr. 2). At http://reporting.sunlightfoundation.com/outside-spending/super-pacs/, accessed Apr. 2, 2013.

Valentino, N. A., Hutchings, V. L., and Williams, D. (2004). The impact of political advertising on knowledge, Internet information seeking, and candidate preference. *Journal of Communication* 54: 337–354.

Counterargument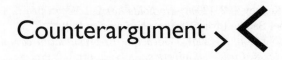

Why negative political advertising is bad advertising

Albert R. Tims

University of Minnesota, USA

Negative political discourse or what commonly is called "mudslinging" has a 200-year history in American national political campaigns. So why are we still debating if "going negative" or "going dirty" is good or bad? This is a fair question since some scholars, political consultants, and pundits tell us that negative advertising helps win elections (Grey 2012; Lariscy 2012) and might actually enrich democratic processes (Geer 2006). Political advertising scholar Ruthann Lariscy (2012) says that in 2012 "negative ads are a virtual must-have component of every political campaign." And political scientist John Geer's *In defense of negativity* details how in presidential campaigns between 1960 and 2004 "attack" ads tended to carry more issue-relevant information important for voters than what we might call "positive" image advertising. In terms of the mechanisms of persuasion, empirical research suggests that, all other things being equal, negative political information can be more memorable and influential than positive information (Lau 1985; Kahn and Kenny 1999).

Spending on political advertising has skyrocketed during the past 30 years (McAdams 2012) with much of the new spending going to fuel negative messages

(Brooks and Murov 2012). According to survey results from the 2010 midterm election by the Pew Research Center for People and the Press "77% of voters say there was more negative campaigning or mud-slinging than in previous elections; 69% of voters expressed this view after the 2006 election" (Pew Research Center 2010).

Given that candidates and their supporters want to win elections, it may seem obvious that they invest in negative "mudslinging" attack advertising simply because it works. But might the opposite be true? Might candidates be locked in a negativity arms race costing millions of dollars, fueled by the media's love of conflict and the urging of campaign consultants who make their living using "win at all costs" and "earned media" strategies? And might this mudslinging be reinforced by fervent financial supporters, special interest groups, and a belief that the most ardent supporters of the candidate (aka the "base") have come to expect no-holds-barred attacks on the opponent? Might candidates be wasting their money and in the process contributing to public cynicism, alienation, and malaise? (Ansolabehere and Iyengar 1995; Lau and Rovner 2009) Might all this negativity actually generate a "backlash" reaction against candidates perceived as too mean and nasty to govern (Kaid 2004; Lau et al. 2007)? Might the recent meteoric rise in campaign spending by super PACs (Political Action Committees) be putting candidates at unprecedented risk of being perceived as having gone too far in attacking an opponent? And, in the end, might the use of attack ads run counter to much of what we know about what constitutes good advertising?

Social scientists have long observed a tendency for us to not reliably remember the source of messages we may have read, heard, or seen (Lariscy and Tinkham 1999). Think about how often you have shared something you heard or read but can't quite recall the original source. The messages coming from the candidate's own campaign and those of rabid special interest super PACs run the risk of being dissociated from the source over time and landing squarely in the lap of the candidate. A candidate forced to disavow or distance himself or herself from groups attacking an opponent may run the risk of losing control of the campaign, although during the 2004 presidential campaign President George Bush tried to distance himself from the "Swift Boat Veterans for Truth" ads attacking Senator John Kerry's combat record in Vietnam by publicly criticizing the ads, though only after they had stopped running, describing them as "bad for the system." He is correct.

Campaign consultants sell their services, in part, by demonstrating their ability to generate "earned media," or coverage of their campaign by the news media. It will come as no surprise, of course, that the news media treat attacks as controversial news. And controversy drives the news cycle. By covering the controversy stirred up by a particularly nasty ad, far more people may end up seeing the ad on the news than those who saw it when it ran as an ad. And it gets into blogs, becomes fodder for talk shows, opinion magazines, and news satires like *The Daily Show*. This is what "earned" media means. In essence, the news media incentivize negativity for the campaign. This process does not mean attacks are, in the end, good for the candidate, the public, or democracy. Just because something might generate earned media coverage doesn't make it a good idea or even the best approach for determining who will govern.

The result of this campaign controversy is that the news agenda is shifted from coverage of real issues of importance to the attack itself. The news agenda in turns affects what the public perceives as the most important issues in the campaign and the salience of information when we think about the candidates (McCombs and Reynolds 2002). Democracy is not served if our perceptions of what is important and what we can most easily recall is built around campaign controversy as opposed to constructive issue controversy.

Existing partisan views exert significant influence on the way we process and interpret political messages (Sigelman and Kugler 2003). This means that what we define as unfair, mean, and untrue is intimately linked to how it squares with what we already believe. Attack ads that outrage supporters of an opposing candidate as being malicious lies could seem to be perfectly consistent truths to the attacking camp. In a very real sense, the ad is experienced in completely different ways.

Given we know this psychological process is at work, what is the point of spending billions on attack advertisements? Mobilization of the "base" is one argument often used, but it would be far less expensive to use other communication channels such as the Internet for that purpose, especially given how costly it is to buy air time in major markets. Another far more disturbing reason is to demobilize, or discourage, voting (Ansolabehere and Iyengar 1995; Lau and Rovner 2009).

The demobilization hypothesis advances three primary means by which negative advertising creates demobilization. Essentially, the demobilization strategy, if it can be called that, is to get weak partisans, independent voters, ethnic groups, and so on to dislike the opponent, even if they don't come to support the attacking candidate. It is easy to imagine how suppressing voting by certain groups could decide a close election.

Equally troubling is demobilization arising from the corrosive effects of highly partisan attacks on how citizens feel about their leaders and political institutions and their sense of empowerment. Ansolabehere and Iyengar's seminal research found that political independents were particularly susceptible to the demobilization effects of negative ads. These findings stimulated many subsequent studies by both political scientists and advertising researchers (Lau et al. 2007). Scientific uncertainty persists surrounding the demobilization effect hypothesis with as many studies finding little or no statistically significant evidence of demobilization as studies that find support for the hypothesis. As Lau and Rovner note, "Despite the volume of research already available on the decision to attack and its impact on political behavior, a myriad of questions remain for future research to address" (2009: 305).

There are other legitimate reasons for serious concern about the potential threats posed by unbridled attack advertising, even if the scientific literature remains unclear. Fowler and Ridout (2010) report that during 2010 roughly 36 percent of candidate ads could be classified as "negative," compared to a whopping 87 percent for independent groups. Without question, the use of negative advertising is center stage in an ongoing controversy over the political campaign upheavals ushered in by the 2010 US Supreme Court's 5 to 4 decision in the case of *Citizens United v. Federal Election Commission*. Heralded by many as an affirmation of First Amendment protections for political speech, this landmark decision effectively abolished many of the previous restrictions on campaign advertising by outside groups. Now groups do not have to abide by spending limits, can avoid reporting on the source of their funding, and can shield contributors' identities. The sponsorship message can simply say "Sponsored by Citizens Who Love America" or any other innocuous, nonpartisan-sounding names that might hide affiliation, celebrate a cherished value, or just seem wonderfully patriotic.

These political action groups can accept unlimited funding from domestic and multinational corporations based in the United States, labor unions, trade associations, wealthy private citizens, or virtually anyone with the resources and interest in supporting an election outcome. And to the chagrin of many, they may do so in a manner that effectively hides their identity. During his 2010 State of the Union address, President Obama attacked this decision, saying "I don't think American elections should be bankrolled by America's most powerful interests, or worse, by foreign entities. They should be decided by the American people."

With no spending limits and virtually no accountability, these independent groups are ushering in an era of vicious negative campaigning unprecedented in American history and with largely unknown consequences. In terms of accountability Brooks and Murov argue "when negative ads are run by groups unaffiliated with campaigns, it is harder for the public to judge the veracity of the ads or blame anyone directly if they think the messages are problematic" (2012: 388). What may seem like a windfall of campaign allies may well result in disaster for candidates if it appears to the electorate that secretive and well-funded special interests have hijacked the campaign. Absent anyone else to blame, the candidate will likely be viewed as the source of the problem, even if these independent groups are "technically" unaffiliated with the candidate's official campaign. The use of negative advertising is taking on a new dimension that makes past concerns about backlash seem quaint by comparison.

To appreciate this controversy in its proper context we need to take a very brief look at the origins of negative election campaigning in America. The contest between Vice President John Adams and Secretary of State Thomas Jefferson in 1796 was the first in which two different political parties and philosophies were pitted against one another. Because of the way the Electoral College functioned at the time, Adams was elected president and Jefferson his vice president, even though Adams was a Federalist and Jefferson a Democratic-Republican. That election set the stage for what many regard as one of the nastiest political campaigns in US history in 1800, between the incumbent Adams and his vice presidential rival Jefferson (Swint 2006).

The campaign was carried out primarily through the highly partisan press of the day, rather than by the candidates, with newspapers clearly aligned with the Federalists or the Democratic-Republicans publishing hostile articles and making claims about the personal failings of the opposing candidate. Handbills (posters) and pamphlets were directed at the small number of white, male land-owning citizens eligible to vote for the electors who would cast the deciding ballots for president and vice president in the Electoral College (Jamieson 1996). Adams's supporters claimed that Jefferson had "financially cheated his creditors, obtained his property by fraud, robbed a widow of an estate worth ten thousand pounds, and behaved in a cowardly fashion as governor of Virginia during the revolution." Jefferson's supporters countered that Adams was "a fool, a hypo-crite, a criminal and a tyrant, and said that his presidency was one continued tempest of malignant passions" (Swint 2006: 184).

Almost from the founding of the nation, candidates and their partisan sup-porters moved beyond the bounds of the democratic ideal of civil political dis-course around the important issues of the day to ad hominem arguments and fearmongering. Johnson and Johnson tell us that ad hominem arguments "involve questioning the motives of the opponent, accusing the opponent of acting on personal interest, accusing the opponent of inconsistency, or accusing the oppo-nent of past misconduct" (2000: 294).

As the partisan press slowly evolved during the mid to late nineteenth century into the advertising-supported mass medium we recognize today, political cam-paigns began to target their messages to the electorate through advertising as well as through more traditional means of communication. Once movie news-reels, radio, and television came on the scene, political campaigning took full advantage of paid advertising opportunities to exercise unprecedented control over their campaigns. The monopoly that newspapers had on the electorate's attention was broken forever (Jamieson 1996). While powerful interests have always found ways to influence elections, it wasn't until the Bipartisan Campaign Reform Act of 2002, also known as the McCain–Feingold Act, that spending on ads by PACs and tax-exempt 507 and 501(c)(4) groups began radically changing the complexion of election campaigns (Brooks and Murov 2012).

Election campaigns are by their nature competitive. Candidate positions on issues, qualifications, and leadership credentials must be compared and con-trasted. This type of critical inquiry and analysis is essential for a functioning democracy. Advertising highlighting the strengths and weaknesses of candidates is not, per se, negative advertising. Johnson and Johnson (2000) define it as constructive controversy. It is the ad hominem tactic of appealing to prejudices and fears or viciously attacking character that legitimately defines what we mean by negative advertising. And, of course, it includes the grossly unethical, if legally protected, tactic of spreading outright lies designed to misinform the electorate.

Surveys of voters in Virginia (Freedman et al. 1999) provide confirming evi-dence that going after an opponent's voting record, past business practices, or ties to special interest groups are regarded as fair game by 70 to 80 percent of voters. Ad hominem attacks, however, are considered "fair game" by fewer than 30 percent of voters. Candidates and their supporters risk alienating voters when they cross the line, even if voters can't tell them where that line may be in any given election. Furthermore, Lau and Rovner's authoritative review of the scientific literature concludes that the literature reflects "an overall indictment of baseless attacks and unwarranted character assaults" (2009: 304). Baseless attacks have not proven effective.

Truth-in-advertising regulations enforced by the Federal Trade Commission (FTC) do not apply to political advertising. And the Federal Communications Act enforced by the Federal Communications Commission states that

> if any licensee shall permit any person who is a legally qualified candidate for any public office to use a broadcasting station, he shall afford equal opportunities to all other such candidates for that office in the use of such broadcasting station: Provided, That such licensee shall have no power of censorship over the material broadcast under the provisions of this section. No obligation is imposed under this subsection upon any licensee to allow the use of its station by any such candidate. (US Code: Title 47, sec. 315 – Candidates for public office)

Candidates and their supporters can, if they wish, distort an opponent's record, make unsupported claims of fact, or accuse an opponent of any horrific thing they wish without risking federal government interference or attempts to hold them accountable for accuracy. The lack of accountability to government regulations designed to protect the public from false and misleading advertising is one of the most significant differences between political and commercial advertising in America.

The First Amendment to the US Constitution is unambiguous about protecting the political speech rights of citizens. And with the landmark *Citizens United v. Federal Election Commission* decision in January 2010, the US Supreme Court ruled that corporations and unions were deemed to enjoy the same unfettered political speech protections as candidates and individual citizens. Moreover, the donors to these campaigns, even foreign-owned corporations, have the ability to remain largely hidden from public view. The majority opinion asserted that the government should in no way seek to limit the marketplace of ideas or the free exercise of speech.

But just because a candidate, and now the super PACs, can communicate without limitations doesn't mean that negative attacks are an effective campaign strategy, ethical conduct for those aspiring to govern, or ultimately good for democracy. Groups like the League of Women Voters, FactCheck.org, and Politifact.org are endeavoring to hold candidates and their supporters accountable, but the decline of the traditional watchdog function of the press is clearly in evidence.

In a recent essay in *Columbia Journalism Review*, Downie and Schudson (2009) assert that independent reporting is under threat – the type of reporting that "provides information, investigation, analysis, and community knowledge." Cable news networks, talk radio, and the Internet make it much easier for partisans to filter out opposing views or what might otherwise be called balanced reporting and analysis. And with this has come increased negativity, ideological extremism, and an increased inability of legislative bodies to reach bipartisan agreement or compromise. The rise of super PACs, with their documented propensity to run attack advertising, are fueling a bitter divide in the United States.

Equally troubling is the fact that just six media conglomerates own the majority of media outlets in the nation and are the primary financial beneficiaries of the many millions of dollars spent on advertising for election campaigns. The rise of the Super PACs has been a windfall of new revenue for these corporations. They have a vested interest, many argue, in capturing as much campaign advertising spending as they can. Nichols and McChesney (2012) report that during the 2012 election cycle political advertising might well have accounted for as much as 20 percent of the annual advertising revenue for many television stations. Should we really expect these corporations to report on the veracity or fairness of attack ads?

Television, both broadcast and cable, will remain, at least for a few more national election cycles, the place where most political advertising takes place. This statement isn't a failure to grasp the increasing importance of the Internet or social media, but is premised on the fact that most national elections are fought over the swing voters in the middle. Online sources (websites, blogs, etc.) are highly selective for engaged partisans, making them quite useful for energizing and engaging base supporters and powerful campaign tools for fund-raising. But television is where most campaigns for national political office go to tell their stories to those most likely to determine national election outcomes.

Without question, there are powerful reasons both for candidates and for the public to have serious concerns about the skyrocketing use of negative attack advertising and their harmful consequences, not to mention the ethical issues associated with deliberately misinforming the public.

Vitriolic attacks on character and outright lies are not what the First Amendment was designed to advance and protect. The protection was granted to insure that issues were debated and decided in full public view and that no law could suppress a citizen's right to speak. Zealots have always had outrageous things to say, but this rhetoric has rarely dominated campaigns the way negative attacks have since 2010. We may find that public backlash will cause super PACs to rethink their no-holds-barred attacks and that Congress will eventually institute "Stand by Your Ad" and public disclosure requirements for these groups, which are now required of candidates.

Negative attack advertising uses character assassination and distortion to discredit and alienate. In the process these ads debase respect for our leaders and political institutions. Imagine if Coke were to start running ads saying that Pepsi wants you to get diabetes, that Pepsi wants kids to get fat, and that Pepsi uses high-fructose corn syrup because Pepsico is in the pocket of powerful corn growers. Consumption of too much sugar can contribute to the development of type 2 diabetes and can contribute to obesity, but to link these outcomes to a specific product pretty much identical to your own product and to the alleged harmful intentions of Pepsico is self-destructive, not to mention illegal. Political attack ads are created as weapons of destruction. What democracy needs and deserves are campaigns that help us engage in constructive controversy over real issues, to build trust in the integrity of political institutions and faith in those we elect to govern.

References

Ansolabehere, S. and Iyengar, S. (1995). *Going negative: How political advertising shrinks and polarizes the electorate.* New York: Free Press.

Brooks, D. J. and Murov, M. (2012). Assessing accountability in a post-citizens united era: The effects of attack ad sponsorship by unknown independent groups. *American Politics Research* 40(3): 383–418.

Downie, L., Jr. and Schudson, M. (2009). The reconstruction of American journalism. *Columbia Journalism Review* (Oct. 19). At http://www.cjr.org/reconstruction/the_reconstruction_of_american.php?page=all, accessed Mar. 20, 2013.

Fowler, E. F. and Ridout, T. N. (2010) Advertising trends in 2010. *Forum* 8(4): 2–16.

Freedman, P., Lawton, D., and Wood, W. (1999). Do's and don'ts of negative ads: What voters say. *Campaign Elections* 20: 20–25.

Geer, J. G. (2006). *In defense of negativity.* Chicago: University of Chicago Press.

Grey, J. (2012). *Dem pollster Mark Mellman weighs in on negative ads. Daily Beast* (Feb. 4). At http://www.thedailybeast.com/articles/2012/02/03/dem-pollster-mark-mellman-weighs-in-on-negative-ads.html, accessed Mar. 20, 2013.

Jamieson, K. H. (1996). *Packaging the presidency: A history and criticism of presidential campaign advertising,* 3rd edn. New York: Oxford University Press.

Johnson, D. W. and Johnson, R. T. (2000). Civil political discourse in a democracy: The contribution of psychology. *Peace and Conflict: Journal of Peace Psychology* 6(4): 291–317.

Kahn, K. F. and Kenney, P. J. (1999). Do negative campaigns mobilize or suppress turnout? Clarifying the relationship between negativity and participation. *American Political Science Review* 93: 877–889.

Kaid, L. L. (2004). Political advertising. In L. L. Kaid (ed.), *Handbook of political communication research.* Mahwah, NJ: Lawrence Erlbaum, pp. 155–202.

Lariscy, R. (2012). Why negative political ads work. *CNN* (Jan. 2). At http://edition.cnn.com/2012/01/02/opinion/lariscy-negative-ads, accessed Mar. 20, 2013.

Lariscy, R. and Tinkham, S. F. (1999). The sleeper effect and negative political advertising. *Journal of Advertising* 28(4): 13–30.

Lau, R. (1985). Two explanations for negativity effects in political behavior. *American Journal of Political Science* 29(Feb): 119–138.

Lau, R. and Rovner, I. B. (2009). Negative campaigning. *Annual Review of Political Science* 12: 285–306.

Lau, R., Sigelman, L., and Rovner, I. B. (2007). The effects of negative political campaigns: A meta-analytic reassessment. *Journal of Politics* 69: 1176–1209.

McAdams, D. D. (2012). $8 Billion: 2012 Political Advertising Forecast II. *TV Technology* (Jan. 9). At http://www.tvtechnology.com/article/billion – political-advertising-forecast-ii/211212, accessed Mar. 20, 2013.

McCombs, M. and Reynolds, A. (2002). News influence on our pictures of the world. In J. Bryant and D. Zillmann (eds.), *Media effects: Advances in theory and research*, 2nd edn. Mahwah, NJ: Lawrence Erlbaum.

Nichols, J. and McChesney, R. W. (2012). The assault of the super PACs. *Nation* (Feb. 6), 11–17.

Pew Research Center (2010). Mixed reactions to Republican midterm win. *Pew Research Center for the People & the Press* (Nov. 11). At http://www.people-press.org/2010/11/11/mixed-reactions-to-republican-midterm-win/, accessed Mar. 20, 2013.

Sigelman, L. and Kugler M. (2003). Why is research on the effects of negative campaigning so inconclusive? Understanding citizens' perception of negativity. *Journal of Politics* 65: 142–160.

Swint, K. C. (2006). *Mudslingers: The top 25 negative political campaigns of all time*. Westport, CT: Praeger.

5

Tobacco Advertising

> *Advertising is legalized lying.*
>
> H. G. Wells

Recently I spent a couple of weeks in the country of Georgia, a land with a rich and incredibly interesting history – and delicious food! I spent most of my time in the capital city of Tbilisi, known as "the city that loves you." The city was different from every American city I've ever visited for a number of reasons. But the most extreme difference to me was that it seemed that *everyone* smoked – *everywhere*. It was particularly noticeable in restaurants where my Georgian friends would smoke cigarette after cigarette while I was trying to enjoy my kachapuri. It also reminded me how much the smoking culture in the United States has changed in the last 50 years. It used to be cool to smoke, but it seems that we have finally gotten the message that it's not so cool to damage your health.

Ever since 1982 when the United States Surgeon General C. Everett Koop released a report stating that cigarette smoking was the major cause of cancer death, the number of smokers in the United States has declined. Today, estimates are that about 19 percent of adults smoke. In comparison, in the early 1900s nearly 80 percent of men smoked at least one cigar a day.

Advertising and Society: An Introduction, Second Edition. Edited by Carol J. Pardun.
© 2014 John Wiley & Sons, Inc. Published 2014 by John Wiley & Sons, Inc.

The relationship between tobacco and cancer has been a long one. As soon as smoking in the United States became a market bonanza (taxes on tobacco helped to fund the Civil War, for example), experts have questioned the benefit of smoking. During World War I, General John J. Pershing reportedly declared: "You ask me what we need to win this war. I answer tobacco as much as bullets; Tobacco is as indispensable as the daily ration; we must have thousands of tons without delay." Savvy tobacco marketers saw a potential goldmine with the war and quickly connected patriotism to smoking. For example, Bull Durham, a popular brand during the war used the line "When our boys light up, the Huns will light out."

While health issues with tobacco emerged very early in tobacco's popularity, by the 1930s and 1940s many tobacco ads actually pushed the healthy aspect of smoking. For example, a 1930s ad for Philip Morris indicated that cigarettes helped throat irritation: "Every day millions actually confirm what a distinguished group of doctors discovered: when smokers changed to Philip Morris, every case of nose or throat irritation due to smoking, cleared completely or definitely improved" (Vintage Ad, n.d.).

Very few products on the market have absolutely no redeeming value. Even dubious products like weight loss pills and spray-on hair claim to do some good. But is there any potential positive outcome for smoking? While lawmakers have tried to restrict cigarette consumption, it is still lawful for adults to smoke.

As Michael Hoefges and Tim Dewhirst, authors of the essays in this chapter, point out, the to-regulate or not-to-regulate tobacco advertising debate has been raging for a long time. What is the role of the government? To keep us safe? Or to keep us from hurting others? Clearly, at times the government steps in and makes laws to protect us from ourselves. We are supposed to wear a seatbelt. In many states it is against the law to ride a motorcycle without a helmet. Some states do not allow you to buy firecrackers for fear you may blow up your neighbor. How do we know where to draw the line?

At this point, even with the scientific data that basically proves food with trans fat is bad for you, it is not against the law to eat it. It's also not against the law to advertise it. So, can this analogy be applied to smoking? Yes, we know it's bad. (Okay, it's real bad.) But, can't people make up their own minds whether they want to kill themselves? Or shorten their lives by several years, or at the very least, develop premature wrinkles and brittle hair?

Some people argue that adding restrictions is not going to change the amount of media exposure tobacco companies can garner, so the instigation of bans may have a reverse effect. For example, when the voluntary ban on television commercials for cigarettes began, the tobacco industry did not fight hard against it. In fact, some would say it even encouraged it. Why? Some have argued that, with the removal of cigarette commercials, there would also be a removal of anti-cigarette commercials. (And there was.) Besides, there were other media to explore, such as movies, sporting events, and other venues – many of which would eventually end up on television. In fact, there is evidence that this was what happened. So perhaps an all-out ban on the presence of tobacco in any kind of media is warranted.

Trying to figure out what side you come down on in the advertising and tobacco controversy pits free speech purists against health advocates, advertising haters against free market gurus. This is one of those topics that tends to get heated rather quickly. Debating the merits of regulating tobacco advertising (or arguing against it, for that matter) is a hard battle to win because the result is problematic whichever side you take. What if a complete ban on advertising were promoted by the government because of the proven harmful effects of smoking: what would be next?

On the other hand, what if there were no restrictions? There is evidence that countries with fewer advertising restrictions have higher numbers of smokers – and, subsequently, higher numbers of smoking-related deaths. Of course, even with this compelling evidence it's difficult to know if the relationship is coincidental or causal.

Trying to work your way through the quagmire of the pros and cons of advertising regulation for tobacco is difficult. Michael Hoefges and Tim Dewhirst do an admirable job, each laying out a compelling argument for the regulation of advertising or the protection of free speech. What's the right side? *You decide.*

Ideas to Get You Thinking . . .

1   Make a list of all the products you can think of that are extremely dangerous to a consumer. Do you recall any advertising for them? If so, what kinds of strategies do you think the advertisers used to get their messages across?
2   Could you come up with a code of ethics to decide when you might want to restrict advertising for a harmful product such as tobacco? What kinds of things would you put into the code?
3   Ask some young teens who smoke why they smoke. Do you think the media have a role in why they started to smoke?
4   The next time you rent a movie, make a list of every time you see someone smoking. What did you observe?

Other Topics to Debate

1   Tobacco should be treated as a drug, for which the advertising needs to come under the same regulations as other controlled substances.
2   Warning labels on cigarettes need to correspond more closely to teens' concerns.
3   Advertising for tobacco products should be treated in the same manner as for other harmful products (such as foods high in trans fat).

If You'd Like to Know More . . .

Calvert, C. et al. (2010). Playing politics or protecting children? Congressional action & First Amendment analysis of the Family Smoking Prevention and Tobacco Control Act. *Journal of Legislation* 36: 201–248.

Hoefges, M. (2003). Protecting tobacco advertising under the Commercial Speech Doctrine: The constitutional impact of Lorillard Tobacco Co. *Communication Law and Policy* 8(3): 267–311.

Hoefges, M. & Rivera-Sanchez, M. (2000). "Vice" advertising under the Supreme Court's Commercial Speech Doctrine: The shifting Central Hudson analysis. *Hastings Communications and Entertainment Law Journal* 22(3–4): 345–390.

Master Settlement Agreement (1998). At http://ag.ca.gov/tobacco/pdf/1msa.pdf, accessed Mar. 20, 2013.

Pennock, P. E. (2007). *Advertising sin and sickness: The politics of alcohol and tobacco marketing, 1950–1990.* DeKalb: Northern Illinois University Press.

Redish, M. (1996). Tobacco advertising and the First Amendment. *Iowa Law Review* 81: 589–639.

Stoll, E. (2010). The Family Smoking Prevention and Tobacco Control Act and the First Amendment: Why a substantial interest in protecting public health won't save some new restrictions on tobacco advertising. *Food and Drug Law Journal* 65: 873–900.

Reference

Vintage Ad (n.d.). Tobacco/cigarette ads of the 1930s: Call for Philip Morris. At http://www.vintageadbrowser.com/tobacco-ads-1930s/12, accessed Apr. 5, 2013.

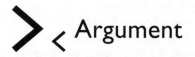 Argument

The strong First Amendment right to promote lawful products

R. Michael Hoefges

University of North Carolina, USA

In 2009 the United States Congress passed the Family Smoking Prevention and Tobacco Control Act (FSPTC Act) on public policy grounds of protecting minors from the harms of tobacco products (Pub. L. No. 111-31, Div. A, Stat. 1776, June 22, 2009). Significantly here, the FSPTC Act gave the Food and Drug Administration (FDA) regulatory jurisdiction over tobacco products and instructed the agency to enact sweeping restrictions on the advertising and promotion of cigarettes and smokeless tobacco. The FSPTC Act also strengthened existing federal statutory warning requirements for advertising and packaging for these products. In the FSPTC Act, Congress did not address, and thus allowed, continued enforcement of the current federal ban on most tobacco advertising on electronic media regulated by the Federal Communications Commission, like broadcast and cable television (15 U.S.C. §§1335, 4402(f)).

The major tobacco advertising restrictions required by the FSPTC Act, including the enhanced warnings with color graphics for cigarette and smokeless tobacco advertising, were all supposed to have been in effect already but were not at the time of this publication. Why? Basically, because federal courts have found specifically that some of these advertising restrictions violate the protection provided by the First Amendment of the US Constitution against governmental interference with the free flow of protected speech – in this instance, free-flowing commercial speech or, as most call it, advertising.

But why does the First Amendment provide protection for messages that arguably encourage people to purchase and use tobacco products when the health-related dangers and addictive nature of these products are medically established? Why does the First Amendment sometimes prevent the government from restricting tobacco advertising as a means of attempting to prevent minors using these products which, while legal for adults, everyone knows are unhealthy and even deadly, and difficult to stop using once started? Is that one of the functions of the First Amendment? Should it be? Answering these questions requires a detailed look at the extent to which the First Amendment provides protection for commercial speech in general and then for tobacco product advertising under current Supreme Court jurisprudence specifically. And this analysis suggests that, indeed, the First Amendment does and ought to protect truthful and non-misleading commercial advertising of legalized products targeted at lawful purchasers, including tobacco products, unpopular – and dangerous – though they may be, and even though minors might be exposed to some of these messages.

Turning first to the main tobacco advertising restrictions, in the 2009 FSPTC Act, Congress ordered the FDA to enact a rule limiting most print advertisements for regulated tobacco products to black text on a white background, among other restrictions (black-and-white text rule). The main exception that Congress allowed to the black-and-white text rule was for regulated tobacco advertising that appears in "adult publications" – meaning newspapers and magazines that have an underage readership (under the age of 18) of no more than 15 percent, and, in any event, the total number of underage readers must be fewer than two million. In 2010 the FDA enacted a final rule – titled "Regulations Restricting the Sale and Distribution of Cigarettes and Smokeless Tobacco to Protect Children and Adolescents" – that included these provisions, among others (75 Fed. Reg. 13225, codified at 21 C.F.R. pt. 1140).

In addition, the FSPTC Act amended the federal statutory warning requirements for cigarette and smokeless tobacco advertising and packaging in the
Federal Cigarette Labeling and Advertising Act (FCLAA – an acronym commonly
pronounced "*fick*-lah") (15 U.S.C. §§1331, *et seq.*) and the Comprehensive Smokeless Tobacco Health Education Act (15 U.S.C. §§4401, *et seq.*). Most significantly,
in the 2009 FSPTC Act, Congress ordered the FDA to design a set of "color
graphics depicting the negative health consequences of smoking" for use in rotation with nine textual warning statements, which include "WARNING: Cigarettes
are addictive," "WARNING: Cigarettes cause cancer," and "WARNING: Smoking
can kill you," among others (123 Stat. at 1842–1846; 15 U.S.C. §1333). In addition,
in the FSPTC Act, Congress amended the FCLAA to require that warning boxes
comprise the top 20 percent, at least, of cigarette advertisements and include
one of the nine textual warning statements in rotation with one of the color
graphic warnings designed by the FDA, also used in rotation. In 2011 the FDA
enacted a final rule – titled "Required Warnings for Cigarette Packages and
Advertisements" – which approved a controversial set of nine color graphics for
the enhanced warning boxes required by Congress in the revised FCLAA, including graphic depictions of a corpse with its chest sewn up, a diseased lung, and
smoke emanating from a tracheostomy hole in a person's throat (78 Fed. Reg.
36628, codified at 21 C.F.R. pt. 1141). The entire set of FDA-approved color
graphics for cigarette advertising warnings may be downloaded to view at the
FDA website at http://www.fda.gov/TobaccoProducts/Labeling/ucm259214.htm
(accessed March 20, 2013). In the FSPTC Act, Congress did not require color
graphic warnings for other tobacco products but strengthened the textual warnings required for smokeless tobacco advertising and packaging.

Not surprisingly, tobacco companies challenged the advertising restrictions
required by the FSPTC Act, including the black-and-white text rule and the
enhanced warning requirements with the color graphic warnings, on First
Amendment free speech grounds in lawsuits filed in the federal courts. These
cases were not the first time tobacco companies had been in federal court to
challenge government restrictions on tobacco advertising. In a 2001 decision,
the United States Supreme Court sided with tobacco companies and ruled that
a statewide ban in Massachusetts on tobacco billboards and signs within 1,000
feet of locations like schools and playgrounds – where children are likely to
be – was unconstitutional under the First Amendment's protection for commercial speech. This case – *Lorillard Tobacco Co. v. Reilly* – is discussed in more
detail later in this essay, along with recent federal court rulings in First Amendment challenges to various advertising restrictions required by the 2009 FSPTC
Act and corresponding FDA rules.

But first, given that the First Amendment of the United States Constitution
reads, in relevant part, "Congress shall make no law . . . abridging the freedom
of speech" without defining "speech" in any way, how is it that "speech" today
is widely understood to include protection for advertising? That has come from
a series of Supreme Court decisions including the landmark *Virginia State
Board of Pharmacy v. Virginia Citizens Consumer Council, Inc.* (1976) case,

in which the Court – for the first time – explicitly extended First Amendment protection to pure commercial speech, meaning speech that does no more than propose a commercial transaction. The Court in that case concluded that free-flowing commercial information from advertisers to consumers is critical to informed consumer decision-making in the marketplace and that these choices in the aggregate facilitate the function of our free market economy. Thus, the Court acknowledged in that case that while advertisers have a First Amendment right to truthfully and nondeceptively promote lawful goods and services, consumers have an equally important concomitant constitutional right to receive this information and use it to make purchase and other economic decisions based on their own self-determined interests free from excessive government intervention. In other words, the Court concluded, the First Amendment stands strongly against government attempts to manipulate lawful consumer choices in the marketplace by depriving them of information.

Thus, the *Virginia Board of Pharmacy* Court ultimately held that a state regulation that banned licensed pharmacists from advertising prescription drug prices violated the First Amendment because consumers – especially the elderly and those on fixed incomes – would benefit by knowing where to purchase their prescribed medications most economically. Writing for the majority in the case, Justice Harry Blackmun stated: "As to the particular consumer's interest in the free flow of commercial information, that interest may be as keen, if not keener by far, than his [or her] interest in the day's most urgent political debate" (425 U.S. at 763).

However, it bears mentioning here that the *Virginia State Board of Pharmacy* Court did not extend First Amendment protection to false or deceptive advertising, or advertising for unlawful transactions. Therefore, federal and state governments remain relatively unencumbered by the First Amendment to prohibit false or deceptive advertising on grounds of consumer protection in the marketplace. In other words, the First Amendment speech clause is not synonymous with the term "buyer beware." In addition, the *Virginia State Board of Pharmacy* Court did not extend full and complete First Amendment protection to commercial speech for lawful goods and services, even when truthful and nondeceptive, but instead it extended an intermediate level of constitutional protection. What this means today is that protected commercial speech – under some circumstances – can still be constitutionally regulated under the First Amendment. But how does the government know how much regulation is too much under the First Amendment when it comes to protected commercial speech?

In a 1980 case, *Central Hudson Gas & Electric Corp. v. Public Service Commission*, the Supreme Court determined more specifically the circumstances under which the government can constitutionally regulate protected commercial speech. In *Central Hudson*, the Court held that protected commercial speech can be constitutionally regulated only if the government asserts a substantial governmental interest – meaning an important public policy goal – and also demonstrates that the regulation will directly advance that asserted interest and also is narrowly tailored. In other words, to constitutionally regulate protected commercial speech, the government must have a reasonably strong public policy goal at stake, and must prove both that the regulation in question effectively serves that goal without sweeping too broadly by burdening protected commercial speech more than is reasonably necessary. In recent commercial speech decisions, the Court has applied this First Amendment analysis referred to as the *Central Hudson* test to strike down federal restrictions on direct-to-consumer advertising for compounded prescription drugs (*Thompson v. Western States Medical Center*, 2002) and state restrictions on in-person marketing of prescription drugs to physicians by pharmaceutical companies – a practice called "detailing" (*Sorrell v. IMS Health Inc.*, 2011).

And, what all of this means today is that advertisers have a constitutional right to promote lawful products and services in a truthful and nondeceptive manner. On the other hand, the government retains a good bit of leeway to constitutionally regulate unprotected false or deceptive advertising, and advertising for an illegal product or service, and still may constitutionally regulate even protected truthful and nondeceptive advertising for lawful products and services within the parameters of the *Central Hudson* test. In other words, the regulatory hands of the government are not completely tied by the First Amendment in terms of regulating advertising when there are important public policy goals at stake and the restrictions on protected commercial speech are demonstrated to be directly and materially effective and reasonable in scope.

So, what does all of this have to do with tobacco advertising? Well, specifically, the government has the constitutional authority to prohibit false and deceptive advertising for tobacco products and, probably, the related authority to constitutionally prohibit a specific unfair business practice, on a case-by-case basis, like a tobacco advertiser specifically targeting minors with its advertising. And, of course, the government generally may lawfully impose any number of direct tobacco product regulations that do not involve advertising (often referred to as "nonspeech alternatives") including age restrictions for purchases, and limitations on places of purchase, taxes on purchases, and even a ban on the use or sale of tobacco products.

In addition, as indicated, the government can even constitutionally regulate truthful and nondeceptive advertising for lawful tobacco products so long as the regulations directly and materially serve a reasonable public policy goal such as curbing underage tobacco use without unreasonably burdening the ability of tobacco advertisers and marketers to continue to advertise and promote their products to adult consumers. Needless to say, developing a constitutional regulatory scheme that withstands scrutiny under the *Central Hudson* test is challenging, especially when the government has opted to legalize products like tobacco and then wishes to restrict protected First Amendment *speech* about those products. In addition, the government can – and does – constitutionally require advertisers to disclose fact-based information to prevent false or deceptive advertising before the purchase decision is made. For example, as mentioned above, provisions in the FCLAA had required rotating textual health warnings in all cigarette advertising and packaging for years before Congress passed the FSPTC Act in 2009. And, in a different context, the Supreme Court has held that advertisers do not have a First Amendment right to refuse to disclose pertinent factual information in advertising when to do so would render an advertisement actually or inherently deceptive to consumers and the disclosure requirement is reasonably related to this goal – a more lenient standard than the *Central Hudson* test (*Zauderer v. Office of Disciplinary Council*, 1985; *Millavetz, Gallop & Millavetz, P.A. v. United States*, 2010). Therefore, the regulatory option of reasonable disclosure requirements in advertising related to the goal of preventing actually or inherently deceptive claims, along with all of the other regulatory options listed above, remain constitutionally viable without the need to strip tobacco product advertising of its constitutional protection under the First Amendment and thus eliminate truthful and nondeceptive commercial communication between tobacco advertisers and their adult customers without overly burdensome government interference.

But should that be the case? If the government can impose all of these regulations on a product and even ban the sale and use of the product altogether – especially a harmful or "vice" product like tobacco – should it not then have additional leeway under the First Amendment to regulate advertising for such products more stringently than advertising more socially acceptable products? Basically, no, the Supreme Court has told us in several important commercial speech decisions. And, one could argue, rightly so. Why is this? Well, the First Amendment generally does not make such normative judgments and instead protects speech without regard to viewpoint, including speech that many would find repugnant and disagreeable. In fact, arguably, such is the type of speech that is most needy and deserving of First Amendment protection because it can be most at risk of being banned legislatively in response to popular sentiment. Therefore, for example, the First Amendment generally protects noncommercial political and social messages quite strongly, even those that are dissident and repugnant to most, and thus allows each individual in society to decide in the "marketplace of ideas" whether a certain message is "good" or "bad," agreeable or disagreeable.

The First Amendment commercial speech doctrine treats advertising for products and services somewhat similarly. So long as the government has legalized a commercial product or service, there is a fairly strong constitutional right to promote that product to consumers in a truthful and nondeceptive manner. In other words, there may not be a constitutional right to sell, purchase, or use particular consumer products like tobacco products but when the government has legalized these products, there is a strong First Amendment right to *speak* about the products, including commercially in the form of truthful and nondeceptive advertising. And consumers have the corresponding right to receive this information and use it to make lawful decisions in the economic marketplace and, ultimately, to make a judgment on the product or service being advertised.

Along these lines, the Supreme Court has extended First Amendment protection to truthful and nondeceptive commercial speech related to conceded harmful products and activities – so-called "vice" products and activities – like high-alcohol malt beverages (*Rubin v. Coors Brewing Co., Inc.*, 1995), liquor (*44 Liquormart, Inc. v. Rhode Island*, 1996), casino gambling (*Greater New Orleans Broadcasting Association v. United States*, 1999) and, most relevant here, tobacco products (*Lorillard Tobacco Co. v. Reilly*, 2001). In these cases, the Court refused to create a "vice" exemption under the First Amendment that would allow the government to more freely regulate advertising for such harmful but legal products and services than it may for other types of products and services that are considered more socially acceptable. For example, writing for the Supreme Court in a 1999 case in which the Court struck down a federal ban on broadcast advertising for casino gambling, Justice John Paul Stevens explained that the Court had "rejected the argument that the power to restrict *speech* about certain socially harmful activities [is] as broad as the power to prohibit such *conduct*" (*Greater New Orleans Broadcasting*, at 193; emphasis added). And, in all of these cases, the government had nonspeech regulatory options available to curb asserted harmful secondary effects stemming from consumers choosing to use these products or to patronize such activities, rather than restricting protected commercial speech.

Especially pertinent to tobacco advertising, in a 2001 decision the Supreme Court refused to allow the state of Massachusetts to prohibit truthful and non-misleading outdoor advertising for tobacco products, including signs in retail establishments visible from outside, within 1,000 feet of locations where children were likely to be, including schools and playgrounds (*Lorillard Tobacco Co. v. Reilly*). In the majority opinion written by Justice Sandra Day O'Connor, the Court concluded under the *Central Hudson* test that Massachusetts indeed had established a sufficiently substantial – even compelling – regulatory goal of protecting children from the harms of tobacco products and also that reducing the extent to which children are exposed to tobacco advertising would effectively serve this goal sufficiently to withstand the constitutional challenge in the case. Indeed, Justice O'Connor, writing for the *Lorillard Tobacco* Court, stated that "[f]rom a policy perspective, it is understandable for States to attempt to prevent minors from using tobacco products before they reach an age where they are capable of weighing for themselves the risks and potential benefits of tobacco use, and other adult activities" (*Lorillard Tobacco Co.*, at 570–571).

However, the *Lorillard Tobacco* Court presumed that "[i]n some geographical areas, [the 1,000-foot rule] would constitute nearly a complete ban on the communication of truthful information about [tobacco products] to adult consumers" and found that the state had not conducted the "careful calculation of the speech interests involved" as required by the First Amendment (*Lorillard Tobacco Co.*, at 562). Again, writing for the Court, Justice O'Conner explained:

> The First Amendment . . . constrains state efforts to limit advertising of tobacco products, because so long as the sale and use of tobacco products is lawful for adults, the tobacco industry has a protected interest in communicating information about its products *and* adult consumers have an interest in receiving that information. (*Lorillard Tobacco Co.*, at 571; emphasis added)

In other words, the *Lorillard Tobacco* Court concluded, Massachusetts should have developed an evidentiary record to demonstrate that the 1,000-foot rule for outdoor advertising did not sweep more broadly than reasonably needed to effectively combat underage tobacco usage and did not overly burden lawful tobacco advertising to adults as constitutionally mandated by the First Amendment. And, as mentioned, the Court did not ignore the importance of preventing minors from using tobacco products and reducing their exposure to tobacco advertising. However, the Court had to balance that important concern with the long-standing First Amendment requirement, as the Court had applied it previously in cases including a 1983 decision striking down a federal ban on unsolicited direct-mail contraception advertising (*Bolger v. Youngs Drug Products Corp.*), that constitutionally protected communications to adults not be broadly capped at the level of what is appropriate only for minors (*Lorillard Tobacco Co.*, at 564). In addition, mostly as an aside here, it bears mentioning that the *Lorillard Tobacco* Court also considered and rejected as unconstitutional related state regulations that would have prevented retailers that permitted minors inside, say, a convenience store located in one of the 1,000-foot zones from using any indoor tobacco advertising lower than five feet from the floor. The Court concluded that Massachusetts had failed to demonstrate that the five-foot rule would effectively serve the goal of reducing underage tobacco usage and, in any event, noted that minors in such locations might well be taller than five feet and that those who were not could simply raise their heads to look up.

Therefore, according to the *Lorillard Tobacco* Court, the Massachusetts regulations unconstitutionally prohibited tobacco advertisers, especially local retailers, from communicating with adult consumers and, for instance, could have been more narrowly tailored to target the most highly visible outdoor tobacco advertisements or those with advertising messages with demonstrated youth-oriented appeals. Instead, the Court pointed out, the regulations would even have prohibited retailers located within a specified 1,000-foot zone from simply informing the adult passerby, in any manner whatsoever, that they sold tobacco products inside. In the case, Justice Clarence Thomas, in a strongly worded concurring opinion, specifically warned about the dangers of allowing restrictions on messages that some may find harmful. On this point, he wrote:

> Calls for limits on expression always are made when the specter of some threatened harm is looming. The identity of the harm may vary. People will be inspired by totalitarian dogmas and subvert the Republic. They will be inflamed by racial demagoguery and embrace hatred and bigotry. Or they will be enticed by cigarette advertisements and choose to smoke, risking disease. It is therefore no answer for the State to say that the makers of cigarettes are doing harm: perhaps they are. But in that respect they are no different from the purveyors of other harmful products, or the advocates of harmful ideas. When the State seeks to silence them, they are all entitled to the protection of the First Amendment. (*Lorillard Tobacco Co.*, Thomas, J., concurring in part and concurring in the judgment, at 590).

Justice Thomas warned that allowing the Massachusetts ban on outdoor tobacco advertising to stand under the First Amendment likely would open the door to similar restrictions on such products as fast food and alcohol, which are also deemed by many in society to be harmful yet are perfectly lawful.

What of the constitutional fate of the advertising restrictions required in the 2009 Family Smoking Prevention and Tobacco Control Act and described above? At the time of this publication, in cases decided by two federal circuit courts of appeals – courts that sit one level below the Supreme Court in the federal judicial system – the black-and-white text requirements for cigarette and smokeless tobacco advertising had been ruled unconstitutional and thus unenforceable under the *Central Hudson* test by the Sixth Circuit in *Discount Tobacco City & Lottery, Inc. v. United States* (2013); and the color graphic warnings approved by the FDA had been ruled unconstitutional and unenforceable also under the *Central Hudson* test by the District of Columbia Circuit in *R. J. Reynolds Tobacco Co. v. Food and Drug Administration* (2012). The *Discount Tobacco City* case was not a total First Amendment victory for the tobacco parties, however, because although the Sixth Circuit struck down the black-and-white text requirements required by the FSPTC Act, the court *upheld* other restrictions required by the Act including those that prohibit tobacco advertisers from claiming that a tobacco product is less risky than other similar products available in the marketplace – including using the terms "light," "mild," or "low" – unless approved in advance by the FDA; and prohibiting tobacco companies from engaging in branded sponsorships of musical and athletic events, among others (*Discount City Tobacco*, at 543–544, 536–537). And, although the Sixth Circuit generally upheld the enhanced warning requirements specified in the FSPTC Act, the court did *not* have the occasion to rule on the specific color graphic warnings ultimately approved by the FDA because the case was filed before the FDA had enacted that particular rule.

However, later in 2012, the District of Columbia Circuit did rule on the constitutionality of the FDA-approved color graphic warnings in the *R. J. Reynolds* case and concluded under the *Central Hudson* analysis that the FDA had failed to prove the requisite level of effectiveness of the color graphic warnings in serving the government's asserted interest in reducing smoking rates, especially among children, as stated in the preamble to the FSPTC Act and the FDA's final rule approving the color graphic warnings. On this point, the appeals court in *R. J. Reynolds* concluded that although the FDA had presented a substantial record, including various social scientific studies, only two of them "directly evaluate[d] the impact of graphic warnings on actual smoking rates, and neither set of data show[ed] that graphic warnings will 'directly' advance [the] asserted interest in reducing smoking rates 'to a material degree'" as required by the *Central Hudson* test (*R. J. Reynolds*, at 1220, quoting *Rubin v. Coors Brewing Co. Inc.* (1995), at 487). In 2013 the US government announced that it would not appeal the D.C. Circuit Court of Appeals ruling in the *R. J. Reynolds* case. In addition, in the 2009 FSPTC Act, Congress required the FDA to enact a 1,000-foot rule similar to the one that the Supreme Court struck down in the *Lorillard Tobacco* case but to take that decision into account and make any necessary accommodations to address the constitutional deficiencies found by the Court in that case (123 Stat. at 1831). At the time of this publication, the FDA had not yet enacted a final 1,000-foot rule for outdoor tobacco advertising so the constitutional fate of such a rule when enacted remained unknown.

However, given that First Amendment protection for tobacco advertising has never been considered absolute, and that the government retains the right to regulate, tax, and even ban tobacco products, it seems quite dangerous indeed to assert that commercial *speech* about such a lawful product – tobacco advertising – should be rendered entirely devoid of First Amendment protection and permitted to be banned by the government even when truthful and nondeceptive. And, of course, should the government decide to remove tobacco products from the list of legalized products available to the public by banning their sale, the First Amendment would no longer recognize any right to promote the sale or use of these products once criminalized. But, so long as the government has chosen to allow the legalized sale of tobacco products, the First Amendment does – and should – protect the right of advertisers to speak commercially about these products to lawful consumers in a truthful and nondeceptive manner as well as the concomitant right of consumers to receive these communications. Specifically, this means that even when the government seeks to restrict nondeceptive advertising lawful transactions and has demonstrated a substantial regulatory goal like protecting minors from the harms of tobacco use, the government must demonstrate that its regulation will be directly and materially effective in serving that interest and, even if it does so, that it is not so broad that it unreasonably burdens or restricts the free flow of protected commercial messages to lawful purchasers. Supreme Court decisions indicate that burden is not an easy one, but anything less would violate the spirit and intent of free commercial speech rights, and the importance of free-flowing commercial information facilitating informed consumer decision-making and efficient functioning of the economic marketplace.

References

44 Liquormart, Inc. v. Rhode Island, 517 U.S. 484, 1996.

Bolger v. Youngs Drug Products Corp., 463 U.S. 60, 1983.

Central Hudson Gas & Electric Corp. v. Public Service Commission, 447 U.S. 557, 1980.

Discount Tobacco City & Lottery, Inc. v. United States, 674 F.3d 509 (6th Cir.), 2012.

Family Smoking Prevention and Tobacco Control Act, Pub. L. No. 111-31, Div. A, 123 Stat. 1776, June 22, 2009 (codified in various sections of the United States Code).

Greater New Orleans Broadcasting Association v. United States, 527 U.S. 193, 1999.

Lorillard Tobacco Co. v. Reilly, 533 U.S. 525, 2001.

Millavetz, Gallop & Millavetz, P.A. v. United States, 130 S.Ct. 1326, 2010.

R. J. Reynolds Tobacco Co. v. Food and Drug Administration, 696 F.3d 1205 (D.C. Cir.), 2012.

Regulations Restricting the Sale and Distribution of Cigarettes and Smokeless Tobacco to Protect Children and Adolescents, 75 Fed. Reg. 13225, 2010 (codified at 21 C.F.R. pt. 1140).

Rubin v. Coors Brewing Co., Inc., 514 U.S. 476, 1995.
Sorrell v. IMS Health Inc., 131 S.Ct. 2653, 2011.
Thompson v. Western States Medical Center, 535 U.S. 357, 2002.
Virginia State Board of Pharmacy v. Virginia Consumer Council, Inc., 425 U.S. 748, 1976.
Zauderer v. Office of Disciplinary Council, 471 U.S. 626, 1985.

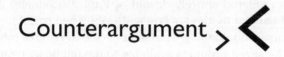

Counterargument

Rationales for the regulation of tobacco advertising and promotion

Timothy Dewhirst

University of Guelph, Canada

In this essay, rationales for government intervention and the regulation of tobacco advertising and promotion are provided, including discussion about the health consequences and addictiveness of tobacco use, the unavoidable exposure of youth to many tobacco promotional campaigns, the deceptive and misleading nature of several tobacco promotional campaigns, the minimal role of factual information being made available in several tobacco promotional campaigns, and the role of tobacco advertising and promotion in increasing tobacco use in the population, especially among youth.

Tobacco Is a Highly Distinctive Product

Tobacco use is a major public health problem, representing the single most important preventable cause of death in the world. Globally, if current trends continue, it is estimated that tobacco use will be attributable for more than eight million deaths each year by 2030 (WHO 2008). In the United States, an estimated 443,000 people die prematurely each year as a result of smoking, which represents roughly one of every five deaths domestically (USDHHS 2012). Tobacco use is responsible for a greater number of deaths among Americans than the total number of deaths caused by motor-vehicle crashes, suicides, murders, AIDS, and illicit drug use combined (USDHHS 2004).

Despite being a lawful product (for adults), tobacco has been identified as an obvious example of an inherently harmful and addictive product. Thus limitations on marketing efforts have been recommended regardless of whether the target market is considered a sophisticated, at-risk, or vulnerable consumer (Rittenburg and Parthasarathy 1997). Youth are considered to be a group particularly worthy of protection from tobacco inducements given that smokers usually begin during their preteen or teenage years, and they are known to highly underestimate the addictiveness of cigarettes. Industry-commissioned research indicates that adolescents who start smoking do not generally disbelieve the overall health consequences of smoking, but they almost universally assume these risks are nonapplicable because they do not anticipate becoming addicted (Kwechansky Marketing Research 1982). Moreover, most existing smokers regret their behavior and express a desire to quit (i.e., between 80% and 90% of American smokers state that, if they had to do it again, they would not have started smoking), yet attempts at quitting are typically unsuccessful (Slovic 2001; Fong et al. 2004; Hyland et al. 2004). Tobacco represents a highly distinctive product category given its devastating health consequences and addictiveness, the recognized strategic importance of youth and recruitment of new smokers by tobacco companies, as well as most consumers stating that they do not want to continue using the product.

"Starters" and "Pre-Quitters": Two Key Typologies of Cigarette Consumers

Despite the importance of conducting a standard market segmentation analysis, British American Tobacco (BAT 100575008) identifies that basic consumer segmentation consists of "current smokers, starters, temporary quitters, 'confirmed' ex-smokers, and non-smokers." Moreover, reviews of internal tobacco industry documents, made public from litigation, reveal that two key typologies of cigarette consumers, as perceived by tobacco firms and their advertisers, are "starters" and "pre-quitters" (Pollay 2000).

First, the documents make known that cigarette brands are successfully marketed to youth, including consumers who are classified as "starters" or "new smokers" (Pollay and Lavack 1993; Perry 1999; Cummings et al. 2002; Dewhirst and Sparks 2003; Dewhirst 2008). The rationale for tobacco companies directing their promotions toward youth is that the pivotal period for smoking initiation in the United States has historically been during adolescence and smokers are known to be extremely brand-loyal (USDHHS 2012). It is highly likely that someone who starts smoking Marlboro during adolescence, for example, will continue smoking the brand if he or she is still smoking 20 years later; changes in product selection are commonly within the same brand family (e.g., from Marlboro Red to Marlboro Smooth).

Second, the documents make known that cigarette brands are successfully marketed to "pre-quitters," which represents those who continue to smoke despite being anxious about the health consequences that are likely to ensue. Quitting is not an easy option for many smokers, thus the opportunity to switch to a lower machine-measured yield cigarette (historically offered as "light" or "mild" on the package) offers an attractive and reassuring alternative (Pollay and Dewhirst 2002; Hoek and Dewhirst 2012). According to documentation from BAT (1985: 100501593), "it is useful to consider lights more as a third alternative to quitting and cutting down – a branded hybrid of smokers' unsuccessful attempts to modify their habit on their own." Advertising and promotions that point to a cigarette brand's supposed low-tar delivery (e.g., 1.0 mg) are regarded as misleading, as tar and nicotine yields generated for cigarettes smoked by machines are appreciably lower than the yields actually delivered to compensating smokers (Canova et al. 2001; Kozlowski and O'Connor 2002; Benowitz et al. 2005). Given the addictiveness of nicotine, smokers often engage in subconscious, compensatory behavior when smoking lower-yield cigarettes, including smoking the cigarette closer to the butt, taking deeper puffs from the cigarette, increasing the number of puffs taken while smoking the cigarette, and smoking more cigarettes per day (National Cancer Institute 2001).

The Importance of Communicating Image/Lifestyle and Minimal Information

Most American cigarette brands have historically been positioned on the basis of lifestyle and expressing a brand image or personality. In the seminal article on dimensions of brand personality, Marlboro is offered as an example of a ruggedness brand, which "tend to glamorize American ideals of Western, strength, and masculinity" (Aaker 1997: 353). More generally, several content analysis studies reveal that health and vitality, risk and adventure, independence, status redemption, sophistication and social acceptance, masculinity or femininity, romance, recreation, and relaxation are common themes that are associated with cigarette products in advertising (USDHHS 1994; Dewhirst 2008).

Internal corporate documents, made public from litigation, reveal that tobacco firms recognize cigarettes as a product category in which the marketing of a brand's image – and the portrayal of lifestyle – is paramount (Dewhirst 2004; Dewhirst and Davis 2005; National Cancer Institute 2008). Communicating brand image is considered particularly crucial for product categories, such as cigarettes, that are classified as low involvement and emotional (exciting) goods (Vaughn 1980; Zaichkowsky 1987). For such products, it is recommended that advertising adopt a "feel good" theme, in which appeals typically have a lifestyle orientation and account for sensory pleasures. According to Richard Vaughn, "imagery and quick satisfaction are involved" (1980: 32). Advertising strategy should be developed with the aim of gaining the consumer's attention. There is likely to be a strong emphasis on visuals and minimal ad copy (i.e., few words are used in providing a short and simple message, which may be limited to a catchy slogan or tagline) in advertising strategy or such products. Thus, such advertising is comparatively less informative, given there are few rational reasons for purchasing products such as cigarettes. Outdoor advertising (e.g., billboards) and point of purchase are regarded as particularly useful mediums of marketing communication (Tuckwell 2008).

Shifts in Tobacco Industry Promotional Spending

Tobacco control policies have historically been approached in a piecemeal manner, in several jurisdictions, in which particular mediums of tobacco promotion are prohibited whereas other mediums remain permissible. Such a regulatory environment has facilitated shifts in promotional spending, with overall tobacco industry promotional spending levels persisting. In other words, *partial* tobacco advertising bans do not generally result in reduced advertising output, but rather in media substitution and reinvestment (Saffer and Chaloupka 2000). For example, in accordance with the Public Health Cigarette Smoking Act, cigarette advertising was no longer permitted in the US broadcast media, effective January 2, 1971. Consequently, the tobacco industry shifted promotional spending, including toward print media and sponsoring broadcast sports events as a means of compensating for lost broadcast advertising exposure (Feinberg 1971; Teel et al. 1979; Warner 1979, 1985; Cornwell 1997). To demonstrate that sport sponsorship was used by tobacco companies to circumvent the cigarette broadcast advertising ban, a videotaped recording of the Marlboro Grand Prix, from July 16, 1989, revealed that Marlboro was seen or mentioned 5,933 times (Blum 1991). A ban on billboard advertising in the United States, in accordance with the 1998 Master Settlement Agreement, prompted an increase in the prevalence of both interior and exterior tobacco advertising at retail outlets (Celebucki and Diskin 2002; Wakefield et al. 2002). Stringent regulatory environments have facilitated retail merchandising becoming a central focus of tobacco marketing efforts. According to US advertising trade press, retail merchandising contracts are now the most potent part of a tobacco company's marketing arsenal, and "the contracts are cigarette marketers' primary marketing tool since the 1998 Master Settlement Agreement prohibited most tobacco advertising" (Beirne 2002: 3).

The Point of Purchase Advertising Institute monitors in-store advertising expenditures for 22 industries, and their market research reveals that the tobacco industry is the top spender on in-store media (Gottesman 1997). Merchants receive significantly more money for tobacco display allowances relative to other product categories. One study, comparing incentive programs among small retail outlets in Santa Clara, California, for tobacco, beer and wine, soft drinks, snack foods, and candy, found that, among the five measured product categories, approximately 78 percent of incentive payments came from tobacco firms (Feighery et al. 1999).

US tobacco firms now spend most of their promotional dollars via the retail sector (e.g., convenience stores, gas stations). Federal Trade Commission (FTC) data reveal that in 2001, 85 percent of cigarette advertising and promotional dollars were spent via retailers when point-of-sale advertising, promotional allowances (e.g., payments to retailers for shelf space and passing along price reductions to consumers), and retail value added (e.g., costs associated with bonus items distributed at retail when cigarettes are purchased) categories are combined (FTC 2003). In 2006, $12.5 billion was spent on tobacco promotion by the major US tobacco firms, with 81 percent of total spending allocated to promotional allowances alone, and 90 percent of total spending via retailers and wholesalers (FTC 2009).

The $12.5 billion figure and *intensive* channel intensity level (i.e., the product has widespread market coverage and is readily available) speaks to the notable persistence and pervasiveness of tobacco promotion. A dense environment of cigarette promotion and imagery gives the impression that tobacco use is socially acceptable, desirable, and prevalent (Pollay 2002). The large promotional budgets that are apparent for leading cigarette brands reinforce and elevate consumer perceptions about the popularity of those brands, and popularity is considered to be a crucial factor in brand desirability among youth. Academic research shows that US youth disproportionately smoke heavily advertised brands (Pollay et al. 1996). Moreover, for existing and former smokers, point-of-sale advertising and displays can function to stimulate unplanned or impulse purchases through discount prices (e.g., a "good deal" being offered such as buy two packs, get one free) or the mere visibility of smoking cues (e.g., tobacco packaging, a photo of a cigarette or of someone smoking) that bring about physiological cravings among smokers and ex-smokers (Hoek et al. 2010).

Product Category Growth

Internal corporate documents from the tobacco industry recognize that their marketing activities, including retail merchandising, goes beyond influencing market share and serves to affect overall consumption levels. According to BAT documentation, the company has four global in-store marketing objectives: category leadership, increased brand presence, volume growth, and profit. For volume growth, the company seeks to "achieve long-term dependable growth of the category and our brands. Use of innovative in-store marketing techniques by trade channels will help us to achieve our growth objectives" (BAT 500316637). In reaching their growth objectives, it is important to note that BAT is referring to both their portfolio of brands and the tobacco product category generally. Moreover, in discussing partnership benefits at the category product level, the company states that in-store marketing techniques "[grow] new segments," and for trade partners "insures volume/profit growth" (BAT 500316657). Additional BAT documentation indicates that while the tobacco company benefits through "increased share, sales and profit," trade partners, such as wholesalers and retailers, benefit from merchandising marketing activities due to "increased *category* sales and profits" (Niederman 1994).

After extensive reviews of studies with a diversity of research approaches, sample sizes, time frames, and settings, a major conclusion of the 2012 Surgeon General's report is "advertising and promotional activities by tobacco companies have been shown to cause the onset and continuation of smoking among adolescents and young adults" (USDHHS 2012: 8). Additionally, the National Cancer Institute concluded that the total weight of evidence "demonstrates a causal relationship between tobacco advertising and promotion and increased tobacco use" (2008: 12).

The WHO FCTC

A global treaty has taken effect, known as the World Health Organization's (WHO) Framework Convention on Tobacco Control (FCTC), which is legally binding for those countries that ratify the treaty. To date, 176 parties have ratified the WHO FCTC, which "requires parties to adopt a comprehensive range of measures designed to reduce the devastating health and economic impacts of tobacco" (see www.fctc.org for details). The WHO FCTC is an evidence-based treaty that consists of several measures meant to reduce both the supply and demand of tobacco. Article 6, for example, identifies price and tax measures to reduce the demand for tobacco, whereas Articles 9 and 10 call for a ban on cigarette flavors such as vanilla and honey, given their appeal to youth with increasing the palatability of cigarettes. According to Article 11, tobacco packaging and labeling should not include terms, such as "low tar" and "ultra-light," that are likely to be misleading about the product's harmfulness. Article 13 stipulates that each party shall have a comprehensive ban on tobacco advertising and promotion, in accordance with its constitutional principles, within five years of ratification. To date, the United States has not ratified the treaty.

Summary and Conclusions

A review of internal corporate documents from the tobacco industry reveals its strategic interest and intention to appeal to "starters" as well as "pre-quitters." Marketing initiatives, including retail merchandising, meant to influence both of these key typologies of tobacco consumers, impacts the overall size of the market. By influencing "starters," who are usually in early adolescence, the industry insures that new smokers enter the market, either contributing to the product category's growth or mitigating its decline by serving to replace smokers leaving the market by quitting or dying.

Retail settings have generally become the principal site of paid promotion for tobacco firms. Tobacco retail merchandising (e.g., product displays, promotional signage) is likely to be influential toward those in adolescence, at the stage of potential initiation, for a variety of reasons. First, tobacco products remain widely available and visible, if permitted, which contributes to the perception that, if they are as widely available as products like milk and bread, and likely more visible, they can't be that harmful and addictive. Second, the mere exposure effect, in which objects encountered frequently are more likely to be viewed favorably, is well established from research. Third, research supports the contribution of a strong presence of tobacco products at retail outlets to the perception that tobacco products are popular and more socially acceptable, prompting overestimates regarding the proportion of people that actually smoke. Moreover, a retail setting with a strong presence of tobacco products is likely to contribute to the perception, among adolescents, that cigarettes can be easily acquired. Fourth, it is evident that tobacco brands are rich in symbolic and lifestyle imagery; consequently, allowing tobacco packages and promotional signage to be visibly on display establishes an environment where tobacco brands being an expression of independence, ruggedness, femininity, success, and so on is enhanced and reinforced. For existing and former smokers, tobacco retail merchandising is likely to be influential for many of the same reasons cited above for adolescents, although impulse purchases may also play an important role.

Left unregulated, tobacco promotion is pervasive. Advertising theory specifies that promotions for tobacco, as a product category, are likely to be image- and lifestyle-oriented, with minimal information being communicated. In the United States, laws regulating tobacco advertising and promotion appear justified given that a considerable amount of tobacco advertising has been targeted toward youth or been misleading (e.g., promotion that has pointed to a cigarette's supposed low yield and made used of product descriptors such as "light," "mild," and "low tar"). In a 1,742-page decision issued on August 17, 2006, federal Judge Gladys Kessler ruled that the major US cigarette firms violated civil (i.e., noncriminal) provisions of the Racketeer Influenced Corrupt Organizations (RICO) Act:

> For several decades, Defendants have marketed and promoted their low tar brands as being less harmful than conventional cigarettes. That claim is false, as these Findings of Fact demonstrate. By making these false claims, Defendants have given smokers an acceptable alternative to quitting smoking, as well as an excuse for not quitting. (Kessler 2006: 740)

There is also a substantial government interest to be served by the regulation of tobacco advertising and promotion given its effect and influence on overall consumption levels and the devastating health consequences of cigarette smoking.

References

Aaker, J. L. (1997). Dimensions of brand personality. *Journal of Marketing Research* 34 (Aug.): 347–356.

Beirne, M. (2002). Tobacco row: Cigarette makers step up retail war. *Brandweek* (Dec. 2), 3.

Benowitz, N. L. et al. (2005). Carcinogen exposure during short-term switching from regular to "light" cigarettes. *Cancer Epidemiology, Biomarkers and Prevention* 14(6): 1376–1383.

Blum, A. (1991). The Marlboro Grand Prix: Circumvention of the television ban on tobacco advertising. *New England Journal of Medicine* 324: 913–917.

BAT (British American Tobacco). Brand concepts and image design: The general law of cigarette marketing. Bates No. 100575008. At http://legacy.library.ucsf.edu/tid/cuk76a99/pdf;jsessionid=D60D6DA58F4376BA59EBE98E70FB40F6.tobacco03, accessed Apr. 5, 2013.

BAT (British American Tobacco). In-store marketing manual. Bates No. 5003166520–500316665.

BAT (British American Tobacco) (1985). R&D/marketing conference. Bates No. 100501593. At http://legacy.library.ucsf.edu/tid/sxf34a99/pdf, accessed Apr. 5, 2013.

Canova, D., Myers, M. L., Smith, D. E., and Slade, J. (2001). Changing the future of tobacco marketing by understanding the mistakes of the past: Lessons from "lights." *Tobacco Control* 10(Suppl. 1): i43–4.

Celebucki, C. C. and Diskin, K. (2002). A longitudinal study of externally visible cigarette advertising on retail storefronts in Massachusetts before and after the Master Settlement Agreement. *Tobacco Control* 11(Suppl. 2): ii47–53.

Cornwell, T. B. (1997). The use of sponsorship-linked marketing by tobacco firms: International public policy issues. *Journal of Consumer Affairs* 31: 238–254.

Cummings, K. M. et al. (2002). Marketing to America's youth: Evidence from corporate documents. *Tobacco Control* 11(Suppl. 1): i5–17.

Dewhirst, T. (2004). Smoke and ashes: Tobacco sponsorship of sports and regulatory issues in Canada. In L. R. Kahle and C. Riley (eds.), *Sports Marketing and the Psychology of Marketing Communication*. Mahwah, NJ: Lawrence Erlbaum, pp. 327–352.

Dewhirst, T. (2008). Tobacco portrayals in U.S. advertising and entertainment media. In P. E. Jamieson and D. Romer (eds.), *The Changing Portrayal of Adolescents in the Media since 1950*. New York: Oxford University Press, pp. 250–283.

Dewhirst, T. and Davis, B. (2005). Brand strategy and integrated marketing communication (IMC): A case study of Player's cigarette brand marketing. *Journal of Advertising* 34(4): 81–92.

Dewhirst, T. and Sparks, R. (2003). Intertextuality, tobacco sponsorship of sports, and adolescent male smoking culture: A selective review of tobacco industry documents. *Journal of Sport and Social Issues* 27(4): 372–398.

Feighery, E. C., Ribisl, K. M., Achabal, D. D., and Tyebjee, T. (1999). Retail trade incentives: How tobacco industry practices compare with those of other industries. *American Journal of Public Health* 89: 1564–1566.

Feinberg, B. M. (1971). Content analysis shows cigarette advertising up twofold in 14 magazines. *Journalism Quarterly* 48: 539–542.

Fong, G. et al. (2004). The near-universal experience of regret among smokers in four countries: Findings from the International Tobacco Control Policy Evaluation Survey. *Nicotine and Tobacco Research* 6(Suppl. 3): S341–351.

FTC (Federal Trade Commission) (2003). *Federal Trade Commission cigarette report for 2001*. Washington, DC: Federal Trade Commission.

FTC (Federal Trade Commission) (2009). *Federal Trade Commission cigarette report for 2006*. Washington, DC: Federal Trade Commission.

Gottesman, A. (1997). Store wars. *Adweek* (Dec. 1), 20.

Hoek, J. and Dewhirst, T. (2012). The meaning of "Light" and "Ultralight" cigarettes: A commentary on Smith, Stutts, and Zank. *Journal of Public Policy and Marketing* 31(2): 223–231.

Hoek, J., Gifford, H., Pirikahu, G., Thomson, G., and Edwards, R. (2010). How do tobacco retail displays affect cessation attempts? Findings from a qualitative study. *Tobacco Control* 19(4): 334–337.

Hyland, A. et al. (2004). Predictors of cessation in a cohort of current and former smokers followed over 13 years. *Nicotine and Tobacco Research* 6(Suppl. 3): S363–369.

Kessler, G. (2006). Amended final opinion. U.S. v. Philip Morris USA, Inc., Civil Action No. 99-2496 (D.D.C.), August 17, 2006. At http://www.tobacco.neu.edu/litigation/cases/DOJ/20060817KESSLEROPINIONAMENDED.pdf, accessed Mar. 20, 2013.

Kozlowski, L. T. and O'Connor, R. J. (2002). Cigarette filter ventilation is a defective design because of misleading taste, bigger puffs, and blocked vents. *Tobacco Control* 11 (Suppl. 1): i40–50.

Kwechansky Marketing Research Inc. (1982, May 7). Project plus/minus. Prepared for Imperial Tobacco Ltd. Exhibit AG-217, *RJR-Macdonald Inc. v. Canada (Attorney General)*.

National Cancer Institute (2001). *Risks associated with smoking cigarettes with low machine-measured yields of tar and nicotine*. Smoking and Tobacco Control Monograph No. 13. Bethesda, MD: US Department of Health and Human Services, National Institutes of Health, National Cancer Institute.

National Cancer Institute (2008). *The role of the media in promoting and reducing tobacco use*. Smoking and Tobacco Control Monograph No. 19. Bethesda, MD: US Department of Health and Human Services, National Institutes of Health, National Cancer Institute.

Niederman, H. (1994, Nov.). In-store marketing manual: Principles and applications. British American Tobacco. Bates No. 503896000.

Perry, C. L. (1999). The tobacco industry and underage youth smoking: Tobacco industry documents from the Minnesota litigation. *Archives of Pediatrics and Adolescent Medicine* 153(9): 935–941.

Pollay, R. W. (2000). Targeting youth and concerned smokers: Evidence from Canadian tobacco industry documents. *Tobacco Control* 9(2): 136–147.

Pollay, R. W. (2002). How cigarette advertising works: Rich imagery and poor information. Exhibit D-57, Expert report prepared for *JTI-Macdonald Corp., Imperial Tobacco Canada Ltd., and Rothmans, Benson & Hedges Inc. v. The Attorney General of Canada*. Quebec Superior Court.

Pollay, R. W. and Dewhirst, T. (2002). The dark side of marketing seemingly "Light" cigarettes: Successful images and failed fact. *Tobacco Control* 11(Suppl. 1): i18–31.

Pollay, R. W. and Lavack, A. M. (1993). The targeting of youths by cigarette marketers: Archival evidence on trial. *Advances in Consumer Research* 20: 266–271.

Pollay, R. W. et al. (1996). The last straw? Cigarette advertising and realized market shares among youths and adults, 1979–1993. *Journal of Marketing* 60: 1–16.

Rittenburg, T. L. and Parthasarathy, M. (1997). Ethical implications of target market selection. *Journal of Macromarketing* 17(2): 49–64.

Saffer, H. and Chaloupka, F. (2000). The effect of tobacco advertising bans on tobacco consumption. *Journal of Health Economics* 19: 1117–1137.

Slovic, P. (2001). Cigarette smokers: Rational actors or rational fools? In P. Slovic (ed.), *Smoking: Risk, Perception, & Policy*. Thousand Oaks, CA: Sage, pp. 97–124.

Teel, S. J., Teel, J. E., and Bearden, W. O. (1979). Lessons learned from the broadcast cigarette advertising ban. *Journal of Marketing* 43: 45–50.

Tuckwell, K. J. (2008). *Integrated marketing communications: Strategic planning perspectives*, 2nd edn. Toronto: Pearson Prentice Hall.

USDHHS (US Department of Health and Human Services) (1994). *Preventing tobacco use among young people: A report of the Surgeon General*. Atlanta, GA: US Department of Health and Human Services, Public Health Service, Centers for Disease Control and Prevention, National Center for Chronic Disease Prevention and Health Promotion, Office on Smoking and Health.

USDHHS (US Department of Health and Human Services) (2004). *The health consequences of smoking: A report of the Surgeon General*. Atlanta, GA: US Department of Health and Human Services, Centers for Disease Control and Prevention, National Center for Chronic Disease Prevention and Health Promotion, Office on Smoking and Health.

USDHHS (US Department of Health and Human Services) (2012). *Preventing tobacco use among youth and young adults: A report of the Surgeon General*. Atlanta, GA: U.S. Department of Health and Human Services, Centers for Disease Control and Prevention, National Center for Chronic Disease Prevention and Health Promotion, Office on Smoking and Health.

Vaughn, R. (1980). How advertising works: A planning model. *Journal of Advertising Research* 20(5): 27–33.

Wakefield, M. A. et al. (2002). Tobacco industry marketing at point of purchase after the 1998 MSA billboard advertising ban. *American Journal of Public Health* 92: 937–940.

Warner, K. E. (1979). Clearing the airwaves: The cigarette ad ban revisited. *Policy Analysis* 5: 435–450.

Warner, K. E. (1985). Tobacco industry response to public health concern: A content analysis of cigarette ads. *Health Education Quarterly* 12: 115–127.

WHO (World Health Organization) (2008). *Mpower: A policy package to reverse the tobacco epidemic*. Geneva: World Health Organization.

Zaichkowsky, J. L. (1987). The emotional affect of product involvement. *Advances in Consumer Research* 14: 32–35.

6

Alcohol Advertising

> *They who drink beer, will think beer.*
>
> Washington Irving

While academics often pair alcohol advertising and tobacco advertising together in the ethical debate on advertising regulation, in reality these two "vice" products are really worlds apart. For example, people tend to be smokers or not. Many smokers want to quit, but can't. It's rare to find a "social" smoker (one who only smokes on rare, social occasions). Those who don't use cigarettes can't stand being around smoke. Many restaurants have become completely nonsmoking. People tend to appreciate this – even the smokers. By 1998 smoking was banned on all commercial planes. Smoking on an airplane seems inconceivable now, but there was a time when a smoker couldn't imagine flying from New York to London without a cigarette. By contrast, many people can't imagine that flight without at least a couple of glasses of wine or beer.

Drinking is different from smoking in many ways. It is very possible to be a social drinker, an "at home" wine connoisseur, an occasional celebra-

---

Advertising and Society: An Introduction, Second Edition. Edited by Carol J. Pardun.
© 2014 John Wiley & Sons, Inc. Published 2014 by John Wiley & Sons, Inc.

tory champagne drinker, and so on. Medical reports espouse the value of a glass of red wine to keep our circulation systems healthy. Drinking can even be a bit of a religious experience. Some monks make beer in their monasteries. For example, St Sixtus of Westveteren, a Trappist monastery in Brussels, brews a consistently top-rated (and high alcoholic content) beer to support the monastery. And, of course, many churches use wine for Communion.

The problems with advertising alcohol on television are legion. Beer commercials are often present at televised sporting events. But it's not just the association of beer and sports that's problematic. Kids are in the grandstands watching the sporting event. And they're also at home watching – often with their dads (who may very well be guzzling beer and chowing down on salty foods galore, all of which require more beer). Beer and basketball is bad enough. But beer and NASCAR? Whose idea was it to associate drinking and really fast cars, anyway?

Then there are all the other television programs that include beer commercials. If we think kids are watching only children-appropriate television, we're even more naive than the naysayers say we are!

And it's not just about beer advertising any more. While broadcast television has tended to uphold its voluntary ban on advertising distilled spirits for a quarter of a century, this resolve looks soon to be a thing of the past. As the lines between cable television and network television continue to blur, it's only a matter of time. According to the Center on Alcohol Marketing and Youth, distilled spirits advertising increased nearly 6,000 percent from 2001 to 2004! That's a lot of ads.

No one really debates the problem of alcohol abuse. Recent estimates are that over 15 million Americans have problems with binge drinking. As both Jon Nelson and Esther Thorson point out, there are plenty of perils that come with drinking too much.

However, what does all this have to do with advertising? Nelson presents solid research-based evidence that restricting alcohol advertising does not curb drinking. Thorson presents equally research-based evidence that it does.

What is the balance between free speech and the government taking responsibility to stop bad behavior? The belief that individuals have the power to think for themselves – and that they should exercise that power – is a strong one in our society.

But alcohol abuse is clearly a problem. Does advertising contribute to this problem? And, if it does, should its advertising be curtailed? Critics of regulation argue that we open ourselves up to all sorts of other restrictions once we put our trust in the government to watch over us. Some critics would argue that we're already seeing this. They use the soda ban (limiting soda drinks to 16-oz glasses or smaller) that New York City Mayor Bloomberg was able to see passed in fall 2012 as an example of a slippery slope that we should all be hesitant to ride. What's next? Banning food at all state fairs where deep-fried cola, fried bacon, and even fried butter tend to be big sellers? Can advertising influence our decision to drink in the first place? Or is it more about brand awareness and trying to grab competitors' customers? *You decide.*

Ideas to Get You Thinking . . .

1   Find 10 different beer ads in magazines or newspapers. What do you learn about the beer from the ads? What do you not learn?
2   Find some magazine ads touting wine or spirits. List the creative strategies that you see in these ads. Can you make any general observations from what you've found?
3   Watch some primetime television programming and look for beer advertising. When you find it, make some observations about the programming. Do some research and try to find the statistics about what age groups are watching. (Start by going to the Nielsen website at www.nielsen.com.) What did you discover?
4   Compare some alcohol print ads with television ads. Does it look like the advertisers are targeting the same or different markets?

Other Topics to Debate

1   Advertisements touting alcoholic beverages are simply more unethical than all other kinds of advertisements and, as a result, should be more highly regulated than any other category of advertising.
2   As long as alcohol ads include warning labels for dangers of overuse, there should be no limitations on where or when these ads can be seen.
3   The only problem for alcohol advertising is related to underage drinking.

If You'd Like to Know More . . .

Cohen, E. L., Caburnay, C. A., and Rodgers, S. (2011). Alcohol and tobacco advertising in black and general audience newspapers: Targeting with message cues? *Journal of Health Communication* 16(6): 566–582. doi:10.1080/10810730.2011.551990

Duhachek, A., Agrawal, N., and Han, D. (2012). Guilt versus shame: Coping, fluency, and framing in the effectiveness of responsible drinking messages. *JMR (Journal of Marketing Research)* 49(6): 928–941. doi:10.1509/jmr.10.0244

Shin, D. and Kim, J. (2011). Alcohol product placements and the third-person effect. *Television & New Media* 12(5): 412–440. doi:10.1177/1527476410385477

Weber, K., Dillow, M. R., and Rocca, K. A. (2011). Developing and testing the anti-drinking and driving PSA. *Communication Quarterly* 59(4): 415–427. doi:10.1080/01463373.2011.597285

>< Argument

Not so fast! Evidence-informed alcohol policy requires a balanced review of advertising studies

Jon P. Nelson

Penn State University, USA

The *Central Hudson* Test: Balancing Benefits and Costs

In a landmark decision, the Supreme Court in 1980 laid out a balancing test to be applied to public policies restricting commercial speech. The Court in *Central Hudson Gas & Electric Corp. v. Public Service Commission* (447 U.S. 557, 1980) rejected the view that governments have complete power to suppress or regulate advertising, and reasoned that First Amendment protection depends on the nature of the expression and interests served by the proposed regulation. The four-prong *Central Hudson* test provides that:

1   the speech must concern lawful activity and may not be false or misleading;
2   the government's interest asserted to justify regulation must be substantial;
3   the regulation must directly advance the governmental interest asserted; and
4   the regulation must not be more extensive than necessary to serve that interest. (447 U.S. 566)

The first prong articulates a "strict scrutiny" standard or necessary condition for government regulation, while the remaining prongs are sufficient conditions for a regulation to pass a balancing test or intermediate level of scrutiny. The third prong provides that the proposed restriction must have a material effect or, in the words of Justice Powell, "the regulation may not be sustained if it provides only ineffective or remote support for the government's purpose" (447 U.S. 564). For the fourth prong, he noted that this criterion "recognizes that the First Amendment mandates that speech restrictions be 'narrowly drawn'" (447 U.S. 565). Hence, courts generally uphold content-neutral restrictions that are carefully tailored with regard to time, place, and manner of advertising, such as anti-leafleting ordinances and complete bans of billboards.

The *Central Hudson* test has been applied several times to important cases involving alcohol advertising. In *Rubin v. Coors* (514 U.S. 476, 1995), the Court unanimously struck down a Federal law passed in 1935 prohibiting labels on beer containers from displaying alcohol content, including words suggesting high content. The Court reasoned the government had provided only anecdotal evidence and educated guesses that the labeling ban inhibited "strength wars" between brewers. In *44 Liquormart, Inc. v. Rhode Island* (517 U.S. 484, 1996), the Court struck down a state law banning price advertising of alcohol beverages. Rhode Island asserted the ban advanced its interest in temperance, but this and similar state laws were blatantly anti-competitive in origin (McGahan 1995). On the third and fourth prongs, the decision noted: "the State has presented no evidence to suggest that its speech prohibition will *significantly* reduce marketwide consumption . . . [and] it is perfectly obvious that alternative forms of regulation . . . would be more likely to achieve the State's goal of promoting temperance" (517 U.S. 506–507; emphasis original). This decision also made clear that the government's power to ban a product completely did not carry with it the lesser power to restrict advertising. In *Pitt News v. Pappert* (379 F.3d 96, 2004), then District Court Judge Alito invalidated a Pennsylvania statute banning advertisers from paying for alcohol advertising contained in media affiliated with an educational institution, such as college newspapers. Applying the third prong, he reasoned that the state had failed to adequately prove a material advancement of its interest because students were exposed to alcohol ads in other media, including free newspapers handed out on campus.

Central Hudson and its progeny provide the basis for this essay. Do empirical studies support additional restrictions of alcohol advertising that would survive a *Central Hudson* challenge? I argue the evidence is not supportive. It is obvious that governments have a substantial interest in preventing underage and other illegal or abusive uses of alcohol. It is not obvious that the best way to do this is to ban alcohol advertising or to restrict various marketing methods. However, such regulations and restrictions enjoy enormous popularity among public health advocates and critics of advertising. For example, it is the policy of the American Medical Association to actively support and work for a total statutory prohibition of alcohol advertising, except for inside retail outlets (AMA 2010). A report by the Center on Alcohol Marketing and Youth argues: "research clearly indicates that, in addition to parents and peers, alcohol advertising and marketing have a *significant* impact on youth decisions to drink" (CAMY 2007; emphasis added). Are the AMA's position and CAMY's statement credible? Does the evidence support a ban of alcohol advertising or narrower regulations aimed at reducing youth exposure to alcohol marketing, such as audience-composition codes? Arguing that advertising bans should be imposed solely because they receive popular support is the *argmentum ad populum* fallacy. Failure to carefully examine all of the evidence makes a mockery of scientific inquiry. Using scientific evidence to inaccurately support misleading statements or false conclusions is equally troubling. This essay seeks to avoid these mistakes.

Econometric Studies: Proof That Bans Don't Accomplish Much

Two types of empirical studies provide insight into the possible effects of alcohol advertising and marketing regulations. First, studies by economists examine the influence of advertising and advertising bans on alcohol consumption. Econometric studies are usually conducted using aggregate data at the state, national, or international level. Second, studies by social psychologists and public health researchers use surveys of youth and self-reported exposure to alcohol advertising and marketing. The best of these studies, referred to as "longitudinal surveys," involve an initial or baseline survey and a follow-up survey at a later point in time. However, a body of literature never yields empirical evidence that is uniform across investigators, countries, time periods, statistical methodologies, and so forth. Rather, there is a blizzard of methods and results that may appear daunting to a student. Given this diversity, there are several ways researchers review and summarize empirical literature. First, there are traditional study-by-study examinations of methods and results. Examples for alcohol advertising include Calfee and Scheraga (1994), the National Institute on Alcohol Abuse and Alcoholism (NIAAA 2000), and Nelson (2001, 2008). Second, systematic surveys attempt to define comparable studies based on method, media, or context. Examples for alcohol advertising are Anderson et al. (2009), Smith and Foxcroft (2009), and Nelson (2004, 2010a). Third, meta-analyses use statistical methods to combine empirical estimates from a sample of comparable studies, with possible controls for basic differences in data, methods, context, and precision. Examples of meta-analyses of alcohol advertising studies are Gallet (2007) and Nelson (2011). The last analysis also examines the issues of "publication bias" and "dissemination bias." These problems are discussed below.

Several econometric studies use cross-national panel data on alcohol consumption and advertising bans. (Panel data is another technical term for longitudinal data.) The most recent is Nelson (2010b), which includes an index or control variable for "other alcohol policies" that was missing in earlier studies. Briefly, omitting a relevant variable creates a misspecification bias that contaminates other variables of interest, such as advertising bans. Some of the omitted effect of other alcohol policies is falsely attributed to the included variable for bans. Nelson (2010b) also provides a detailed history of advertising bans in 17 countries and discusses cultural differences in drinking patterns between countries. My study also controls for income, prices, tourism, unemployment, demographics, drinking sentiment, panel fixed effects, and the possible endogeneity of advertising bans. The empirical results indicate statistically significant negative effects for the policy index and alcohol prices. The study also finds that neither comprehensive nor limited ad bans reduce alcohol consumption. Moreover, many of the bans in question have existed for many years. If advertising bans negatively affect drinking decisions by youth and young adults, it is difficult to see why this is not reflected in the empirical results. Several other international panel data studies provide similar results (Nelson 2001, 2004).

Two other types of econometric studies provide evidence on the possible effects of advertising bans. First, there are studies of selective bans, such as bans of alcohol advertising on billboards. In Nelson (2003), I report on a panel data study of state bans of billboard advertising. The study allows for substitution among beverages as a response to regulations targeting a specific beverage. I also control for income, prices, tourism, unemployment, demographics, minimum legal age, retail monopolies, state-specific time trends, and regional fixed effects. The study demonstrates that selective bans of advertising do not reduce total alcohol consumption, which partly reflects substitution among beverages. Second, many econometric studies use advertising expenditures as an explanatory variable for alcohol consumption. The relationship between alcohol demand and advertising outlays has been investigated using annual, quarterly, and monthly time-series data for Australia, Canada, United Kingdom, and the United States, with null results found in most studies (e.g., Lee and Tremblay 1995; Lariviere et al. 2000). Sometimes it is claimed that too little variation exists in annual time-series data, so studies using quarterly and monthly data are of special interest. Nelson (1999) is an econometric study of quarterly alcohol consumption and advertising in the United States, which differentiates advertising by beverage (beer, wine, spirits, total alcohol) and medium (broadcast, print, outdoor, total ads). Advertising does not have a significant effect on total alcohol consumption. Broadcast advertising is not a significant factor and does not differ from print advertising, despite different rates of use by marketers. If total alcohol consumption is held constant, regressions at the beverage level allow for own-advertising effects (e.g., effect of beer ads on beer demand) and cross-advertising effects (e.g., effect of beer ads on wine demand). Outdoor ads for spirits are insignificant, but wine broadcast ads have a small positive effect on wine demand. Broadcast advertising of beer does not have a statistically significant effect on the demand for beer, indicating that beer ads affect brand shares and not marketwide demand. Overall, the effects of advertising at the beverage level are unimportant in terms of magnitude or material effect. For example, a 50 percent increase in print and broadcast advertising of wine would increase annual demand for wine by only 4 percent or an additional 0.1 gallons of wine per capita.

Do econometric studies support the third prong of the *Central Hudson* test? No, not if the evidence is examined carefully. Econometric studies of advertising bans demonstrate that regulations have had an immaterial effect on alcohol consumption. Studies of alcohol demand provide further support for the argument that persuasive advertising is a "weak" force. For many economists, this conclusion is not surprising as the main effect of ads for familiar products is to alter brand shares or enhance brand loyalty (Calfee 1997; Bagwell 2007; Desmond and Carveth 2007). However, noneconomists often argue these results are of little concern. First, most econometric studies do not directly address drinking by youth and young adults. However, I argued above that this is not strictly true for long-standing comprehensive bans of advertising. Second, most econometric studies do not use individualized data, so the decisions modeled are average marginal responses and may fail to detect behaviors by at-risk groups, such as youth and young adults. For alternative evidence, I next review survey studies of youth drinking. My summary is based on Nelson (2010a, 2011), which include many details that for reasons of space will not be covered here.

Survey Studies: Inconsistent and Faulty Research

Nelson (2010a, 2011) examines 20 longitudinal studies of youth drinking and alcohol advertising, including 14 US studies. In a longitudinal study, a baseline survey collects information on current drinking behaviors (if any) by youth and exposure to one or more methods of alcohol advertising and marketing. The youth surveyed are about 12–15 years of age, and respondents' drinking and advertising-marketing exposures are self-reported. Measures of advertising exposure include mass media (TV, radio, magazines, etc.), other marketing methods (branded merchandise, cinema displays, in-store displays), and subjective indexes (liking of ads, awareness of ads and brands, receptivity). The follow-up survey collects information on subsequent drinking outcomes. The basic idea in longitudinal surveys is that the baseline advertising-marketing exposure *caused* the subsequent drinking. There are several problems with this interpretation. First, the statistical results are not robust; rather, the evidence is conflicting and inconsistent. Numerous empirical estimates are null or statistically insignificant, and these poor results are ignored by other systematic reviews. For example, my reviews examine and summarize comparable results in 12 longitudinal studies. These studies yield 23 estimates of the effect of advertising-marketing exposure on youth drinking onset and 40 estimates of the effects on other drinking behaviors (frequency, amount, bingeing). Only 21 of 63 estimates, or 33 percent, are statistically significant and positive.

Second, the statistical results are weak for mass media, where additional regulations are more likely to occur. There are 16 estimates of the effect of TV viewing, which are significantly positive in only six cases. Two estimates for magazine advertising are insignificant. There are also 15 estimates for subjective indexes and only one estimate is statistically significant. Third, exposure and receptivity measures are not shown to be related in any particular way to actual advertising outlays. Thus, it is impossible to determine how the measures and drinking behavior would change in light of particular public policies. As a consequence, longitudinal surveys usually recommend complete bans of all forms of alcohol advertising, but this is not a statistical application or even logical extension of the results. Fourth, many longitudinal surveys examine only one or two measures of advertising or marketing. For example, several studies examine the effect of alcohol-branded merchandise on youth drinking. Using the same data, a separate study examines the effect of alcohol displays in motion pictures. These duplicative studies suffer from omitted variable bias, which overstates any possible effect. Fifth, many of the studies are ad hoc representations of "social learning theory," with little attention given to the variables required to provide a robust test of this theory. For example, only 12 of 20 longitudinal surveys control for "peers' drinking"; only 10 studies control for "parental drinking"; and only 11 studies include a personality variable for "sensation seeking." These omissions will bias the empirical results, but are ignored by other reviews. Even survey studies using the same data fail to yield comparable results for similar advertising-marketing variables.

There are two additional statistical areas where the survey studies are faulty. First, sampling bias arises when a rule other than random sampling is used to sample from the underlying population. More subtle is the bias introduced by self-selection, whereby youth (or their parents) make a conscious decision to not participate in the baseline survey or refuse to participate in the follow-up survey. Researchers conducting longitudinal surveys are generally careful to avoid investigator bias when selecting the initial sample, but this does not rule out self-selection by survey participants. For example, Hanewinkel et al. (2008) report higher sample attrition among younger participants, males, sensation-seekers, having parents who drink less frequently, and less movie exposure to drinking displays. These results illustrate self-selection in the survey, which is another form of specification bias. Second, all survey studies fail to consider the possibility that the advertising variables are endogenous. In other words, exposure to alcohol advertising and marketing is not randomly assigned among survey participants. Rather, individuals (even youth!) make conscious decisions to acquire an alcohol-branded item, watch an R-rated movie containing alcohol displays, or view TV sports programs containing beer ads. Failure to model explicitly the exposure decision is another form of specification bias (Heckman et al. 2008). Overall, these biases rule out any causal interpretation of longitudinal surveys. The inconsistent statistical results alone are enough to render the studies of little use for policy purposes under *Central Hudson* or as definitive support for other governmental restrictions, such as audience-composition codes.

Publication and Dissemination Biases in Survey Research

Publication bias is defined as the publication of empirical results depending on the direction, statistical significance, or magnitude of the results. Owing to emphasis on significance, published studies are likely to be skewed toward larger effects or outcomes, especially when mainstream theory supports a specific effect or there is overwhelming professional consensus. Using a variety of statistical procedures, Nelson (2011) examines the extent of publication bias in 12 longitudinal survey studies of youth drinking and alcohol marketing. Using meta-analysis, I show that the results are skewed for drinking onset and behavior. Average effect sizes in the studies are biased toward larger positive coefficients. Using meta-regressions, I show the degree of bias depends on precision, journal quality, and specification errors in the primary studies. I conclude the "results are consistent with lack of genuine effects of marketing on adolescent drinking" (Nelson 2011: 217).

Dissemination bias arises when there is selection bias in the interpretation and use of results by researchers and health policy advocates. Scientific studies tend to be complex and diverse, so a journalist or health advocate may seize on any positive result to help support a story or policy proposal. This bias also is referred to as "cherry-picking" or "overreaching." However, the problem is more general as even investigators may distort the results in the paper's conclusion or abstract. Nelson (2011) examines 15 studies of adolescent drinking and advertising, where evaluative statements by either the investigators or outside supporters are distorted. For example, a nationwide survey by Fleming and colleagues (2004) finds that exposures to liquor ads on billboards and in magazines are unrelated to alcohol expectancies, youths' intentions to drink, and alcohol use by young adults. They also report that TV beer ads have a significant *negative* association with alcohol expectancies and radio ads for liquor have a *negative* association with drinking intentions. For the attitude and perception variables, Fleming and colleagues (2004: 15) report 30 estimates of the indirect effects of advertising, with only eight positive coefficients, one significantly *negative* coefficient (liquor billboards), and 21 insignificant coefficients. The study concludes that "greater exposure to alcohol advertising . . . was not a determining factor that predicted the 15–20-year-olds' intentions to drink and the young adults' consumption" (23). However, it is inaccurate to conclude – as Fleming and colleagues (2004) and CAMY (2007) do – that these weak results demonstrate an indirect effect of advertising on youth alcohol expectancies and intentions. It is difficult to see how effective public policy can be based on non-transparent claims, unbalanced reviews, and misleading or false representations of scientific studies.

Brand Advertising Affects Alcohol Brands, and Not Market Demand

Why do alcohol producers advertise so much? Well, it's not because they want to expand the overall product market or because they desire to recruit youth. For familiar products, the message in this essay is that brand advertising affects brands and no marketwide spillovers exist. I think this point is amply illustrated by the following example. Absolut Vodka is an advertising icon and often the leading advertiser among all distilled spirits brands (Hamilton 2000; Nelson

2001). Absolut's advertising campaign, which hit the US market in 1980, is known for its creative print ads, which feature the brand's distinctive bottle and a two-word message that plays on its name, such as "Absolut Perfection" and "Absolut Joy." By 1999, Absolut was the second-best seller among vodkas and the third leading brand of spirits in the United States (behind Bacardi rum and Smirnoff vodka). Case sales of Absolut in the United States rose from about 2.25 million in 1989 to 4.05 million in 1999, an increase of 80 percent (Nelson 2001: 282). However, total case sales of vodka during the same period remained constant at about 35 million cases per year. No marketwide spillover from Absolut ads is apparent here.

In 1980 vodka consumption in the United States was about 0.53 gallon per capita adult and total spirits consumption was 2.90 gallons. However, by 1999 the two amounts had declined to 0.41 and 1.80 gallons per capita adult, respectively. In 2004 these amounts rose marginally to 0.50 and 1.89 gallons, but remained below 1980 levels. In 2010 the amounts were 0.67 and 2.06 gallons. Absolut's share of the vodka category was 6.44 percent in 1989, 11.6 percent in 1999, 10.5 percent in 2004, and 7.5 percent in 2010 as its sales stagnated after 1999. Advertising success is often short-lived, and Absolut was unable to sustain its growth rate even though it was among the top three distilled spirits advertisers.

The early success of Absolut did not translate into success for the vodka category or into marketwide gains for distilled spirits. Successful brand advertising translates into increased brand sales and any market spillovers are extremely small in magnitude, thus refuting claims of an industry advertising–sales response function. It is puzzling that some commentators, including the judiciary and legislators, confuse brand-level success with possible market outcomes. Evidence-informed policies on alcohol advertising require a clear focus on essential issues, not quick responses or distorted claims.

References

AMA (American Medical Association), Council on Scientific Affairs (2010). Youth access to alcohol. At http://www.ama-assn.org/resources/doc/alcohol/alcohol_availability.pdf, accessed Mar. 21, 2013.

Anderson, P., de Bruijn, A., Angus, K., Gordon, R., and Hastings, G. (2009). Impact of alcohol advertising and media exposure on adolescent alcohol use: A systematic review of longitudinal studies. *Alcohol and Alcoholism* 44: 229–243.

Bagwell, K. (2007). The economic analysis of advertising. In M. Armstrong and R. Porter (eds.), *Handbook of Industrial Organization*, vol. 3. Amsterdam: North-Holland, pp. 1701–1844.

Calfee, J. E. (1997). *Fear of persuasion: A new perspective on advertising and regulation*. Washington, DC: AEI Press.

Calfee, J. E. and Scheraga, C. (1994). The influence of advertising on alcohol consumption: A literature review and an econometric analysis of four European nations. *International Journal of Advertising* 13: 287–310.

CAMY (Center on Alcohol Marketing and Youth) (2007). Alcohol advertising and youth. At http://www.camy.org/factsheets/sheets/Alcohol_Advertising_and_Youth. html, accessed Mar. 21, 2013.

Desmond, R. and Carveth, R. (2007). The effects of advertising on children and adolescents: A meta-analysis. In R. W. Preiss et al. (eds.), *Mass media effects research*. Mahwah, NJ: Lawrence Erlbaum, pp. 169–179.

Fleming, K., Thorson, E., and Atkin, C. K. (2004). Alcohol advertising exposure and perceptions: Links with alcohol expectancies and intentions to drink or drinking in underaged youth and young adults. *Journal of Health Communication* 9: 3–29.

Gallet, C. A. (2007). The demand for alcohol: A meta-analysis of elasticities. *Australian Journal of Agricultural and Resource Economics* 51: 121–135.

Hamilton, C. (2000). *Absolut: Biography of a bottle*. London: Texere.

Hanewinkel, R., Morgenstern, M., Tanski, S. E., and Sargent, J. D. (2008). Longitudinal study of parental movie restriction on teen smoking and drinking in Germany. *Addiction* 103: 1722–1730.

Heckman, J. J., Flyer, F., and Loughlin, C. (2008). An assessment of causal inference in smoking initiation research and a framework for future research. *Economic Inquiry* 46: 37–44.

Lariviere, E., Larue, B., and Chalfant, J. (2000). Modeling the demand for alcoholic beverages and advertising specifications. *Agricultural Economics* 22: 147–162.

Lee, B. and Tremblay, V. J. (1992). Advertising and the US market demand for beer. *Applied Economics* 24: 69–76.

McGahan, A. M. (1995). Cooperation in prices and advertising: Trade associations in brewing after repeal. *Journal of Law and Economics* 38: 521–559.

Nelson, J. P. (1999). Broadcast advertising and U.S. demand for alcoholic beverages. *Southern Economic Journal* 65: 774–790.

Nelson, J. P. (2001). Alcohol advertising and advertising bans: A survey of research methods, results, and policy implications. In M. R. Baye and J. P. Nelson (eds.), *Advertising and differentiated products*. Amsterdam: JAI, available from Emerald Group, Bingley, pp. 239–295.

Nelson, J. P. (2003). Advertising bans, monopoly, and alcohol demand. *Review of Industrial Organization* 22: 1–25.

Nelson, J. P. (2004). Advertising bans in the United States. *EH.Net Encyclopedia* (pp. 1–20). At http://eh.net/encyclopedia/article/Nelson.AdBans, accessed Mar. 21, 2013.

Nelson, J. P. (2008). Reply to Siegel et al.: Alcohol advertising in magazines and disproportionate exposure. *Contemporary Economic Policy* 24: 493–504.

Nelson, J. P. (2010a). What is learned from longitudinal studies of advertising and youth drinking and smoking? A critical assessment. *International Journal Environmental Research and Public Health* 7: 870–926.

Nelson, J. P. (2010b). Alcohol advertising bans, consumption and control policies in seventeen OECD countries, 1975–2000. *Applied Economics* 42: 803–823.

Nelson, J. P. (2011). Alcohol marketing, adolescent drinking and publication bias in longitudinal studies: A critical survey using meta-analysis. *Journal of Economic Surveys* 25: 191–232.

NIAAA (National Institute on Alcohol Abuse and Alcoholism) (2000). Alcohol advertising: What are the effects? In *10th special report to the U.S. Congress on alcohol and health*. Washington, DC: National Institute on Alcohol Abuse and Alcoholism, pp. 412–426.

Smith, L. A. and Foxcroft, D. R. (2009). The effect of alcohol advertising, marketing and portrayal on drinking behavior in young people: Systematic review of prospective cohort studies. *BMC Public Health* 9: 51–73.

Counterargument ＞◀

Abandonment of alcohol advertising regulation carries a high social cost

Esther Thorson

University of Missouri–Columbia, USA

In the late 1990s I wrote position papers for attorneys in Chicago and Los Angeles who were aiding city councils to try to restrict alcohol billboards. Research showed how many alcohol billboards were so close to American schools that schoolchildren had to walk by them every day. Alcohol billboards were particularly prevalent in inner city areas where alcohol abuse problems were higher than in suburban areas. I argued from social science research that alcohol advertising influenced children and youth to begin experimenting with alcohol use, that early use increased the likelihood of adult alcohol abuse, and all the negatives associated with that abuse (think about drunk driving and the tragedies it causes). Both Chicago and Los Angeles, among other American cities, passed alcohol billboard restrictions. But in June 2001 the Supreme Court (*Lorillard Tobacco Co. v. Reilly*, 533 U.S. 525, 2001) ruled that even though concern about youthful alcohol use was a significant issue, outdoor advertising restrictions of tobacco ads in Massachusetts were "too broad and not narrowly tailored." This ruling led to rescinding of the city's restrictions on alcohol billboards as well. Furthermore, as a result, all of the city efforts nationwide were also killed. Today alcohol billboards are unrestricted and highly prevalent everywhere in the United States. My belief at that time, and even more now that there is much more sophisticated research on the effect of alcohol advertising on people, especially children and teens, is that failure to restrict alcohol advertising is a costly mistake for our society. In this essay I will give a brief overview of how we came to treat alcohol advertising as we do, why people are underestimating the damage that alcohol advertising does, especially to the young, and what the research is that supports my position.

How Did We Get Here?

In the United States, alcohol is a legal product except for those under the age of 21. It is, of course, regulated in the sense that blood alcohol level while driving is limited. Just as for all legal products, alcohol advertising is protected by our laws about the protection of commercial speech. And indeed, the only question about alcohol regulations concerns its presence on television. But excessive alcohol consumption is associated with death and injury throughout the world – and levels of risky drinking are increasing, especially among women (Jones and Jernigan 2010). Arguments can be made that broadcast (and other forms of television like cable and Internet-based) alcohol advertising should be completely banned because of its effects on both youth and adults. But the strongest argument for alcohol advertising regulation lies in its effects on those under the age of 21, and thus that will be the focus of my argument here.

In spite of years of efforts by citizens and public health activists, the US government has never regulated the marketing of alcohol advertising. The spirits (hard or grain liquor) industry in the 1940s developed a self-regulation code that disallowed advertising on the radio. In 1948 the National Association of Broadcasters put into its code a regulation disallowing spirits advertising on all airwaves. Beer and wine, however, were always allowable on air. In the 1950s codes were developed that disallowed any alcohol consumption in broadcast commercials. Interestingly, efforts to put governmental regulation into place changed fundamentally in their nature over time. After World War II, those pushing for regulation were generally religious people who objected to drinking. By the 1970s, however, activists were parents and public health professionals who argued that alcohol advertising was unfair and deceptive to children and underage youth (Pennock 2005). In spite of years of Congressional hearings, it was concluded that Federal Trade Commission (FTC 2008) instituting of alcohol advertising regulations even as it related to the young violated the commercial First Amendment rights of alcohol companies (Neuendorf 2009). Except for a requirement to have a warning on alcohol products (a law passed in 1988), National Association of Broadcasters' self-regulation keeps spirits advertising off networks, although not cable television and not the Hispanic networks (Neuendorf 2009). Although there is no national regulation of alcohol advertising, there is a complex web of local and state laws that do prevent some forms of alcohol marketing. For example, in 17 states there is regulation of out-of-home advertising venues like billboards, signs on the fronts of stories, and transit advertising (Goldfarb and Tucker 2011).

Today the main self-regulation for network television advertising of alcohol is the unwritten rule that spirits should not be advertised. Beer and wine, however, are allowed, the only proviso being that no more than 30 percent of the audience of the program in which the advertising appears can be underage. In 2008 the FTC (2008) conducted a study to determine the extent to which beer and wine advertisers were complying with the 30 percent rule. It found that 92 percent of companies were complying.

In spite of this compliance, however, there are problems with the effectiveness of the rule. First, there is clear evidence that many youth under the age of 21 watch "adult" programming – which is untouched by the 70 percent rule. Second, "70 percent of the audience" is just an estimate based on past viewing patterns, which are not accurate. If the percentage of youth watching borderline programs increases, the advertising will continue to run in that programming. Perhaps most troubling is that the audience for network television has decreased greatly since the 1990s, while the audiences for cable television and Hispanic networks have grown. In these media, the 70 percent rule does not apply and spirits can be and are advertised. Finally, there is evidence that Internet-based alcohol advertising is providing additional uncontrolled exposure (Goldfarb and Tucker 2011).

Probably as a result, the exposure of US youth to alcohol advertising increased by more than 70 percent between 2001 and 2009, as shown by the most recent analysis (CAMY 2010). Youth exposure to alcohol advertising of spirits on cable television was 30 times greater in 2009 than in 2001. Furthermore, the study found that in 2009 nearly 8 percent of alcohol ads on television were in shows with more than 30 percent underage viewers and on cable this level was 9 percent.

So why, after more than 60 years of debate with very little movement toward regulation of alcohol advertising, would I argue here that we need it? First and foremost, the cost to our society of alcohol abuse, and specifically underage drinking, is phenomenal. And second, it is clear that alcohol advertising increases the likelihood that youth will drink, drink more, and start drinking earlier. We'll look first at the damage that underage drinking does and then at the research that shows alcohol advertising's role in underage drinking.

Underage Drinking

The Centers for Disease Control and Prevention (CDC) say that "alcohol is the most commonly used and abused drug among youth in the United States, more than tobacco and illicit drugs" (CDC 2011). And alcohol is not just abused by high school and college students. The biennial "Youth Risk Behavior Survey" (2009) found that 37 percent of eighth graders had tried alcohol, and 15 percent of them had drunk alcohol during the past month. A CDC study of seventh to ninth graders reported that 35 percent of them had started drinking before age 13 (Swahn et al. 2008).

Children and youth who drink have a whole host of problems: more failing grades, more fighting, more arrests for driving or hurting someone while drunk, more unprotected sex, higher risk of suicide and homicide, and greater likelihood of death from alcohol poisoning. Youth who started drinking before age 15 are five times more likely to become alcoholics than those who didn't drink until the legal age of 21 (CDC 2011).

The leading cause of death in teenagers aged 15–20 in the United States is motor vehicle crashes. Thirty-one percent of those crashes involve alcohol and 25 percent of the drivers are legally intoxicated. Of the youth involved in deadly crashes who had been drinking, 73 percent were not wearing seat belts. Crashes are worse when alcohol is involved. In 2008, 2 percent of drunk youthful drivers were involved in property-only crashes; 4 percent of these young drinkers were involved in injury crashes; and a staggering 22 percent were involved in fatal crashes (CAMY 2012).

Unprotected and unwanted sex is also extraordinarily high among drinking youth. In a study of thousands of college students, students who got drunk before the age of 13 were twice as likely to report they had had unplanned sex because of drinking. Sexually transmitted diseases are another cost of youthful drinking. Males who drank heavily were four times as likely as nondrinkers to have a sexually transmitted disease, while heavy-drinking females were three and a half times as likely as nondrinkers (CAMY 2012).

The newest finding for brain development indicates that adolescents who were heavy drinkers scored much lower on tests of verbal and nonverbal recall and other cognitive skills than nondrinking adolescents (Brown et al. 2000). In fact, heavy-drinking adolescents have been shown to have smaller areas in their brain (the hippocampus) that are memory centers than nondrinkers (Nagel et al. 2005).

But Can We Blame Alcohol Advertising for Youth Drinking?

We have seen that alcohol use in those below 21 is clearly a major public health problem in the United States. But can we blame alcohol advertising and therefore support much tighter regulation of it? Today the evidence is very strong. There are many ways to test the impact of alcohol advertising, and nearly every one of those shows significant effects. Let's take a quick trip through all the evidence amassed in the last 30 years. The strength of these findings, particularly in recent studies, is such that it leaves one gasping at the ignorance of our society for failing to regulate alcohol advertising, especially as it affects youth (Thorson 1995).

Ways to Test How Advertising Affects People

There are four main research approaches to looking at how advertising influences alcohol attitudes, knowledge, beliefs, and consumption. These methods are used for studying effects on both the underaged and in adults. All of these methods and their applications to the question of alcohol advertising have become much more sophisticated since they were initially deployed in studies prior to 2000. We look briefly at each method and how it boosts the argument that alcohol advertising should be more restricted, especially as it relates to underage youth.

Experiments

There have been only a handful of experiments that examined the immediate effects of viewing commercials for alcohol. Most of the studies involved showing youth alcohol ads mixed with other ads in programming and comparing their responses to questions about drinking to youth shown the same programming without any alcohol ads. In general, these studies failed to show major effects on actual drinking or intention to drink. Importantly, however, some of the studies showed that viewing alcohol advertising (usually beer was used in the studies) had some effect on young people's expectations about the positive values of alcohol on self, for example, "it will make me feel relaxed, happy, worry less about my problems, feel more outgoing or friendly, and have a lot of fun" (e.g., see Grube and Wallack 1994). This is important because survey studies consistently show that alcohol expectancies play a crucial role in youth drinking or intention to drink.

It is important to keep in mind that there are problems with using experiments to test the effects of alcohol advertising. First, the viewing situation is very different from what a teen would experience watching a favorite program at home or with friends. Second, the experimental stimulus is usually just a one-shot experience, nothing like exposure day after day in program after program. Further, different commercials have different effects on different targeted groups. Given the findings on how many alcohol ads youth are exposed to, and the variety of those ads, it only makes sense to posit that it is crucial to show youth commercials that would be expected to have high impact on them. Males and females like different kinds of alcohol ads, as do Caucasian, African American, and Latino youth (Connolly et al. 1994; Herd and Grube 1996). While the main experimental studies have shown a small- to medium-level immediate effect on the intention to drink, there have not yet been studies of the impact of ads chosen because they are most likely to break through to attention from various groups of youth, and be persuasive to them.

Econometric Studies

Econometric studies basically look at the relationship between how much is spent on alcohol advertising and how much alcohol is consumed in terms of sales. Some of the studies also look at the relationship between advertising dollars spent and indicators of alcohol damage like the number of drunk driving arrests and crashes that involved alcohol. Econometric studies also have compared areas or countries where there were alcohol advertising bans or severe restrictions and the consumption or abuse of alcohol.

Of course any student of advertising will immediately surmise that alcohol advertising expenditures are a very rough estimate and therefore a potentially flawed measure to use in testing the effects of advertising. If the expenditures are examined across all media, we lose the opportunity to see how magazine versus newspaper versus television advertising may have differential effects. If some but not all media expenditures are examined, advertising dollars may flow into media that are not measured, like, for example, the Internet. Any student of advertising knows that the same dollars can produce a high-impact campaign or one that falls with a thud. Econometric studies summarize overall campaigns. And finally, there are many other variables that change over the time period being examined (like how much drunk driving law enforcement is in effect) and these variables may affect alcohol consumption, masking the relationship between advertising expenditures and drinking.

Probably as a result, in the early econometric studies there was only weak support for links between alcohol advertising expenditures and alcohol consumption (e.g., Calfee and Scheraga 1994). Nevertheless there were a small handful of very sophisticated studies that did find effects. Henry Saffer of the National Bureau of Economic Research was an important player. In comparisons between countries with and without bans on alcohol advertising, Saffer (1991) showed that those with bans had 16 percent lower alcohol consumption levels than those without bans. Saffer (1997) also looked at the relationship between how much alcohol advertising there was in the largest 75 media markets in the United States and motor vehicle fatalities. Based on the positive relationship, even after a number of controls were taken into account (e.g., regional price differences for alcohol), Saffer estimated that a total ban of alcohol advertising was likely to reduce road fatalities by 5,000 to 10,000 lives per year.

More recently, however, econometric methodology has become much more nuanced and sophisticated. In a recently published study, Goldfarb and Tucker (2011) looked at more than 61,000 online respondents across the nation, who were asked about their intentions to purchase and drink alcohol. People who were not exposed to online alcohol ads and who lived in one of the 17 states where outdoor alcohol advertising was restricted (note that states can still regulate some kinds of alcohol advertising like signage outside liquor stores) were 8 percent less likely to indicate intention to drink, but when people in the ban states were presented with online alcohol ads, the 8 percent difference was reduced to 3 percent. Many controls were employed to insure that it was not factors other than the bans that were giving rise to the differences. The study provides a micro-level look at the effects of advertising bans and uncontrolled exposure, for example from Internet ads and other forms of persuasive communication. In addition, statistical power in the study shows a strong econometric link between alcohol advertising and its influence. This is in spite of all the challenges to the validity of econometric analyses we discussed earlier.

Content Analysis of Alcohol Ads

Another important area of study that links alcohol advertising to drinking involves looking at the nature of content of alcohol ads and its relationship to youth appeals. One of the earliest studies (Finn and Strickland 1982) showed that only about 17 percent of television beer and wine commercials contained product information. The dominant themes in the beer ads were humor, camaraderie, relationships, and physical activity. The dominant themes in the wine commercials were humor, camaraderie, sex, love or romance, and physical activity. A more recent study (Kelly and Edwards 1998) again showed alcohol ads tend to appeal to "image," that is, they do not talk specifically about the product attributes of alcohol (taste, price) but rather depict the desirable lifestyle of drinkers. There are not only quantitative content analyses of alcohol commercials but also qualitative ones based on cultural theories of communication. Strate describes one example in a beer ad:

> There is a cowboy on horseback herding cattle across a river. A small calf is overcome by the current, but the cowboy is able to withstand the force of the river and come to the rescue. The voiceover says: "Sometimes a simple river crossing isn't so simple. And when you've got him back it's your turn. Head for the beer brewed natural as a mountain stream." (Strate 1991: 116)

At that point in the commercial, the cowboy pulls a six-pack out of the river. As Strate explains, here the beer ties itself into the cultural image of the cowboy and his brave role on the western frontier. The beer becomes synonymous with water. The meaning of drinking beer then comes to mean being part of frontier courage and of the beauty and challenge of nature. As we shall see in the survey research on the effects of alcohol advertising, it is images like these that become inextricably linked with the meaning of alcohol products to young and old alike.

Surveys of Alcohol Ads

Surveys have consistently found the smoking gun evidence that exposure to alcohol advertising has major effects on underage attitudes toward alcohol, perceptions of alcohol's positive values, and youthful intentions to drink in the future.

Surveys show that how strong a young person's memory is for advertising at age 15 predicts how much they will drink at age 16 (Connolly et al. 1994). It has also been shown that alcohol commercials become increasingly salient and attractive to children from ages 10–14 (Grube 1993). Fourteen- to 16-year-olds read more into the meaning of alcohol commercials. These findings provide strong evidence that the cultural meanings of alcohol commercials are not lost on teens. This advertising, to which the young, as we have seen, are extensively exposed, comes to define alcohol not in terms of its intoxicating effects or even its taste, but in terms of desirable, glamorous, brave, sexy images.

It turns out that surveys also show that one, if not the biggest, predictor of underage drinking is alcohol expectancy. What do the young expect from drinking? Clearly they expect to become part of the cultural images of alcohol to which they have been exposed. Simons-Morton and his colleagues (1999) showed in a survey of more than 4,000 youth (sixth to eighth grade) that positive alcohol expectancies were associated with drinking for both boys and girls. In a longitudinal study where researchers looked at teens from 12 to 14, first in 1989 and then three years later, found that those with the highest alcohol expectancies in 1989 were much more likely to be drinking alcohol three years later (Smith et al. 1995).

A major contributor to a large survey literature that shows just how this happens and how strong the effect is psychologist and media researcher Joel Grube. In numerous early studies (Grube 1993; Grube et al. 1995) Grube has shown that alcohol expectancies are one of the best predictors of underage drinking. Fleming and colleagues (2004) showed that the more teens were exposed to alcohol advertising, the more they had strong positive expectations about advertising and the more likely they were to drink.

This body of research shows clearly how alcohol advertising wields its persuasive impact on the young. Alcohol commercials focus on the wonderful things that happen to those who drink, who are also good-looking, brave, glamorous, athletic, and a great sense of humor: they have fun; they lead adventurous lives. The steady drip of exposure to these images is highly appealing and very salient to the young. From this endless diet of images, they develop expectancies about how wonderful alcohol will make their own lives – and their own selves or identities. It is these expectancies that play a key role in the decision to drink before reaching 21. Of course, there are other variables involved, but the power of alcohol expectancies is inarguable. This is why those who claim that alcohol advertising either fails to reach America's children and youth, or that it has no effect on their alcohol consumption, are so wrong.

One final area of research provides even more evidence for the causal impact of alcohol expectancies. Media literacy studies take the approach that if you can teach youth to understand and arm themselves against alcohol advertising, you will reduce the likelihood of their drinking. Austin and Johnson (1997) provided training for third graders in which they had to look specifically at two beer commercials and talk about how important it was to question what was real on television, and what was right or wrong. Students were asked to pledge not to drink and as a reinforcement got a cookie each month for three months. These children developed a better understanding of the selling intent of television commercials: they thought the characters in the commercials were less positive role models, that there were fewer positives about the experience of drinking alcohol, and said they were less likely to begin drinking than children in various control groups. The same pattern appeared in a follow-up test conducted three months later.

What this shows is that if children are actually taught to engage cognitively with the intended cultural messages of alcohol advertising, the impact on their expectations about drinking and eventual adoption of alcohol consumption can be lessened. This is not only encouraging, but also demonstrates the impact that alcohol advertising has on the young.

Conclusion

I have argued here that alcohol advertising has a great effect on underage drinking, that the self-regulation of network and cable television's alcohol advertising is a failed experiment, and therefore the only reasonable alternative is for the government to apply a ban on television alcohol advertising. Given the "leakage" effects of the Internet, there should also be discussion of the degree of impact this medium has in providing alcohol video advertising to children, and an appropriate response.

Researcher Lance Strate summarized the situation very well: "the real question is not about the existence of advertising's effects, but about the nature of those effects" (1991: 115). Alcohol advertising has a major impact on underage drinking – and underage drinking causes great social and individual harm.

References

Austin, E. W. and Johnson, K. K. (1997). Effects of general and alcohol-specific media literacy training on children's decision making about alcohol. *Journal of Health Communication* 2: 17–42.

Brown, S. A., Tapert, S. F., Granholm, E., and Delis, D. C. (2000). Neurocognitive functioning of adolescents: Effects of protracted alcohol use. *Alcoholism: Clinical and Experimental Research* 24(2): 164–171.

Calfee, J. E. and Scheraga, C. (1994). The influence of advertising on alcohol consumption: A literature review and an econometric analysis of four European nations. *International Journal of Advertising* 13: 287–231.

CAMY (Center on Alcohol Marketing and Youth) (2012). The toll of underage drinking. At http://www.camy.org/factsheets/sheets/The_Toll_of_Underage_Drinking. html, accessed Mar. 21, 2013.

CDC (Centers for Disease Control and Prevention (2011). Alcohol and public health. At http://www.cdc.gov/alcohol/fact-sheets/underage-drinking.htm, accessed Mar. 21, 2013.

Connolly, G. M., Casswell, S., Zhang, J.-F., and Silva, P. A. (1994). Alcohol in the mass media and drinking by adolescents: A longitudinal study. *Addiction* 89: 1255–1263.

Finn, T. A. and Strickland, D. E. (1982). A content analysis of beverage alcohol advertising. *Journal of Studies on Alcohol* 43(9): 964–989.

Fleming, K., Thorson, E., and Atkin, C. (2004). Alcohol advertising exposure and perceptions: Links with alcohol expectancies and intention to drink in teens and young adults. *Journal of Health Communication* 9(1): 3–29.

FTC (2008). FTC reports on alcohol marketing and self-regulation. *Federal Trade Commission.* At http://www.ftc.gov/opa/2008/06/alcoholrpt.shtm, accessed Mar. 21, 2013.

Goldfarb, A. and Tucker, C. (2011). Advertising bans and the substitutability of online and offline advertising. *Journal of Marketing Research* 58(Apr.): 207–227.

Grube, J. W. (1993). Alcohol portrayals and alcohol advertising on television. *Alcohol Health and Research World* 17(1): 61–66.

Grube, J. W. and Wallack, L. (1994). Television beer advertising and drinking knowledge, beliefs, and intentions among school children. *American Journal of Public Health* 84: 254–259.

Grube, J. W., Chen, M.-J., Madden, P., and Morgan, M. (1995). Predicting adolescent drinking from alcohol expectancy values: A comparison of additive, interactive, and nonlinear models. *Journal of Applied Social Psychology* 25(10): 839–857.

Herd, D. and Grube, J. (1996). Black identity and drinking in the US: A national study. *Addiction* 91(6): 845–857.

Jones, S. C. and Jernigan, D. H. (2010). Editorial: Alcohol advertising, marketing and regulation. *Journal of Public Affairs* 10: 1–5.

Kelly, K. J. and Edwards, R. W. (1998). Image advertisements for alcohol products: Is their appeal associated with adolescents' intention to consume alcohol? *Adolescence* 33(129): 47–59.

Nagel, B. J., Schweinsburg, A. D., Phan, V., and Tapert, S. (2005). Reduced hippocampal volume among adolescents with alcohol use disorders without psychiatric comorbidity. *Psychiatry Research* 139: 181–190.

Neuendorf, K. A. (2009). Alcohol advertising: Regulation can help. In Ruth C. Engs (ed.), *Controversies in the addiction field*. Dubuque, IA: Kendall-Hunt.

Pennock, P. (2005). Televising sin: Efforts to restrict the television advertisement of cigarettes and alcohol in the United States, 1950s to 1980s. *Historical Journal of Film, Radio and Television* 25(4): 619–636.

Saffer, H. (1991). Alcohol advertising bans and alcohol abuse: An international perspective. *Journal of Health Economics* 10: 65–79.

Saffer, H. (1997). Alcohol advertising and motor vehicle fatalities. *Review of Economics and Statistics* 79: 431–442.

Simons-Morton, B., Haynie, D. L., Crump, A. D., Saylor, K. E., Eitel, P., and Yu, K. (1999). Expectancies and other psychosocial factors associated with alcohol use among early adolescent boys and girls. *Addictive Behaviors* 24(2): 229–238.

Smith, G. T., Goldman, M. S., Greenbaum, P. E., and Christiansen, B. A. (1995). Expectancy for social facilitation from drinking: The divergent paths of high-expectancy and low-expectancy adolescents. *Journal of Abnormal Psychology* 104(1): 32–40.

Strate, Lance (1991). The cultural meaning of beer commercials. *Advances in Consumer Research* 18: 115–119.

Swahn, M. H., Bossarte, R. M., and Sullivent, E. E. (2008). Age of alcohol use initiation, suicidal behavior, and peer and dating violence victimization and perpetration among high-risk, seventh-grade adolescents. *Pediatrics* 121(2): 297–305.

Thorson, E. (1995). Studies of the effects of alcohol advertising: Two underexplored aspects. In Susan E. Martin (ed.), *The effects of the mass media on the use and abuse of alcohol*. Washington, DC: National Institute of Alcohol Abuse and Alcoholism, pp. 159–196.

7

Sex in Advertising

> *But, you know, sex is controversial, it just is and it always will be.*
>
> Liam Neeson

No doubt about it. Sexual content in the media has increased. Just think about any episode of *The Big Bang Theory* (where PhDs Leonard and Raj talk about sex a lot more than they talk about physics), *Grey's Anatomy* (where the surgeons spend as much time performing various sex acts as they do performing surgery), *Glamour* and *Seventeen* magazines (which help women learn how to improve their sex lives) and it's easy to believe that portrayals of sex in the media have increased over the years. By comparison, sex in advertising is often much more subtle than the "in your face" approach we see in programs and articles, for example.

It's not unusual for people to think that sex in advertising is unethical, but Tom Reichert presents another thoughtful perspective. While he admits that some use of sex in advertising may be problematic, for the right product it's a useful attention-grabbing creative device. Sounds good. But just when we think we have the answer, Kathy Forde presents another side. She argues just as persuasively that using sex in advertising is lazy. It's an abuse of tired clichés and visual boredom. Plus she throws in this ringer: Does an ad that uses sexual appeal tell the truth? *Ouch.*

Advertising and Society: An Introduction, Second Edition. Edited by Carol J. Pardun.
© 2014 John Wiley & Sons, Inc. Published 2014 by John Wiley & Sons, Inc.

What do we know about sex in advertising, other than it's used a lot?

There's an interesting article from the South African *Sunday Times*, where author Chris Moerdyk (2004) argues that sex doesn't sell any more, so we should be seeing less of it soon. He says that part of the reason is because of 9/11: a move back toward family values. He also argues (as Kathy Forde does) that consumers are looking for something they can trust. Maybe. But according to my TV, sex in advertising has not diminished. If anything, it has increased.

It's easy to point the finger and complain about sex in advertising, but the creators of the advertising message aren't necessarily the only ones to blame. What about the company marketing executives who create products assuming the need for sex appeal, like Procter & Gamble's creation of a deodorant body spray for prepubescent boys? What about magazine editors who approve storylines about improving our sexual performance? What about those of us who buy a brand of cereal because we believe it will give us the body we long for – sleek, sexy, and sensational?

No one questions that sex in advertising exists. But the question remains: Is sex in advertising ever a good idea? Read the following essays. *You decide.*

Ideas to Get You Thinking . . .

1   Grab a magazine, or spend an evening flipping through the TV channels. Note all the ads you see. Try and determine which ones are using sex appeal. How many are there? Can you decide where the line is between creativity and indecency? Are there any "sexy" ads that have made you more interested in buying the product?

2   A lot of the controversy about sex in advertising is based on the premise that it denigrates women. Look at some ads that use sex appeal. What do you think?

3   Find an ad in a magazine that is sexual in nature. Make sure it's an ad that you think is particularly well done. Now, try to reconceptualize it without the sex. Can you rewrite the headline and the body copy? How would you change the photo? Do you think your version could potentially be as compelling? Why, or why not?

4   Some researchers have argued that some products would rightly be deemed more sexual than others. Without looking at any ads, make a list of at least 10 products that you think might inherently be sexual and 10 products that wouldn't be sexual. (Obvious examples would be perfume (sexual) and milk (not sexual). Now find ads for these products. What did you discover?

Other Topics to Debate

1   Since women have been sexualized in advertising for decades, and it is inappropriate to perpetuate that. However, using sex in advertising for men is fine.

2   Products that are sexual in nature rightly rely on sex as a creative strategy.
3   Sexual innuendos in advertising are worse then overt sexual messages because you have to spend more energy to understand the "joke."

If You'd Like to Know More . . .

Dahl, D. W., Sengupta, J., and Vohs, K. D. (2009). Sex in advertising: Gender differences and the role of relationship commitment. *Journal of Consumer Research* 36(2): 215–231.
Gunter, B. (2002). *Media sex: What are the issues?* Mahwah, NJ: Lawrence Erlbaum.
O'Barr, W. M. (2012). Sexuality, race, and ethnicity in advertising. *Advertising & Society Review* 13(3). At http://muse.jhu.edu/journals/advertising_and_society_review/v013/13.3.o-barr.html#fig02, accessed Apr. 2, 2013.
Reichert, T. (2003). *The erotic history of advertising*. Amherst, NY: Prometheus Books.
Savoir, L. A. (2007). *Sex in design*. Antwerp: Tectum.

Reference

Moerdyk, C. (2004). Clothes back on as sex in advertising proves a turn-off. *Sunday Times* (South Africa) (Nov. 14), 7.

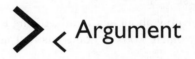 Argument

Sex in advertising:
No crime here!

Tom Reichert
University of Georgia, USA

Introduction

Bodies in a tight embrace. A bead of perspiration trickles across a dark, well-defined abdomen. Moist lips trace their way from below the ear to the base of the neck as clothing slips to the floor. His eyes are closed as a sigh of pleasure escapes his lips. Reacting without thinking, she reaches down expectantly for . . . an Uncle Ben's microwavable rice bowl.

Did I get your attention?

Good. Once you regain your train of thought, continue with me as I attempt to persuade you that sexual information in advertising (aka sex in advertising) is not the felony some make it out to be. In fact, I argue that scenes like the one just described are more often used for the types of brands most relevant to sex appeal: fragrance, fashion, beauty and personal care products, and entertainment. And far from being a simple attention getter, sex is used to position brands as a means to enhance attractiveness, intimacy, and romance.

Don't get me wrong. Sex in advertising isn't found under "virtue" in the dictionary. Unfortunately, there are sexual ads out there that cross the line with regard to explicitness, taste, and degradation. One need only think of Calvin Klein and his ability to spark controversy to know what I am referring to. As with most things in this world, a few bad apples cast a poor light on those who act responsibly. The same is true for sex in advertising.

Why should you listen to me? Good question. I've been researching sex in advertising for over 18 years. During that time I've coedited three books on the promotional uses of sex in the media and I wrote a book about the history of sex in advertising. I only mention this so that you'll know I've thought a lot about the issues raised in this essay. Sex in advertising is not inherently a bad thing. It sells products, and can do so in a healthy, respectful manner. Let me begin by defining sex in advertising and then address two common objections regarding its use.

Definition

First, let's be sure we're on the same page. What is sex in advertising? Like most advertising, it is a persuasive message that contains sexual information. Advertisers try to get people to think, feel, or become aware of a product or idea, and sexual information can be related to that idea to greater or lesser degrees. According to sexuality research, sexual information is that which elicits sexual thoughts and/or feelings.

In some research I conducted with Art Ramirez, we asked students to think of a sexual ad and to describe what it was about that ad that made it sexual to them. Revealing displays of desirable physiques was number one. Sexual behavior was number two. An array of supporting variables such as photographic techniques, what the model said, and the context of the action constituted number three. These findings in light of other research confirm that most instances of sexual information are visual images of people.

But we shouldn't forget the text. Sexual innuendo, entendre, suggestiveness, and double meaning usually involve the interplay of text and image. For example, a recent magazine ad for Harlequin books features the innocuous headline: "Has he been reading your Harlequin books?" Paired with a full-page image of an attractive couple in a heated embrace, however, the implication is that reading romance novels will get him in the mood. Now that we know what sex in advertising is, let's see if it works.

Objection 1: Sex in Advertising Doesn't Work

This objection comes in several varieties. One is that sex is only used to grab attention. Some people refer to this usage as "borrowed interest." In other words, advertisers attempt to take the interest generated by sexual information and use it to generate interest for their brands. In a related sense, detractors argue that, while sex may stop traffic, it only produces – at best – a one-time sale that won't build brand value needed to sustain long-term growth.

To some degree the critics are correct. Sex information does grab attention. Sex evokes a hardwired emotional response that is linked to species survival. We can't help that our eyes and ears are drawn to it because emotional information has a way of piercing our perceptual fields by rising above other environmental information trying to get our attention. So, yes, it does grab attention. And if sex is used merely to draw attention to a product that has no relevance to sex, then long-term success is not likely.

But consider the statement: "Sex is only used to grab attention." These critics should update their thinking because research indicates that sex is used for more than attracting attention. I did some work with Jacque Lambiase and we discovered that 73 percent, almost three-quarters, of sexual ads in magazines contained a sex-related brand benefit. Common themes followed the "buy this, get this" formula. That is, if you buy our product: (1) you'll be more sexually attractive, (2) you'll have more or better sex, or (3) you'll just feel sexier for your own sake. Recall the commercials used by Unilever to introduce Axe body spray. A young man sprays it on, and attractive women (even physicians and mothers of girlfriends) find him irresistible. Credible? Doubtful. Tongue-in-cheek? Sure. I'm convinced that the agency handling Axe found through extensive research that these appeals resonated with members of the target audience (teens and young men 14–34 years old).

Again, almost three times as many ads use sex as a selling message – in most cases as the primary reason for buying and using the brand – than solely for attention-getting purposes. Axe, Tag, and Old Spice body sprays have produced a lot of revenue for their parent companies in a relatively short period of time (Axe was introduced in 2000), and all three are positioned as sexual-attractant enhancers.

In addition, there are plenty of cases in which sexual positioning strategies have resulted in long-term success. One of those is Calvin Klein. He has successfully imbued his brand's identity with sexuality. For well over 30 years, sex in one form or another has been a mainstay in Calvin Klein fragrance, fashion, underwear, and accessories ads. The result? In 2005 products with Calvin's name generated at least $1 billion in annual revenue.

The same is true for Victoria's Secret. With its stable of supermodels clad only in panties and bras, the company has grown from three boutiques in San Francisco to the most successful and recognizable intimates brand in the United States, if not the world. Much of that success was achieved through an aggressive catalog effort and inventive promotional techniques such as Super Bowl commercials, streaming fashion shows, and primetime fashion shows on network television. These promotional efforts rarely vary from Victoria's Secret's carefully crafted, sexually sophisticated image. Women who want to be associated with that image, either for their own pleasure or for that of someone else, willingly pay for it.

Many other firms have successfully used sex in advertising for sustained periods of time, and sex in advertising works in other ways beyond gaining attention and offering sex-related benefits. Suffice to say that as long as people desire to be attractive to others, and as long as people desire romance, intimacy, and love, and all the wonderful feelings they involve, advertisers can show how their products help meet those needs and desires. Whether we like it or not, products play a role in society's intimacy equation.

Objection 2: Sex in Advertising Contains Degrading Images of Women

I agree. Advertisers need to do a better job of portraying women not only in sexual ads but in all advertising. Obviously, however, not all sexual ads are degrading, and the industry, especially the Madison Avenue agencies that produce nationally visual campaigns, is improving the tone of those images.

But, first, let's look more closely at the objection, because it is an important one. Essentially feminists have argued that decorative images of women – women shown as one-dimensional objects present merely to look good – influence people's attitudes and perceptions about women's contributions and roles in society. Research shows that the feminists are right. Both women and men who are exposed to these decorative images place more value on women's physical attractiveness and role as a mate, and devalue their intellect, skills, and competencies. One ad won't do it, but who sees just one ad? We see thousands of them every day. Over time, and unannounced, sexist attitudes work their way into our belief system.

How does this relate to sex in advertising? Although beefcake images have made inroads in the last 20–25 years, provocatively dressed women in suggestive poses constitute a fair portion of sexual images. In some cases women are subservient to their male counterparts. Men watch as their women strip, dance, or playfully tease them in some other manner.

As a whole, these images are unacceptable. The advertising industry is increasingly aware of the sexism inherent in these types of images, and it is cleaning up its act. In some cases, the industry is policing itself. For example, there is a very influential industry group known as Advertising Women of New

York (AWNY). At their annual meeting they give out awards to advertisers who portray women in the most positive and negative ways. Several instances of sex in advertising have received the "Grand Ugly" award. These awards publicly identify particularly offensive ads (and their sponsors) and result in a lot of bad press. Several years ago Candie's won the "Grand Ugly" award for a print ad featuring Jodi Lyn O'Keefe astride a computer monitor, and Sugar Ray's Mark McGrath sitting at the keyboard. On the screen a space shuttle is shown blasting upward toward O'Keefe's crotch.

Today, ads like the one for Candie's are the exception, not the rule. In fact, many sexual ads often contain humor that pokes fun at the objectifying male characters. For those of you who are too young to remember, in 1994 a very popular Diet Coke commercial turned the tables as women ogled a shirtless male construction worker. Also note that Madison Avenue isn't the primary source of sexist ads these days. Many offending ads are placed by local businesses in newspapers and major urban alternative weeklies such as the *Dallas Observer* and *Phoenix New Times*. Last, keep in mind that sexual information isn't inherently degrading to women, or men. Sexual ads that portray couples in healthy relationships, with equal power dimensions, can capture a unique and compelling slice of life with no hint of sexism (for an example, reread this essay's first paragraph).

Conclusion

In addition to these two primary complaints, there are other concerns regarding sex in advertising. For example, some, including me, have claimed that sexual ads unfairly target teens and young people. Raging hormones, sexual discovery, and newly minted critical thinking skills can cloud judgment and make teens especially susceptible to sexual appeals that advocate brands as sexual attractants. Advertisers who are guilty of targeting young adults obviously should be held accountable. Abercrombie & Fitch have felt the heat recently as public pressure is mounting to compel them to tone down the sexual explicitness of their quarterly "magalogs."

In sum, sex in advertising can be a very effective creative strategy if:

1   it is relevant to the product it is promoting;
2   it isn't sexist; and
3   it doesn't target susceptible populations.

In other words, advertising creators – perhaps like yourself someday soon – need to be aware of these issues and to act in good faith. If they don't, as research by LaTour and Henthornem (2003) has shown, consumers are more likely to boycott products sold with sexist images. Also, Advertising Women of New York (AWNY) may feature your ad as a "Grand Ugly." I hate to imagine you trying to explain that award to your client. Last, remember that advertising's job is to tell consumers how products fulfill their needs and desires. As long as people use products to attract others (e.g., fashion, fragrance, mouthwash, cosmetics, even automobiles), what's so bad about advertising helping people get what they really want – romance, intimacy, and the affection of others? In the meantime, are you going to finish that rice bowl?

Reference

LaTour, M. and Henthornem T. L. (2003). Nudity and sexual appeals: Understanding the arousal process and advertising response. In T. Reichert and J. Lambiase (eds.), *Sex in advertising*. Mahwah, NJ: Lawrence Erlbaum, pp. 91–106.

Further Reading

Lambiase, J. and Reichert, T. (2003). Promises, promises: Exploring erotic rhetoric in sexually oriented advertising. In L. Scott and R. Batra (eds.), *Persuasive imagery: A consumer perspective*. Mahwah, NJ: Lawrence Erlbaum, pp. 247–266.

Pardun, C. J., L'Engle, K. L., and Brown, J. D. (2005). Linking exposure to outcomes: Early adolescents' consumption of sexual content in six media. *Mass Communication and Society* 8(2): 75–91.

Reichert, T. (2003). *The erotic history of advertising*. Amherst, NY: Prometheus Books.

Reichert, T. and Lambiase, J. (2003). How to get "kissably close": Examining how advertisers appeal to consumers' sexual needs and desires. *Sexuality and Culture* 7(3): 120–136.

Reichert, T. and Ramirez, A. (2000). Defining sexually oriented appeals in advertising: A grounded theory investigation. In S. J. Hoch and R. J. Meyer (eds.), *Advances in consumer research*, vol. 27. Provo, UT: Association for Consumer Research, pp. 267–273.

Counterargument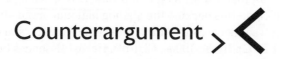

Using sex in advertising is never a good idea

Kathy Roberts Forde

University of South Carolina, USA

Advertising has long filled nearly every nook and cranny of public life in the United States. As you watch a New York Yankees game on television, you also take in an AT&T advertisement behind home plate. As you wait for your morning train in Grand Central station, you notice rows of split-flap departure boards promoting the opening of Apple's largest retail store ever, in the train station itself. When you get off the subway in Columbus Circle, you walk alongside a moving image of elite marathoner Ryan Hall on an Asics-sponsored 60-foot video wall promoting the New York City Marathon and, of course, Asics running gear. Can you keep up with Hall's 4:46 mile pace for only 60 feet? The video advertisement invites you to try.

In the last several years, advertising has extended in new ways into our private lives too. With the advent of social media and increasingly powerful handheld devices that keep us tethered to the Internet, advertising has become more personalized and interactive. Apple's iAd embeds interactive and immersive "rich media" ads in apps targeting particular demographic groups of iPod, iPad, and iPhone users around the world. Social networks like Facebook and Twitter deliver local ads to local target audiences.

The content of new media advertisements has, in some cases, become notably intimate. In 2009, capitalizing on the popularity of "manscaping" among younger men, Gillette produced a series of instructional shaving videos promoting the Fusion razor. The videos, posted on YouTube, quickly went viral. The most popular was titled "How to shave your groin." The calming voiceover in the how-to cartoon informed viewers, "When there's no underbrush, the tree looks taller." The point of the video? To increase demand for – and thus sales of – Gillette razors.

Ours is a society of desire, and commerce is the deep structure of our daily lives. We speak and dream in the language of commodity and consumption. Even sex – or at least the idea of sex – has become something we readily consume at the click of a mouse or turn of the page. And sex pervades contemporary advertising in the United States (Reichert et al. 2007).

There's no doubt that sex sells certain products to certain people. As early as the 1890s, Duke cigarettes became the leading national brand after the company began including trading cards featuring portraits of female stars in its cigarette packs (Reichert 2002). In the 1990s, Clairol's Herbal Essences became a leading brand of shampoo, largely due to an ad campaign touting the "organic" (read "orgasmic") experience the shampoo offered women (Fass 2001). But research has found that sexual appeal doesn't work very well for products with no plausible sexual meaning (Reichert 2002: 254). And even when ads feature products popularly sexualized, such as fashion and alcohol, sexual content tends to damage brand recall, especially for men, who tend to focus on breasts and legs and neglect the product and brand (Nudd 2005). What's more, most women don't even care for sexual ads (Nudd 2005).

Despite the ubiquity of sexual appeal in today's advertising landscape, most Americans believe there is too much sexual imagery in the ads they view (Dolliver 1999). It's time to rethink the use of sex in advertising. In fact, let's get rid of the sexual appeal altogether. We're collectively exhausted with sexual messages intended to persuade us to buy this or that, usually through tired cliché or norm-shocking visuals.

We've come a long way, baby, since Virginia Slims advertisements touted smoking as a sexy and emancipated pastime for women and Herbal Essence commercials shocked us with women shampooing their hair in sexual excitement. These ads seem practically demure in our contemporary marketplace where Gucci shows off its couture in a print ad featuring an impossibly thin young woman pulling down her underpants to expose pubic hair shaved in the shape of the iconic G, while a young man kneels in front of her, grasping her thigh (Kilbourne 2005).

It's shocking, at least when you see such an image in the pages of a glossy women's magazine rather than on replays of *Sex and the City*. But when you recover from your surprise, the overwhelming feeling is boredom. Enough already.

Ennui is hardly the only suffering caused by the glut of sex in advertising. Sexual ads contribute to serious social ills, such as unhealthy sexual attitudes, beliefs, and behavior in adolescents, teens, and young adults; the objectification of women – and men – as sexual commodities; body image problems; and disordered eating. Other possible harmful effects are harder to measure, such as the trivialization of intimacy and what Jean Kilbourne (2005) has identified as the "sexual dissatisfaction" of many Americans.

Teens and Sex

A study conducted by researchers at the University of North Carolina found that the more sexual content young teens aged 12 to 14 consume in the media, the more likely they are to have had sex and to engage in sexual activity in the future (Pardun et al. 2005: 88). Sexual advertisements are but one element of a measure this study termed the "Sexual Media Diet (SMD)" – which included television and movie viewing, magazine and newspaper reading, music listening, and Web surfing – but they contribute to the overall sexual content of teens' media world. It is the amount, not the kind, of sexual media teens consume that influences sexual behavior and attitudes.

In the United States today, almost half of high school students have had sex (CDC 2006: 3). Although teen pregnancy and birth rates have steadily declined in the United States since 1991, these rates are still higher than in other Western developed countries. Sexually transmitted disease and abortion rates are higher too. Teens in all these countries are exposed to sexual media, including advertisements, that rarely depict the risks involved in sexual activity such as pregnancy and sexually transmitted diseases. A devastating difference is that US cultural attitudes have prevented more robust sex education and contraceptive programs, like those that exist in Sweden and France, from developing. There are fewer social buffers in the United

States to counteract the negative effects of sexual media messages on youth (Darroch et al. 2001).

While stronger sex education campaigns in the United States are key, we also need a less sexually charged media environment. Young people today primarily learn about sex from the media (Brown and Keller 2000). If advertisements dropped the sexual appeal – especially advertisements aimed at teens and adolescents – that would be one step in the direction of better public health for American youth.

Objectification

In its attempt to sell merchandise and services, advertising often represents women's bodies as sexual objects. Ads for jeans show women in underwear, focusing on breasts, rear ends, and exposed skin without a shred of denim in sight. The female body parts – not the product – are the visual subject. If you wear our jeans, the ad suggests, you too can have a sexy body that any man would want to see and touch. It's an age-old advertising technique. It's time-worn too.

Today women are the major consumers in the US economy – spending 88 percent of a household's disposable income – and advertising continues to offer up objectified images of female bodies that many of these female consumers find offensive and even stupid (Crawford 2004). The advertising industry is simply out of touch with today's marketplace and the contemporary woman.

The sexual objectification of women in advertisements conditions girls and women to view themselves as objects – a phenomenon called self-objectification. This way of viewing one's own body can lead to shame, disgust, and appearance anxiety, which in turn can contribute to eating disorders, sexual dysfunction, and depression. Self-objectification appears to be activated more readily by print media such as fashion magazines, in which large numbers of objectified images of women appear in advertisements, than by television (Roberts and Gettman 2004).

Men too can be adversely affected by ads objectifying women. Research has shown a relationship between male acceptance of both sex role stereotypes and violence against women and viewing of such advertisements (Lanis and Covell 1995). Research also suggests that advertisements depicting sexualized violence against women by men appear to appeal more to younger men than any other group and may socialize these men "into a culture of aggression" (Capella et al. 2010: 47).

But it's not only women who are objectified in advertising these days. Men too have become sexual objects. The body size of men has increased substantially over time in advertising depictions, with an emphasis on large, muscular physiques (Roberts and Gettman 2004). Sexual portrayals of men have increased too (Reichert et al. 1999). Although the effects of these "beefcake ads" are uncertain, some believe they have influenced men to body-build obsessively in a kind of "reverse anorexia" (Roberts and Gettman 2004).

Body Image and Beauty

In a country where sales in the diet industry totaled $1.9 billion in 2004, weight is on the mind of many Americans. In 1980, 47 percent of the US population was overweight; the figure has risen sharply in the past 25 years to 65 percent (Mintel Reports 2005). High-fructose corn syrup runs through the arteries of supermarkets and the fast food industry, conditioning our bodies to store rather than burn fat, and fast food giants push supersized meals and feed children in school cafeterias (Critser 2004). Yet just as economic and social forces drive the US obesity epidemic, they also drive the beauty and fashion industries, which glorify thinness and youth. We live in a culture of insanely mixed messages and competing social pressures. Simply consider the message one Carl Jr. television and Internet commercial sends to women and girls. Eat this half-pound hamburger! But be sure to maintain the body of a Paris Hilton – and while you're at it, work on your seductive car-washing skills!

Advertising for the fashion and beauty industries relies on making consumers feel that they just aren't attractive or sexy enough. The ideal female body is ultrathin, young, and without wrinkle, cellulite, or blemish – an ideal no woman can attain. And yet advertisements tell women repeatedly that if they use this face lotion, wear this bra, try this diet they can achieve the ideal. For many women and girls, the idealized female bodies they see in advertisements produce body shame and appearance anxiety (Monro and Huon 2005). For men and boys, these images provide unrealistic expectations of what their girlfriends, wives, sisters, and mothers should look like and a diminished appreciation for who these women can be and are in their full humanity.

America needs major social reform to address the obesity epidemic, including public health campaigns and increased regulation of the food industry. But we also need media depictions of bodies in a range of shapes, sizes, ages, and physical capacity. Let's replace the thin, youthful, sexy ideal in advertisements with images of real women: muscular athletes, women in wheelchairs, breast cancer survivors, women over the age of 50. Let's believe there is more to women and girls than the sex objects and stereotypes we often see in advertising. And then let's insist that advertisers believe it too.

Eating Disorders

It is estimated that one in 10 college women suffer from an eating disorder such as anorexia and bulimia, and that 15 percent of young women exhibit disordered eating. It is likely no coincidence that as eating disorder rates have climbed in recent years, the media's body ideal for women has become thinner and thinner.

Although many factors contribute to eating disorders, for some women and girls the media's ultrathin body ideal is a strong influence (Stice et al. 1994).

Eating disorders affect men and boys too. About 10 percent of those with eating disorders in the United States are male. Whether mediated messages contribute to this problem is unclear.

The good news is that advertisers can counteract such negative messages and their results by providing more realistic images of women. Research shows that young women who view average-weight models in media depictions appear to develop resistance to the negative effects of the thin body ideal. There is hope, then, that advertisements depicting real women can lessen the prevalence of eating disorders (Fister and Smith 2004).

Regulating Sex in Advertising

Although plenty of consumers object to sex in advertising purely on moral or religious grounds, such an argument is hard to advance in a heterogeneous society with diverse social and religious practices and beliefs. A legal argument is hard to mount too. The Federal Trade Commission rules prohibit deceptive and unfair advertising, but regulatory law has little to say about the often irrational lifestyle claims an advertisement may make, such as the attribution of a woman's sexiness to the perfume or jeans she wears (Preston 1998: 73). It's important to note too that commercial speech enjoys substantial First Amendment protection, although less robust than that afforded political and social discourse. At present, the only realistic means for changing the advertising industry's over-reliance on sexual appeal is through self-regulation, media regulation (the power of the media to choose the advertising it will publish), and public pressure.

Public and governmental alarm over the recently recognized obesity epidemic in the United States has resulted in increased scrutiny of food advertising directed at children. In response, the food industry has made positive changes in products and packaging aimed at children and strengthened self-regulation of its marketing techniques (Parnes 2006). Although these efforts have only just begun, similar self-regulation in the arena of sexual advertisements (directed at all audiences) may do much to ameliorate associated public health problems and social issues.

The American Association of Advertising Agencies' Standards of Practice (2011) dictates that advertisements should tell the truth, avoid misleading the public through omission of important facts, and adhere to public standards of good taste and decency. Does an ad that uses sexual appeal tell the truth? Does it provide all significant facts the consumer needs to make an informed purchasing decision? Is it in keeping with current social standards of good taste? These are questions advertisers should ask themselves before using a sexual appeal. But there is another question that should be encapsulated in any ethical code of advertising. Does the message in the ad tend to contribute substantively to documented public health concerns and social ills? If yes, the ad message is ethically suspect and needs to be revised.

Conclusion

Beyond the substantive ethical and social research arguments against many sexual advertisements, there is another argument against the use of the sexual appeal in advertising – and it is this argument that may be most persuasive. Sexualized sales messages have permeated the world of advertising to such an extent that they are just plain uninteresting and, in many cases, ineffective.

What would the media landscape look like without sex in advertising? Would the creative minds in advertising come up with better, more entertaining, more publicly useful messages? O brave new world that has such ads in it! It's a world we all deserve.

References

American Association of Advertising Agencies (2011). Standards of practice. At http://www.aaaa.org/about/association/Pages/standardsofpractice.aspx, accessed Mar. 22, 2013.

Brown, J. D. and Keller, S. N. (2000). Can the mass media be healthy sex educators? *Family Planning Perspectives* 32(5): 255–256.

Capella, M. L., Hill, R. P., Rapp, J. M., and Kees, J. (2010). The impact of violence against women in advertisements. *Journal of Advertising* 39(4), 37–51.

CDC (Centers for Disease Control and Prevention) (2006). *Youth Risk behavior surveillance – United States, 2005.* Morbidity and mortality weekly report No. SS-5. At http://www.cdc.gov/mmwr/PDF/SS/SS5505.pdf, accessed Mar. 22, 2013.

Crawford, K. (2004). Ads for women are "Miss Understood." *CNNMoney* (Sept. 22). At http://money.cnn.com/2004/09/22/news/midcaps/advertising_women/index.htm, accessed Mar. 22, 2013.

Critser, G. (2004). *Fat land: How Americans became the fattest people in the world.* Boston: Houghton Mifflin.

Darroch, J. E., Frost, J. J., Singh, S., and Study Team (2001). *Teenage sexual and reproductive behavior in developed countries: Can more progress be made?* Occasional Report No. 3. New York: Alan Guttmacher Institute.

Dolliver, M. (1999). Is there too much sexual imagery in advertising? *Adweek* 40(11) (Mar. 15): 21–22.

Fass, A. (2001). Clairol tones down a campaign in an effort to give its new hair products a separate personality. *New York Times* (June 25), C8.

Fister, S. M. and Smith, G. T. (2004). Media effects on expectancies: Exposure to realistic female images as a protective factor. *Psychology of Addictive Behaviors* 18(4): 394–397.

Kilbourne, J. (2005). What else does sex sell? *International Journal of Advertising* 24(1): 119–122.

Lanis, K. and Covell, K. (1995). Images of women in advertisements: Effects on attitudes related to sexual aggression. *Sex Roles* 32: 639–649.

Mintel Reports (2005). *Weight control – US – April 2005*. Chicago: Mintel Group. At http://oxygen.mintel.com/display/121269/, accessed July 11, 2006.

Monro, F. and Huon, G. (2005). Media-portrayed idealized images, body shame, and appearance anxiety. *International Journal of Eating Disorders* 38(1): 85–90.

Nudd, T. (2005). Does sex really sell? *Adweek* 46(40) (Oct. 17), 14–17.

Pardun, C., L'Engle, K. L., and Brown, J. D. (2005). Linking exposure to outcomes: Early adolescents' consumption of sexual content in six media. *Mass Communication and Society* 8(2): 75–91.

Parnes, L. B. (2006). Remarks. 2006 Annual Advertising Law & Business Conference, Association of National Advertisers, Orlando, FL, Jan. 25. At http://www.ftc.gov/speeches/parnes/0601lydiaanaspeech.pdf, accessed Mar. 22, 2013.

Preston, I. L. (1998). Puffery and other "loophole" claims: How the law's "don't ask, don't tell" policy condones fraudulent falsity in advertising. *Journal of Law and Commerce* 18: 49–114.

Reichert, T. (2002). Sex in advertising research: A review of content, effects, and functions of sexual information in consumer advertising. *Annual Review of Sex Research* 13: 241–273.

Reichert, T., Lambiase, J., Morgan, S., Carstarphen, M., and Zavoina, S. (1999). Cheesecake and beefcake: No matter how you slice it, sexual explicitness in advertising continues to increase. *Journalism & Mass Communication Quarterly* 76(1): 7–20.

Reichert, T., LaTour, M. S., and Kim, J. Y. (2007). Assessing the influence of gender and sexual self-schema on affective responses to sexual content in advertising. *Journal of Current Issues and Research in Advertising* 29(2): 63–77.

Roberts, T. and Gettman, J. Y. (2004). Mere exposure: Gender differences in the negative effects of priming a state of self-objectification. *Sex Roles* 51(1–2): 17–28.

Stice, E., Schupak-Neuberg, E., Shaw, H. E., and Stein, R. I. (1994). Relation of media exposure to eating disorder symptomatology: An examination of mediating mechanisms. *Journal of Abnormal Psychology* 103(4): 836–840.

8

Stereotypes in Advertising

> We don't have milk cows. People
> have so many stereotypes of
> people from where I come from –
> Oklahoma. We don't ride around
> in covered wagons, either.
>
> Carrie Underwood

There's an automobile television commercial that has been running incessantly on the TV programs I like to watch. In it, there is a back-in-the-home 20-something kid complaining about his clueless parents. The parents, meanwhile, are out having a blast – either riding mountain bikes across treacherous terrains or gathering with hip friends to take in an outdoor concert of an equally hip band. These commercials annoy me to no end. It might be because I don't like how the advertiser is using an "anti-stereotype" in what, to me, seems like a stereotypical way. Or perhaps, I'm annoyed with the portrayal of these clueless "adult children." (Move out of the house right now!)

While I find this advertising campaign irksome, I have to admit that it does touch a nerve. First, I'm the target market of the campaign. (I'm in the same age group as the hip parents.) And, second, the car actually sounds like it might be

Advertising and Society: An Introduction, Second Edition. Edited by Carol J. Pardun.
© 2014 John Wiley & Sons, Inc. Published 2014 by John Wiley & Sons, Inc.

a good one for me. So, maybe this is an example of a commercial that is full of stereotypes used in a very effective way.

It's easy to make a list of stereotypes we see in advertising. In fact, I'm not sure I can recall an advertisement that *doesn't* use stereotypes! While it may be easy to say stereotyping is wrong, when an advertiser has 15 or 30 seconds to tell a story, it's more challenging to explain the importance of eating oatmeal to control cholesterol if the viewer can't quickly see that the person on screen obviously needs the product! And, really, aren't some stereotypes just another way to good-naturedly poke fun at others – and ourselves?

Even if we think stereotypes are expected – even necessary – in advertising, the issue is only going to continue being controversial. Here's why.

First, our society is becoming more segmented, so even if stereotypes are indeed helpful, as Margaret Morrison argues, it is becoming more difficult to create a meaningful stereotype that the audience can resonate with right away. For example, consider the aging population. There are currently more than 40 million Americans who are over 50 years old. Where a generation ago, "over 50" might have meant middle age – or even "over the hill" – being 50+ today is more complicated. Yes, many people in their fifties are indeed grandparents, but some are also new parents themselves. Some are competitive athletes, some are on the "most beautiful people" list, some are college students, and some are Florida retirees, spending their days on the golf courses around the state.

Second, it is harder than ever to get a viewer's attention when it comes to commercials. Now that digital video recorders and other technologies are common, advertisers have to be more daring, more targeted, more "in your face" to get your attention for even a few seconds. It could be that the days of gentle stereotyping are over! If an advertiser is too subtle, the message is most likely to get lost.

Third, in this media-saturated world, consumers have become more sophisticated about what the media can (and can't) do. Many look suspiciously at the message advertisers provide. So if it's not authentic, the consumer may very well ignore the message. If an advertiser doesn't use a stereotype, there is probably just as much chance that audience members will criticize the advertiser for being "too real" (i.e., the company is trying too hard) and thus the advertiser ends up being criticized as much as (or more than) if it had just gone ahead and used the stereotype.

So, what's the right way to handle stereotypes in advertising? Do we get offended if we're made fun of by way of stereotypes? Or do we decide that it's a technique to quickly grab our attention and then let us choose what to make of the message? Are all stereotypes bad? Or can a "good stereotype" (hardworking, patriotic blue-collar employee, for example) benefit the demographic that is getting praised?

Finally, we need to wrestle with the issue of why stereotypes in advertising may be an ethical issue in the first place. How important is it for us to get the whole picture before we make a judgment about a person? Does it matter if we judge fictional people (characters in advertising) quickly? Some people might argue that if we don't see a person accurately – even in an advertisement – then we are setting ourselves up to treating "real" people too simplistically, and therefore not ethically. Or, as Jane Marcellus mentions in her essay, when we believe stereotypes, we begin to expect that people will act in a certain way, which may be short-sighted and ignores the complexity of the person. Other people would say a stereotype is only an entrance into a person's life – not a definition of it. These are tough questions. What ethical role – if any – do stereotypes have in advertising? *You decide.*

Ideas to Get You Thinking . . .

1   Make a list of all the stereotypes you can think of. Start with the most obvious (housewife, football player, grandmother, etc.). Then write a one-word description of the label. Now see if a classmate or friend can match the descriptions with the stereotypes. How many did they get right? What did you learn?
2   Watch your favorite television program. List every kind of stereotype that you come across in the show. Be as specific as possible. Do you think these stereotypes are necessary? Why, or why not?
3   Flip through a magazine. Every time you come across a stereotype, make a note of it. Are there certain groups that come up more than others? Which ones?
4   Tape one of your favorite television programs (or access it online or through YouTube). You will most likely need to view it more than once. Make a list of all the commercials you see during the show. List all the main characters in the commercials and indicate whether you think the characters are portrayed in stereotypical ways. What did you discover?

Other Topics to Debate

1   Only negative stereotypes are really negative.
2   Stereotypes in the media outside of advertising are bad because those vehicles have plenty of time to develop the characters. However, because advertisers have just a few seconds to make a point, it's a necessary mechanism.
3   Stereotypes that mock successful individuals (such as doctors) are perfectly acceptable.

If You'd Like to Know More . . .

Gilmore, J. and Jordan, A. (2012). Burgers and basketball: Race and stereotypes in food and beverage advertising aimed at children in the US. *Journal of Children and Media* 6(3): 317–332. doi:10.1080/17482798.2012.673498

Hirshman, E. C. (2011). Motherhood in black and brown: Advertising to U.S. minority women. *Advertising & Society Review* 12(2). doi:10.1353/asr.2011.0015.

O'Barr, W. M. (2012). Niche markets: Gay consumers. *Advertising & Society Review* 12(4). At http://muse.jhu.edu/journals/advertising_and_society_review/v012/12.4.o-barr.html#fig02, accessed Apr. 2, 2013.

Van Hellemont, C. and Van den Bulck, H. (2012). Impacts of advertisements that are unfriendly to women and men. *International Journal of Advertising* 31(3): 623–656. doi:10.2501/IJA-31-33-623-656

Yeh, M. A., Jewell, R. D., and Hu, M. Y. (2013). Stereotype processing's effect on the impact of the myth/Fact message format and the role of personal relevance. *Psychology & Marketing* 30(1): 36–45. doi:10.1002/mar.20587

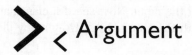

❯❮ Argument

What's the harm in advertising stereotypes?

Jane Marcellus

Middle Tennessee State University, USA

In the November 2011 issue of *Esquire* magazine, a foldout poster of Rihanna shows the performer lying on her side, wearing nothing but what looks like strategically draped seaweed. On the flip side is a color photograph of the 2012 Shelby GT500 Mustang. Both the poster and the ad follow a lengthy profile of Rihanna, who was named *Esquire*'s "Sexiest Woman Alive" in a contest sponsored by Ford.

Immediately following the poster, a Ford ad proclaims that "How you hang this poster says a lot about you." It offers three choices. Choosing the "Sexiest Woman Alive side" shows that "You're a red-blooded American male." Choosing the Mustang side also shows that "You're a red-blooded American male." Hanging the poster on a plate-glass window, so both sides can be seen reveals that "You're a genius."

There are a number of criticisms about this spread. It blurs the line between editorial copy and advertising and suggests that a woman and an automobile are equal in value. Just as troubling, however, is the suggestion that if a man does *not* select the car, the woman, or both, his masculinity – and his

Americanism – will be in question. The ad degrades women, but it *stereotypes* both women and men, reducing them, as British cultural studies theorist Stuart Hall observes, "to a few, simple, essential characteristics, which are represented as fixed by Nature" (1997: 257).

Stereotypes in advertising are unacceptable. They are limiting, often demeaning, and simply not necessary to sell products. In fact, ad stereotypes are so troubling that, in 2008, the European Parliament voted 504–110 to adopt a nonbinding report aimed at convincing the ad industry not to use them. Focused primarily on gender stereotypes, the report states that ad stereotypes can "straitjacket women, men, girls and boys by restricting individuals to predetermined and artificial roles that are often degrading, humiliating and dumbed-down for both sexes" (Carvajal 2008).

Understanding the problem with stereotypes is easier if you understand that the word "stereotype" comes from early printing, where it had to do with using a metal plate to produce the same image over and over. Nowadays, according to the *Oxford English Dictionary*, it refers to an "oversimplified idea" that is used, like those metal plates, over and over again. Media scholar Kim Sheehan (2004) likens the concept to modern-day photocopying. The word "cliché" has similar roots. Unoriginal ideas multiplied without thought, stereotypes limit our ability to see people, things, and ideas in nuanced ways. As Walter Lippmann (1922) writes in his classic work *Public opinion*, stereotypes are "pictures in our heads" (1922: 81) that construct the way we see the world around us before we have a chance to look for ourselves:

> For the most part we do not first see, and then define, we define first and then see. In the great blooming, buzzing confusion of the outer world we pick out what our culture has already defined for us, and we tend to perceive that which we have picked out in the form stereotyped for us by our culture. (Lippmann 1922: 81)

Media ethicist Thomas Bivins calls stereotypes a "Platonic shadow-show put on by our own culture – a figment of reality at best" (2009: 206). Limiting our ability to see would be bad enough, but as Hall observes, stereotyping often occurs where one group is more powerful than another. Difference is emphasized as the less powerful group becomes "the Other" (1997: 258) and social dominance is maintained. In the Ford ad from *Esquire*, the dominant group is the "red-blooded American male" who sees both cars and women as interchangeable. Measured against one another in a contest, women are disempowered, but male readers who do not wish to disempower them are also, implicitly, "the other" – unmasculine and un-American.

Of course, stereotypes are often justified as the fastest way to communicate in the blink of time that an advertiser has to capture audience attention. Certainly, they leave lasting impressions. We are all familiar with the "choosy moms" who select a certain brand of peanut butter or women who debate the best way to mop their floors, clean their bathrooms, or get the stains out of their rowdy little boys' clothes. It seems dads rarely worry about such things, and girls are never rowdy. Instead, at very young ages, girls are found in fashion magazines like *Teen Vogue* and *Cosmo Girl*. Ultra-skinny, with flawless skin, they tout everything from mascara to jeans. Such images are perfect illustrations of Laura Mulvey's point that the "male gaze" constructs women as sexual objects in an "erotic spectacle" (2006 [1975]: 346). In other words, the way men see women determines their value, so women evaluate themselves according to how they think men will evaluate them. Both sexes are encouraged to see women as objects, and anything else is unnatural in this system of mutually reinforcing stereotypes.

One might argue that there is nothing wrong with having a clean house, playing outside in the dirt, or wearing nice clothes and makeup. But many ads present people in what cultural historian Roland Marchand calls "social tableaux" (1985: 165), a strategy that emerged in the 1920s. Many tableaux suggest there is no *other* way to see moms, little boys, or teen girls. As Bivins says, stereotypes "present only a single cultural picture, and reinforce certain cultural expectations" (2009: 207). "How many believe that the Irish are heavy drinkers, that Mexicans are lazy, that blondes are dumb, that white men can't jump?" he asks (208). Although many people know such egregious stereotypes are wrong, other stereotypes – subtle but just as powerful – tell us that men are slobs, single people are desperate to mate, and anything fleshier than "sixpack abs" is obese.

Both Sheehan (2004) and Bivins (2009) cite two media theories to help explain why stereotypes are so powerful. *Cultivation theory*, developed by George Gerbner (1973) holds that the media (particularly television) have such power over the way we see the world that, as Denis McQuail writes, it "gradually leads to the adoption of beliefs about the nature of the social world which conform to the stereotyped, distorted and very selective view of reality" (2005: 497). For example, those who see a lot of ads where only women scrub bathrooms and men objectify women begin to believe that these are natural behaviors for real people. *Media expectancy theory*, similarly, holds that over time we not only believe that certain behaviors are normal but we expect all people in that group to conform to them. As Sheehan argues, expectancy theory suggests that "the use of stereotypes hinders one's view of any individual as a complete person" (2004: 83). An example is Richard Dyer's list of common gay and lesbian stereotypes – "the butch dyke and the camp queen, the lesbian vampire and the sadistic queer, the predatory schoolmistress and the neurotic faggot" (2006 [1984]: 353). He notes that even some gay people in the past believed they were true, perpetuating self-oppression. Similarly, Bivins says, "If you are a young woman and you consistently see women portrayed as air-headed 'shopaholics,' you may, over time, begin to adopt that cliché as an actual way of life" (2009: 208).

It is important to remember that not all stereotypes are communicated visually; accents also stereotype. "Who would think that a German car company could break ground in Spartanburg, Carolina and call it home?" asks the announcer in a BMW commercial, his speech heavy with "good old boy" Southern inflections. The voiceover continues as images of working-class people in a diner and football players on a field are interspersed with visuals of the factory (which makes luxury cars). Similarly, a series of BP ads that appeared in the wake of the 2010 Gulf of Mexico oil spill used announcers with Southern accents as part of the company's crisis management. In both, the "folks like us" attitude and Southern dialect are clearly intended to convey "Americanness" and to ward off the perceived threat of large foreign corporations. Yet when there is no foreign "other," regional accents can be negative. As linguist Dennis R. Preston notes,

> Just as US popular culture has kept alive the barefoot, moonshine-making and drinking, intermarrying, racist Southerner, so has it continued to contribute to the perception of the brash, boorish, criminal, violent New Yorker. Small wonder that the varieties of English associated with these areas have these characteristics attributed to them. (Preston n.d.)

British accents also convey stereotypes about social class and education. The little green gecko who sells GEICO car insurance actually speaks with a Cockney accent from East London – the one-time poor, working-class area immortalized in Charles Dickens's *Oliver Twist*. Although the gecko's charm appeals to many, it may offend those sensitive to defining "Englishness" in a way that both capitalizes on but ignores the cultural complexity of an area known for overcrowding, poverty, and crime, but which is today a rich hodgepodge of ethnicities. To those who understand the regional nuances of British culture, "English" is no more defined by the Cockney accent than it is by the stuffy upper-class accent of the stereotypical English butler. Out of place in America (and on a Southwestern lizard), the gecko's accent may not amuse viewers sensitive to its cultural implications. After all, how would people in the United States (particularly in the South) feel if a "redneck" accent were used in British ads for British products?

But maybe you're still not convinced.

Sometimes, it helps to take a step back in time and gain a historical perspective. Let's consider the African American woman featured in a bathtub cleaner ad that aired regularly in 2006. Did she just happen to be black? Or did she have what Raymond Williams calls "cultural ancestors" (1961: 53), whose presence in media of the past make her presence in media now seem natural?

Go to the store (or maybe to your kitchen cabinet) and look at the image of the black woman on Aunt Jemima pancake mix. She has the bright smile, neat white collar, and pearl earrings that any professional woman today would be proud to wear to an executive job. But she used to look quite different. From the 1890s, when the product was introduced, until the mid twentieth century, she was an overweight black woman with a rag around her head – the typical mammy from the antebellum South. In fact, the first model for Aunt Jemima actually *was* a 59-year-old former slave named Nancy Green (Advertising Age, n.d.). In a 1919 ad from *Ladies' Home Journal*, Aunt Jemima was called, paradoxically, "the cook whose cabin became more famous than Uncle Tom's" – a reference to Harriet Beecher Stowe's antislavery novel *Uncle Tom's Cabin.*

Back in those unapologetically racist times, the black "mammy" who spoke in dialect was common in ads for household products. The woman in a 1928 ad for an insecticide called Flit declares, "Dat little easy contraption do de wuk of six of dem giggling house gals in de old days" – referring to slave times. A 1931 ad in *Forbes* magazine urges businessmen to use "Clarinda" (another mammy with a rag on her head) along with the new imaging process of rotogravure to sell their products. "Fresh, savory, delightful – ten thousand such words would not tell the sales story of freshness as vividly and dramatically as the camera and Clarinda tell it here," claims this ad, which features Chase and Sanborn coffee as an example of what "Clarinda" could sell. The popularity of such images changed only when people became more sensitive to racism. Have they gone away completely? If you think so, then why does it seem natural in American culture for bathroom cleaner (or, in another ad that aired in the early 2000s, medicine for constipation) to be sold by plump black women with "down home" plainspokenness, even if they do not wear rags around their heads? Who are their cultural ancestors?

Other groups are also stereotyped. As Debra Merskin argues, "Trade characters such as Aunt Jemima (pancake mix), Uncle Rastus (Cream of Wheat), and Uncle Ben (rice) are visual reminders of the subservient occupational positions to which Blacks often have been relegated" (2001: 160). In the same way, "Crazy Horse Malt Liquor, Red Chief Sugar, and Sue Bee Honey similarly remind us of an oppressive past" (160) for Native Americans. Today's images of Native Americans are heir to such stereotypes, for they draw on ideas of "Indianness" that many people learned as children. In the case of African Americans, the cultural purpose of many stereotypes was originally to help "make Whites feel more comfortable with, and less guilty about, maintenance of distinctions on the basis of race well after Reconstruction" (Merskin 2001: 160). Their daily use had the effect of "constantly and subtly reinforcing stereotypical beliefs" (160). The same can be said for any other group that is made "other."

For advertising students seeking alternatives, it is useful to remember Dyer's distinction between *stereotypes* and *social types*, which "are open-ended, more provisional, more flexible," creating "the sense of freedom, choice, self-definition" (1984: 355). Social typing suggests that there are many ways to see oneself as a man or woman, mom or dad, girl or boy. In contrast, stereotypes are designed to limit and exclude those who do not fit narrow ideas of normalcy. "You appear to choose your social type in some measure, whereas you are condemned to a stereotype" (Dyer 1984: 355). Dyer argues that "righteous dismissal does not make stereotypes go away" (353) and calls for better understanding of how stereotypes function in society. Sheehan (2004) argues that stereotypes are mitigated by factors such as valence (emotional significance) and frequency, and whether the stereotypes are positive or negative. However, it is important to remember that these may vary with audiences, as we saw with the GEICO gecko example.

Advertising creates an imaginary world that teaches us how to see the real world – and how to see ourselves. As Anthony J. Cortese writes, ads "seem to seep quietly into the back room of our consciousness," where they "try to tell us who we are and who we should be" (1999: 12). For this reason, stereotypes have no place in advertising. They harm us all by diminishing our ability to see and to be seen as the thinking, feeling, unique individuals we are. If, as Lippmann (1922) says, we define first, then see, we don't really see at all. Because ads have so much social power, those who create them have a responsibility to do so in a way that does not reinforce unequal power structures. The ability to do that is one indication, in the twenty-first century, of a truly creative, responsible advertising professional.

References

Advertising Age (n.d.) "Aunt Jemima". *Special report: The advertising century.* At http://adage.com/article/special-report-the-advertising-century/aunt-jemima/140176/, accessed Mar. 22, 2013.

Bivins, T. (2009) *Mixed media: Moral distinctions in advertising, public relations, and journalism*, 2nd edn. New York: Routledge.

Carvajal, D. (2008) Europe takes aim at sexual stereotyping in ads. *New York Times* (Sept. 9). At http://www.nytimes.com/2008/09/10/business/media/10adco.html, accessed Mar. 22, 2013.

Cortese, A. (1999) *Provocateur: Images of women and minorities in advertising.* Lanham, MD: Rowman & Littlefield.

Dyer, R. (2006 [1984]) Stereotyping. In M. G. Durham and D. M. Kellner (eds.), *Media and cultural studies: Key works*, rev. edn. Oxford: Blackwell, pp. 353–365.

Gerbner, G. (1973) Cultural indicators – the third voice. In G. Gerbner, L. Gross, and W. Melody (eds.), *Communication Technology and Social Policy*. New York: Wiley, pp. 553–573.

Hall, S. (1997) *Representation: Cultural representation and signifying practices.* London: Sage.

Lippmann, W. (1922) *Public opinion.* New York: Macmillan.

Marchand, R. (1985) *Advertising the American dream: Making way for modernity, 1920–1940.* Berkeley: University of California Press.

McQuail, D. (2005) *McQuail's mass communication theory*, 5th edn. London: Sage.

Merskin, D. (2001) Winnebagos, Cherokees, Apaches, and Dakotas: The persistence of stereotyping of American Indians in American advertising brands. *Howard Journal of Communications* 12: 159–169.

Mulvey, L. (2006 [1975]) Visual pleasure and narrative cinema. In M. G. Durham and D. M. Kellner (eds.), *Media and cultural studies: Key works*, rev. edn. Oxford: Blackwell, pp. 342–352.

Preston, D. R. (n.d.) Language myth #17: They speak really bad english down south and in New York City. PBS. At http://www.pbs.org/speak/speech/prejudice/attitudes, accessed Mar. 22, 2013.

Sheehan, K. (2004) *Controversies in contemporary adverting.* Thousand Oaks, CA: Sage.

Williams, R. (1961) *The long revolution.* New York: Columbia University Press.

Counterargument ＞ ❮

Stereotypes are a necessary and appropriate strategy for advertising

Margaret Morrison

University of Tennessee, USA

You come across a lot of estimates of how many advertisements the average person sees every day. J. Walker Smith, principal with the Futures Company, former president of Yankelovich, a prominent market research firm, and writer of one of the essays in Chapter 3, says that we've gone from being exposed to about 500 ads daily in the 1970s to as many as 5,000 today (Johnson 2009). Obviously we can't possibly pay attention to all those ads. And advertisers have only seconds to capture the attention of consumers. To do so they use a variety of techniques designed to catch consumers' attention. They place their ads in the media vehicles that their target markets use (i.e., Gatorade on ESPN.com or Wells Fargo in the *Wall Street Journal*). They make their ads as relevant to the target as possible (for instance, a lot of college-age men like beer and women and that's why you often see very attractive women in beer commercials). They'll use things like catchy headlines, popular music, quick edits, and metaphorical devices, all with the goal of catching your attention.

And they often use stereotypes.

Yes, stereotypes. And most advertising would be a failure without them.

So what is a stereotype? Let's start at the beginning. "Stereotype" is derived from the Greek ("stereos" or solid) and Romance languages and originally referred to a method of printing from a plate. The meaning of the word has changed over time. Today we use "stereotype" to refer to an oversimplified idea about a group based on some preconceived assumptions.

We use stereotypes to help make sense of all aspects of our lives. Think of them as shorthand for living. For example, belongings like cowboy boots or flag pins communicate to others something about the individuals to whom they belong (we might be quick to stereotype the former as a fan of country music and the latter as an extremely patriotic person) (Cheryan et al. 2009). Given the complex nature of our world – all the information you are exposed to every day, all the stimuli present in your environment, and the myriad things you encounter every day like countless advertising messages – you can begin to see how stereotypes may be vital to help you understand the world.

So stereotypes have been around as long as humans and are useful in helping us organize our thoughts.

There are many theories about how the brain processes knowledge, including advertising. One of these – schema theory – is particularly useful in understanding how stereotypes work. A schema is a cognitive framework or concept that helps organize and interpret information. Schemas can be useful because they allow us to take shortcuts in interpreting a vast amount of information (like the amount of advertising to which we're exposed). However, these mental frameworks can also cause us to ignore pertinent information in favor of information that confirms our pre-existing beliefs and ideas. For instance,

> prejudice is an example of a schema that prevents people from seeing the world as it really is and inhibits them from taking in new information. By holding certain beliefs about a particular group of people, this existing schema may cause people to interpret situations incorrectly. When an event happens that challenges these existing beliefs, people may come up with alternative explanations that uphold and support their existing schema instead of adapting or changing their beliefs. (Cherry, n.d.)

Because we tend to gravitate toward mental images that reinforce what we already know about the world, schemas contribute to stereotypes and make it difficult for us to be receptive to or to retain new information that does not conform to what we already believe. Incorrect pre-existing information about other groups is hard to correct because it is reinforced through the use of stereotypes. As such, we develop ideas about people who are different (in psychology these are known as "out-groups") that become intractable. That's the main reason why the word "stereotype" often conjures up all sorts of negative associations. White people don't have rhythm. African Americans are good at basketball. All Asians know kung fu. Middle Easterners hate America. Germans are cold and rigid. These are some common and enduring negative stereotypes about racial groups. And such examples abound. But stereotypes can just as often be positive. Mothers are loving and nurturing human beings. Children are born innocent. Best friends are loyal and would give you the shirt off their backs. Your dog loves you no matter what you do. Hard work seldom goes unnoticed. All of these are stereotypical ideas with positive connotations.

Stereotypes simplify reality and advertisers use them to make an impression on you. And it makes sense. Think about television. Advertisers have approximately 30 seconds to explain their products to you. Some of these products might be quite complex (think of technological things like computers, or high-priced luxury vehicles with a myriad options), so explaining them in such a short time frame is a challenge. Short cuts are needed and that's where stereotypes are useful. If an advertiser can give you a cue via a stereotype, that makes for an efficient message. For instance, classical music used in a luxury car advertisement, combined with actors wearing expensive clothing, signals that the car is prestigious. You expect that rich people dress well and that they drive nice cars.

Similarly, inner city youth and rap music in an ad for a clothing brand tells you that the brand has "street cred" and is hip. And advertisers hope these qualities will be associated with their product; they use very specific tactics to create a brand with a personality that is attractive to the target market.

Common Stereotypes in Advertising

The United States is a large and complex country, comprising an almost infinite number of different groups. And, similarly, an almost infinite number of stereotypes. Below, we discuss some common ones found in advertising.

- *Children*: In children's advertising, boys are often portrayed as rough or aggressive. They are more likely to be seen in sporting or athletic roles or in positions of power. They are presented as more independent than girls. Girls, on the other hand, are portrayed as more dainty or feminine. They are often shown playing house or cooking and they play with dolls (boys, on the other hand, play with action figures). They like the color pink. They are more concerned than boys with being popular and beautiful. If a girl is shown in an advertisement with a boy, she is often smaller and gazes up at the boy or is portrayed as in some way subordinate to him (Browne 1998).
- *Shallow or incompetent men*: A fixture of many beer commercials, young men are often portrayed playing childish pranks on each other. They are old enough to drink alcohol, but their mental development seems to have regressed. They will drop their friends in a heartbeat if a pretty blond pays them the slightest bit of attention. Incompetent males are also often shown in advertising. Who hasn't seen an ad in which a bewildered husband is out-foxed by his smarter spouse? Males are often portrayed as bumblers around the home, incapable of performing even the easiest of household tasks (that is, unless they have the advertised product).
- *Senior citizens*: Older consumers are often portrayed in advertisements as infirm and doddering. They are shown as out of touch with reality and may be unattractive.
- *Females*: Apparently, men don't do the laundry, as virtually every advertisement for laundry detergent features a woman. Even though the majority of women work outside the home, they are still depicted as being in charge of all household chores. They are also more likely than men to be shown as responsible for food selection and meal preparation in the home (unless it is barbecuing, which is almost exclusively the domain of men).
- *Race*: Advertising can perpetuate racial stereotypes that have lasted for generations. Native Americans have been portrayed in advertising as wild, primitive, and uncivilized. Or as noble or peaceful people who live in harmony with nature. African Americans are often shown to be great athletes and superb singers and dancers. African American women are sometimes portrayed as angry and loud. When Asians appear in advertising, they are typi-

cally presented as technical experts or otherwise intellectually gifted. They appear in ads for business-oriented or technical products. They are seldom shown in a domestic setting. Hispanics are often portrayed as lively and fun-loving, or violent (but great lovers). When whites are portrayed in advertisements with those of another race, they are perceived to be in charge and typically pictured in the forefront of the ad. Additionally the majority of ads for luxury goods feature white people, thus creating a stereotype of privilege.

So obviously, stereotypes are pervasive in advertising. Why should you care? Stereotypes create expectations that members of a group will act a certain way. And if all you have to go on is a stereotype, then members of the group *become* the stereotype in your mind. Think, for example, of a teenager growing up in a tiny town. This person has never met an Asian person. But, he thinks they're probably all really smart because they program computers, or at least that's the message that advertisers have been sending him. Imagine his surprise when an Asian student transfers to his school and turns out to be a mediocre student except in the area of art, at which he excels. To take this further, think about the pressures that the Asian student himself encounters owing to stereotypes. All around, he sees signals (stereotypes) that Asians are exceptionally smart and technologically savvy. He feels like a misfit with his dream of being an artist.

The Right Way to Use Stereotypes

We've discussed what stereotypes are, and why they are vital to advertising. We've also discussed some of the negative things associated with them. At this point it's relevant to ask: Can stereotypes be used responsibly? If so, how?

I believe they can. But first, it's necessary to distinguish between good and bad uses of stereotypes. Stereotypes can be functional when they are accepted as a natural process to guide expectations. Stereotypes become dysfunctional when they are used to judge an individual incorrectly (Mooij 2005). Advertising messages are typically short and thus they depend on stereotypes to attract attention and generate awareness, but they can also result in harm. Let's look at an example. Elderly people have been stereotyped as feeble and senile. In reality, many are physically fit and as sharp as tacks. But let's say that you are an insurance provider looking at an application for supplemental insurance and all you have to go by is a piece of paper that says the person applying is 80 years old. A dysfunctional stereotype might lead you to deny the applicant, causing harm to him or her.

The best thing for an advertiser to do is to use stereotypes in functional ways. This is particularly effective in these times of niche marketing, as functional stereotypes can be used to make advertising that is relevant to target segments. For example, after 9/11, many negative stereotypes of Middle Easterners emerged. When you see stories about Muslims, they are often accompanied by images of stern-looking men with turbans and beards. If we were advertising a product to a Muslim, we might create a functional stereotype that shows a Muslim man laughing with his little daughter or enjoying a happy feast with his family. This new stereotype, seen often enough, might replace the older one.

Concept or copytesting your ad with members of the target audience also helps avoid dysfunctional stereotypes. In such cases, members are shown several concepts or rough advertisements and asked such questions as: What was the main thing the concept/advertisement was saying? Were there any other ideas in the concept/ad? Discovering in advance that you are sending a wrong or unintended message can help avoid a disaster for both you and your client.

If you're planning to work in advertising, stereotypes will become vital to you because they are vital to advertising. The key is to use them in a manner that is respectful and does not perpetuate negative ideas about a group.

References

Browne, B. A. (1998). Gender stereotypes in advertising on children's television in the 1990s: A cross-national analysis. *Journal of Advertising* 27(1): 83–97.

Cherry, K. (n.d.). What is a schema? At http://psychology.about.com/od/sindex/g/def_schema.htm, accessed Mar. 22, 2013.

Cheryan, S., Plaut, V. C., Davies, P. G., and Steele, C. M. (2009). Ambient belonging: How stereotypical cues impact gender participation in computer science. *Journal of Personality and Social Psychology* 97(6): 1045–1060.

Johnson, C. A. (2009). Cutting through advertising clutter. *CBS News* (Feb. 11). At http://www.cbsnews.com/stories/2006/09/17/sunday/main2015684.shtml, accessed Mar. 22, 2013.

Mooij, M. K. de (2005). *Global marketing and advertising: Understanding cultural paradoxes*. Thousand Oaks, CA: Sage.

Part II

Emerging Issues

9

Direct-to-Consumer Pharmaceutical Advertising

I want a schedule-keeping,
waking-up-early,
wallet-carrying, picture-hanging
man. I don't care if he takes
prescription drugs for
cholesterol or hair loss.

Mindy Kaling

You've seen these ads in magazines and on your favorite television shows (and more recently on your Facebook pages). Some of them are quite compelling. We are told to ask our doctors whether we need cholesterol-lowering drugs, eye health vitamins, or something to help us cope with our COPD (which I had never heard of until I saw the commercial!).

Before we started seeing direct-to-consumer (DTC) pharmaceutical ads on a regular basis, conventional thinking was that medicine was far too complex for the patient; the only person who knew enough about the drugs you needed was your own family physician. How times have changed!

This is a complicated issue that warrants multiple voices weighing in. First, Beth Barnes lays out a clear and compelling argument that questions putting so

Advertising and Society: An Introduction, Second Edition. Edited by Carol J. Pardun.
© 2014 John Wiley & Sons, Inc. Published 2014 by John Wiley & Sons, Inc.

much drug information (and misinformation) into consumers' hands. Michael Capella answers that call with the opposite approach – basically that advertising is information; therefore, DTC drug ads make sense. And finally, Debbie Triese and Wan Seop Jung build on that argument with additional reasons that imply DTC pharmaceutical ads are a smart prescription for all.

What these three essays do together is provide a comprehensive literature review and analysis of the issues surrounding DTC advertising. But, who is right? *You decide.*

Ideas to Get You Thinking . . .

1   Take a few minutes and list all the names of drugs you've heard of. Now, think about any ads for them. Do you think the advertising has an impact on your ability to name the drug? Why, or why not?
2   Are there certain drugs that you might think are okay to advertise on television? If so, which ones would be okay? Are there other drugs that should not be advertised? Which ones? How would you argue that one kind is okay, but another is not?
3   Spend a couple of hours watching television. Every time a commercial hawking a drug of some kind comes on, write down the name of the drug and the basic message you take away from the commercial. When you have a list of five to 10 drugs, do some research, trying to find out how much money has been spent on marketing them – compared to their competition. What have you discovered?

Other Topics to Debate

1   Only drugs that are nonsexual in nature (so no Cialis or Viara!) should be allowed to be advertised on television.
2   DTC pharmaceutical television commercials should not have to list all the side effects possible. No one pays any attention to them anyway!
3   It should be required that drugs that are about to lose their patents (and open up the possibility of generic drugs) need to aggressively provide this information to the consuming public.

If You'd Like to Know More . . .

Jung, W., Rhee, E., and Kim, J. (2012). The influence of message framing and message familiarity on direct-to-consumer (DTC) antidepressant advertising. *Journal of Communication in Healthcare* 5(1): 23–31. doi: 10.1179/1753807611Y.0000000019

Krezmien, E., Wanzer, M., Servoss, T., and LaBelle, S. (2011). The role of direct-to-consumer pharmaceutical advertisements and individual differences in getting people to talk to Physicians. *Journal of Health Communication* 16(8): 831–848. doi: 10.1080/10810730.2011.561909

Mackert, M. (2011). Health literacy knowledge among direct-to-consumer pharmaceutical advertising professionals. *Health Communication* 26(6): 525–533. doi: 10.1080/10410236.2011.556084

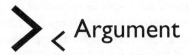

Argument

Doctor knows best: Why DTC advertising of prescription medications is bad for patients

Beth E. Barnes

University of Kentucky, USA

Direct-to-consumer pharmaceutical advertising is big business. While spending on DTC advertising in the United States has declined somewhat from its highest levels, US drug manufacturers still spent an estimated $2.42 billion on advertising prescription drugs to consumers in the first nine months of 2012 (Nielsen 2012). That level of spending made the pharmaceutical category the fifth highest expenditure category during that time period.

The United States is one of only two countries that allow DTC advertising (the other is New Zealand (Richardson and Luchsinger 2005). When the US Food and Drug Administration (FDA) acted in 1997 to make it easier for pharmaceutical firms to advertise their products directly to consumers through television and print ads and online, the reasoning was that more information would lead to better-informed patient decisions (Kaiser Family Foundation 2003). But information does not always equal knowledge. This essay will examine reasons why DTC advertising actually hurts patients rather than helping them.

Doctor–Patient Relationships

The relationship between patients and their health-care provider is a delicate thing, based on trust on the patient's part that his or her doctor is a highly trained professional with the expertise to diagnose and treat ailments in the most effective way possible. To the extent that DTC advertising leads patients to second-guess their physician, this type of advertising erodes the foundation of the doctor–patient relationship. In a 1998 report, shortly after the rules for broadcast

DTC ads were relaxed and DTC ads began to proliferate, the American College of Physicians reported that its members "are besieged with requests for specific products patients have seen in advertisements" (American College of Physicians 1998). For example, Singh and Smith (2005) found that 40 percent of the adults they surveyed reported asking about a drug they had seen advertised and 17 percent asked to be prescribed a specific brand of drug. A survey of members of the National Medical Association, a group for African American doctors, revealed many complaints about DTC advertising. Among the 322 doctors who responded to the survey, 76 percent said "ads make people think meds work better than they do"; 76 percent said the ads "confuse[s] people about the relative risks and benefits of drugs"; and 65 percent said that "ads cause patients to second-guess diagnoses." Fifty-four percent of the doctors said "they feel pressured to prescribe particular drugs because of ads" (Arnold 2007).

Bradford and colleagues (2006) reviewed patient visit records for practices specializing in treating osteoarthritis. They compared the visit data with advertising expenditures and placement for two osteoarthritis drugs, Celebrex and Vioxx. Their analysis showed an increase in osteoarthritis patient visits to doctors that was associated with increased advertising for the two drugs. And their results suggested that patient visits led to prescriptions: "Once patients arrived at the physician's office, it was clear that DTC advertising tended to change the rate at which COX-2 inhibitors were prescribed . . . In summary, DTC advertising for COX-2 inhibitors appears to have affected physician practices and patients" (Bradford et al. 2006: 1376).

In a 2010 article summarizing a number of previous studies, Frosch and colleagues concluded that "Overall, physicians are less likely than patients to endorse the positive aspects of DTCA (direct-to-consumer-advertising) and more likely to worry that DTCA promotes longer, unnecessary visits and inappropriate medication requests."

Patients, however well informed they might be through advertisements and websites, do not have the rigorous training of physicians. They cannot understand all the issues related to drug interactions, possible side effects, and the like. While it is the physician's ultimate responsibility whether or not to prescribe a specific drug, the time it takes to talk patients out of a drug they have seen advertised that may not be right for them is not only costly, but has the potential to erode the patients' trust in the physician.

Quality of Information

There are also questions about the usefulness of the information provided in DTC ads and on DTC websites. The Federal Trade Commission (FTC) relaxed the requirements for DTC ads on television in 1997. The major change that was made was that DTC television ads were no longer required to include the so-called "brief summary" (Macias and Lewis 2003–4), a list of "side effects, contraindications, and effectiveness" (FDA, n.d.).

Without the information included in the brief summary, patients who only see DTC television advertising are at best ill informed about the drugs advertised and may even be misinformed. While all advertising is one-sided, talking only about the possible benefits of a drug without noting any of its negative qualities provides very little in the way of useful information for making an informed decision about the medication. The potential risks are too high, and the potential consequences too great, for such advertising to be the basis on which patients make decisions about which drugs are right for them. And yet, as the research cited above shows, many do just that.

In a content analysis of television ads for prescription medications, Frosch and colleagues (2007) found that the ads studied relied heavily on emotional appeals and that those emotional appeals often overrode any factual claims made in the ads. Few of the ads studied talked about the factors leading to the particular medical condition the drug was intended to treat, or the risks associated with taking the advertised medication. Frosch and colleagues conclude that:

> By ambiguously defining who might need or benefit from the products, DTCA implicitly focuses on convincing people that they may be at risk for a wide array of health conditions that product consumption might ameliorate, rather than providing education about who may truly benefit from the treatment. (2007: 10)

What about DTC advertising that does carry the brief summary? Who hasn't seen a magazine ad for a prescription drug where the eye-catching, image-building message is followed by a page or more of tiny type listing all the things required by the brief summary and more? The information is certainly there, but is it in a form that is likely to be used by patients? Singh and Smith found that "consumers are not comfortable with the format in which drugs are advertised, they do not feel competent to evaluate the claims made in such advertising, and they are not aware of the various avenues to get more information" (Singh and Smith 2005: 376).

Problems with DTC advertising continue. In a Food and Drug Law Institute review of the most common violations of the FDA's guidelines between January 2011 and August 2012, four major categories emerged: leaving out or minimizing information on risks associated with using the advertised medication, misleading claims on the effectiveness of the drug, misleading claims on the drug's superiority to other medications or forms of treatment, and ads that promoted uses of the drug for conditions other than those approved by the FDA (Abrams 2012). If the ads themselves are not conforming to the conditions laid out by the FDA, how good can the quality of information provided be?

Websites are fairly well-known possible sources of additional information. Macias and Lewis (2003–4) conducted a content analysis of prescription drug websites and found mixed results as to information content. Among the 83 sites they examined, only 21 percent addressed misconceptions about the condition the drug was intended to treat, and only 23 percent indicated the drug's success rate in treating that condition. Only half the sites included information on how long treatment with the drug would last, and only 52 percent indicated how long it would be before the patient would start to see an effect once they had begun taking the drug.

Advertising messages are used to inform and persuade; sales promotion messages are used to provide an incentive to buy the product. Macias and Lewis (2003–4) found that 52 percent of the websites they analyzed offered some type of financial incentive: rebates, coupons, free samples, or value-added offers of merchandise. Only 47 percent of the sites studied offered more information (video, audio, or printed material) as an incentive. Only three out of the 83 sites offered a patient support program to prospective drug users. So consumers who turn to prescription drug websites find incomplete information combined with monetary or other incentives to use the promoted drug. That hardly seems a situation that promotes informed decision-making.

The rise of social media has added another dimension to the concerns regarding DTC advertising. Greene and Kesselheim (2010) identified three potential problems: the need for medical personnel to better understand how consumers use and react to drug messages in social media; the need for explicit disclosure of any financial interests a posting individual or entity may have in the drug being discussed; and the need for the FDA and drug companies to take responsibility for making sure drug information presented through social media is credible. Their implied preference was for the FDA to act to prevent the promotion of pharmaceuticals in social media.

The FDA has not taken that step, although it is trying to keep track of how social media are being used to promote pharmaceuticals. An October 2012 column by Brad Friedman of Social Media Today gave a number of examples of social media postings that had come under FDA scrutiny for being being misleading or not providing sufficient risk information (Friedman 2012). While this area is still evolving, the FDA, having opened the door to DTC promotion of pharmaceuticals, must either come up with policies for social media as well or run the risk of greater consumer misinformation.

At-Risk Audiences

One intended audience for many prescription drug advertisements is older consumers. They are the people most likely to suffer from many ailments the advertised medications claim to treat, and so the most likely to pay attention to such messages (Richardson and Luchsinger 2005). DeLorme and colleagues (2006) found that senior citizens do pay attention to DTC advertising, but believe that the effects of such advertising will be greater for other people than for themselves, the classic third-person effect.

Baca and colleagues (2005) studied college students' reactions to DTC advertising. They found that those most interested in and potentially most influenced by DTC advertising were students who self-reported their own health status as poor; students who rated their health status as good were less interested in and less favorable toward DTC advertising.

The FDA's own website makes it clear that DTC ads should raise many questions for consumers. In a section titled "Prescription drug advertising: Questions to ask yourself" the FDA lists 13 questions consumers should ask both themselves and a doctor or pharmacist about any drug advertisement they see (American College of Physicians 1998). The range and detail of the topics listed calls into question whether all consumers could, or would, bother to work through the list.

This evidence should raise questions about the ethics of DTC advertising. In the United States, there is a history of both legislation (Levin 2006) and industry self-regulation (OAAA 2006) to try and avoid harm to disadvantaged or at-risk groups through advertising practices related to specific products; why should prescription medications be treated differently? If those most likely to be influenced are also the most vulnerable, should there not be protections put in place for these groups?

Economic Consequences

In a statement made to a Federal Trade Commission (FTC) Health Care Workshop, Steven D. Findlay, Director of Research for the National Institute for Health Care Management Research and Educational Foundation, pointed out that one of the most important arguments against DTC advertising is the cost of such advertising and the impact of that cost on the price of the advertised medicines (Findlay 2002). Findlay's analysis pointed out that a dramatic increase in health insurance and health plan coverage of prescription drugs overlapped with the loosening of restrictions on DTC advertising and the increase in those messages:

> Sales of the top 50 most heavily advertised drugs rose an aggregate 32% from 1999 to 2000 compared to 13.6% for all other drugs combined. Increases in the sales of these 50 drugs heavily advertised accounted for almost half (47.8%) of the overall $20.8 billion rise in spending on drugs in the retail sector from 1999 to 2000. (Findlay 2002: 3)

Given that pattern, Findlay argued that health-care insurers, and, by extension, the Food and Drug Administration, would need to work to make sure that consumers could continue to get appropriate medication while not overmedicating needlessly based on demand fueled by DTC advertising.

Shin and Moon (2005) asked the direct question: "is [DTC advertising] the best way to spend nearly $3 billion on health communications to the American public"? Specifically, their concern is that "DTC advertising for prescription drugs conveys the information that mislead[s] viewers to lean more on the drugs whose prices embed the advertising costs even when they are aware of the availability of cheaper and equally effective alternatives."

FDA Oversight

If DTC advertising is to be conducted appropriately, a high level of oversight by the Food and Drug Administration is essential. A 2006 study of the FDA's approach conducted by the US Government Accountability Office identified a number of problems with the FDA's procedures. Among the shortcomings listed were that the FDA reviews only a sample of the promotional materials submitted, does not appear to have a systematic process for deciding what materials will be reviewed, and takes an increasingly longer time to conduct reviews. In addition, the effectiveness of the review process, based on companies' records of compliance with FDA recommendations, has also been weak (GAO 2006). If the FDA cannot conduct timely reviews following accepted procedures, then the effectiveness of its oversight is questionable, and DTC advertising of pharmaceuticals should either be stopped or significantly limited to a level where the FDA can exercise appropriate oversight.

Conclusion

Perhaps the person best qualified to comment on the negative aspects of DTC advertising is former FDA Commissioner David Kessler, now a faculty member in medicine at University of California, San Francisco. Kessler and Dr Douglas A. Levy summarized the situation in these words:

> consumers who make health decisions based on what they learn from television commercials ultimately take medicines they may not need, spend money on brand medicines that may be no better than alternatives, or avoid healthy behaviors because they falsely think a medicine is all they need. (Kessler and Levy 2007: 5)

While there are certainly many benefits to increased consumer information, such information is truly useful only if it can be interpreted appropriately. Without the medical knowledge and the full range of information needed to appropriately assess a drug to know if it is indeed the right treatment in a particular situation, and without sufficient oversight by the FDA, DTC advertising does more harm than good.

References

Abrams, T. (2012). OPDP update on oversight of prescription drug promotion. Presentation at the Food and Drug Law Institute, Washington, DC, Oct. 1, 2012. At www.fda.gov/downloads/AboutFDA/.../CDER/UCM330855.pdf, accessed Mar. 22, 2013.

American College of Physicians (1998). Direct-to-consumer advertising for prescription drugs: Position paper of the American College of Physicians (Oct. 9). At http://www.acponline.org/acp_policy/policies/direct_to_consumer_advertising_for_prescription_drugs_1998.pdf, accessed Apr. 8, 2013.

Arnold, M. (2007). Black docs warm to DTC ad benefits. *Medical Marketing and Media* 42(4): 26.

Baca, E. E., Holguin, J., Jr, and Stratemeyer, A. W. (2005). Direct-to-consumer advertising and young consumers: Building brand value. *Journal of Consumer Marketing* 22(7): 379–387.

Bradford, W. D., Kleit, A. N., Nietert, P. J., and Steyer, T. (2006). How direct-to-consumer television advertising for osteoarthritis drugs affects physicians' prescribing behavior. *Health Affairs* 25(5): 1371–1377.

DeLorme, D. E., Huh, J., and Reid, L. N. (2006). Perceived effects of direct-to-consumer (DTC) prescription drug advertising on self and others: A third-person effect study of older consumers. *Journal of Advertising* 35(3): 47–65.

FDA (US Food and Drug Administration) (2011). OPDP frequently asked questions (FAQs). http://www.fda.gov/AboutFDA/CentersOffices/OfficeofMedicalProductsand Tobacco/CDER/ucm090308.htm, accessed Apr. 8, 2013.

FDA (US Food and Drug Administration) (2012). Evaluation of consumer-friendly formats for brief summary in direct-to-consumer (DTC) print advertisements for prescription drugs, executive summary. Division of Drug Marketing, Advertising, and Communications, Office of Medical Policy, Center for Drug Evaluation and Research, Food and Drug Administration (May 2011). At http://www.fda.gov/AboutFDA/Centers Offices/OfficeofMedicalProductsandTobacco/CDER/ucm258483.htm, accessed Apr. 5, 2013.

Findlay, S. D. (2002). DTC advertising: Is it helping or hurting? Statement before the Federal Trade Commission Health Care Workshop (Sept. 10). National Institute for Health Care Management (NIHCM) Foundation. At http://www.ftc.gov/ogc/health-care/findlay.pdf, accessed Apr. 8, 2013.

Friedman, B. (2012). Is the Federal Drug Administration (FDA) embracing social media? *Socialmediatoday* (Oct. 15). At http://socialmediatoday.com/bradfriedman/ 910606/federal-drug-administration-fda-embracing-social-media, accessed Mar. 22, 2013.

Frosch, D. L., Krueger, P. M., Hornik, R. C., Cronholm, P. F., and Barg, F. K. (2007). Creating demand for prescription drugs: A content analysis of television direct-to-consumer advertising. *Annals of Family Medicine* 5(1): 6–13.

Frosch, D. L., Grande, D., Tarn, D. M., and Kravitz, R. L. (2010). A decade of controversy: Balancing policy with evidence in the regulation of prescription drug advertising. *American Journal of Public Health* 100(1): 24–32.

GAO (U.S. Government Accountability Office) (2006) Prescription drugs: Improvements needed in FDA's oversight of direct-to-consumer advertising. At http://www.gao.gov/ assets/260/253778.pdf, accessed Mar. 22, 2013.

Greene, J. A. and Kesselheim, A. S. (2010). Pharmaceutical marketing and the new social media. *New England Journal of Medicine* 363: 2087–2089.

Kaiser Family Foundation (2003). Impact of direct-to-consumer advertising on prescription drug spending. At http://www.kff.org/rxdrugs/upload/Impact-of-Direct-to-Consumer-Advertising-on-Prescription-Drug-Spending-Summary-of-Findings.pdf, accessed Mar. 22, 2013.

Kessler, D. A. and Levy, D. A. (2007). Direct-to-consumer advertising: Is it too late to manage the risks? *Annals of Family Medicine* 5(1): 4–5.

Levin, P. (2006). Tobacco. *National Association of Attorneys General.* At http://www. naag.org/tobacco.php, accessed Mar. 22, 2013.

Macias, W. and Lewis, L. S. (2003–4). A content analysis of direct-to-consumer (DTC) prescription drug web sites. *Journal of Advertising* 32(4): 43–56.

Nielsen (2012) Top 10 U.S. Advertisers of 2012 – Product Categories. At http://blog. nielsen.com/nielsenwire/media_entertainment/nielsen-tops-of-2012-advertising/, accessed Mar. 22, 2013.

OAAA (Outdoor Advertising Association of America) (2006) OAAA code of industry principles. At http://www.oaaa.org/about/oaaacodeofindustryprinciples.aspx, accessed Mar. 22, 2013

Richardson, L. and Luchsinger, V. (2005). Direct-to-consumer advertising of pharmaceutical products: Issue analysis and direct-to-consumer promotion. *Journal of American Academy of Business* 7(2): 100–105.

Shin, J. and Moon, S. (2005). Direct-to-consumer prescription drug advertising: concerns and evidence on consumers' benefit. *Journal of Consumer Marketing* 22(7): 397–403.

Singh, T. and Smith, D. (2005). Direct-to-consumer prescription drug advertising: A study of consumer attitudes and behavioral intentions. *Journal of Consumer Marketing* 22(7): 369–378.

Counterargument 1 ><

Pharmaceutical DTC advertising provides valuable information to health-care consumers

Michael L. Capella

Villanova University, USA;

Charles R. Taylor

Past President, American Academy of Advertising, USA

Since its inception in the United States in the early 1980s, the impacts of direct-to-consumer prescription drug advertising on consumers has been a source of controversy. Prescription drugs are a product category that has a profound impact on public health. Thus, it is particularly important to look at the economic and societal effects of prescription drug advertising. Those arguing that DTC advertising is beneficial cite several benefits, including patients making more informed decisions, addressing undertreatment by informing consumers, improving the economic value of health care, improved drug treatment compliance, and improved communication between doctors and patients.

These arguments are grounded in the classic school of thought (Advertising = Information), which emphasizes the informative value of advertising (Farris and Albion 1980). This school argues that advertising informs consumers about product attributes and allows them to make better choices. It also argues that better-informed consumers make better purchase decisions, as opposed to simply purchasing products they do not need. Another tenet of the Advertising = Information view is that consumers can compare competitive offerings and new entrants can thrive if they are able to advertise wanted features. Thus, competition is encouraged, and there is downward pressure on pricing as a result of advertising.

In this essay, I review the literature and summarize evidence related to two major points of debate relative to the impact of DTC advertising:

1   Does DTC advertising lead to consumers being more informed about the availability of prescription drugs?
2   Do consumers have more informed interactions with doctors, or does the advertising merely lead patients to request products they do not need?

Advertising = Information School

The "advertising = information" school also has some noted adherents, including Telser (1964) and McAuliffe (1987). This view emphasizes a positive role that advertising plays in giving the consumer information on product features, prices, and quality, thereby enhancing consumer knowledge. The increased knowledge provided by advertising, according to this school, both reduces search costs and forces producers to improve the quality of their products. With respect to industry concentration, the "information" school predicts that advertising actually facilitates entry by allowing innovative products or product features to be effectively communicated to consumers. By allowing new products to gain rapid acceptance if they have an advantage, firms are allowed to exploit economies of scale and offer lower prices. Thus, advertising's impact on prices is to lower them, according to the "information" school.

Informative Value of DTC Advertising

The "information" school would clearly argue that DTC advertising plays a positive role by informing consumers about the benefits of new and existing drugs. In this view, DTC advertising helps consumers to become more knowledgeable about ailments and what treatments are available. It would follow from this logic that better-informed consumers communicate more effectively with their doctors, are more likely to understand usage of the pharmaceuticals and hence to use them more effectively. The improved communications and compliance should, in turn, lead to better health outcomes, according to this view.

DTC Advertising and Informing the Consumer

Over the past decade, several studies have examined the impact of DTC prescription drug advertising on consumers. Much of this work has focused on whether DTC advertising helps to better inform consumers, as opposed to having them ask for drugs they do not need. Below, we detail the empirical evidence regarding the impacts of DTC advertising on consumers and doctors, examining US studies. This review will be used to assess whether the research evidence is supportive of the "information" school.

Evidence from Studies of DTC Advertising in the United States

The issue of the impacts of DTC advertising on consumers has drawn widespread attention from regulators and academics alike. For example, the US Food and Drug Administration conducted national telephone surveys in 1999 and 2002 to examine this issue. The results of these studies suggest that DTC advertising acts as a stimulus for consumers to search for more information about their health and the pharmaceutical products being advertised, including the risks associated with the use of them (Aikin et al. 2004). For example, among those who indicated that a DTC ad had caused them to search for more information in 2002, 61 percent reported searching for information about side effects.

The 2002 sample included 943 respondents who had consulted a physician within the last three months. Results of the survey indicated that approximately 45 percent of respondents in the two surveys said that an advertisement for a prescription drug had led them to seek more information. In addition, 27 percent of the survey respondents in 1999 and 18 percent in 2002 who had seen a physician indicated that the DTC advertising had led them to discuss a medical condition they had not previously discussed with a physician.

Additionally, in a FDA survey of 500 physicians, a majority indicated that DTC advertising played a positive role in their interactions with patients. Specifically, most agreed that because of exposure to DTC advertising, patients asked more insightful questions. In addition, many physicians believed that the ads made their patients more involved in their health care. At the same time, 8 percent of physicians felt "very pressured" and 20 percent felt "somewhat pressured" to prescribe a specific brand-name drug when requested by the patient. In these cases, however, most physicians suggested alternative courses of action such as prescribing a more appropriate drug because of possible side effects and/or it is less expensive.

In a study using monthly time-series regression data on DTC advertising for the statin class of cholesterol-lowering drugs from 1995 to 2000, Calfee and colleagues (2002) estimated the effect of DTC advertising on demand. The authors did not find a statistically significant relationship between the level of DTC advertising and new statin prescriptions. However, the study did find that prescription drug advertising had increased the proportion of cholesterol patients who were successfully treated, suggesting that better information provision was aiding in improved treatment. In general, the authors concluded that there are no adverse effects from DTC advertising, such as unnecessary prescriptions with regard to the cholesterol-reducing drug market.

The findings of a survey conducted by Mintzes and colleagues (2002) also support the notion of little or no adverse impact of DTC advertising on physician prescribing behavior. Specifically, these authors examined the relationship between DTC advertising and patients' requests for prescriptions as well as the relationship between patients' requests and physician prescribing decisions. The results showed that patients requested prescriptions in 12 percent of surveyed visits. Of these requests, 42 percent were for pharmaceutical drugs advertised to consumers. Nonetheless, physicians prescribed the requested drugs to just 9 percent of patients and the requested advertised drugs to only 4 percent of patients.

In a national telephone survey of 3,000 adults conducted in 2001 and 2002, Weissman and colleagues (2003) report that approximately 86 percent of consumers had seen or heard a DTC advertisement in the prior year. About 35 percent of all respondents reported being prompted by a prescription drug ad to have a discussion about the advertised drug or other health concern during a physician visit. Nearly one in four of these physician visits resulted in patients being given a new diagnosis for a previously untreated condition. Regarding DTC advertising, the authors failed to find large negative consequences for patients and, thus, concluded that there is no widespread adverse effect of prescription drug advertising.

A content analysis of 30 national circulation magazines conducted by Main and colleagues (2004) investigated whether DTC advertising presents consumers with information regarding the prescription drug, the disease it is designed to treat, as well as the drug's risks and benefits. The data came from issues of magazines published in December of 1998, 1999, and 2000, and involved a total of 195 DTC advertisements over that period. The study found that virtually all of the DTC ads did, indeed, contain information about the drug, the disease it is designed to treat, and risks and benefits. In terms of appeal type, the authors also found that the DTC advertisements relied more on emotional appeals than rational appeals.

In the largest sample of its kind, the MARS database tracks over 21,000 adults by means of a 20-page self-administered questionnaire mailed annually to a representative sample of the US population. Results from 2002 and 2003 indicate that 36 and 39 percent, respectively, made an appointment with a physician as a result of DTC advertising, presumably seeking additional information. In addition, 12 percent of respondents in 2002 and 13 percent in 2003 asked physicians to prescribe specific drugs as a result of prescription drug advertising (White et al. 2004). These findings, as the authors conclude, are consistent with the

FDA research previously mentioned which found relatively little consumer pressure to prescribe specific drugs reported by doctors.

As described by Huh and Becker (2005) in summarizing the results of prior studies, the goal of DTC advertisers is to have consumers perform one of the following four tasks: (1) seek more information about the drug; (2) discuss the drug with a physician; (3) discuss the drug with a pharmacist; or (4) communicate with family and friends about the merits of the drug. In the same article, Huh and Becker analyze an FDA mail survey from 343 respondents and determine that DTC advertising is a strong predictor of seeking drug information, but a rather weak predictor of communication with the doctor. As a result, the authors conclude that "consumers do not blindly rush to their doctors to get a prescription for the advertised drug but try to find more information from other sources" (Huh and Becker 2005: 463).

In general, the studies that have been conducted on consumer perceptions of prescription drug *advertising suggest that the public has favorable perceptions*. For example, using data from the FDA national telephone survey of 1,081 adults, Herzenstein and colleagues (2004) found that consumers were favorable toward DTC advertising, particularly when they searched for more information and discussed treatment options with their doctor. These researchers also found that the more favorable a consumer's attitude toward DTC advertising, the more likely he or she was to search for additional information and to ask a physician about the prescription drug.

A mail survey of 288 Midwestern respondents aged 21 or above by Singh and Smith (2005) also found that consumers generally have favorable perceptions of prescription drug advertising. They also found that consumers feel empowered by the enhanced knowledge gained by the information provided in DTC *advertising and, because of this*, there is concern about any governmental attempts to regulate prescription drug advertising.

Recent research indicates that web-based DTC advertising has educational value for consumers as well because of the ability to actively involve them in their own health-care management (Macias and Lewis 2005). Indeed, the Internet offers consumers a significant benefit because of the reduced search costs involved in obtaining relevant information regarding pharmaceutical drugs. For instance, in a comprehensive review of all 90 accessible DTC prescription drug websites as of March 2001, Macias and Lewis (2005) demonstrate that 43 percent of the websites included a form to assist patient–doctor communication. Also, 94 percent of the websites encourage the patient to discuss the drug with either a doctor or a pharmacist.

More recent research by Iizuka and Jin (2005) concluded that the argument that DTC advertising prompts patients to "pressure" the physician to prescribe unnecessary medications is not accurate. The authors examined data covering 151 drug classes over 72 months and found that DTC advertising does encourage more patients to seek treatment without exerting undue pressure on physicians for explicit brand-name drugs. Thus, as previous research has suggested, Iizuka and Jin assert that DTC advertising has been successful in prompting patients to discuss their health conditions with physicians without requesting specific drugs (e.g., Calfee et al. 2002; Iizuka and Jin 2005; White et al. 2004).

The aforementioned findings are further supported by a nine-year trend survey conducted by *Prevention* magazine (Thomaselli 2006) which suggests that direct-to-consumer pharmaceutical advertising helps increase disease awareness, educate consumers about treatment options, increase information-seeking behavior, and encourage prescription compliance. Specifically, the national sample of 1,504 US adults conducted from March 2 through March 19, 2006 indicates that 41 percent of consumers had talked to their doctors after seeing an advertised prescription drug, a 7 percent increase over the prior year. Furthermore, the results show DTC ads increased information-seeking behavior, with an 11 percent increase since 2003 in the number of respondents who had seen a prescription drug advertisement that prompted them to seek out more information (Thomaselli 2006).

In a review of the literature, Calfee (2002) suggests that DTC advertisements provide multiple benefits to consumers. For example, one is giving valuable information to consumers, including risk information for prescription drugs. Second, DTC advertising is found to induce patient information-seeking, mainly from physicians. Third, it prompts patients to communicate about conditions not previously discussed. Finally, according to Calfee, DTC advertising may improve patient compliance with drug therapy. This conclusion is not surprising, given the prior content analysis research that suggests consumers have a desire for more information about pharmaceutical products (Kopp and Bang 2000). As a consequence, some researchers such as Calfee have concluded that DTC advertising satisfies this need for increased medical information on the part of the consumer.

In addition to Calfee's studies, additional research has concluded that the result of increased DTC advertising has been an improvement in the undertreatment of certain diseases and an increase in drug compliance which have been associated with an overall enhancement of patient health outcomes (e.g., Calfee et al. 2002; Auton 2006). In general, our review of the US literature provides strong evidence in support of the advertising = information school of thought. There is consistent and compelling evidence that consumers are better informed about prescription drugs, have favorable attitudes about DTC advertising, and are encouraged to have constructive conversations with their doctors. Meanwhile, the extant research does not appear to support the argument that large numbers of consumers demand prescription drugs that they do not need or place undue pressure on physicians to prescribe pharmaceuticals that they believe they need.

Discussion

The literature review above suggests that, overall, the advertising = information school received considerable support from empirical studies conducted on the impact of DTC advertising of pharmaceutical products. The research questions focused on whether DTC advertising leads consumers to be more informed about the availability of prescription drugs and to have more informed interactions with doctors, as opposed to simply asking for drugs they do not really need. The empirical evidence on this topic, from the United States strongly supports the "information" school. Most notably, DTC advertising provides useful information to consumers, and consumers believe they are better informed about the availability of prescription drugs (e.g., Weissman et al. 2003; Huh and Becker 2005; Macias and Lewis 2005; Singh and Smith 2005). Additionally, consumers are more likely to initiate conversations with physicians and to seek out other information about the advertised drugs (Weissman et al. 2003; Aikin et al. 2004; Herzenstein et al. 2004; Thomaselli 2006). Coupled with evidence that patients are more likely to discuss medications with their doctors, as opposed to directly asking for a prescription, our findings are consistent with the observation of Carey Silver, Director of Consumer and Advertising Trends for Rodale Publishing who, with reference to the impact of DTC advertising stated, "The net effect is that the doctors are still in charge, but the patient is still knowledgeable. There is also some evidence that DTC improves under-treatment of ailments and improves drug compliance" (Calfee et al. 2002; Auton 2006).

In addition to some of the evidence of positive impacts of the information provided to consumers, the weight of the evidence appears to support a lack of significant negative impacts on consumers. There is evidence that doctors do not feel that they frequently face undue pressure to prescribe drugs that patients do not need and, in fact, they believe that patients are asking more insightful questions. In contrast, the empirical studies are not suggestive of any kind of widespread problem with consumers misdiagnosing themselves or unduly wasting physicians' time. It is notable that the evidence suggests that the physician's role as the learned intermediary appears to be intact, in that survey evidence demonstrates that the patients continue to rely on the physician's opinion (e.g., Calfee 2002; Mintzes et al. 2002; White et al. 2004).

In sum, this chapter set out to examine the compelling predictions of the advertising = information school of thought in the context of DTC prescription drug advertising. A review of empirical studies provides convincing evidence that the benefits of DTC advertising to consumers are consistent with what is predicted by the "information" school and are substantial. The evidence indicates that consumers like DTC advertising, are better informed about available drugs, and are more likely to initiate conversations with their physicians and to have more effective interaction with physicians. There is also some evidence of improved compliance with drug regimens and improvement in undertreatment of some diseases. Meanwhile, there does not appear to be compelling empirical evidence of potential adverse effects, such as misinformed consumers or consumers putting excessive pressure on doctors to prescribe drugs they do not need.

References

Aikin, K. J., Swasy, J. L., and Braman, A. C. (2004). Final report: Patient and physician attitudes and behaviors associated with DTC promotion of prescription drugs. Washington, DC: US Department of Health and Human Services, Food and Drug Administration, Center for Drug Evaluation and Research.

Auton, F. (2006). Direct-to-consumer advertising (DTCA) of pharmaceuticals: An updated review of the literature and debate since 2003. *Institute of Economic Affairs* 26(3): 24–32.

Calfee, J. (2002). Public policy issues in direct-to-consumer advertising of prescription drugs. *Journal of Public Policy and Marketing* 21(2): 174–193.

Calfee, J., Winston, C., and Stempski, R. (2002). Direct-to-consumer advertising and the demand for cholesterol-reducing drugs. *Journal of Law and Economics* 45(2): 673–690.

Farris, P. W. and Albion, M. S. (1980). The impact of advertising on the price of consumer products. *Journal of Marketing* 44(3): 17–35.

Herzenstein, M., Misra, S., and Posavac, S. S. (2004). How consumers' attitudes toward direct-to-consumer advertising of prescription drugs influence ad effectiveness, and consumer and physician behavior. *Marketing Letters* 15(4): 201–212.

Huh, J. and Becker, L. B. (2005). Direct-to-consumer prescription drug advertising: Understanding its consequences. *International Journal of Advertising* 24(4): 441–466.

Iizuka, T. and Jin, G. Z. (2005). The effects of prescription drug advertising on doctor visits. *Journal of Economics and Management Strategy* 14(3): 701–727.

Kopp, S. and Bang, H. K. (2000). Benefit and risk information in prescription drug advertising: A review of empirical studies and marketing implications. *Health Management Quarterly* 17(3): 39–56.

Macias, W. and Lewis, L. S. (2005). How well do direct-to-consumer (DTC) prescription drug web sites meet FDA guidelines and public policy concerns. *Health Marketing Quarterly* 22(4): 45–71.

Main, K. J., Argo, J. J., and Huhmann, B. A. (2004). Pharmaceutical advertising in the USA: Information or influence? *International Journal of Advertising* 2: 119–142.

McAuliffe, R. E. (1987). *Advertising, competition, and public policy: Theories and new evidence.* Lexington, MA: D. C. Heath.

Mintzes, B., Barer, M. L., Kravitz, R. L., Kazanjian, A., Bassett, K., et al. (2002). Influence of direct to consumer pharmaceutical advertising and patients' requests on prescribing decisions: Two site cross sectional survey. *British Medical Journal* 324(7332): 278–279.

Singh, T. and Smith, D. (2005). Direct-to-consumer prescription advertising: A study of consumer attitudes and behavioral intentions. *Journal of Consumer Marketing* 22(7): 369–378.

Telser, L. (1964). Advertising and competition. *Journal of Political Economy* 72(Dec.): 537–562.

Thomaselli, R. (2006). DTC ads prompt consumers to see physicians. *Advertising Age* 77(May 6): 30.

Weissman, J. S., Blumenthal, D., Silk, A. J., and Zapert, K. (2003). Consumers' reports on the health effects of direct-to-consumer drug advertising. *Health Affairs* (Jan.–June), 82–95.

White, H. J., Draves, L. P., Soong, R., and Moore, C. (2004). Ask your doctor! Measuring the effect of direct-to-consumer communications in the world's largest healthcare market. *International Journal of Advertising* 23: 53–68.

Counterargument 2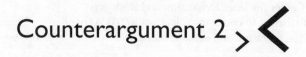

Feel empowered! Enhanced health knowledge!

Debbie Treise

University of Florida, USA;

Wan Seop Jung

University of Dubai, UAE

Americans are increasingly talking to their health providers about the prescription medicines they see advertised for problems from indigestion to "Captain Winky doesn't salute anymore" (Treise and Rausch 2007). Studies have shown that direct-to-consumer advertisement ads can influence perceptions not only about an advertised drug, but also about the disease it treats (Zachry et al. 2003). It is estimated that Americans who watch even average amounts of television are exposed to more than 30 hours of DTC advertising each year from this source alone (Rabin 2004). Additionally, a 2011 study reported that viewers see nine DTC advertisements per day across a variety of media (Krezmien et al. 2011). Is this too much? critics ask.

The Food and Drug Administration itself has recognized the value of DTC advertising. Prescription pharmaceuticals have been marketed to the public since the 1980s. In 1997, however, the FDA eased restrictions on broadcast DTC advertisements, and its rationale for doing so was simple: the more restrictive guidelines prevented consumers from obtaining product information (D'Souza et al. 2003).

These relaxed restrictions led to a dramatic increase in pharmaceutical advertising expenditures, followed swiftly by an onslaught of debate and criticism. Much of the research conducted on DTC advertising since then suggests there are numerous important and unexpected benefits to consumers that go far beyond the FDA's original reasoning. Indeed, a report issued by the National Health Council in 2002 concluded:

The preponderance of evidence indicates that most consumers and physicians, as well as the Food and Drug Administration, support DTC advertising as long as it complies with FDA's regulations and guidelines and refers consumers to their physicians. The benefits are viewed as outweighing any negative impacts. (NHC 2002: 2)

Just What Are Those Benefits?

Past studies have found a bounty of benefits to consumers, including:

1   Increased awareness of and education about conditions, symptoms, and treatment options leading to better-informed health decision-making, and more involvement in and responsibility for health care, including increased prescription medication regimen compliance.
2   More constructive and informed discussions with health-care providers.
3   Empowering consumers to come forward to discuss conditions thought to be too embarrassing before being addressed in DTC advertising.
4   DTC advertising's role in enhancing health literacy.

Each of these benefits will be addressed in turn.

Increased Awareness of and Education about Disease and Treatment

Several studies focusing on DTC advertising's influence on consumers and physicians have found surprising and supportive results in terms of increased consumer awareness of health (Holmer 2002; Aikin et al. 2004; Cline and Young 2004; Treise and Rausch 2007). Indeed, a 2003 FDA study (Aikin et al. 2004), conducted with a random sample of 500 American Medical Association (AMA) physicians, found that 72 percent of the participants agreed "somewhat" to "a great deal" that DTC advertising made their patients more aware of possible treatments – up from 67 percent reported in NHC (2002) – while 80 percent believed that patients understood "somewhat" to "very well" what condition the advertised drug treated. The same FDA AMA study found that 58 percent of the physicians agreed "somewhat" to "a great deal" that DTC advertising made patients more involved in their health care.

The perceived downside of a more informed consumer is ostensibly the increased pressure felt by physicians to prescribe the advertised medication to their patients. However, 82 percent of the physicians in the FDA study indicated that their patients understood "somewhat" or "very well" that only doctors could decide if a certain medication was correct for them, and 91 percent said the patient did not try to influence the course of treatment if the physician felt that it would be harmful to them. It is clear, therefore, that patients believe doctors remain the ultimate gatekeepers in medication decisions. More important, only

8 percent of the surveyed doctors said they felt very pressured; indeed, 72 percent indicated they felt little or no pressure. Asked whether a patient having seen DTC advertising created a problem for their interactions, 82 percent said no (Aikin et al. 2004). Isn't it ludicrous to assume that the same doctor who does not give in to a patient requesting narcotics who doesn't legitimately need them, would give in to a patient asking for an advertised drug for erectile dysfunction or depression?

Perhaps the clearest endorsement of a more informed consumer comes from the same FDA AMA study (Aikin et al. 2004): 88 percent of patients asking about a specific DTC-advertised medication had the condition the drug treats. So, for the 18 percent of surveyed physicians who indicted DTC advertising for causing problems for their interactions with patients – and, mostly, the major problem they encountered was the time they spent correcting misconceptions about the drug – it seems a small sacrifice if 88 percent of the patients do indeed have the condition which the requested drug treats.

Although the reasons are unclear, DTC advertising appears to increase patient compliance with a prescribed drug regimen and to induce patients to use the medications properly (Pines 2000; Calfee 2002). The 2003 FDA study (Aikin et al. 2004) found that 57 percent of the physicians surveyed agreed "somewhat" or "a great deal" that DTC advertising would make patients adhere to a treatment regimen. Perhaps an explanation for that compliance can be found in the results of the NHC 2002 study indicating that about half of those using prescription drugs said the ads make them feel better about the drug's safety.

Additionally, millions of Americans have diseases of which they are unaware, such as diabetes, depression, and high cholesterol, which untreated can have devastating consequences not only for the individual, but also for their family and community (Holmer 1999). Many of these conditions can be treated by prescription medications, often those that are advertised, and so DTC ads may prompt people to seek additional information about the drugs or the symptoms they treat.

In addition to increasing consumers' knowledge and awareness, DTC advertising may enable patients to notice a disease in its early stages. A number of studies have addressed potential effects of DTC advertising, and have posited that DTC advertising increases the likelihood of patients' intention to discuss symptoms with their physicians or to visit their physicians, thereby increasing the likelihood that diseases will be detected earlier (Yuan 2008).

More Constructive and Informed Discussions with Health-Care Providers

Yes, DTC advertising may increase the amount of time health-care providers spend with their patients discussing medication, but not all health-care providers feel this is a bad thing. In fact, Murray and colleagues (2004) confirm that, from the patient perspective, 81 percent reported getting positive responses from their doctors when they discussed drugs they had seen advertised. A study conducted in 2007 by Treise and Rausch found that nurse practitioners, a growing group of health-care providers, use DTC advertising to "jumpstart conversations" about health. Additionally, the 2003 FDA study (Aikin et al. 2004) indicated that 51 percent of the surveyed physicians felt DTC advertising facilitated better discussions about health, and 56 percent agreed "somewhat" to "a great deal" that DTC advertising helped patients ask better questions. Other studies have found DTC advertising may enhance doctor–patient relationships (Bonaccorso and Sturchio 2002; Young and Cline 2003). The traditional doctor–patient relationships have been hierarchical because health-care decisions were previously dominated by doctors who controlled medical treatment and treatment information. This relationship leads to patient unwillingness to ask about advertised prescription drugs. A 1995 study suggested that many patients believed their doctors might view patient inquiries or prescription requests as a sign of distrust or even disrespect (Petroshius et al. 1995). However, DTC advertising develops horizontal doctor–patient relationships (Berger et al. 2001). It can empower consumers to take an active role in the treatment of their medical conditions via the knowledge they provide.

Destigmatizing Effects

DTC advertising can be credited with removing or easing some of the fears about diseases or conditions previously felt to be too embarrassing to discuss with patients' health-care providers. Treise and Rausch provide an example:

> A lot of times patients are reluctant to come in and talk about depression. And they may have watched a Zoloft ad. In the ad they are describing symptoms of depression: feeling sad, decreased energy, not sleeping well, fearful, worrying, things like that. A patient will come in and say, "You know, I've been really wrestling with some of the very same things that they've been talking about on this television commercial." So at times it gives them the freedom and permission to come in and relate to something they may have been self conscious about. The ad gives them a little bit of freedom to express that. (Treise and Rausch 2007)

Increasing Health Literacy

DTC advertising also plays a somewhat unexpected role in enhancing health literacy, which has become a national priority (US Department of Health and Human Services 2000) by helping health providers not only to better assess the health literacy of their patients but also to address it on an individual basis (Treise and Rausch 2005). A 2004 Institute of Medicine study indicated that 90 million people – about half of US adults – have difficulty understanding and using health information, and estimates suggest these deficiencies of health literacy cost the US health-care system $58 billion a year (Alspach 2004).

Health literacy has been shown to result in a number of benefits, including "improved self-reported health status, lower healthcare costs, increased health knowledge, shorter hospitalizations, and less frequent use of healthcare services" (Speros 2005: 637). Erlen suggests that "functional health illiteracy is a silent and hidden disability and a significant barrier to healthcare" (2004: 151), which can decrease People's sense of self-worth and make them vulnerable to decisions made by others that they don't understand.

Health information is critical to health decisions, and research suggests that consumers who are better informed make healthier choices, and have different interactions with health-care providers. Therefore, the issue of health literacy is compounded when considering disparities in consumer information about health. Avery and colleagues suggest that "The link between medical progress and health disparities raises the concern that the rapid advances in the pharmaceutical industry lead to increased disparities in pharmaceutical use" (2007: 1). But as these researchers suggest, "Because the pharmaceutical industry tends to advertise new drugs, DTC advertising has the potential to reduce innovation-related disparities in pharmaceutical utilization" (5) and can address vital health disparities. Indeed, their survey found that DTC advertising had a positive impact on addressing health disparities among both African American physicians and patients.

Thus, promotion of health literacy is essential, and DTC advertising affords occasions for increasing health information and for discussion with providers at the precise times that patients are likely to be most open and responsive to these efforts. By seizing these DTC advertising opportunities, providers are not only able to better educate patients about medications, but they can also enhance patient–provider communication and patient health more generally by providing individualized health literacy training. Such endeavors can have only positive ramifications by enhancing the patient–provider relationship and also by contributing to a nation of better-informed, more satisfied, and healthier consumers. As the president of the National Consumers League said about DTC advertising: "In health care, there is a general trend toward having consumers more responsible for their own health. Now, consumers can go to their physicians with a little more information" (Holmer 1999).

References

Aikin, K. J., Swasy, J. L., and Braman, A. C. (2004). *Patient and physician attitudes and behaviors associated with DTC promotion of prescription drugs: Summary of FDA survey research results*. Washington, DC: US Department of Health and Human Services, Food and Drug Administration, Center for Drug Evaluation and Research.

Alspach, G. (2004). Communicating health information: An epidemic of the incomprehensible. *Critical Care Nurse* 24(4): 8–13.

Avery, R., Kenkel, D., Lillard, D., Mathios, A., and Wang, H. (2007). Health disparities and direct-to-consumer advertising of pharmaceutical products. Paper presented at Beyond Health Insurance: Public Policy to Improve Health, Nov., University of Illinois at Chicago.

Berger, J., Kark, P., Rosner, F., Packer, S., and Bennett, A. (2001). Direct-to-consumer drug marketing. *Mount Sinai Journal of Medicine* 68: 197–202.

Bonaccorso, S. N. and Sturchio, J. L. (2002). Direct to consumer advertising is medicalising normal human experience. *British Medical Journal* 324: 910–911.

Calfee, J. E. (2002). Public policy issues in direct-to-consumer advertising of prescription drugs. *Journal of Public Policy and Marketing* 21: 174–193.

Cline, R. J. W. and Young, H. N. (2004). Marketing drugs, marketing healthcare relationships: A content analysis of visual cues in direct-to-consumer prescription drug advertising. *Health Communication* 16: 131–157.

D'Souza, A. O., Lively, B. T., Siganga, W., and Goodman, M. H. (2003). Effects of direct-to-consumer advertising of prescription drugs: Perceptions of primary care physicians. *Journal of Pharmaceutical Marketing and Management* 15: 61–75.

Erlen, J. A. (2004). Functional health illiteracy. *Orthopaedic Nursing* 23(2): 150–153.

Holmer, A. F. (1999). Direct-to-consumer prescription drug advertising builds bridges between patients and physicians. *Journal of the American Medical Association* 281: 380–382.

Holmer, A. F. (2002). Direct-to-consumer advertising: Strengthening our healthcare system. *New England Journal of Medicine* 346: 526–528.

Krezmien, E., Bekelja Wanzer, M. B., Servoss, T., and LaBelle, S. (2011). The role of direct-to-consumer pharmaceutical advertisements and individual differences in getting people to talk to physicians. *Journal of Health Communication* 16(8): 831–848.

Murray, E., Lo, B., Pollack, L., Donelan, K, and Lee, K. (2004). Direct-to-consumer advertising: Public perceptions of its effects on health behaviors, health care, and the doctor–patient relationship. *Journal of the American Board of Family Practice* 17: 6–18.

NHC (National Health Council) (2002). Direct-to-consumer prescription drug advertising: Overview and recommendations (abstract). At http://www.healthyskepticism.org/global/library/item/1978, accessed Apr. 6, 2013.

Petroshius, S., Titus, P., and Hatch, K. (1995). Physician attitudes toward pharmaceutical drug advertising. *Journal of Advertising Research* 35(6): 41–51.

Pines, W. (2000). Direct-to-consumer advertising. *Annals of Pharmacology* 34: 1341–1344.

Rabin, K. (2004). DTC advertising for prescription medicines: Research and reflections as the second decade ends. *Journal of Health Communication* 9: 561–562.

Rausch, P. and Treise, D. (2006). Direct to consumer advertising: Enhancing patient–provider communication and health iteracy. Paper presented at the Association for Education in Journalism and Mass Communications annual conference, San Francisco, Aug. 3.

Speros, C. (2005). Health literacy: Concept analysis. *Journal of Advanced Nursing* 50(6): 633–640.

Treise, D. and Rausch, P. (2005). The prescription pill paradox: Nurse practitioners' perceptions about direct-to-consumer advertising. *Journal of Pharmaceutical Marketing and Management* 17(2): 35–60.

US Department of Heath and Human Services (2000). *Healthy people 2010: Understanding and improving health*, vol. 1. At http://www.cdc.gov/nchs/data/hpdata2010/hp2010_general_data_issues.pdf, accessed Mar. 22, 2013.

Young, H. N. and Cline, R. J. W. (2003). "Look George, there's another one!" The volume and characteristics of direct-to-consumer advertising in popular magazines. *Journal of Pharmaceutical Marketing and Management* 15: 7–21.

Yuan, S. (2008). Public responses to direct-to-consumer advertising of prescription drugs. *Journal of Advertising Research* 48(1): 30–41.

Zachry, W. M., Dalen, J. E., and Jackson, J. R. (2003). Clinicians' responses to direct-to-consumer advertising of prescription medications. *Archives of Internal Medicine* 163: 1808–1812.

10

Hyper-Niche Markets and Advertising

> *The thing that we are trying to do at Facebook, is just help people connect and communicate more efficiently.*
>
> Mark Zuckerberg

This morning when checking my Facebook page, I noticed two advertisements. One headline stated "Remove skin tags safely." Yuck, but realistically, probably appropriate for my age. The other was in a language I didn't even recognize. (It looked a little like German but was definitely not German.) So, as far as super-accurate hyper-targeting advertising might go, it appears that Facebook still needs some work.

The debate about bull's-eye precise niche advertising tends to revolve around privacy. The logic is that in order for an advertiser to deliver advertising to me in a manner that demonstrates an innate knowledge of my buying behavior and preferences for certain kinds of products, some company somewhere knows more about me than I may be comfortable sharing with complete strangers.

Obviously, there are no easy answers to what advertising ought to look like in our new cyber-world. But no matter what people might think about privacy

Advertising and Society: An Introduction, Second Edition. Edited by Carol J. Pardun.
© 2014 John Wiley & Sons, Inc. Published 2014 by John Wiley & Sons, Inc.

expectations related to advertising, hyper-targeted advertising is here to stay – especially in the online world.

Ultimately, someone has to pay for content on the Web. While many companies continue to experiment with different kinds of market models, it usually comes down to paying a subscription for access, being willing to be exposed to advertising, or some combination of the two. The subscription model is working in some areas, but so many consumers are used to a free and open Internet that clearly the subscription approach has limited appeal.

So that leaves advertising. The arguments in this chapter focus on Facebook – a phenomenon so ubiquitous that it's no longer a question of whether or not we're on Facebook, but how it's incorporated into our lives.

Online Auctions

Additionally, our commercial life extends far beyond Facebook of course. For example, we are buying more of our goods online and often within an auction site. While eBay may be the best-known online auction, the company is not alone in trying to capture online consumers' hearts and minds. Companies like QuiBids, BidMax, BidCandy, ZBiddy, AlwaysAtAuction are all looking for ways to convince us to move our buying patterns onto the Internet.

According to eBay's website, as of 2011 there were 97 million active users. For a company that began in 1995, that's meteoric growth – even by Internet standards. EBay's website reports $62 billion worth of goods sold in 2010. And, that's just eBay. It's mind-boggling.

And Other Ways to Make Money in the Digital World

As the Web continues to develop as commercial marketplace, Google has been at the forefront, figuring out ways to help advertisers reach their customers. With Google AdSense and other programs, more companies are moving more of their ad dollars into an online presence. According to Joe Mandese's *Online Media Daily* posting on March 12, 2012, digital advertising grew from 10 percent of US advertising to 18 percent between 2007 and 2011. In addition, Mandese's March 13 posting posits an increasing attention to "predictive" audience data-targeting, which is only going to continue to raise concerns about privacy.

Clearly, it's a balancing act. We all understand that the digital world has to figure out how to make money in order to sustain the content that we not only expect but demand. But, as technology improves and companies continue to find better ways to figure out what we want to buy and how to provide ads that are targeted just for us, we will continue to debate how much privacy we're willing to give up in order have the digital world that we love.

Advertising on Facebook is at the forefront of this debate. Joe Bob Hester and Tom Weir, both advertising professors with extensive media planning experience, have different interpretations on whether ads on Facebook are fantastic – or a creepy invasion of privacy. Who's right? *You decide.*

Ideas to Get You Thinking . . .

1   Think about a casual acquaintance of yours – someone you don't know very well, but well enough to tell the person what you're planning to do. Go online and see how much information you can find out about the person within an hour. After you compile the information, share your findings with your acquaintance and get the person's reaction. Were you surprised about the kinds of information you were able to find? Why, or why not?

2   Keep track of the ads that show up on your Facebook page every day for about a week. What do these ads say about you? Are they an accurate representation of the kinds of goods and services that you like?

3   Examine your list of "friends" on Facebook. How many of them are strangers to you? Try and figure out why you agreed to "friend" them. Did you discover anything interesting about how these strangers became your friends?

4   For the next week (or month if you're really ambitious!), keep a list of everything over $10 that you buy (not counting food). When you have compiled your list, check eBay or another auction site and see how many of these products you could buy at auction. Watch a few of the auctions. Could you have bought the products at a lower price than you paid in the store? What other observations can you make?

Other Topics to Debate

1   There should be stronger regulations for marketers' use of social media.

2   Social media are so effective that "traditional" advertising is no longer necessary for a company's product or service to reach the target market.

3   How people present themselves on Facebook and other social media sites is an accurate description of how they really view themselves.

4   Rather than being advertising-based, Facebook should give users a choice of advertising or subscription base as an option for profitability.

If You'd Like to Know More . . .

Anderson, B., Fagan, P., Woodnutt, T., and Chamorro-Premuzic, T. (2012). Facebook psychology: Popular questions answered by research. *Psychology of Popular Media Culture* 1(1): 23–37.

Debatin, B., Lovejoy, J. P., Horn, A. K., and Hughes, B. N. (2009). Facebook and online privacy: Attitudes, behaviors, and unintended consequences. *Journal of Computer-Mediated Communication* 15: 83–108.

Taylor, D. G., Lewin, J. E., and Strutton, D. (2011). Friends, fans, and followers: Do ads work on social networks? How gender and age shape receptivity. *Journal of Advertising Research* 51(1) (Mar.): 258–275.

References

Mandese, J. (2012). From iAd to launching pad, new "predictive" data platform could be organizing principle mobile advertising has been waiting for. *OnlineMediaDaily* (Mar. 12). At http://www.mediapost.com/publications/article/170038/#axzz2Oe5Zu 590, accessed Mar. 26, 2013.

Mandese, J. (2012). Big 5 outpace ad industry two to one, emphasis on digital cited. *OnlineMediaDaily* (Mar. 13). At http://www.mediapost.com/publications/article/ 170026/#axzz2Oe5Zu590, accessed Mar. 26, 2013.

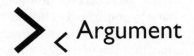 Argument

Hyper-targeted and social: Why Facebook advertising may be advertising at its best

Joe Bob Hester

University of North Carolina, USA

Social networking is the leading content category in terms of the number of online display ads delivered, accounting for more than 25 percent of US impressions, and Facebook is the single largest publisher of all US display impressions. In the third quarter of 2011, Facebook delivered more display ad impressions than Yahoo!, Microsoft, Google, and AOL combined (comScore 2011). And, with an audience of more than 800 million worldwide, Facebook was predicted to double its ad sales to $3.8 billion in 2011. Why? Facebook advertising combines hyper-targeting with social networking, "converting the primary gesture of social media – sharing – into something potentially even better for branding than TV ads: a supercharged version of word of mouth" (Hof 2011a).

Hyper-Targeting

Whether you are watching a television show, reading a magazine, listening to a radio station, or browsing a website, you will see advertisements that are obviously not meant for you. That's because traditional media advertising is based on target audience concentration. Advertisers select media vehicles in which a high percentage of audience members fit a particular demographic, psychographic, lifestyle, and/or usage profile. Messages exposed to audience members who do not fit the profile are essentially wasted. When the target audience is very broad (i.e., adults ages 25–54), the percentage of audience members who fit the profile may be quite high, but there will still be wasted exposures. When the target audience is more specific (i.e., married women ages 25–34 with one or more children living at home), advertisers are often forced to use more wasteful media vehicles in order to reach enough of their target audience members.

Hyper-targeting greatly reduces waste. A term originally coined by MySpace, "hyper-targeting" refers to delivering advertising targeted to specific interest-based segments of a social network based on very specific criteria (Riley 2007). Facebook and other social networking sites have three primary sources of information about users (Gold 2009): registration information (basic information gathered when users set up an account), profile information (posted by the user on his/her profile: favorite movies, music, books, etc.), and behavioral data (things that users do or look at online, pages they're fans of, events they respond to, etc.). According to Facebook's ad guidelines (Facebook 2012), this translates into being able to target based on how your audience "and their friends interact and affiliate with the brands, artists, and businesses they care about," and involves factors such as:

- location, language, education, and work;
- age, gender, birthday, and relationship status;
- likes and interests such as "camping," "hiking," or "backpacking" instead of "tents" or "campers";
- friends of connections (friends of users already connected to your page or app);
- connections (fans of your page).

Hof (2011b) sums it up nicely: "Facebook's value proposition to advertisers is precisely that it can offer more data on its users – and not just behavioral data like many Web sites and ad networks, but accurate personal data provided by users themselves." With so much data and personalization available, advertising becomes as targeted as it could possibly be. However, Facebook goes even farther by integrating advertising directly into the social networking experience.

Social Networking

At the end of 2011, the research firm comScore, Inc. reported that social networking was the most popular online activity, accounting for nearly one in every five minutes spent online and reaching 82 percent of the world's Internet population. The leading social network, Facebook, reached 55 percent of the world's global audience and accounted for one in every seven minutes spent online and three in every four social networking minutes.

In addition to interacting with their friends, Facebook users can interact with a brand by liking a brand, interacting with a brand's app, or checking in at a brand's location. These "organic" interactions between people and brands can be used to enhance Facebook advertising. It works like this. Brand X creates a short post that is transformed into an ad (Facebook calls it a "sponsored story") which appears in the right-hand column of Facebook under a "Sponsored" heading for members of the target audience. If one of your friends, Suzie, has clicked the "Like" button on this post, a line of text will appear in the ad reading "Suzie likes Brand X." In addition, a story about this activity will be generated on all of Suzie's friends' news feeds. People have an average of 130 Facebook fans. When they "like" a brand, that fact spreads to the news feeds of those friends, and those friends may spread it further. When Mars Chocolate introduced M&M's Pretzel by offering samples to 40,000 fans, each of whom could spread the offer to two friends, 120,000 samples went out in under 48 hours (Hof 2011a).

This type of "social" advertising is important because, according to Nielsen Co., it is more effective. When your friend is in the ad, you are twice as likely to remember it, more likely to click on it versus traditional display ads, and your purchase intent quadruples (Hof 2011a).

Optimization

In addition to being able to hyper-target very specific groups and to present them with more effective "social" ads, Facebook provides the tools for advertisers to optimize their ad dollars by providing numerous metrics of campaign and ad performance. Some of these metrics include:

- *social percent*: the percentage of impressions where the ad was shown with names of viewers' friends;
- *clicks*: the number of times users click on ads;
- *impressions*: the number of times an ad is shown to a user;
- *click-through rate* (CTR): the number of clicks divided by the number of impressions in a given time period;
- *average cost per click* (CPC): ad cost relative to the number of clicks.

Using these and other metrics along with demographic information, advertisers can determine which ad is performing best and reallocate budget to the highest-performing ad within a campaign.

What about Consumers?

So far, we've outlined the advantages of Facebook advertising from the standpoint of the advertiser. Consumers gain substantial advantages from Facebook advertising as well. A recent report from McCann Worldgroup revealed that 71 percent of consumers are willing to share shopping data with a brand online, and 86 percent see that there are major benefits associated with sharing this data. Part of this willingness to share is based on the type of data. As one American woman in the report stated, "My shopping data is not ME" (McCann Truth Central 2011: 11).

First and foremost, because of both hyper-targeting and "social" advertising, Facebook users are more likely to be exposed to more relevant advertising that is based on what they are interested in or where they live. Just look at the ads on your own Facebook page. Chances are that you can probably figure out why you are being shown the ads that you are seeing by thinking about the information/interests you've provided in your profile. While the system is not perfect and you may still be exposed to some nonrelevant advertising, the situation should improve as more and more brands begin to use Facebook advertising. In addition, Facebook continues to refine and improve its algorithms for using data in advertising.

Facebook's web interface is also less cluttered by advertising than many web properties, and certainly less cluttered than traditional media. Facebook users typically see only one or two ads in the right-hand column of their news feed. There are no pop-ups, pop-unders, expanding banners, or any of the other annoyances associated with typical banner ads. The simple text designs have more in common with Google AdWords than with traditional banner advertising.

Facebook users also have a tremendous amount of control over what ads they see. If you see an ad you don't like, simply click on the cross in the upper right-hand corner to hide the ad or to hide all ads from that particular advertiser. On the other hand, if you would like to see more ads, click on the "See all" link to see "Ads and sponsored stories you may like."

Finally, advertising revenue allows Facebook to provide its services free of cost to users. Facebook's total current annual revenue, which comes mostly from online advertising, is estimated to be about $5 billion and growing. This business model is in line with many traditional media forms in the United States, where advertising provides the majority of revenue while users receive the service free (television and radio) or at a reduced cost (newspapers and magazines). Every so often a rumor goes around online that Facebook is going to start charging for use, but Facebook has repeatedly stated that it has no plans to do so.

Some argue that there is a hidden cost of using Facebook: loss of privacy. However, given the types of information available on Facebook, user controls, and the company's privacy policy, it is difficult to make this argument. Facebook's privacy policy (2011) is quite specific: you own your own data and it is not shared unless you give your permission, Facebook has given you notice, or personally identifying information has been removed. As far as using your data for advertising purposes, the policy states that

> We only provide data to our advertising partners or customers after we have removed your name or any other personally identifying information from it, or have combined it with other people's data in a way that it is no longer associated with you. Similarly, when we receive data about you from our advertising partners or customers, we keep the data for 180 days. After that, we combine the data with other people's data in a way that it is no longer associated with you. (Facebook 2011)

Users even have control of the use of their names in social ads. You can edit social ad settings so that when you take an action such as liking a page, that action does not end up in an ad displayed to your friends.

The Future

Facebook's success has other social networks working to connect advertising with the social experience they provide. For instance, Twitter announced plans in 2011 to let advertisers place ads in front of Twitter users who are similar to ones following their Twitter accounts. That means users who aren't following a particular brand on Twitter might still see an ad for that brand in their timeline because Twitter thinks they have things in common with people who do follow the brand (Kafka 2011).

Where will it go from here? Predicting the future is difficult. Who could have foreseen the dramatic changes in the advertising industry, or society for that matter, in the last 20 years? The marriage of hyper-targeting and social networking as practiced by Facebook advertising could be just a passing fad, but that seems unlikely. On the other hand, while it is equally unlikely that we "will see the extinction of all ads that don't incorporate social" (Shih 2011), the combination of hyper-targeting and social, this "supercharged word of mouth," seems to be here to stay.

References

comScore (2011). It's a social world: Top 10 need-to-knows about social networking and where it's headed (Dec. 21). At http://www.comscore.com/Press_Events/ Presentations_Whitepapers/2011/it_is_a_social_world_top_10_need-to-knows_ about_social_networking, accessed Mar. 26, 2013.

Facebook (2011). Data use policy. At http://www.facebook.com/about/privacy/, accessed Mar. 26, 2013.

Facebook (2012). Facebook advertising guidelines (Dec. 17). At http://www.facebook.com/ad_guidelines.php, accessed Apr. 3, 2013.

Gold, H. (2009). Hypertargeting registered users. *ClickZ*. At http://www.clickz.com/clickz/column/1710063/hypertargeting-registered-users, accessed Mar. 26, 2013.

Hof, R. (2011a). Facebook's new advertising model: You. *Forbes* (Nov. 16). At http://www.forbes.com/sites/roberthof/2011/11/16/facebooks-new-advertising-model-you/, accessed Mar. 26, 2013.

Hof, R. (2011b). What Facebook's FTC privacy settlement means to marketers. *Forbes* (Nov. 29). At http://www.forbes.com/sites/roberthof/2011/11/29/what-facebooks-ftc-privacy-settlement-means-to-marketers/, accessed Mar. 26, 2013.

Kafka, P. (2011). Twitter ramps up its ad plan again, with ads you haven't asked to see. *All Things D* (Aug. 31). At http://allthingsd.com/20110831/twitter-ramps-up-its-ad-plan-again-with-ads-you-havent-asked-to-see/, accessed Mar. 26, 2013.

McCann Truth Central (2011).The truth about privacy: Executive summary. *McCann Truth Central*. At http://www.scribd.com/doc/69322060/The-Truth-About-Privacy, accessed Mar. 26, 2013.

Riley, D. (2007). MySpace to announce self-serve hyper targeted advertising network. *TechCrunch* (Nov. 4). At http://techcrunch.com/2007/11/04/myspace-to-announce-self-serve-advertising-network/, accessed Mar. 26, 2013.

Shih, C. (2011). Beyond targeting: The convergence of social and advertising. *Online Media Daily* (Oct. 25). At http://www.mediapost.com/publications/article/161149/beyond-targeting-the-convergence-of-social-and-ad.html, accessed Mar. 26, 2013.

Counterargument ﹥ ◀

Today is the new 1984: Big Brother is not only watching you – he is selling to you

Tom Weir

University of South Carolina, USA

Welcome back to Oceania. It is really a shame that George Orwell left us before he had the opportunity to see the extent to which we are able to pry into people's lives today. In *1984* (Orwell 1949) he envisioned "telescreens" that broadcast constant messages in support of the Party, but were also able to see into your living room and check up on you. We have Computers that we use to look at the world, but they are also able to look into our lives to see what we are doing, buying, reading, watching, and thinking. The Ministry of Truth has been replaced by the Ministry of Marketing. Once the Party had taken over all aspects of life and was intent on eliminating all thoughts of individuality. Now, the Sellers have taken over all aspects of life and are intent on prying into our private lives to a degree we used to think was unimaginable. Once we learned that "Ignorance is strength," never suspecting that the idea was ignorance for the consumer and strength for the Seller. Well, we are there again. Welcome home.

The Present

The United States Patent Office granted patent number 7,809,740 B2 to Yahoo! Inc. on Oct. 5, 2010. The patent was for a "Model for generating user profiles in a behavioral targeting system." Below is the description of the system listed on the application:

> A behavioral targeting system determines user profiles from online activity. The system includes a plurality of models that define parameters for determining a user profile score. Event information, which comprises online activity of the user, are received at an entity. To generate a user profile score, a model is selected. The model comprises recency, intensity and frequency dimension parameters. The behavioral targeting system generates a user profile score for a target objective, such as brand advertising or direct response advertising. The parameters from the model are applied to generate the user profile score in a category. The behavioral targeting system has application for use in ad serving to online users. (Chung et al. 2007)

A patent for a behavioral targeting system for advertisers? Is this a joke? We have gone around a great, dark corner and are forging headlong into an abyss unknown in our history. More about that later.

Facebook and other less dominant social media sites have become useful appliances for millions of people. They are also monsters devouring the advertising budgets of thousands of marketers. Because users supply so much personal information, marketers can use these systems to target prospects to a previously unheard of level. That level of specificity in identifying the web navigation, personal likes and dislikes, and countless other variables of unsuspecting users has never been available to marketers before. Of course, the first response was elation – an opportunity to target at this level was a wonderful opportunity – but now it has become a concern (Fullerton et al. 2011). This extensive personal and behavioral targeting is bordering on (some would say extending beyond) a violation of individual privacy.

There are 618 million active users of the social networking site, Facebook (Facebook 2012). More than half of them log on to the site on any given day. The average user has 130 friends, and is connected to 80 community pages, groups, and events. The amount of personal information willingly provided by users, either in their personal profile or in posts is astonishing, and because the company has access to all of that information, Facebook provides an unprecedented opportunity for advertisers to target prospects that they believe will be receptive to their messages. Although Facebook does not share personal information of users with advertisers, the site allows them to search their immense database by location, demographics, likes, keywords, and any other information they hold. Not only that, but the search is capable of identifying individuals based on information that can be inferred from their profiles. This ability presents advertisers with the opportunity to target prospects based on their behavior. The resulting search provides advertisers with the estimated reach, and the site can deliver advertising messages to all, or to a subset of them.

This situation has changed the way market segmentation is done, and it has certainly made millions of people open to receive advertising based on factors they can only guess at. The ethical implications are serious for marketers and consumers alike. Examining the way people use Facebook tells us a lot about how it has become a central part of their lives. The casual observer will conclude that writing brief notes on someone's "wall," or reviewing postings and photos from friends consume the vast majority of time spent on Facebook. But some studies indicate there may be more social benefit, including a relationship between usage and building social capital (Ellison et al. 2007).

By 2010, 98 percent of adults between the ages of 18 and 24 used some sort of social media, a larger percentage than any other age group (although 97 percent of adults 24–34 are so engaged). From there usage drops off, but 73 percent of adults over the age of 65 are using some sort of social media (Ellison et al. 2007). FaceBook dominates this environment, particularly in the younger age categories. But other social networking sites are increasingly getting into the game because advertisers want targeted contact with potential consumers. It is hard to overestimate the potential market.

All the "friends" on Facebook have a personal profile that is searchable by advertisers, and increasingly those friends consist of parents, siblings, and members of extended families (Experian Marketing Services 2011). In Google's free email program, Gmail, the contents of user messages are scanned for key words, with appropriate advertising appearing on subsequent log-ins. To me, this crosses the line.

A study of privacy concerns of both Facebook and MySpace users demonstrated that the former had more faith both in the protection of their personal data and fellow members, and were more willing to share personal information (Dwyer et al. 2007). Whether Facebook actually does a good job in protecting privacy is yet to be seen.

Facebook proudly cites its privacy policy in defense of accusations that nothing is really "private" in the conventional sense of the word. The site consults with what it refers to as a "global Safety Advisory Board" regarding the security of personal information (Facebook 2011).

We are beginning to see a backlash against the infectious use of behavioral targeting through social networks sites. Facebook has been in discussions with the Federal Trade Commission about possible violations of their members' personal information. Also, increasing anxiety has arisen about the service's maintenance of a log of all the websites visited by members for the last 90 days, although the company maintains users have the option of opting out of this feature (Arcohido 2011).

Social science research is now beginning to show increasing concern among Facebook users about the privacy of their personal information. Questions have been raised about individual privacy concerns and misunderstandings about the visibility of personal information (Acquisti and Gross 2006). Further, research seems to be showing that trust and privacy concerns are less important in online relationships than in interpersonal ones (Dwyer et al. 2007).

I recently asked students from four different colleges about their social media use. While the sample was not random, the 430 responders demonstrated strong Facebook use – to the tune of 99 percent. And, of those students, 94 had been involved in Facebook for three or more years.

To get at expectations of privacy in dealings with others in the network, I asked participants if they had ever accepted a "friend" request from someone they did not know, and was surprised to find that 69 percent had done so. Slightly fewer than half (45%) reported that they believed the information they posted on Facebook was protected and private. One-third noted that someone had retrieved some personal information from their account without their permission at least once. Finally, when asked to rate their concern about being targeted by advertisers as a result of their personal information, 47 percent said they did not like the practice.

At what point does the ability to collect personal information about a person become a violation of their personal space? Can we consider behavioral or personal targeting in this manner to be invasive at all? How is it different from an advertiser reaching potential consumers through a magazine that serves a particular lifestyle or interest group?

There is a significant difference between placing advertising in a magazine directed to runners, and placing advertising only on the pages of Facebook users whom you have learned are runners through serendipitous examination of information they believed to be personal and (relatively speaking) confidential.

There has long been an accepted practice to collect information about individual purchase patterns in order to make marketing decisions on a broad scale. Few people seem to object to a marketer noticing that a particular brand of cat food is favored more by women than men, and adjusting advertising to appeal more directly to this group. But that is distinctly different than the sort of targeting we are discussing. I often ask my advertising classes to answer this question: If I had all of your grocery receipts for six months, what could I tell about you? To think about this is enlightening for them because it lets them examine how much personal information really is available to marketers. Each time we conduct this exercise my students quickly determine that I would know their gender, relative age, eating habits, lifestyle, pet ownership, hair type (possibly color), and an entire range of other information they consider to be highly personal. When I ask them if they would be comfortable sharing all of that information with marketers, the response is almost universally negative. Guess what? You are sharing that, and more, every time you post to your Facebook account.

The Future

Be honest with me for a second. When was the last time you actually read through the privacy policy before you clicked the "I agree" button? You can't remember? I can't either. I don't think it has ever happened. I doubt anyone has ever read the policy before agreeing to it. It is shocking, considering the amount of personal information that we are so willing to submit to people or organizations we do not know.

We all have an expectation of privacy – rightly or wrongly – that allows us to do stupid things. We assume our privacy is safe, off limits to peering eyes and ears. But we are wrong. We rail about identity theft, but say nothing about having mountains of personal information stored somewhere we don't know by people we don't know or trust. The expectation of privacy is treated differently by younger versus older people. As people age, they tend to care more about privacy – perhaps because they have more to hide, perhaps because they become more cynical with age, or perhaps because they learn more about the ability of marketers to mine personal data.

Many consumers continue to live a carefree life in Internet-world, oblivious to the fact that their every move is being watched and stored. It's important to understand that we are moving toward a world in which there simply is no privacy at all, and the consequences are staggering. Marketers can and will learn anything about you they want to know. Your response might be that if you have nothing to hide, you have nothing to fear. But think again.

There are important implications to having your life spread-eagled all over the Internet. If you are an employer, you can easily find out all sorts of information about prospective employees. If you are a politician, or ever plan to be, you had better quickly become a lot more careful about what you post on your Facebook page. The government, school admissions offices, the Internal Revenue Service, and, yes, advertisers are all impacted by the freedom of information that floats through the ether.

It appears that Orwell was right. Oceania is a nice place, after all. I know that no one will do anything shady with all of that information. I trust them: they like me. I am no longer an individual, which is fine with me. Who needs it? I don't like to worry and think and have to find my own stuff. I will leave all of that to the Sellers. Freedom is slavery.

References

Acohido, B. (2011). Facebook tracking is under scrutiny. *USA Today* (Nov. 16). At http://usatoday30.usatoday.com/tech/news/story/2011-11-15/facebook-privacy-tracking-data/51225112/1, accessed Mar. 26, 2013.

Acquisti, A. and Gross, R. (2006). Imagined communities: Awareness, information sharing, and privacy on the Facebook. In P. Golle and G. Danezis (eds.), *Proceedings of 6th Workshop on Privacy Enhancing Technologies*. Cambridge: Robinson College, pp. 36–58.

Chung, C. Y., Koran, J. M., Lin, L.-J., and Yen, H. (2007). U.S. Patent Application No. 20070239518, Class 705010000. Washington, DC: U.S. Patents and Trademark Office.

Dwyer, C., Hiltz, S., and Passerini, K. (2007). Trust and privacy concern within social networking sites: A comparison of Facebook and MySpace. In *Proceedings of the Thirteenth Americas Conference on Information Systems, Keystone Colorado, August 9–12 2007*. At http://csis.pace.edu/~dwyer/research/DwyerAMCIS2007.pdf, accessed Apr. 3, 2013.

Ellison, N. B., Steinfield, C., and Lampe, C. (2007). The benefits of Facebook "friends": Social capital and college students' use of online social network sites. *Journal of Computer-Mediated Communication* 12(2007): 1143–1168.

Experian Marketing Services (2011). The 2011 social media consumer trend and benchmark report. At http://www.experian.com/assets/simmons-research/brochures/2011-social-media-consumer-report.pdf, accessed Mar. 26, 2013.

Facebook (2012). Key facts. At http://newsroom.fb.com/Key-Facts, accessed Mar. 26, 2013.

Fullerton, J., Kendrick, A., and Weir, T. (2011). Advertising student opinion of ethical issues – online behavioral targeting – controversial issues. *Journal of New Communications Research* 5(1): 61–76.

Orwell, G. (1949). *1984*. New York: Penguin.

11

Advertising and Product Placement in Entertainment Media

> *Everything I learned, I learned from the movies.*
>
> Audrey Hepburn

When we talk about "product placements," we usually mean brand-name items (including products, packaging, signs, and corporate names) that are *intentionally* placed in movies and on television programs – and more recently, in other forms of entertainment. Some of these placements are paid, but other branded products are placed in programming at the discretion of the creative directors.

Interest in product placement continues to be strong – and to grow. Yet the phenomenon is not new. Back in the early days of television, advertisers sponsored entire programs, infusing their brand's name throughout the program. Kraft Television Theatre, General Electric College Bowl, and Mutual of Omaha's Wild Kingdom are only three well-known examples from the past.

Researchers D'Astous and Chartier (2000) list three reasons why advertisers might want to place their products in entertainment programming. First, watching a movie involves high attention, so the assumption is that some of that "super-"attention might fall on the product. Second, movies can produce large audiences. Even if the movie isn't a box-office blockbuster, after international

Advertising and Society: An Introduction, Second Edition. Edited by Carol J. Pardun.
© 2014 John Wiley & Sons, Inc. Published 2014 by John Wiley & Sons, Inc.

sales and rentals, lots of people may potentially see the product placement. And with shrinking television audiences, audience exposure is becoming even more important. Third, the "natural" placement may make audience members less irritated than they sometimes are with in-your-face advertising. And a happy viewer is potentially a happy customer.

While some people have argued that using product placements is a form of "stealth" advertising (slipped into the programming so no one realizes it might be an ad) and, in turn, is unethical, others champion the approach as innovative and effective. Sometimes there is even a quirky use of a named brand product that almost creates a cult following. Often, this is seen in television where fans watch the program over time and get "involved" with the characters, so much so that they feel it's up to them to save the show when the network decides to cancel it. For example, NBC was not at all convinced it would bring back *Chuck* for a second season until fans started buying sub sandwiches from Subway and telling the chain that "Chuck had sent them." Apparently, NBC and Subway have continued and expanded their partnership. For example, a Subway is prominently included in the cafeteria of the fictional community college that is home to the quirky faculty and students of *Community*.

With the increase (and popularity) of reality shows, the ease with which products have found a happy home should be no surprise. *American Idol* is one of the earliest champions, with its arrangement with Coke. Is it any surprise then that *X Factor* followed with Pepsi? (You *did* play the Fan Experience Contest sponsored by Pepsi, didn't you?) *The Biggest Loser* likes to tell us that Jenni O's turkey is really lean (I guess you're supposed to think that it's leaner than Perdue!) And, please, don't hurt the environment by using plastic bottles of water when you work out. Instead, use the Brita water purifier system. These products make sense for a show like *The Biggest Loser*, but many would argue that when the trainers stop and talk for minutes about a product (and they do this more and more), it starts to look staged – the exact opposite of what a well-placed product is supposed to do.

And then there are the cooking channels and the home improvement channels. If ever there was a perfect match for products and programming, these channels would be it. I don't know if Ina Garten (*Barefoot Contessa*) has an arrangement with KitchenAid, but I recognize a KitchenAid when I see one – and I like seeing her use hers. I feel like I am becoming a chef because I have the same equipment in my kitchen as my favorite celebrity cook does. Believe me, if Ina tells me I have to have a Henckels knife in my arsenal of kitchen gadgets, I'll go get one. (Okay, I already have one, but I would get another!)

Placing products in movies and television is just the beginning. According to Ammar Faruki, a Pakistani designer who studies product placement, products are regularly being placed in music, board games (Starbucks in Monopoly, for example) and even on eggs! According to news reports, in 2006 CBS announced its programming on 35 million eggs using a company called EggFusion. CBS called this "egg-vertising." Whether this is product placement or just weird marketing, it's a good example of creative people thinking up new ways to promote products. Is it any wonder product placement would seem like a win–win for all?

Except when it's not a win – at least from the product's perspective. For example, in the recent film *Flight* (released in 2012), Denzel Washington plays a pilot with a drinking issue. He drinks a Budweiser beer when he shouldn't be drinking. Anheuser-Busch was not pleased to have their wildly popular beer associated with Washington's character. They asked to have the logo removed from the movie because it placed the company's product in a negative light. But, in what might be a surprise to many, directors of films do not need to get permission (let alone pay) for the use of products in movies. Whether a "negative" placement is really negative, however, is also up for debate. It turns out that Anheuser-Busch may have been worried for nothing. Some researchers have demonstrated that even a placement in a negative environment can lead to higher recall and higher desirability of the product. I guess there is a little bit of a rebel in all of us!

Product placement may seem fairly innocuous after we have been assaulted by overt advertising all day, every day. The "egg" example makes this point. The more viewers move toward "on demand" media consumption (watching when you want), the more "traditional" commercials are in danger – and the more advertisers will look for ways to incorporate their products into movies, TV shows, music, and so on. With the never-ending content demands of Twitter, Facebook, Pinterest, and other social media outlets, chatting about brands, "liking" brands, having actors being shown in photos in brands, and so on, the onslaught of product promotions is only going to increase.

The James Bond movie *Skyfall* (2012) reportedly collected a record $45 million in placement fees. There is an entire website called "Bond lifestyle: The real thing," which lists all the products used in all the Bond films (all with links to the brands' websites). The list is long, but some of the products placed in *Skyfall* include Heineken beer (apparently controversial, since this is not the beer that Bond would be expected to drink, according to Bond afficionados), Land Rover, a Sony Xperia T phone, an Omega Seamaster watch, and lots of other high-end products we can only dream of owning.

Are all the products placed in *Skyfall* manipulative persuasion – or just great advertising strategy?

Whether you think product placement is a good idea or not, advertising agencies have had to struggle with how to figure out adequate payment. Some have moved toward a "time on screen" approach or a "product prominence" approach, and others have tried to develop a form of gross rating points for quantifying a branded placement in order to run comparisons for different media platforms. But even with these approaches, most agree that it is difficult to control product placements in movies (and more recently on television, in video games, and even in mass market paperback books) – let alone understand the impact that they may have. Whether or not media planners understand how to "count" product placements, it is clear that they are trying.

As the use of product placement as an effective strategy in media planning becomes more pervasive, it is inevitable that people will start to question the ethics of the practice – seeing it either as a form of privacy invasion ("I paid to see the movie once, why do I have to pay again by watching the ads in the movies?") or from a pragmatic perspective. What happens when a client purchases a placement and doesn't get the box-office numbers – or the scene gets cut because of the creative director's prerogative? What happens if the new television show flops after just a few episodes? What is the media planner going to do if a big part of the advertising strategy revolved around that television show?

Why Are Product Placements Potentially So Important?

As Geah Pressgrove and Kathy Richardson both observe, product placement as an advertising strategy will only become more important as Tivos and other kinds of digital recorders become more prevalent. As it becomes easier for consumers to skip commercials, advertisers will become even more creative at finding ways to make sure the message slips in. With estimates of over 85 percent of viewers now skipping commercials (via remote controls, DVRs, or other controlled viewing options), advertisers need to find a way to get their messages across – otherwise, they may withdraw from television all together. Embedding products in programs is a logical way to assure audience exposure.

As Pressgrove and Richardson point out, product placements are here to stay. But are they unethical? *You decide.*

Ideas to Get You Thinking . . .

1   Watch a favorite television show. Look carefully and see if you can find any branded products. How many did you find? Do you think the products are there because the advertiser asked for them to be there?

2   Rent a movie with a friend and watch it for the action. After the movie, ask your friend to write down all the branded products he or she can remember. Now go back and watch the movie again, noting every time you see a product placement. Did your friend catch most of them? If not, why not? Based on this "experiment," do you think these product placements were a good idea?

3   Watch a reality program and list all the products you see on the show. Pick a program that will have a variety of products, such as something on HGTV or the FoodNetwork. Now find those products on the Web and look to see if the advertiser connects to the show. For example, you might see something like "As seen in *Iron Chef America*." What are your observations? Do you think this is good advertising strategy? Why, or why not?

Other Topics to Debate

1   All products placed in entertainment media need to be clearly labeled.

2   All products placed in entertainment media should be approved by the advertiser.

3   It doesn't matter whether a product is shown in a negative or a positive light. Ultimately, all advertising is good advertising.

If You'd Like to Know More . . .

A-B (2012). InBev wants to ground Bud's appearance in "Flight." *Advertising Age* 83 (41): 1.

Gillespie, B., Joireman, J., and Muehling, D. D. (2012). The moderating effect of ego depletion on viewer brand recognition and brand attitudes following exposure to subtle versus blatant product placements in television programs. *Journal of Advertising* 41(2): 55–65. doi: 10.2753/IOA0091-3367410204

Lehu, J. (2007). *Branded entertainment: Product placement and brand strategy in the entertainment business*. London: Kogan Page.

Matthes, J., Wirth, W., Schemer, C., and Kissling, A. (2011). I see what you don't see. *Journal of Advertising* 40(4): 85–100.

Redondo, I. (2012). The behavioral effects of negative product placements in movies. *Psychology & Marketing* 29(8): 622–635. doi: 10.1002/mar.20548

Steinberg, B. (2012). Why so many brands want to be on "Modern Family" . . . and so few will. *Advertising Age* 83(4): 2–36.

Reference

D'Astous, A. and Chartier, F. (2000). A study of factors affecting consumer evaluations and memory of product placement in movies. *Journal of Current Issues and Research in Advertising* 22(2): 31–40.

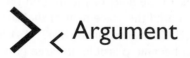

Argument

Product placement is simply good advertising strategy

Geah Pressgrove

West Virginia University, USA

Product placement marketing, branded entertainment, product integration, advertainment, no matter what you call it, is a strategy that has become an increasingly powerful tool to seize the attention of consumers in a fragmented traditional marketing landscape. According to PQ Media, which has been tracking branded entertainment since 1975, paid placement spending in 2011 was at $4.26 billion, a 10.2 percent increase over the previous year. The company forecasts continued growth in the coming years (PRWeb 2012). This burgeoning corporate marketing line item provides an important stream of capital for underwriting production costs for entertainment programming, an opportunity for brand strategists to weave marketing messages into popular programming, which results in decreased consumption costs for the consumer wishing to enjoy entertainment media.

In this essay, I will briefly outline the reasons why product placement in entertainment media enhances the media experience. First, I summarize the critical role of corporate partnerships in the evolution of entertainment media. Next, I provide examples of the potential impact of product placement in terms of sales and market research. Then I explain the advantages and benefits of product placements for brand strategists competing for consumer attention. In conclusion, I provide a few examples of things to watch for as product placement continues to be an important part of the entertainment media landscape.

History

Long before the lovable extra-terrestrial followed a trail of Reese's Pieces to Elliot's house in the mid-1980s, corporate brands were supporting the production of entertainment media. In fact, most popular sources credit the advent of product placement to the nineteenth-century publishing of Jules Verne's adventure novel, *Around the World in Eighty Days*, which features shipping and transport companies. The origins of product placement in contemporary media can also be traced back to the start of the motion pictures itself in the 1890s when Lever Brothers secured the placement of their branded soaps in some of the earliest films made (Hudson and Hudson 2006). As time passed, the evolution of entertainment media became possible, in large part, owing to corporations and entertainment properties recognizing the mutual benefit of partnering.

At its inception, product placement provided an avenue for studios and television networks to reduce the cost of production through borrowed props (Newell et al. 2006). In time, the barter arrangement gave way to fiscal support for production expenses. Coinciding with the rise in popularity of talking films in the late 1920s, product placement became an organic part of, and a mainstay among, movies. By the 1930s, a substantial portion of radio programming was created by advertisers and ad agencies. By the late 1950s, most television programs were underwritten by corporations strategically aligning their brand with popular programming (Turner 2004). So prominent were these sponsorships that "soap operas" are so named because of their early association with consumer, packaged-goods companies like Procter & Gamble and Unilever. While these sponsorships are far less prominent today, companies such as Hallmark continue this tradition in the twenty-first century by sponsoring programs on networks like Lifetime.

The Business of Product Placement

Today, product placement in entertainment media ranges from the subtle public broadcasting model of "supported by viewers like you," to the ubiquitous in-program placement of products in domestic box-office films and television shows, to the more pragmatic placement of game-show awards. While some critics have called product placement shameless, intrusive, or an affront to preferred programming, these strategies have demonstrated themselves to be an extremely efficient way for marketers to connect to consumers. Elusive target audiences, advances in technology, and the transformational shift in entertainment programming delivery have made it ever more important for brands to invest in strategies that draw associations, create emotional connections, and engage consumers in captive locations.

To illustrate the extent that product placement can have on sales, here are a few examples of silver screen placements that delivered big dividends for the partnering corporation (CNBC 2011):

E.T. the Extra-Terrestrial (1982): Spielberg initially planned to use M&Ms in the movie, but was turned down by the candy giant Mars. Mars' loss was Hershey's gain. Profits rose 65 percent as a result of Hershey's $1 million partnership with what became one of the highest-grossing films of all time.

Risky Business (1983): Not only is this movie credited with launching Tom Cruise's career, but it also saved Ray-Ban's Wayfarer sunglasses, of which more than 360,000 pairs were sold that year.

Top Gun (1986): Aviator sunglass sales increased by 40 percent when the film became an overnight box-office hit. The US Navy capitalized on the prominent role of the armed forces in the plot by setting up information booths in movie theater lobbies, effectively increasing recruitment efforts.

Golden Eye (1995): BMW's three-film commitment to the saga of James Bond paid off with 9,000 orders for the Z3 the month the movie opened, months before the sportster was scheduled for release.

The Italian Job (2003): While the movie performed modestly, BMW's contribution of 30 Mini Coopers during production leveraged a 22 percent increase in sales after the iconic car became the star of the film.

Transformers (2007): General Motors got in on the profit-making product placement action when it provided a tricked-out Chevrolet Camaro to star in this film. The *Transformer*-branded car did not exist for purchase initially, but the public demand was so intense that the company produced the car and proceeded to sell over 60,000 units.

The success of effective product placement in entertainment media is also noted in the demand created for fictional products prior to their production and release, commonly referred to as reverse product placement. Notable examples include the creation of a chain of Bubba Gump Shrimp Co. restaurants after the 1994 release of *Forrest Gump*, Staples' creation of Dunder Mifflin brand paper based on the hit TV show *The Office* (Sauer 2011), and Cap Candy's creation of Bertie Bott's Every Flavor Beans which first appeared in the *Harry Potter* books and movies (Edery 2006).

Other corporate marketers are moving into the online realm to generate buzz. In 2006 American Apparel launched a brand of jeans in the virtual world Second Life months prior to release in its bricks and mortar stores (Lavallee 2006). Also in 2006, Starwood Hotels and Resorts launched a sub-brand, called Aloft, in Second Life, just before it appeared in the real world (Wasserman 2007).

Advantages/Benefits

While a shaky economy, digital competition, and DVRs in a third of US homes may contribute to the rise in product placement in entertainment media, the benefits of this branding strategy cannot be overlooked. If asked, many people would likely say that they do not care for traditional ads interrupting their entertainment viewing. Also, if asked, these same people could likely quickly tick off a list of their favorite movies, television shows, videos, and games. These programs are often made available at minimal cost because of the advertising support of corporations. In sum, viewers react to, talk about, and engage with what happens in their favorite entertainment media, while they actively try to avoid (fast forward through) commercials. This marriage of anti-commercial sentiment and programming loyalty laid out a very natural path for product placement success. Some of the key benefits to marketers and production houses are as follows.

Return on Investment

When was the last time you heard someone talk through a movie, fast forward their favorite program, skip past a great video, or stop playing in the middle of a video game? You've likely answered, "Not recently." This captive audience is exactly what brand strategists and corporate marketers are hoping for. This simple illustration highlights one of the key benefits of product placement over other forms of commercial advertising: value for dollars spent in terms of audience reach. In other words, the cost to produce witty, edgy, and memorable commercial television spots far exceeds the expense of placing a product in a well-targeted film, which also helps to offset rising production costs for producers. This investment further improves with the longevity of the film, video, show, or game.

Increased Realism and Realistic Storytelling Portrayals

A character's choice of cars, clothes, and tools; food eaten in a particular scene; and technological gadgets incorporated into the plot, not only provide marketers with the chance to reach a wider audience, but also allow script writers to add depth to character portrayals and enhance aesthetic setting depictions without blatant explanation. These visual cues help to move the story along in a way not possible in their absence.

Perceived Endorsement and Brand Image Development

For decades, marketers have understood the power of celebrity spokespersons. In the form of product placement, when your favorite star uses a branded product, there is an implied endorsement. This endorsement leads to a stronger emotional connection for the target audience through product associations dovetailing with preferred entertainment media and personalities. This pairing of brand and entertainment also serves to improve the affective or emotional positioning of the product. Associations become aligned with the emotional connection to the entertainment medium, effectively developing the affective positioning of the product in consumers' minds.

Increased Brand Awareness

Fed-Ex in *Cast Away*, Junior Mints in *Seinfeld*, Sears in *Extreme Makeover: Home Edition*, Coke in *American Idol*, Ray-Ban in *Men in Black* . . . the list of products and brands appearing in entertainment media is familiar to even the most casual media consumer. These subtle (and sometimes not so subtle) brand integrations have been proven to increase product recall and brand awareness. Further, consumers have indicated that they feel products or services that are integrated into programming have a higher perceived value than the same product advertised during a commercial interruption (Gupta and Balasubramanian 2000).

Conclusion and the Future

The evolution, continued growth, and powerful benefits of product placement in entertainment media likely mean this is a trend that will only become more common. As early marketers recognized, and I hope you've come to agree, product placement is a powerful promotional tactic in the contemporary marketing arsenal. As this brand strategy continues to evolve, marketers are likely to learn, experiment with, and demand more from their investment. The following are some things to watch for in the future.

Effectiveness of Measurement Metrics

In the last two decades, Nielsen Media Research has been tracking product placements in broadcast programming. Currently, their only metric for determining the effectiveness of a placement is brand recall. This measurement is incomplete, however, as it does not tell us if the consumer intends to or actually does purchase the product. Further, Nielsen (2011) found that, of the 10 most remembered brand integrations, three were in the show *The Big Bang Theory*. The fact that one show accounts for so many recalled placements may actually tell us more about the audience for the show than the memorability of the brand or product placement.

Alternative Product Placement Formats

Some academic studies have shown that viewers push back when they know they are being sold products, leading to greater need for subtlety in product placement (Mandese 2006; Wei et al. 2008). However, in response to overt endemic product placement strategies, parody placement has emerged as an avenue for clever marketers and production houses. In 2012 several such parodies became viral successes. Among the first to successfully execute such a parody was NBC's *30 Rock* television show, which spoofed its part-nership with Snapple. Following this lead, IFC's show *Comedy Bang! Bang!* dedicated a portion of its show to satirically integrating a lengthy drive in a VW Beetle to discuss problems with the faux product placement agreement of a fictional product. Comedy Central's *Colbert Report* also created a stir when the host spent nearly seven minutes mocking a brand memo describing the proper procedures for portraying Wheat Thins as part of their sponsor-ship agreement.

Reverse Product Placement's Role

Another trend worth mentioning and watching is the potential future use of market research in the form of reverse product placement. Fictional products integrated into popular entertainment media provide a way for corporations to gauge public interest prior to costly production.

Effectiveness of Product Placement

Scholarly research investigating consumer attitudes toward product placement as a practice began appearing in the early 1990s (e.g., Nebenzahl and Secunda 1993; Ong and Meri 1994). Advancement in the areas of video game and Internet-based placement, improved matching of entertainment media and audience characteristics, cross-promotional and branded programming, placement time and length on screen, as well as audiovisual formats, are a few of the areas where marketers and researchers will continue to investigate and improve product placement strategies. As investment in product placement continues to grow, so too will research on the efficiency and effectiveness of these place-ments, which will advance our understanding of best practices and current and future trends.

References

CNBC (2011). 10 big successes in product placement. At http://www.cnbc.com/id/43266198/10_Big_Successes_in_Product_Placement, accessed Mar. 26, 2013.

Edery, D. (2006). Reverse product placement in virtual worlds. *Harvard Business Review* (Dec.). At http://hbr.org/2006/12/reverse-product-placement-in-virtual-worlds/ar/1, accessed Mar. 26, 2013.

Gupta, P. B. and Balasubramanian, S. K. (2000). Viewers' evaluations of product placements in movies: Public policy issues and managerial. *Journal of Current Issues & Research in Advertising* 22(2): 41.

Hudson, S. and Hudson, D. (2006). Branded entertainment: A new advertising technique or product placement in disguise? *Journal of Marketing Management* 22(5–6): 489–504.

Lavallee, A. (2006). Now, virtual fashion: Second life designers make real money creating clothes for simulation game's players. *Wall Street Journal* (Sept. 22). At http://www.americanapparel.net/presscenter/articles/20060922wsj.html, accessed Mar. 26, 2013.

Mandese, Joe (2006). When product placement goes too far. *Broadcasting & Cable* (Jan. 1). At http://www.broadcastingcable.com/article/102250-When_Product_Placement_Goes_Too_Far.php, accessed Mar. 26, 2013.

Nebenzahl, I. D. and Secunda, E. (1993). Consumers' attitudes toward product placement in movies. *International Journal of Advertising* 12(1): 1–11.

Newell, J., Salmon, C. T., and Chang, S. (2006) The hidden history of product placement. *Journal of Broadcasting & Electronic Media* 50(4): 30–48.

Nielsen (2011). Nielsen's tops of 2011 advertising. *Nielsen Newswire* (Dec. 20). At http://www.nielsen.com/us/en/newswire/2011/nielsens-tops-of-2011-advertising.html, accessed Apr. 2, 2013.

Ong, B. S. and Mei, D. (1994). Should product placement in movies be banned? *Journal of Promotion Management* 2(3–4): 159–175.

PRWeb (2012). New PQ media data: Global product placement spending up 10% to $7.4 billion in 2011, Pacing for 11% growth in 2012, as wireless technology, changing consumer habits & looser regulations compel brands to invest in alternative marketing solutions. *PRWeb*. At http://www.prweb.com/releases/2012/12/prweb10204688.htm, accessed Apr. 2, 2013.

Sauer, A. (2011). At the movies: The greatest reverse product placements of all time. *BrandChannel* (Dec. 2). At http://www.brandchannel.com/home/post/2011/12/02/At-the-Movies-Greatest-Reverse-Product-Placements-Of-All-Time.aspx, accessed Mar. 26, 2013.

Turner, K. (2004). Insinuating the product into the message: A historical context for product placement. In M. L. Galician (ed.), *Handbook of product placement in the mass media: New strategies in marketing theory, practice, trends, and ethics.* Binghamton, NY: Best Business Books, pp. 9–14.

Wasserman, T. (2007). Forward thinkers push reverse product placement. *Brandweek* (Jan. 29). At http://www.aef.com/industry/news/data/2007/7008 , accessed Mar. 26, 2013.

Wei, M. L., Fischer, E., and Main, K. J. (2008). An examination of the effects of activating persuasion knowledge on consumer response to brands engaging in covert marketing. *Journal of Public Policy & Marketing* 27(Spring): 34–44.

Counterargument >

Placing products in entertainment media does not enhance the media experience

Kathy Brittain Richardson

Berry College, Rome, Georgia

Does placing products in entertainment media enhance the media experience? No! While audiences and consumers live in a brand-enriched environment, product placement doesn't enhance the experiences we have with television programs, movies, games, or videos. Granted, it doesn't necessarily harm the experience, but it seldom makes it better. A prominent soda can resting on a judge's table, a chef touting the value of a sponsor's branded sauce during a cooking program, or the billboards that streak by during a furious video game car chase – these placements intrude, reminding audiences that while the program's overt goal may be to entertain, the covert goal is always persuasive, sometimes intrusive, and occasionally so blatant as to be comical or irritating. While the placements may sell products, they may also repel viewers. Therefore, audience members – and brand strategists – should be wary of product placement for four reasons, which will be discussed below: (1) overt branding frequently interferes with the stories told or constructed within programming; (2) ubiquitous placement takes away the choices that technology now offers consumers; (3) undisclosed placement reaches naive and susceptible audiences in ways that make it difficult for parents or others to intervene; and (4) embedded branding allows harmful products to be featured.

Advertisements or Aesthetics?

Branded products can add reality to the setting for a drama or comedy program or game. Whether a character drives a BMW or a Toyota Prius may provide a quick insight into their motivations or values. Similarly, their choice of clothing, appliances, alcohol, handbags, sports shoes, or hotels offers rich details about their lifestyle and motivations. However, increasingly, the product pitching within programs, films, games, videos, songs, blogs, and social media has often become more than just back-story detail, when major characters seem to stop normal conversation or action to engage in a 15-second promotional spot discussing a product or holding it carefully so that the camera can capture and caress the brand logo. A 2006 study found that every "three minutes of programming" in primetime television has at least one brand appearance, and 10 percent of placements involve a direct mention of the brand by a character within the program (LaFerle and Edwards 2006), which the Screen Actors Guild has questioned as a type of "forced endorsement," according to a report in the *Washington Post* (Byrne 2006). The appearance of products within entertainment programs has become the focus of branding campaigns. For example, the *USA Today* headline from November 18, 2011, describes an upcoming film in this way: "BMWs star in upcoming 'MI,'" detailing the i3 electric vehicle that was to appear in the December 2011 release of *Mission Impossible: Ghost Protocol.* How that impacts on the artistic and editorial decisions made by producers, directors, singers, playwrights, and novelists is difficult to know, but various branding agreements have been documented by case studies or promotions in academic journals, trade journals, and newspapers, as has the occasional lawsuit or compensation agreement filed when decision-makers do not adhere to the agreements (e.g., see Nitins 2005).

Few would argue that having a branded package lying on a counter during a kitchen scene, or the sign for a restaurant appearing as background during an establishing shot in a film or program, is distracting. However, placement can be far less subtle. For example, in the cable reality program, *Project Runway*, hair-care, makeup, and accessory products are often mentioned by host Tim Gunn, signage appears in shots, and contestant designers are encouraged and/ or required to use the products as they prepare their models for the runway. Those products appear relevant to the reality story line and competition, but there are other programs and films in which the story line fades while the promotion occurs – to the point that, at times, the sponsorships are spoofed within scripts. The series *30 Rock* has integrated placement into pivotal moments in some scripts in ways that exploit the ironies of such placements – yet even then, the brand gets the time on screen.

What the story lines would be without the intrusion of branding is unknown, but consumers and audiences do note what they see and hear when branding agreements are honored. Does this internalized and naturalized advertising deter creativity and consistency in writing and directing? It is impossible to know the full impact, but its impact on programming and promotions is observable and, too often, so obvious that spontaneity and authenticity are weakened – and the distinctiveness of entertainment gives way to a bland blending of pitching and storytelling that offers full service to neither.

Transcending Technology

Most agree that entertainment placement has expanded as marketers try to reach audiences whose technologies have given them greater control over exposure to traditional advertising. The DVRs that record programs and skip the advertising, the web or screened downloads that give access to programs without advertisements, and the mobility of viewing that allows audience members to choose time, place, and space for viewing make it harder for marketers to know that they will have access to the eyes and ears of consumers. So, embedding commercial messages within the scenery, the script, or the lyrics seems a better and more convenient way to access the audience.

In a sense, personal technologies may be forcing advertising into becoming an invited messenger, requiring the consent of those who want to be amused, informed, aroused, or persuaded. Those who want to watch the commercials in a television program or before a film in a theater or on screen before the streaming begins may do so. Those who don't want to watch may zip, zap, click through, or arrive at the theater a few minutes late. The necessity for commercial underwriting of programming made more sense in a two or three over-the-air-network world, but in an age when most viewers of programming pay for it directly, technology allows them to opt in or out, and producers and distributors have – or can find – other means of revenue. Product placement takes away consumer and audience choice, making exposure to the pitch a requisite if one wants the rest of the program.

Perhaps most adults are savvy or cynical enough to note and discount the persuasive impact of such embedded branding. However, choosing exposure to entertainment typically means that audiences are in a positive, receptive mode when they likely expect to be able to suspend critical consumptive judgment. Viewers have chosen a film or a television program deliberatively, seeking whatever gratifications present – and then are called to simultaneously suspend disbelief in order to immerse themselves in the involving or amusing narrative while also critically noting (and perhaps discounting) the depiction and association of the products featured within that narrative.

Consenting Children?

Such a process is certainly difficult for adults, but more challenging for children who have not yet developed sufficient media literacy to be able to decode traditional advertising, let alone branding that avoids the traditional signals of a "commercial message." From a marketer or advertiser's viewpoint, the deep involvement children or others may have with characters, plots, and actions provides an open venue for associating brands with pleasure and gratification. The cross-promotions that often accompany film and television placement lead to the toys included with children's meals at fast food chains or the clothing or furnishings in children's bedrooms, thereby creating a seamless stream of branding, with broad and deep persuasive and economic impact. The naive audience member – whether child or adult – may not be aware of the covert or even overt sales pitch that becomes associated with an engaging and entertaining activity, and may be far less questioning or suspicious than more media-savvy consumers.

Children as young as six or seven have been shown to remember brands they've seen in movies with as much accuracy as older children (Auty and Lewis 2004). Think about it – who doesn't remember what department store featured the "real" Santa in *Miracle on 34th Street* or what brand of candy enticed E.T. to emerge from his hiding place? Similarly, children remember the costumes, toys, and gadgets used by characters on Nickelodean, Disney, and the Cartoon Network, as well as in films and video games. This effect is made even more powerful by the merchandising of character-related products as, in effect, the entire program becomes a product placement for brands that then line the aisles of toy stores and the children's departments in department and big-box stores. The sale of products such as *Dora the Explorer* bed sheets, *Hannah Montana* furniture, and *Zach and Cody* T-shirts reinforce the commercialization of children's television – and the power of programming placements.

When surveyed, parents say they object to the overt and covert product placements in children's programs, games, and books and believe such placements should be disclosed so they can make more informed choices about what their children see and hear (Hudson et al. 2007). Groups such as the National Advertising Division of the Council of Better Business Bureaus have indicated they will review product placements on children's television (Edwards 2005); requiring notification would not prevent placement, but it would allow audiences to offer more informed consent for their children to be exposed to the embedded persuasions in much the same way in which rating codes offer information about other program themes.

Perilous Persuasion?

Audience members also report concerns about the placement of products that may not be regularly advertised on television or other general-audience settings (Gupta and Gould 1997; McKechnie and Zhou 2003; Brennan et al. 2004). Products that may not usually be found in children's programming, such as guns, tobacco, and alcohol, may find a place within film content. The number of film characters that smoke and discuss specific brands, for example, has prompted consumer-advocacy groups to argue for increased regulation (Lipman 1989). Glamorizing alcohol use or smoking without the accompanying warning labels required in traditional advertising offers marketers a different route to reach and to persuade audience members.

Perhaps a greater danger lies in the hegemonic impact of the unceasing commercialization of every venue. The integration of promotion and branding into every form of mass communication changes the medium and the message by placing consumption at the center of every exchange. When virtually every cultural vehicle – from films to plays to recording to television programming – carries overt commercial imprimatur, it contributes to a pervasive hegemony of materialism that not only overrides artistic or aesthetic values but also reduces the audience to a commodity to be bought and sold again and again. Kretchmer has noted the advent of what she calls "advertainment," which she describes as "entertainment content that mimics traditional media forms but is created solely as a vehicle to promote specific advertisers" (2004: 39). Put more simply, overt placements turn art, entertainment – and audiences – into commodities.

Is all product placement bad for consumers? Obviously not. Realistic branding may add depth to scenes, humor to some scripts, funding for productions. But audiences as consumers should maintain their right to choose whether they want to be exposed to advertising or to purchasing goods. Open disclosure of placement would not restrict its use, but could empower audiences and consumers in an effective and efficient manner.

References

Auty, S. and Lewis, C. (2004). Exploring children's choice: The reminder effect of product placement. *Psychology & Marketing* 21(9): 697–713.

Brennan, S. P., Rosenberger, P. J., and Hementera, V. (2004). Product placement in movies: An Australian consumer perspective on their ethicality and acceptability. *Marketing Bulletin* 15(1): 16–31.

Byrne, B. (2006). And now, a (scripted) word from our sponsors. *Washington Post* (July 16), N7. Edwards, Jim (2005). Regulators take another look at product placement. *Brandweek* 46(36) (Oct. 10): 15.

Edwards, J. (2005). Regulators take another look at product placement: FTC, NAD consider moves to regulate growing practice. *Brandweek* (Oct. 10), 15.

Gupta, P. B. and Gould, S. J. (1997). Consumers' perceptions of the ethics and acceptability of product placements in movies: Product category and individual differences. *Journal of Current Issues and Research in Advertising* 19(1): 37–50.

Healey, J. R., Meier, F., and Woodyard, C. (2011). BMWs star in upcoming "MI." *USA Today* (Nov. 18), 3B.

Hudson, S., Hudson, D., and Poloza, J. (2008) Meet the parents: A parent's perspective on product placement in children's films. *Journal of Business Ethics* 80: 289–304.

Kretchmer, S. B. (2004) Advertainment: The evolution of product placement as a mass media marketing strategy. In M. Galician (ed.), *Handbook of product placement in the mass media*. Binghamton, NY: Best Business Books, pp. 37–54.

LaFerle, C. and Edwards, S. M. (2006). Product placement: How brands appear on television. *Journal of Advertising* 35(4): 63–86.

Lipman, J. (1989). Outcry over product placement worries movie, ad executives. *Wall Street Journal* (Apr. 7), sect. 2, p. 5.

McKechnie, S. and Zhou, J. (2003). Product placement in movies: A comparison of Chinese and American consumers' attitudes. *International Journal of Advertising* 22(3): 349–374.

Nitins, T. (2005). Are we selling out our culture: The influence of product placement in filmmaking. *Screen Education* 40: 44–49.

12

Advertising in Previously Hands-Off Journalistic Environments

> *Advertisements . . . contain the only truths to be relied on in a newspaper.*
>
> Thomas Jefferson

When I wake up early, nothing makes me happier than to make a pot of coffee and point the remote until *Morning Joe* greets me. I'm a bit of a *Morning Joe* fanatic. I follow both Joe Scarborough and Mika Brzezinski on Twitter and I love their banter. I even appreciate that the show is boldly sponsored by Starbucks. It makes perfect sense to me. You have to drink coffee when you're watching the morning news! It might as well be Starbucks, right?

Regardless of what people say about the future of journalism, news consumption is up. However, in most cases, advertising dollars are down – especially when you spread out the spending across the myriad media outlets we now enjoy. We constantly check our Twitter feeds, our Flipboard sites, our email, our Pinterest pins. And, occasionally we still watch the evening news and pick up an actual newspaper to read (although if we're even half-connected to the world, most likely we've already seen the story). How is any media vehicle ever going to make money in this environment? We are so used to free content that not only do we not want to pay to access it, it seems the news providers don't even want to pay the providers any longer. Just think about all the "citizen news" links that broadcasters use as well as the unpaid post-baccalaureate internships available to our "fortunate" journalism students.

Advertising and Society: An Introduction, Second Edition. Edited by Carol J. Pardun.
© 2014 John Wiley & Sons, Inc. Published 2014 by John Wiley & Sons, Inc.

The easy answer is "Let the advertisers pay for the content." But even that panacea doesn't seem to be the sole answer any longer. Analysts have estimated, for example, that in 2011 Google alone generated about $36 billion in advertising revenue. While not all of that revenue comes at the expense of traditional media outlets, most likely a good chunk of it does. So, as traditional advertising profits continue to disappoint, advertisers must look for new outlets to ply their wares and media content providers must become more willing to allow advertising into places that even a few years ago might have been unthinkable.

As Barnes and Bierbauer demonstrate in the following essays, ad creep has been occurring for many years. Some will argue that it has always been happening. But clearly something has fundamentally changed in recent years. As we continue to wrestle with ways to keep the media profitable enough so we can continue to enjoy our information-overload obsessions, it could be that we have decided that accepting advertising in areas where we previously liked to pretend were off limits (sacred journalistic spaces like the front pages of newspapers, for example) is a small price to pay for that media.

Have we gotten so comfortable with the role of advertising supporting our news media that, in this new financial media environment, we are willing to accept advertisements where just a few years before we would have thought unthinkable? *You decide.*

Ideas to Get You Thinking . . .

1   Watch one or two hours of *Morning Joe*. List every time Starbucks is mentioned. (Don't forget to include "Brewed by Starbucks," which the hosts often say before cutting to a commercial.) How many mentions did you discover? Does the coffee seem intrusive to you?

2   Watch a number of different kinds of news shows. (Check out the local morning news and compare it to an hour of *Hardball with Chris Matthews*, for example.) Keep track of branded products. Did you notice any kind of difference between the programs?

3   Think about branded products promoted on segments of news shows like *The Today Show*. Choose one of those products and see if you can find out whether the product was placed on the show as an intentional product placement. After your research, consider how it has impacted your thinking about products that show up on news shows.

4   Take a look at a couple of different newspapers. Perhaps you'll want to look at *USA Today*, your local paper, and another national paper like the *Wall Street Journal*. Compare the placement of advertisements in the front section of the paper. What similarities and differences do you see?

5   Using the same newspapers, now look at the editorial and see if you can tell if any of the articles are based on press releases. How can you tell? Most likely, several stories were, indeed, generated from press releases. Do you think it's okay if you can't tell the difference?

Other Topics to Debate

1   Some products are inherently more newsworthy than others. Therefore certain products would be appropriate to feature on a news program.
2   Video news releases (for broadcast) and press releases (for print) are not product placement and should not be treated as such.
3   Twitter should be considered a news site and, as such, should not have tweets serving any kind of paid sponsorship.

If You'd Like to Know More . . .

Farhi, P. (2011). Despite law against it, stealth commercials frequently masquerade as TV news. *Washington Post* (Dec. 6). At http://www.washingtonpost.com/lifestyle/style/despite-law-against-it-stealth-commercials-frequently-masquerade-as-tv-news/2011/12/05/gIQANXaxaO_story.html, accessed Mar. 26, 2013.

La Ferle, C. and Edwards, S. M. (2006). Product placement: How brands appear on television. *Journal of Advertising* 35(4): 63–86.

Richardson, K. B. and Pardun, C. J. (2012). The greatest entertainment ever sold: Branded entertainment and public relations agencies' role in product placement across media. Paper presented at the Association of Education in Journalism and Mass Communication, Chicago, IL.

Stelter, B. (2009). Starbucks is now the official joe of "Morning Joe." *New York Times* (June 1). At http://www.nytimes.com/2009/06/01/business/media/01joe.html?_r=0, accessed Mar. 26, 2013.

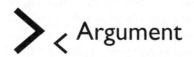 Argument

This is news? Maybe not, but that's okay!

Beth E. Barnes

University of Kentucky, USA

Talk to many professional journalists about the challenges besetting their rapidly changing field and chances are that, before long, someone will bring up "ad creep," the growing prevalence of advertising within news content in places where it would have been unthinkable just a few years ago.

While some recent developments have led to renewed concerns, the issue of possible advertising influence on news content is not new. Brown and Barnes (2001) examined student and practitioner perceptions of advertising influence on broadcast news content and found that news professionals in particular were very concerned about advertising influence. Despite those concerns, though, the blurring of the lines between editorial and advertising is continuing, as the evidence below indicates. But is that necessarily a bad thing?

As advertising spending in the traditional news media has decreased, newspapers and broadcast television programs are looking for new ways to entice advertisers back. One approach has been to offer advertising placements that were previously unavailable due to the strong wall between editorial content ("church") and advertising content ("state").

Newspapers

Belatedly following where others had already gone, the *New York Times* started carrying an advertisement across the bottom of its front page in January 2009 (Perez-Pena 2009); the *Washington Post* followed suit in September 2010 (Calderone 2010). Each time a major newspaper moved to carrying front page ads, journalists in the newsroom and editors proclaimed that this was a terrible thing, a major ethical lapse (Shafer 2009).

Journalism and print design historians know that front page ads and ads that were often indistinguishable from news content were standard in the American press in the eighteenth and nineteenth centuries (Shaw 2007; Shafer 2009). News and advertising were intermixed, and that blending certainly did not kill the American press. Nor will it today.

There does not appear to be any evidence that either the *New York Times* or the *Washington Post* lost subscribers as a result of adding front page ads. Like many major market newspapers, both publications had already seen a decline in subscribers in the months and years preceding the decisions to carry front-page ads. But their "selling out" did not drive readers away. Indeed, the *New York Times* was the third-largest US newspaper based on circulation in the Audit Bureau of Circulation's September 2011 report on the previous six months' circulation (Lulofs 2011). The *Washington Post* was eighth on the list. And the top two circulating newspapers, the *Wall Street Journal* and *USA Today*, have carried advertising on their front pages for longer than either the *Times* or the *Post* (Shaw 2007). Front-page advertising does not drive large numbers of readers away. Perhaps readers didn't notice the change; more likely, they noticed but just didn't care, or at least not enough to cancel their subscriptions.

What is the appeal of a front-page ad? One primary appeal is tied to why many advertisers choose to buy space in newspapers in general: credibility. The hope is that the newspaper's own credibility, built over time by its choice of stories and the careful, accurate reporting of those stories, will transfer over to the products advertised within the newspaper. Because newspapers traditionally put their strongest, most important stories on the front page, ads on the front page might also be seen as more important by association.

The prominence of location is also a factor; just as advertisers have been willing to pay premium prices for the cover locations in magazines for years, the assumed extra exposure that comes with a front-page newspaper ad is very enticing for advertisers who are seeking to increase awareness. (Magazines typically charge their highest rate for the back-cover placement, referred to as the "fourth cover"; placements on the inside front and inside back covers also carry premium prices.) However, it is important to note that many of the newspapers that carry front-page ads put them at the bottom of the page, "below the fold." This means that the ad will not be visible when the newspaper is sitting on a news-stand, or in a newspaper sales box.

To get around that particular challenge, and to offer yet another option to advertisers, many newspapers also sell other front-page advertising formats. Some papers sell advertisers' wraps that cover part or all of the newspaper's actual front page and all of the back page; the *Washington Post* began selling wraps before it started its bottom-of-the-front-page ads (Calderone 2010). The wraps are clearly separate from the editorial content of the front page and so may not convey the same aura of credibility to the advertised product, but they are certainly noticeable from any angle. Similarly, some newspapers offer the ability to have a branded, brightly colored Post-It note stuck over the newspaper's masthead (where the newspaper's name is printed) on the front page (Shafer 2009). The masthead Post-It isn't quite as intrusive as the wrap, but it shares the benefit of being visible on a news-stand stack or in a newspaper sales box.

Each of these formats, the bottom-front-page display ad, the wrap, and the masthead Post-It, is clearly an advertisement. No reader (or journalist, for that matter) is going to confuse one of these messages with a journalistic news story. The ethical dilemma raised comes simply from the proximity of the ad to the front page, the home of the best, most serious news stories. There is no reason to believe, nor evidence to suggest, that allowing ads in proximity to the front page influences the content of front-page news stories to a greater degree than ads within the newspaper's pages.

Problems certainly can, and should, arise when that delineation is blurred. The *Los Angeles Times* received a great deal of criticism in 2009 when an ad for the television program *Southland* was designed to look like a news story and ran on the front page of the *Times* (Schotz 2009). The ad did carry the label "advertisement," but its design and layout were very similar to other, actual, news stories on the front page. The outcry over this blurring of the line between editorial and advertising included criticism of the *Los Angeles Times* by the Ethics Committee of the Society of Professional Journalists, a major watchdog group in the journalism profession. The chair of the committee, Andy Schotz (2009), wrote: "Integrity must anchor our journalism. We serve our readers, listeners and viewers. There's no reason to trick or confuse them with fake news, not even for money."

Given that readers look to newspapers for credible stories, and that advertisers promote their products in newspapers largely to benefit from that perception of credibility, it's difficult to understand why NBC (let alone the *Times*) thought this approach would benefit *Southland*. When advertisers pressure news outlets to bend or stretch their credibility, the long-term outcome will almost certainly be a loss of that credibility, which will in turn lead to a loss of audience, and ultimately make that news outlet far less attractive to advertisers than before. It is actually in advertisers' best interest to promote and support news media credibility, rather than the reverse. While front-page display ads, wraps, and Post-Its may result in some grumbling, the wide outcry that invariably happens when an egregious breach of the wall between editorial and advertising occurs suggests that both journalists and audience members do perceive a difference between these two types of advertising content.

Broadcast News

Concerns over the degree of what is acceptable are more widespread where broadcast news is concerned. As with the newspaper situation, there are varying degrees of blurring the line between editorial and advertising.

A 2008 *New York Times* article reported that several television news stations owned by Meredith Corporation were accepting product placements in their morning news programs. The particular example described by the *Times* was in a Las Vegas station where the morning anchors had "cups of McDonald's iced coffee on their desks during the news-and-lifestyle portion of their morning show" (Clifford 2008). The story went on to quote executives at a number of other news stations who said their programs would not accept such placements.

The Las Vegas station's news director, Adam P. Bradshaw, made it clear that he wouldn't accept a product placement just anywhere: "I would not put product placement into any of my traditional hard newscasts" (Clifford 2008). Bradshaw also asserted that the presence of McDonald's as a sponsor would not prevent the station from reporting negative stories on McDonald's. The *Times* reporter also interviewed people at the advertising agency that had arranged the placement; while they acknowledged that the intent was not to influence news content, they did say that in the case of a negative story, "I would expect that the station would absolutely give us the opportunity to pull our product off set" (Clifford 2008).

MSNBC and Starbucks took product placement to a new level when they announced in June 2009 that Starbucks would become the official sponsor of *Morning Joe*, a news program on the cable network. A *New York Times* article on the partnership termed it "the closest integration between an advertiser and a national news program in recent memory" (Stelter 2009). The naming agreement includes mention of Starbucks in program ID announcements, inclusion of Starbucks in the graphics package for the show, and the co-hosts consuming

Starbucks products on air. As with the McDonald's example above, MSNBC said that the sponsorship would not affect story decisions. The *Times* article quotes Phil Griffin, president of MSNBC, saying "They [Starbucks] understand that we have standards" (Stelter 2009).

Some broadcast stations have rules regarding whether their anchors or other on-air talent can provide voiceovers for advertisements. Many prohibit it out of concern that listeners will assume the person providing the voiceover is personally endorsing the product. In the case of the Las Vegas station and the McDonald's product placement, the *New York Times* reporter said, "The anchors rarely touch the cups" (Clifford 2008). That is not the case with *Morning Joe*; in announcing the sponsorship, MSNBC's Griffin was quoted as saying, "We've been doing this for free for a couple of years" (Stelter 2009), a reference to the co-hosts' personal preference for Starbucks coffee.

The Federal Communications Commission (FCC), the government agency that oversees the communications media, requires television news operations to disclose to viewers when they are using material that is provided by an outside organization (Clifford 2008). Television news programs are also supposed to disclose if persons appearing on the program are being paid, either by the station itself (a big no-no) or by a business (Farhi 2011); the arrangement between Starbucks and MSNBC is obviously clear to viewers. However, it is not always so transparent.

A *Washington Post* article reported on Alison Rhodes, the "Safety Mom" who appears on news programs to talk about products designed to increase child safety. In particular, Rhodes discusses an ADT electronic monitor and a child's backpack rigged with an alarm (Farhi 2011). While Rhodes is paid by both ADT and the maker of the backpack to promote these products, and discloses that on her website, the article reported that at least one news station in the Washington, DC market claimed not to have known about that arrangement when it used Rhodes in a news story on child safety.

A television news station's failure to disclose such a sponsorship arrangement is a violation of the FCC's law and can lead to a fine and even imprisonment (Farhi 2011). The FCC is also looking into expanding its oversight of product placements on television news (Clifford 2008). But the FCC acknowledges that it relies on complaints from viewers to identify problems rather than actively trying to identify these issues itself (Farhi 2011).

Electronic Media

The blurring of the line between news and advertising in the electronic media involves an area that has provoked the attention of the Federal Trade Commission (FTC), another government agency involved in the regulation of promotional messages. The FTC has been keeping an eye on potentially deceptive advertising messages related to diet products for some time (FTC, n.d.). A relatively recent tactic employed by some diet aid firms is creating websites that look and sound like true news sites (Mullin 2011). The sites use actors who look and talk like television news anchors, sitting on what appears to be a news set. They report supposed scientific findings on the wonderful weight loss powers of various products. Related to this practice are fake blogs that appear to be from "real people" who have realized wonderful results by using these products; the blogs are actually run by the companies selling the products (Mullin 2011).

The FTC has rules for how bloggers should disclose any compensation they receive for promoting specific products or services, similar to the FCC's rules on disclosure. The guidelines are outlined in the FTC's "endorsement guides" (Bureau of Consumer Protection 2009). The bottom line, as with the FCC rules, is that readers, viewers, or listeners should be made aware of when content is sponsored. As with our discussion of print media, this admonishment should make sense to a responsible advertiser. Participating in activities that compromise the credibility of a news operation, whether it is a traditional news outlet or an online site or blog, ultimately makes that media vehicle an ineffective place for a product message.

Professional Codes of Ethics

The ethical codes of both the Society for Professional Journalists (SPJ 1996) and the Radio Television Digital News Association (RTDNA 2013) remind journalists of the need to remain objective and free of influence over the stories they report. Journalists' negative reactions to "ad creep" reflect the understandable discomfort they feel when it appears that the relationship between an advertiser and a media outlet is getting too cozy. But ad placement in closer than ever proximity to news content does not necessarily equate to advertiser influence on news content.

There are two primary groups that need to be responsible for making sure that advertising placement within news does not influence the content of the news: journalists and advertisers. The journalists' side of that responsibility should be obvious: journalists and editors need to continue to resist any real or perceived pressure from publishers and ad sales staffs to blur the line between editorial and advertising. When egregious offenses happen, or are suggested, they should be publicized so that the court of professional and public opinion can keep violators in check.

But advertisers must be involved as well. There's actually a very good reason to have journalism programs and advertising programs side by side in colleges and universities. The better advertising people understand and appreciate the benefits of and need for journalistic independence and objectivity, the more vigilant they will be (we hope!) in helping to champion those virtues. Beyond the lofty (and important) ideals of independent journalism lies the hard fact that, simply put, a lousy journalistic product is no place for a legitimate ad. The Brown and Barnes study mentioned earlier also examines perceptions of advertising agency media directors. The media directors included in the study agreed with the statements "It's in advertising's best interest to promote news program-ming free of commercial influence" and "If a news program has no credibility, there's no value to an advertiser in promoting its product near that" (Brown and Barnes 2001: 26).

The economic pressures the news media face are requiring them to think more creatively about how to continue to make their product appealing to potential advertisers. Despite what many journalists (and even some advertising people) may wish, it is not realistic to expect that newspapers will stop running front-page ads anytime soon, or that television news programs will roll back the tide on product placements. Rather than continuing to bemoan the new reality, it is in the best interests of both groups, and ultimately, the audience, to adopt a policy of transparency and full disclosure. Under those conditions, the news media will be able to offer an attractive, credible product to advertisers, and advertisers will not be in a position of potentially killing the goose that laid the golden egg of credibility.

We are in this new reality together, and it's time we set aside the traditional mistrust and suspicion that have characterized interactions between church and state and instead find ways to work together to benefit both sides.

References

Brown, H. W. and Barnes, B. E. (2001). Perceptions of advertising influence on broadcast news. *Journalism & Mass Communication Educator* 55(4): 18–29.

Bureau of Consumer Protection (2009) The FTC's revised endorsement guides: What people are asking. At http://business.ftc.gov/documents/bus71-ftcs-revised-endorsement-guideswhat-people-are-asking, accessed Mar. 26, 2013.

Calderone, M. (2010). Washington Post to start running front-page ads. *Yahoo! News* (Sept. 13). At http://news.yahoo.com/blogs/upshot/washington-post-start-running-front-page-ads.html, accessed Mar. 26, 2013.

Clifford, S. (2008). A product's place is on the set. *New York Times* (July 22).

Farhi, P. (2011). Despite law against it, stealth commercials frequently masquerade as TV news. *Washington Post* (Dec. 6). At http://www.washingtonpost.com/lifestyle/style/despite-law-against-it-stealth-commercials-frequently-masquerade-as-tv-news/2011/12/05/gIQANXaxaO_story.html, accessed Mar. 26, 2013.

FTC (Federal Trade Commission) (n.d.) Weight loss & fitness. At http://www.consumer.ftc.gov/topics/weight-loss-fitness, accessed Mar. 26, 2013.

Lulofs, N. (2011). The top 25 U.S. Newspapers from September 2011 FAS-FAX. *NEWSBulletin Connection* (Nov. 1). At http://accessabc.wordpress.com/2011/11/01/the-top-25-u-s-newspapers-from-september-2011-fas-fax/, accessed Mar. 26, 2013.

Mullin, J. (2011). Acai berry sting: FTC sues fake "news" sites hawking diet products. *paidContent* (Apr. 16). At http://paidcontent.org/2011/04/16/419-acai-berry-sting-ftc-sues-fake-news-sites-hawking-diet-products/, accessed Mar. 26, 2013.

Perez-Pena, R. (2009). The Times to sell display ads on the front page *New York Times* (Jan. 5), B3.

RTDNA (Radio Television Digital News Association) (2013) RTDNA code of ethics. *Radio Television Digital News Association* (Sept. 14). At http://rtdna.org/article/rtdna_code_of_ethics, accessed Apr. 3, 2013.

Schotz, A. (2009). SPJ ethics committee criticizes L.A. Times' fake news story. *Code-words: The SPJ Ethics Committee Blog* (Apr. 21). At http://blogs.spjnetwork.org/ethics/2009/04/21/spj-ethics-committee-criticizes-l-a-times-fake-news-story/, accessed Mar. 26, 2013.

Shafer, J. (2009). Front page for sale. *Slate* (Sept. 7). At http://www.slate.com/articles/news_and_politics/press_box/2006/09/front_page_for_sale.html, accessed Apr. 4, 2013.

Shaw, D. (2007). A fading taboo. *American Journalism Review* (June–July). At http://www.ajr.org/article.asp?id=4342, accessed Mar. 26, 2013.

SPJ (Society of Professional Journalists) (1996) SPJ code of ethics. *Society of Professional Journalists.* At http://www.spj.org/ethicscode.asp, accessed Mar. 26, 2013.

Stelter, B. (2009). Starbucks is now the official joe of "Morning Joe." *New York Times* (June 1). At http://www.nytimes.com/2009/06/01/business/media/01joe.html?_r=0, accessed Mar. 26, 2013.

Counterargument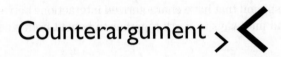

Advertising in strong journalistic environments is never a good idea

Charles Bierbauer

University of South Carolina, USA

In the run up to the 2012 presidential primaries, comedian and scold Stephen Colbert offered the South Carolina Republican Party half a million dollars to fund its cash-strapped party primary. There was just one string attached. It would be called "The Stephen Colbert Super PAC South Carolina Republican Party Primary." How cool for Colbert, a native South Carolinian. The party – hmmm, should we? – declined.

"Basically, the F.E.C. gave me the license to create a killer robot," Colbert told the *New York Times*, referring to the ability to create substantially unregulated Super PACs (McGrath 2012; see also US Supreme Court 2010; FEC 2011).

It is, of course, a slippery slope, if not a lemming's leap. Today the Palmetto primary; tomorrow the White House brought to you by (insert highest bidder). Political cynics will ask rhetorically, "Don't we already do that?"

If this seems off the track of ads in the journalistic milieu, perhaps it is because we've all gone off the track of independent speech and wandered into a morass of wink-wink, nudge-nudge, everything must have an underlying and nefarious meaning, not to mention a deep pocket, source of funds and influence.

We are inured to commercial sponsorships, most straightforward and relatively innocuous. You pays your money and you puts your name on it. And the games go on with most participants and observers oblivious to the message, subliminal or neon. The University of South Carolina football team played in the 2012 Capital One Bowl, once known merely as the Tangerine Bowl. The university's basketball team plays in the Colonial Life Arena. Banks, insurance companies, auto manufacturers, pizza purveyors, and dot.coms sponsor all kinds of athletic and entertainment events and venues. NASCAR circles its rolling ad stock hundreds of times before hundreds of thousands of eyeballs every weekend of its racing season. By the time the M&Ms car has been traced on your memory 500 times, are you going to think of a Snickers?

So if commercial sponsorships and ad placements are good enough – and, need we note, extremely lucrative – for sports and, nearly, for politics, why is it a bad idea in a journalistic environment?

Here are a few reasons: planes crash, autos are subject to massive recalls, pharmaceutical companies make bad batches, *E. coli* gets into hamburgers, banks fail or are beneficiaries of costly federal bailouts, CEOs lie, cheat, steal or create Ponzi schemes. Who would you like to sponsor your newscast when the story is about the sponsor itself? Not that we haven't run the risk. The mere juxtaposition of ads on television and in print necessitates a shuffling of spot locations when the story adjacent – think plane crashes and airlines – is too close for the sponsor's comfort. Frankly, the advertiser is entitled to that, if it is not engaged or at fault in the somber story running next to its cheerful enticement.

Not that we haven't seen sponsored newscasts. From 1948 to 1956, the NBC daily newscast was called the Camel News Caravan with John Cameron Swayze. This was well before cigarettes were fully identified as cancer-causing and tobacco advertising exited the airwaves.

Venerated CBS newsman Edward R. Murrow later used his *See It Now* show to push an inquiry into the link between smoking and cancer. Murrow would admit that he was himself addicted to cigarettes. But he'd been a tacit shill for the tobacco industry. A cigarette in hand while on the air was a Murrow trademark. (If you didn't see it then, see the biopic *Good Night, and Good Luck* (2005).) The curl of smoke drifting through Murrow's interviews was an early wisp of product placement. "Ed Murrow apparently feels he looks his romantic best with arm draped over a chair, cigarette in hand and puffing clouds of smoke," suggested Roy Norr, author of *Cancer by the Carton* (Reporter on Smoking and Health 1963).

Newscasts today are rarely overtly sponsored. They do not need to be. They make good money from the ad blocs – not to be confused with sponsorships – in the newscasts. At most stations and networks, the news departments are now profit centers where once they were loss leaders.

But news divisions are also under considerable pressure to cut costs and raise margins. There are a lot of little, seemingly harmless ways to do that. Trade deals for the anchors' clothing, hair, and makeup. Sponsorships inside the newscasts for sports, weather, and community-oriented features. Video news releases from corporations that are, in essence, letting the people you report about write the story. These practices are rife, but very inconsistent.

They may be seemingly benign. Whose "Joe" is in the cup of Joe on the desk of MSNBC's *Morning Joe* news/talk melange? Well, it's Starbucks. Are the cups removed on days the MSNBC team happens to be reporting on a Starbucks story? Does it matter? What if the floor manager forgets and Joe won't give up his latte? Is this a question the show should even have to confront?

"The world is just different," said MSNBC's chief executive Phil Griffin told the Associated Press in 2009 when the purported $10 million deal was announced. "The rules of 10, 15, 20 years ago just don't apply. You can't live by them. You've got to be creative" (Bauder 2009).

The product infiltration filter is weakest at the local level. In Columbia, South Carolina, for example, four stations with four corporate owners produce local newscasts – WIS, an NBC affiliate owned by Raycom; WLTX, a CBS affiliate owned by Gannett; WOLO, an ABC affiliate owned by Behakel; and WACH, a Fox affiliate owned by Barrington. In late 2011 the four stations showed no consistency within the market. In some cases, managers appeared to operate at their own discretion within their station groups.

"It's all a local decision by each (Gannett) station," said Rich O'Dell, general manager for Gannett's WLTX: "We have no paid product placement. The computers on set are not identified, coffee mugs just have the WLTX logo, no clothing deals, and clothes and hair are paid for by the anchors" (O'Dell 2011).

Across town at Barrington's WACH, interim general manager Ben Tucker said there are "no 'written' guidelines from Barrington corporate regarding product placement in news. The general guideline is to only incorporate 'product placement' in areas that do not create a conflict in doing the 'right thing' when covering any story." Tucker says the issue is "very fluid" (Tucker 2011).

WIS general manager Donita Todd says Raycom's policy is "clear and extensive" and "privileged" (Todd 2011). At WIS and other stations, it also tends to be nuanced. Product placement at WIS is discouraged and requires the general manager to sign off on it. "No talent is ever to mention a product," said Todd. Talent may say, "Here's this week's Deal of the Week" to throw to a promo, but without mentioning the product or service.

Sports and weather segments seem more opportune areas for advertisers to sponsor. WACH's popular Friday high school football report is sponsored by a local auto dealer (I won't name it; no product placement here), and the sports anchor has done promos standing in front of the dealership. Gannett's WIS also has an auto dealership sponsoring its Friday football segment.

WACH's AM weather is sponsored, as is its PM drive time weather. Tucker says he has had "coffee sponsors" at other Barrington stations. WACH runs a "hair style credit" at the end of its newscasts, but covers up the logos on the laptops on set with a WACH Fox sticker. WIS has a spa-sponsored "lake level" graphic showing the water levels on prominent boating venues in the Columbia area. Todd acknowledges there is "more leniency with sports and weather."

Are the sponsorship messages innocuous, subliminal, or pernicious?

During the 2011 Christmas season, CNN's closed captioning was "provided by christianmatch.com," an online religious dating service with a religious orientation. Should we see anything more in that?

ABC's *Nightline* in December 2011 was "brought to you by ConocoPhilips." What's *Nightline*'s take should ConocoPhilips be responsible for an oil spill?

When the *Today* show's Matt Lauer and Savannah Guthrie host the Macy's Thanksgiving parade, there is no escaping the hundreds of embedded promotions on display, starting with the title sponsor department store.

Which deserve a shrug, a wink, a raised eyebrow? If there's Starbucks on one morning TV coffee table, aren't viewers likely to think everyone's filling at the same pot?

"Who would believe us if we started to pitch products," said Kevin Tedesco, executive communications manager for CBS News. "There's no product placement in network news," Tedesco said, adding that when *CBS Morning News* was revamped at the beginning of 2012, "it never entered the discussion" (Tedesco 2012).

American media are not alone in facing this conundrum. In 2011 Ofcom, the independent regulator and competition authority for the UK communications industries allowed product placement in television programs in the United Kingdom. A large onscreen "P" logo "must appear for three seconds at the start and end of programmes, and after any advertising breaks," Ofcom informs broadcasters. The permission for product placement applies only to films, TV series, entertainment shows and sports programs. "It will be prohibited in all children's and news programmes and in current affairs, consumer advice and religious programmes made for UK audiences," Ofcom specifies. But it's not carte blanche even where permissible. EU and UK regulations prohibit product placement of tobacco products, alcohol, baby milk, prescription-only medicines, gambling, and "foods or drinks that are high in fat, salt or sugar" (Ofcom 2011). Whew, the skim latte skims by.

Nescafé broke the barrier on the first day permissible in February 2011 as the first item subtly inserted into the viewer's range on the ITV show *This Morning*. Nescafé paid a reported £100,000 to put its coffee maker on set (Telegraph 2011).

In the United States, FCC regulations focus more on transparency. "FCC rules call for disclosure of any programming sponsorship, including 'product placement' and 'embedded advertising,' that is done in exchange for money, service, or other forms of payment" (FCC 2011). Any product placement deal – in news, entertainment, or any other program – must be disclosed on air.

It's that tiny type at the end of the newscast, somewhere beneath the station or network logo.

But in the news environment, the branded coffee cup, the hairstylist, and the clothing credit are not nearly as insidious as the product or process-favoring report masquerading as reporting. The video news release (VNR), though much exposed as an intrusive promotion, has not disappeared. Shrinking news staffs and tight budgets have only made news organizations more vulnerable to their seductive insertion. VNRs may be as simple as product information produced for a manufacturer or as deceptive as an ersatz reporter or anchor extolling the product's merits. Stations that use them sometimes assign a reporter to voice over the same text.

A 2006 study by the Center for Media and Democracy found that most stations did not disclose the use or source of the sponsored video. The Center documented VNR used by 46 stations in 22 states and found that of 54 VNR broadcasts recorded, there was no disclosure of the source of the video in 48 of the airings (PR Watch 2006).

While the VNR may be held in disdain in many newsrooms, it seems in favor with the US Consumer Product Safety Commission. The Commission's website describes the VNR as "the television version of the printed press release." The site provides lots of help on how to create an effective VNR, including video editing suggestions, "bites and b-roll," buying satellite time, and a tip to "post the VNR on social media sites that your firm utilizes, including YouTube and Facebook." CPSC's Office of Public Affairs offers to "help every step of the way as the video is produced" (CSPC 2011).

The salvation in this, from a news consumer's perspective, is that a VNR too slickly produced may exceed a smaller local station's capacity and give itself away. At some point, viewers may not be as taken in by the external materials. It often doesn't look like the local reporter, set, or style. Do they think they can slip something by us? Well, someone does.

Stations that swoon over their own self-promotion may be more willing to foster someone else's. When I worked as a reporter in a Philadelphia station in the late 1960s, an assistant news director issued a memo encouraging reporters to include a shot of the station's logo-emblazoned microwave truck somewhere in the packaged report, the earlier in the report the better. Our product, our placement.

More difficult to detect is the practice of "plugola" – a seemingly dispassionate expert reviewing products. Morning shows at both the local and network levels are replete with such expertise. What is most likely missing is the full disclosure that the expert may be on the take or even on the payroll of a product manufacturer. The "Safety Mom," according to the Washington Post, in late 2011 was plugging an electronic home monitor and a backpack with a built-in alarm. Thanks to satellite links, Safety Mom has appeared on "as many as 35 morning shows in a single eight-hour stretch." Many of those host stations told the *Post* they were unaware the Safety Mom was paid by the manufacturers (Farhi 2011).

Federal law requires disclosure by the endorser to the broadcaster and by the broadcaster to the viewing audience. Your coffee likely will go cold while you're waiting to hear that. And it's rarely enforced. An FCC spokesman told the *Post*, "The only way we'd know is if someone has complained" (FCC spokesman David Fiske, quoted in Farhi 2011).

Complain they did when the *Los Angeles Times* engaged in a jumbo product promotion with the then new Staples Center arena in 1999. The *Times* and the Staples Center agreed to split the profits of a special *Times Magazine* issue exclusively focused on the opening of the arena. The issue generated more than $2 million in revenue. It also generated a petition from nearly 300 *Times* reporters and editors and an embarrassing apology from publisher Kathryn Downing. Downing said the failure to publicly disclose the deal "stemmed from her 'fundamental misunderstanding' of editorial principles in the newspaper industry" (Hiltzik and Hofmeister 1999). The *Times*–Staples incident has since been held up as an exemplar of what not to do in lowering the firewall between advertising and editorial content.

While product placement may not generally be the issue in print, ad intrusion is. Ads now appear routinely on newspaper front pages, in the guise of seeming news articles, encroaching on the editorial pages.

The *Los Angeles Times*, as the web monitor of the advertising industry *ClickZ* described it, again jumped "down the rabbit hole" with a lucrative mock front page promoting the 2010 movie *Alice in Wonderland*. *ClickZ* said the ad set off calls, emails, and blogs to the *Times*, some in vigorous protest, others amused (Virzi 2010).

The American Society of Magazine Editors guidelines say, "The cover is the editor and publisher's brand statement. Advertising on the cover increases the likelihood of editorial–advertising conflicts. The cover and spine should not be used to advertise products other than the magazine itself." But the guidelines equivocate: "False covers and the front side of cover flaps used for advertising should always be labeled as advertising" (ASME 2011). ASME acknowledges it has little enforcement power.

The Internet is still relatively uncharted terrain. Ads are everywhere – top, sides, bottom, and in between. Irksomely, they pop up in and over what you're reading. The spread to the Web from all conventional media is inexorable. Newspapers and television newsrooms alike have shifted to a "web first" paradigm. Reporters are routinely told to post to the Web first, to their print and broadcast media subsequently. The challenge of the Internet is not making news, but making money. The stock question: How do we monetize it? The ancillary question: Is there sufficient delineation between advertising and content? Many news websites look similar to a newspaper page with headlines, story ledes, and a smattering of announcements and ads. These may be the least of our worries if we take the familiar admixture of ads and content as just a transfer of venues from print to web.

The real terra incognita is occupied by social media – Facebook, YouTube, Twitter, and whatever comes next. Who really knows all their Facebook friends or Twitter followers, even though we have some control over whom we "friend" or "follow"? While social media are in good measure still social, many news organizations have grasped the potential to attract viewers and readers through a social media presence. News consumers are encouraged to "follow us on Facebook" or to "tweet us."

Where the news media go, there are eyeballs. Where there are eyeballs, there are advertisers.

West Wing Report is an entrepreneurial one-man venture into the journalistic use of social media. As of September 2012, Paul Brandus's @westwingreport had 137,870 Twitter followers. Brandus, a seasoned Washington and foreign correspondent, tweets extensively about President Obama's activity, White House events, and presidential history. Periodically, a sponsored tweet arrives:

> WestWingReportWest Wing Report *Sponsor* Time to enjoy some Batdorf & Bronson Coffee. Handcrafted single origin coffees & blends. **@BatdorfCoffee**http://bit.ly/mXbDHd

Brandus tweeted, of course, that WWR's sponsorship policy has three essential points: (1) sponsors are clearly identified; (2) no sponsors are related to issues WWR tweets about; (3) sponsors have no editorial say (Brandus 2012). "I wanted to make sure there is a clear line between content and ads," he explained. While WWR does not mix ads and content in a single tweet, both are similarly formatted.

West Wing Report's online site is more solicitous. Six boxes on the site offer "Your ad here." The site's one item of product placement is forgivable: "You don't have to be a model to look great in a WWR t-shirt. Get yours today – at the WWR store!" (Café Press, n.d.). Self-promotion, we might be willing to concede, is well-placed PR, not ill-placed advertising. The problem is not tooting our own horns, but tooting someone else's in a way that can lead to a conflict in the news environment.

Back to Stephen Colbert. "I always assume that anything that could be for sale probably is," he told the *Times* (McGrath 2012).

In the news business, as many of us have said, the most we have to lose is our integrity and reputation. Why add even a measure of suspicion? It's never a good idea.

References

ASME (American Society of Magazine Editors) (2011). ASME guidelines for editors and publishers. *American Society of Magazine Editors*. At http://www.magazine.org/asme/editorial-guidelines, accessed Mar. 26, 2013.

Bauder, D. (2009). MSNBC, Starbucks in sponsorship deal. *Huffington Post* (June 1). At http://www.huffingtonpost.com/huff-wires/20090601/us-tv-msnbc-starbucks/, accessed Apr. 4, 2013.

Brandus, P. (2012). Interview by phone, email, and Twitter. West Wing Reports @WestWingReport (Jan. 5).

Cafe Press (n.d.). West Wing Report. At http://www.cafepress.com/westwingreport1, accessed Mar. 26, 2013.

CPSC (2011). Video news release guide. United States Consumer Product Safety Commission At http://www.cpsc.gov/en/Business–Manufacturing/Recall-Guidance/Video-News-Release-Guide/, accessed Mar. 26, 2013.

Farhi, P. (2011). Despite law against it, stealth commercials frequently masquerade as TV news. *Washington Post* (Dec. 6). At http://www.washingtonpost.com/lifestyle/style/despite-law-against-it-stealth-commercials-frequently-masquerade-as-tv-news/2011/12/05/gIQANXaxaO_story.html, accessed Mar. 26, 2013.

FCC (Federal Communications Commission) (2011). The policy and regulatory landscape. Federal Communications Commission. At http://transition.fcc.gov/osp/inc-report/INoC-26-Broadcast.pdf, accessed Mar. 26, 2013.

FEC (Federal Election Commission) (2011). Advisory opinion 2011-11. At http://colbert-superpac.com/advisory/Advisory-Opinion.pdf, accessed Mar. 26, 2013.

Hiltzik, M. A. and Hofmeister, S. (1999). Times publisher apologizes for Staples Center deal. *Los AngelesTimes* (Oct. 28). At http://articles.latimes.com/1999/oct/28/business/fi-26983, accessed Mar. 26, 2013.

McGrath, C. (2012). How many Stephen Colberts are there? *New York Times Magazine* (Jan. 4). At http://www.nytimes.com/2012/01/08/magazine/stephen-colbert.html?pagewanted=all, accessed Mar. 26, 2013.

O'Dell, R. (2011). Email exchange with general manager, WLTX, Columbia, SC (Nov. 14).

Ofcom (2011). Product placement logo to be shown on TV screens. *Ofcom* (Sept. 25). At http://media.ofcom.org.uk/2011/02/14/product-placement-logo-to-be-shown-on-tv-screens/, accessed Mar. 26, 2013.

PR Watch (2006). Still not the news: Stations overwhelmingly fail to disclose VNRs. The Center for Media and Democracy's PR Watch (Nov. 3). At http://www.prwatch.org/fakenews2/execsummary, accessed Mar. 26, 2013.

Reporter on Smoking and Health (1963). Ed Murrow – victim of smokers cancer. *Reporter on Smoking and Health* 1(4) (Oct.–Nov.).*Tobacco.org*. At http://archive.tobacco.org/Documents/reporter4.html, accessed Mar. 26, 2013.

Tedesco, K. (2012). Phone interview with executive communications director, CBS News, New York (Feb. 6).

Telegraph (2011). Nescafe coffee machine on This Morning is first product placement on TV. *Telegraph* (Feb. 28). At http://www.telegraph.co.uk/culture/tvandradio/8350382/Nescafe-coffee-machine-on-This-Morning-is-first-product-placement-on-TV.html, accessed Mar. 26, 2013.

Todd, D. (2011). Phone interview with general manager, WIS, Columbia, SC (Nov. 14).

Tucker, B. (2011). Email exchange with interim general manager, WACH, Columbia, SC (Nov. 17).

US Supreme Court (2010). Citizens United v. Federal Election Commission (no. 08-205). At http://www.law.cornell.edu/supct/html/08-205.ZS.html, accessed Mar. 26, 2013.

Virzi, A. M. (2010). Advertising vs. editorial: Can this marriage be saved? *ClickZ* (Mar. 19). At http://www.clickz.com/clickz/column/1692908/advertising-vs-editorial-can-this-marriage-be-saved, accessed Mar. 26, 2013.

13

Advergames

*I like video games, I like tech,
I like being positive.*

Jimmy Falon

One of the challenges for those working in advertising is to uncover "new frontiers" – new places to put ads that a previously untapped market can see, contemplate, and possibly be influenced by. "Advergames" is potentially one of those new markets. Advergames are games that are created by advertisers to get you to interact with a product (or information about the product) in a fun (and sometimes informative) way. The concept has a lot of potential. No one forces you to play, so if you do choose to play, you're already in the mood to like the product. These games can be fun – and maybe even a learning experience.

From a mass communications perspective, the basic idea behind an advergame is that if you play the game for a long time, it means you're connected to the product for a long time, which means (theoretically) that you have connected to the product, and ultimately, will be more likely to buy the product. It's classic involvement theory (the longer I play, or touch, or think about the product, the higher the chance that I will buy the product).

Advertising and Society: An Introduction, Second Edition. Edited by Carol J. Pardun.
© 2014 John Wiley & Sons, Inc. Published 2014 by John Wiley & Sons, Inc.

However, the theory of cognitive dissonance could also be at work here. Here's how this theory works. You've just spent an hour of your life playing a silly game. What a waste of time! Because you've wasted time, you experience cognitive dissonance. (We don't like to waste time.) The theory argues that we will want to get rid of the dissonance. There are a couple of ways to do it. One is to decide that the game was a tremendous learning experience, so it wasn't a waste of time at all. Another is to think that the product that you just spent so much time interacting with is actually a great product and playing this game has helped you learn more about what a great product this is. Either of these reasons is good enough for advertisers to consider incorporating advergames into their advertising strategies.

The authors of these essays help explain how advergames are used as advertising strategies. Adrienne Holz Ivory and James Ivory and focus on children and food advertising – a tremendously huge market for this advertising strategy. Their argument about the danger of this strategy focuses in large part on the advertisers' insistence on reaching this vulnerable market. Kevin Wise and Saleem Alhabash, however, take a different approach, arguing that there is a much larger market that can rightfully be tapped for an advergame advertising strategy. Which argument makes the most sense? *You decide.*

Ideas to Get You Thinking . . .

1   Pick a favorite product (such as your favorite beverage or snack food) and go the company's website and see if you can find an advergame. If you do, play it for a while and record your thoughts and ideas as you progress through the game. What did you learn?

2   Find an advergame for a product you have never used. What kind of experience did you have? Do you think it was impacted by your knowledge (or lack of knowledge) of the product?

3   Spend an hour trawling the Web, looking for advergames. What kind of success did you have? Did you notice any particular kinds of products that tended to use advergames more than others?

4   Talk to some people who have used advergames. If possible, try to find people from a number of different age groups (e.g. your parents, younger brothers and sisters, friends of friends). What have you discovered? Is there an age group that seems to be most appropriate for advergames? Why, or why not?

Other Topics to Debate

1   The mere act of playing the advergame makes it inappropriate as an ethical advertising strategy.

2   Advergames should not be considered advertising at all. It is something else
    entirely.
3   You should have to be at least 18 to play an advergame.
4   As long as advergames are labeled as such, all advertisers should be free to
    use them, regardless of the audience they are trying to reach or the product
    they are trying to promote.

If You'd Like to Know More . . .

Bandura, A. and McClelland, D. C. (1977). *Social learning theory*. Prentice Hall.
Cummings, W. H. and Venkatesan, M. M. (1976). Cognitive dissonance and consumer
    behavior: A review of the evidence. *Journal of Marketing Research (JMR)* 13(3):
    303–308.
Lee, K. M., Jeong, E. J., and Ryu, S. (2011). Computer games and self-efficacy: Effects of
    game experience on various types of self-efficacies. Paper presented at the annual
    meeting of the International Communication Association, May 25.
Sweeney, J. C., Hausknecht, D., and Soutar, G. N. (2000). Cognitive dissonance after
    purchase: A multidimensional scale. *Psychology & Marketing* 17(5): 369–385.

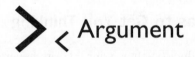

Argument

Food and beverage advergames are playing with children's health

Adrienne Holz Ivory and James D. Ivory

Virginia Tech, USA

Advergames have emerged as an effective tool in advertisers' constant endeavor
to provide potential consumers with as much positive exposure to their products
and brands as possible. An advergame has been described as "a brand-rich environment that merges a video game (usually online) with advertising" (Culp
et al. 2010: 197). In short, advergames are video games designed with the central
purpose of delivering advertising messages to their players (Moore 2006). In the
years since the term "advergame" was coined in 2000 (Culp et al. 2010), the use
of advergames to promote brands and products has become a common practice.
Advertisers spend hundreds of millions of dollars on advergames (Lee et al. 2009;
Harris et al. 2012).

While it may be tempting to see advergames as an innocuous way for advertisers to engage consumers with a fun and harmless diversion, a more sinister side of advergames becomes apparent when we consider that they are often used as an effective method of marketing unhealthy food and drink to children. While much has been made of the possibility that violent video games are a blight on the well-being of our society (see Anderson et al. 2010), it is very likely that food and drink advergames have a much greater tangible negative impact on the public good because they promote unhealthy food and beverage products. In this brief essay, we discuss the frequency and large audiences of food and drink advergames, provide some background about growing obesity rates and poor diets among children, and explain how these advergames and other food and drink advertising can negatively affect children's dietary choices and health.

The Prevalence and Reach of Food Advergames

Of all the industries in the United States that employ advergames to pitch brands and products to players, perhaps none makes more use of advergames than the food and beverage industry. Content analyses of food and beverage websites have identified several hundred online advergames promoting well-known food and beverage brands and products (Moore 2006), with advergames included as a feature on about four in five food-related websites advertised on children's television networks in the United States (Culp et al. 2010). These advergames appear to be effective in attracting young audiences to their host sites. More than two million children and adolescents visit food company sites with advergames each month, with some youth spending up to an hour on a single visit to an advergame site. Children and adolescents also visit food company sites with advergames more often and for longer periods of time compared to food company sites not featuring advergames (Harris et al. 2012). Unfortunately, most of the food and drink promoted by these advergames are unhealthy foods like candy, fast food, carbonated drinks, and salty snacks, and very few food-related sites featuring advergames include information about nutrition (Lee et al. 2009; Harris et al. 2012).

Unhealthy Diets and Obesity among Youth

The frequent use of advergames to promote unhealthy food comes at a time when childhood obesity is already at epidemic proportions. By 2010, 16.9 percent of US children and adolescents were obese (Ogden et al. 2012), and 31.8 percent were overweight or obese. (Obese and overweight statuses are currently often defined using charts of body mass index for age by sex from the Centers for Disease Control, with scores between the 85th and 95th percentile classified as overweight and scores above the 95th percentile classified as obese.) Childhood obesity is not just a problem in the United States either. By 2010, 6.7 percent of youth worldwide were overweight or obese, up from 4.2 percent in 1990, and estimates predict that as many as 9.1 percent of children worldwide may be overweight or obese by 2020 (de Onis et al. 2010).

Consumption of unhealthy fast food and snacks with high amounts of sugar, salt, and fats and low nutritional value is a contributor to the increased prevalence of overweight and obese youth. A 2004 study of more than 6,000 US children between the ages of 4 and 19 found that 30.3 percent ate fast food on a typical day (Bowman et al. 2004). Such high rates of poor-quality food consumption among youth are troubling, as research has consistently found that youth who eat fast food and drink sugar-sweetened drinks more often are more likely to be heavier, eat more calories, and have poorer diets (Ludwig et al. 2001; Bowman et al. 2004; Brownell 2004; Taveras et al. 2005).

While unhealthy food habits are contributing to a rise in obesity rates among youth, do advergames promoting unhealthy food and drink contribute to the problem, or are children's dietary choices unrelated to their exposure to casual video games and the products they feature? Before we even consider the negative effects of advergames on children's diets and health specifically, we can find insight about the effects of advergames in the vast body of literature on the negative influence that food advertising in general has on children's eating habits.

Effects of Food Advertising on Children's Diet and Health

After decades of research, our understanding of how much we are influenced by media content is still far from complete. Although many agree that media can sometimes influence our perceptions and behavior, particularly when used heavily (see Bryant and Oliver 2009), most media effects are far from uniform and vary widely depending on a number of conditions related to a message's content, source, recipient, and context (see McLeod and Reeves 1980; McLeod et al. 1991). One media effects area that has been widely documented as both powerful and relatively uniform, though, is the effects of food and drink advertising on children's dietary attitudes and behaviors.

Children are bombarded with a barrage of food advertising on television. Of the thousands of television ads children are exposed to a year, the most common product type advertised is food and drink (Gantz et al. 2007), and food and drink advertisements are even more common during children's programming (Desrochers and Holt 2007). These food advertisements commonly associate their products with participation in athletic activity, having fun, being cool, and being happy (Folta et al. 2006), even though the majority of food and drink television advertisements targeting children are for products that are high in calories, saturated fat, sugar, or sodium and low in nutritional value, and should not be part of a regular diet (Stitt and Kunkel 2008; Powell et al. 2011).

Perhaps unsurprisingly, all of that advertising for unhealthy food on television has been found to influence its viewers, particularly children who may have limited ability to recognize and understand the advertisements' commercial and persuasive intent (Carter et al. 2011). Television viewing in general has been found to be associated with junk food consumption and greater body mass index in children (Janssen et al. 2005; Livingstone 2006; Dixon et al. 2007; Brown et al. 2011). While it is possible that television viewing influences diet and weight simply because it is a sedentary activity which is also conducive to eating and snacking while watching and not because of the food commonly advertised on television, other research has more specifically implicated food and drink advertising as a culprit for viewers' poor eating choices and health.

In one such example (Gorn and Goldberg 1982), children at a summer camp who were exposed to candy advertisements over a two-week period were more likely to select candy over fruit as snacks compared to children exposed to advertisements for fruit, nutritional public service announcements, or no ads at all. In another study (Halford et al. 2004), children shown food advertisements by researchers ate significantly more after exposure to the advertisements than children who were shown advertisements for products other than food. Advertising has been found to influence selection of specific unhealthy products, as in a study (Auty and Lewis 2004) where children who were shown a movie scene with a product placement for a particular brand of soda were more likely to subsequently select that brand of soda over another compared to children who were shown the same scene without the product placement. The effects of food advertising on product selection may also be more powerful than other influences, as evidenced by a study (Ferguson et al. 2012) which found that when children were shown programs with ads for either French fries or apple snacks from a fast food chain, the majority in each group chose a coupon for whichever product they were shown regardless of whether a parent participating in the study encouraged the children to select the healthy product or not. In other words, the advertisement shown had more influence than parental encouragement on the children's choices of healthy or unhealthy food products.

The effects of food advertising on eating choices are not limited to selection of products, though. Another series of studies (Harris et al. 2009) found that both children and adults exposed to television featuring food advertisements ate greater amounts of food made available to them while viewing compared to others who were exposed to television featuring advertisements for products other than food. The effects of food advertising on eating in that series of studies occurred even though the food made available to the research participants did not include the products advertised in the programs, suggesting that food advertising can have an immediate influence on automatic eating behaviors as well as attitudes toward advertised products and brands. Based on the broad range of research evidence suggesting that exposure to food advertising on television contributes to unhealthy eating and obesity among children, mathematical simulations and expert panels have suggested that anywhere from one to three of every seven obese children in the United States might not have become obese if there were no advertising for unhealthy food on television (Veerman et al. 2009).

Effects of Food Advergames on Children's Dietary Choices

The documented effects of food and drink advertising on television on children's health may alone be enough evidence to indicate that advergames are also harmful simply because they are also a form of food and drink advertising. Beyond the known effects of advertising in general on children's food choices, some research has examined effects of food advergames in particular on children's eating preferences. In one study (Mallinckrodt and Mizerski 2007), children who played an advergame sponsored by a sugary cold cereal brand were more likely to express a preference for the brand over both other cereals and other foods in general, compared to a control group who did not play the advergame. While the majority of children who played the advergame recognized that its intent was to encourage sales of the promoted cold cereal brand, knowledge of this promotional intent did not influence the effects that the advergame had on the children's preference for the advertised brand.

In another study (Harris et al. 2011), children were assigned to play either two advergames for unhealthy food, two advergames for healthy food, or two advergames unrelated to food. When children were offered healthy and unhealthy foods in a subsequent snack break, children who had played the healthy advergames were more likely to eat more healthy food, and children who had played the unhealthy advergames were more likely to eat more unhealthy food. The effect of unhealthy advergames on the amount of unhealthy food eaten was also slightly stronger for children who had played advergames before the study, suggesting that the effects of advergames may grow with additional exposure. Similar studies comparing responses to versions of an advergame manipulated to promote either healthy or unhealthy food within the game have found that the type of food promoted in the game can influence children's subsequent food preferences and choices (Pempek and Calvert 2009; Dias and Agante 2011).

These results, then, indicate that advergames can have similar effects on dietary preferences and behavior as have been observed with television advertising. While some specific long-term effects of advergames on obesity and health are not yet known, the observed parallels between effects of food advergames and other food advertising on children's eating preferences and behavior suggest that food advergames represent a similar threat to children's health as other food advertising.

It is also possible that beyond serving as just another form of harmful food and drink advertising, food advergames may have the potential for even more negative effects than food advertising on television because of the online context in which they are played. While television advertising on children's programming is typically accompanied by messages indicating to children that the program is being interrupted for advertising, the majority of advergame sites have no such indicators of advertising content (Moore 2006). Therefore, the presence of advertising content on an advergame site may be less apparent than with television advertising, possibly limiting children's awareness and processing of advergame content as persuasive commercial messages. Additionally, the cognitive effort and attention children expend playing an advergame may limit the resources they dedicate to critical processing of advergames' persuasive messages, and the entertaining experience advergames can provide may lead children to develop pleasant associations with the advertised product in their minds (Moore and Rideout 2007). Lastly, advergames may simply encourage children to spend more time using them compared to brief television advertisements, extending the amount of time children are exposed to their promotional messages. It is important to note, though, that these arguments for why food advergames may have stronger effects than food advertising on television are speculative and have not yet been supported by research; more study is needed to compare the effects of these two advertising formats, but in the meantime there is plenty of cause for concern about advergames even if their effects on children are not stronger than the troubling effects of television advertising that have already been observed.

Conclusions

Much research has explored the potential effects of video games, particularly the effects of violence in video games on aggression in their users. While the dominant view among many prominent social scientists in the past decade has been that video games can increase aggressive responses among users (Anderson and Bushman 2001; Anderson et al. 2010), a growing body of recent research has challenged that view (Ferguson 2007, 2010). In the meantime, the body of literature indicating powerful negative health effects of food and drink advergames (and other food and drink advertising) on children's health suggests that the most tangible and immediate harms caused by video games on the health of our children are not those of violent games, but of advergames promoting terrible dietary practices.

One piece of good news is that like other forms of advertising, advergames can be used to promote healthy choices as well as unhealthy choices. Just as advertising for unhealthy food can influence unhealthy dietary choices, advertising healthy food can increase healthy eating decisions. Studies have found that advertising healthy food can cause children to have more positive attitudes toward nutritious eating, in the form of both television advertisements (Dixon et al. 2007; Ferguson et al. 2012) and advergames (Pempek and Calvert 2009; Dias and Agante 2011; Harris et al. 2011). Also, research indicates that the addition of "ad breaks" to advergames in order to distinguish the game content from promotional material can reduce children's memory of and preference for the brands promoted by the advergames (An and Stern 2011). Perhaps we will see an increase in the number of advergames promoting healthy food and drink, and an increase in responsible practices, such as "ad breaks" when advergames are implemented to promote unhealthy products. In the meantime, children, parents, teachers, advertisers, and regulators should remember that whatever form it takes, advertising of unhealthy food and beverages to children is never something to play around with.

References

An, S. and Stern, S. (2011). Mitigating the effects of advergames on children: Do advertising breaks work? *Journal of Advertising* 40: 43–56. doi:10.2753/JOA0091–3367400103

Anderson, C. A. and Bushman, B. J. (2001). Effects of violent video games on aggressive behavior, aggressive cognition, aggressive affect, physiological arousal, and prosocial behavior: A meta-analytic review of the scientific literature. *Psychological Science* 12: 353–359. doi:10.1111/1467-9280.00366

Anderson, C. A., Shibuya, A., Ihori, N., Bushman, B. J., Sakamoto, A., et al. (2010). Violent video game effects on aggression, empathy, and prosocial behavior in Eastern and Western countries: A meta-analytic review. *Psychological Bulletin* 136: 151–173. doi:10.1037/a0018251

Auty, S. and Lewis, C. (2004). Exploring children's choice: The reminder effect of product placement. *Psychology and Marketing* 21: 697–713. doi:10.1002/mar.20025

Bowman, S. A., Gortmaker, S. L., Ebbeling, C. B., Pereira, M. A., and Ludwig, D. S. (2004). Effects of fast-food consumption on energy intake and diet quality among children in a national household survey. *Pediatrics* 113: 112–118.

Brown, J. E., Nicholson, J. M., Broom, D. H., and Bittman, M. (2011). Television viewing by school-age children: Associations with physical activity, snack food consumption and unhealthy weight. *Social Indicators Research* 101: 221–225. doi:10.1007/s11205-010-9656-x

Brownell, K. D. (2004). Fast food and obesity in children. *Pediatrics* 113: 132.

Bryant, J. and Oliver, M. B. (eds.) (2009). *Media effects: Advances in theory and research*, 3rd edn. New York: Routledge.

Carter, O. B., Patterson, R. J., Ewing, M. T., and Roberts, C. M. (2011). Children's understanding of the selling versus persuasive intent of junk food advertising: Implications for regulation. *Social Science and Medicine* 72: 962–968. doi:10.1016/j.socscimed.2011.01.018

Culp, J., Bell, R. A., and Cassady, D. (2010). Characteristics of food industry web sites and "advergames" targeting children. *Journal of Nutrition Education and Behavior* 42: 197–201. doi:10.1016/j.jneb.2009.07.008

de Onis, M., Blössner, M., and Borghi, E. (2010). Global prevalence and trends of overweight and obesity among preschool children. *American Journal of Clinical Nutrition* 92: 1257–1264. doi:10.3945/ajcn.2010.29786

Desrochers, D. M. and Holt, D. J. (2007). Children's exposure to television advertising: Implications of childhood obesity. *Journal of Public Policy and Marketing* 26: 182–201. doi:10.1509/jppm.26.2.182

Dias, M. and Agante, L. (2011). Can advergames boost children's healthier eating habits? A comparison between healthy and nonhealthy food. *Journal of Consumer Behavior* 10: 152–160. doi:10.1002/cb.359

Dixon, H. G., Scully, M. L., Wakefield, M. A., White, V. M., and Crawford, D. A. (2007). The effects of television advertisements for junk food versus nutritious food on children's food attitudes and preferences. *Social Science and Medicine* 65: 1311–1323. doi:10.1016/j.socscimed.2007.05.011

Ferguson, C. J. (2007). The good, the bad, and ugly? The meta-analytic review of positive and negative effects of violent video games. *Psychiatric Quarterly* 78: 309–316. doi:10.1007/s11126-007-9056-9059

Ferguson, C. J. (2010). Blazing angels or resident evil? Can violent video games be a force for good? *Review of General Psychology* 14(2): 68–81. doi:10.1037/a0018941

Ferguson, C. J., Muñoz, M. E., and Medrano, M. R. (2012). Advertising influences on young children's food choices and parental influence. *Journal of Pediatrics* 160: 452–455. doi:10.1016/j.jpeds.2011.08.023

Folta, S. C., Goldberg, J. P., Economos, C., Bell, R., and Meltzer, R. (2006). Food advertising targeted at school-age children: A content analysis. *Journal of Nutrition Education and Behavior* 38: 244–248. doi:10.1016/j.jneb.2006.04.146

Gantz, W., Schwartz, N., Angelini, J. R., and Rideout, V. (2007). *Food for thought: Television food advertising to children in the United States.* Menlo Park, CA: Kaiser Family Foundation.

Gorn, G. J. and Goldberg, M. E. (1982). Behavioral evidence of the effects of televised food messages on children. *Journal of Consumer Research* 9: 200–205. doi: 10.1086/208913

Halford, J. C. G., Gillespie, J., Brown, V., Pontin, E. E., and Dovey, T. M. (2004). Effect of television advertisements for foods on food consumption in children. *Appetite* 42: 221–225. doi:10.1016/j.appet.2003.11.006

Harris, J. L., Bargh, J. A., and Brownell, K. D. (2009). Priming effects of television advertising on eating behavior. *Health Psychology* 28: 404–413. doi:10.1037/a0014399

Harris, J. L., Speers, S. E., Schwartz, M. B., and Brownell, K. D. (2012). U.S. food company branded advergames on the Internet: Children's exposure and effects on snack consumption. *Journal of Children and Media* 6: 51–68. doi:10.1080/17482798.2011. 633405

Janssen, I., Katzmarzyk, P. T., Boyce, W. F., Vereecken, C., Mulvihill, C., et al. (2005). Comparison of overweight and obesity prevalence in school-aged youth from 34 countries and their relationships with physical activity and dietary patterns. *Obesity Reviews* 6: 123–132. doi:10.1111/j.1467–789X.2005.00176.x

Lee, M., Choi, Y., Quilliam, E. T., and Cole, R. T. (2009). Playing with food: Content analysis of food advergames. *Journal of Consumer Affairs* 43: 129–154. doi:DOI:10.1111/ j.1745-6606.2008.01130.x

Livingstone, S. (2006). Does TV advertising make children fat? *Public Policy Research* 13: 54–61. doi:10.1111/j.1070-3535.2006.00421.x

Ludwig, D. S., Peterson, K. E., and Gortmaker, S. L. (2001). Relationship between consumption of sugar-sweetened drinks and childhood obesity: A prospective, observational analysis. *Lancet* 357: 505–508. doi:10.1016/S0140-6736(00)04041-1

Mallinckrodt, V. and Mizerski, D. (2007). The effects of playing an advergame on young children's perceptions, preferences, and requests. *Journal of Advertising* 36: 87–100. doi:10.2753/JOA0091-3367360206

McLeod, J. M. and Reeves, B. (1980). On the nature of mass media effects. In S. B. Withey and R. P. Ables (eds.), *Television and social behavior: Beyond violence and children.* Hillsdale, NJ: Lawrence Erlbaum, pp. 17–54.

McLeod, J. M., Kosicki, G. M., and Pan, Z. (1991). On understanding and misunderstanding media effects. In J. Curran and M. Gurevitch (eds.), *Mass media and society.* New York: Edward Arnold, pp. 235–266.

Moore, E. S. (2006). *It's child's play: Advergaming and the online marketing of food to children*. Menlo Park, CA: Kaiser Family Foundation. At http://www.kff.org/entmedia/upload/7536.pdf, accessed Mar. 27, 2013.

Moore, E. S. and Rideout, V. J. (2007). The online marketing of food to children: Is it just fun and games? *Journal of Public Policy and Marketing* 26: 202–220. doi:10.1509/jppm.26.2.202

Ogden, C. L., Carroll, M. D., Kit, B. K., and Flegal, K. M. (2012). Prevalence of obesity and trends in body mass index among US children and adolescents, 1999–2010. *Journal of the American Medical Association* 307(5): 483–490. doi:10.1001/jama.2012.40

Pempek, T. A. and Calvert, S. L. (2009). Tipping the balance: Use of advergames to promote consumption of nutritious foods and beverages by low-income African American children. *Archives of Pediatrics & Adolescent Medicine* 163: 633–637. doi:10.1001/archpediatrics.2009.71

Powell, L. M., Schermbeck, R. M., Szczypka, G., Chaloupka, F. J., and Braunschweig, C. L. (2011). Trends in the nutritional content of television food advertisements seen by children in the United States. *Archives of Pediatrics & Adolescent Medicine* 165: 1078–1086. doi:10.1001/archpediatrics.2011.131

Stitt, C. and Kunkel, D. (2008). Food advertising during children's television programming on broadcast and cable channels. *Health Communication* 23: 573–584. doi:10.1080/10410230802465258

Taveras, E. M., Berkey, C. S., Rifas-Shiman, S. L., Ludwig, D. S., Rockett, H. R. H., et al. (2005). Association of consumption of fried food away from home with body mass index and diet quality in older children and adolescents. *Pediatrics* 116: e518–e524. doi:10.1542/peds.2004–2732

Veerman, J. L., Van Beeck, E. F., Barendredgt, J. J., and Mackenbach, J. P. (2009). By how much would limiting TV food advertising reduce childhood obesity? *European Journal of Public Health* 19: 365–369. doi:10.1093/eurpub/ckp039

Counterargument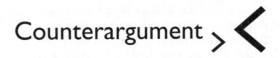

Evidence of advergame effectiveness

Kevin Wise and Saleem Alhabash

Michigan State University, USA; University of Missouri, USA

Overview

Is the advergame an excellent advertising strategy? Though we might not go so far as to say it is excellent, we feel the research suggests that the advergame is an effective advertising strategy. We begin this essay by providing an overview of persuasive gaming in general and advergaming in particular. We then provide brief support for the assertion of advergame effectiveness, propose some reasons for this effectiveness, and identify some features that appear to moderate this effectiveness. We also identify some limitations of the advergame's effectiveness (or at least the evidence thereof) that stand in the way of a conclusion of its excellence. We conclude by discussing whether we think the advergame is an appropriate strategy given its potential for affecting change that might not be in the best interests of certain users (e.g., children). We should state up front that we generally take an agnostic view of this question of societal good, though our conclusion also identifies research demonstrating possible positive outcomes of advergames.

We would like to preface the main body of this essay by stating up front that this is meant to be neither a comprehensive literature review nor a meta-analysis of the existing literature. We are confident that any assertions we make are supported by a preponderance of the existing data, but we also acknowledge that we've been selective in citing only exemplars of these assertions.

What Is Persuasive Gaming/Advergaming?

An advergame is a unique type of video game that falls into a broader, growing category of persuasive games. A persuasive game is simply a game specifically designed to change players' attitudes or encourage their behavior. The advergame is a persuasive game with a branded component: the object of the desired attitude change or behavior is a consumer brand or product. Harris and colleagues defined advergames as "fun, interactive games and other user-directed activities featuring individual products or brands" (Harrison et al. 2011: 4). While this definition gives a structural description of what advergames are, it does not tell what, functionally, advergames do. Advergames, as we see them, are yet another form of presenting a persuasive message, part of the various formats (print, audio, visual, or online), contexts (indoor, outdoor, or mobile), and modalities (newspaper, television, radio, website, etc.). At their core, advergames combine entertainment with a persuasive intent by an individual, a company, or an organization. Similar to a television ad, an advergame is intended to sell you something: a certain product, service, idea, social cause, or political opinion, among others. However, an advergame is different from a traditional TV ad in the sense that the consumer is part of the persuasion process. The power of the game lies in the users' high interactivity with the game, the characters, the gaming environment, and the action and decision taken in the game. Bogost (2007) gives a conceptual framework for understanding persuasive games, where advergames are considered one example. Before discussing the characteristics and effects of persuasive games, it is important to discuss characteristics of video game players. This is especially important owing to the stereotypic nature of how we perceive and visualize video gamers.

Who Plays Games?

The dominant stereotype of a video gamer is a young male, either unemployed or of low income, who plays video games for an excessive amount of time, and has "weird" tendencies, as well as high potential for "violent behavior" as a result of all the violent video games he plays (Reeves and Read 2009). Video games are perceived as a distraction, at best, and a substitution for other media uses and social activities, as well as vital life duties (e.g., homework) that a person could engage in if he or she had not been playing a lot of video games. Video games are also perceived as an extremely powerful medium, somewhat reflective of the traditional and often refuted approach for the powerful effects of media: the magic bullet effect. This negative connotation stems from associations of violent incidents, such as the Columbine High School and Virginia Tech shootings, where the perpetrators of violent acts have been reported by mainstream media as avid players of violent video games (Williams 2003; Egenfeldt-Nielsen et al. 2008; Williams et al. 2008; Lee et al. 2009; Reeves and Read 2009).

While violent video games tend to receive the most publicity, only a fourth of video games are classified as violent (Remondini 2010). It is true that there is a large infiltration of video games among the younger generation. The Pew Internet and American Life Projects reports that 97 percent of teenagers (12–17 years old), 81 percent of college-age young adults, and over half (53%) of adults 18–49 years old report playing video games (Lenhart et al. 2008). While these are impressive numbers, they do not tell the whole story. Pew reports that the average age of video gamers is around 35 years, and four in every 10 gamers are females, who spend significantly more time playing games than males (Lenhart et al. 2008; Williams et al. 2008). Research data reported by Reeves and Read (2009) illustrate that the yearly income of the regular video gamer is $20,000 higher than the average annual income in the United States. These statistics suggest both diversity and relative affluence among the gaming community, contrary to many stereotypes. The video game population also fails to conform exclusively to a violent stereotype. Video games can be bad or good, entertaining or educational, violent or friendly. The way in which video games are used as persuasive tools is really up to the advertiser using them. We simply argue that video games have the potential to ethically persuade consumers, young and old, to change their attitudes and behavior toward an object, issue, product, brand, or person.

Persuasive Games with Good Effects

Now let's get back to exploring persuasive games. In the past few years we've witnessed the growth of video games that are not primarily created for entertainment purposes. These games have many labels: "serious games," "persuasive games," "games for social change," and "advergames" are a few such labels.

Regardless of terminology, these games share one commonality. They combine entertainment with learning and persuasive intent. In other words, these games are designed to change one's attitudes about a certain entity, be it a political issue, a social/political cause, a product, or a brand. What are the mechanisms through which these games are able to persuade us? Scholars have suggested a process called *procedural rhetoric* as one way in which we find games compelling. We briefly describe this process and how it is used to describe different kinds of games.

Bogost (2006, 2007), a scholar and game designer who was part of the team responsible for the Howard Dean for Iowa online game, came up with the idea of procedural rhetoric. A video game, according to Bogost, is designed by using a complex computer algorithm. This algorithm constitutes the procedure by which the players play the game, the rules by which the game should be played. This procedure reflects the narrative that the game designer wishes to convey to the player, hence the second part of the concept: rhetoric. Game designers utilize the computer algorithm (procedure) to convey a certain persuasive message (rhetoric); a story they want the player to go through as he or she progresses in the game from one level to another. The difference between persuasion through a video game and that mediated through any other computer-mediated environment is that in video games the narrative is rather incomplete. It purposefully includes gaps that are filled by the players themselves through actions taken and decisions made through the game-play experience. For example, players start at a similar point in any video game, but can go through different paths of interacting with the virtual environment as a result of decisions and actions they take in the game. In doing so, each player weaves in his or her own narrative through actions taken or decisions made in response to in-game events. This is what differentiates persuasive games from any other type of digital persuasion. It is the convergence of narratives that leads to self-persuasion. The player is not a passive recipient of the persuasive message. Even with the existence of a persuasive intent that is procedurally embedded in the game by the designer, the player controls the actions that are taken and the way the game progresses, thus influencing the persuasive outcome. He or she becomes part and parcel of the persuasion process by determining his or her own *destiny* within the game.

Smith and Just (2009) criticize the generality with which Bogost explains what persuasive games are and how they influence players through procedural rhetoric. To them, Bogost goes too far in attempting to generalize these prepositions to all types of persuasive games. The premise of their argument is that not all games are created equal, meaning that games vary in terms of the level of self-persuasion they facilitate. The authors propose another typology for qualitatively judging the level of self-persuasion in a persuasive game.

According to Smith and Just, games vary in terms of autonomy, integration, and goal overlap. Autonomy refers to the "dialectical or argumentative potential" realized through the game (2009: 58). Games vary in terms of the *pervasiveness* of the persuasion intent, such that those that are fully autonomous provide a clear-cut persuasive message that leaves little to no space for self-deliberation on the players' side, thus leading to a passive reception of the message. On the other hand, games can be found at the other end of the continuum, where persuasion does not deal with a unique and solid preposition, but rather leaves room for the player to utilize pre-existing knowledge and attitudes in performing throughout the game, thus allowing more elastic room for deliberation and self-persuasion. Smith and Just (2009) argue that the less explicit the persuasive argument is, the more persuasive the game.

The second part of the typology, integration, deals with the "abstractness of the argument" (Smith and Just 2009: 58). In an advergaming context, the level of integration depends on how the object of persuasion – the product or the brand – is integrated in the game. Advergames vary in terms of how visible (or invisible) the product or the brand is within the game. With regards to other types of persuasive games, say a more socially or politically oriented game, the concept of integration applies to the level of persuasive object visibility within the game. However, Smith and Just (2009) do not fully succeed in providing empirical evidence as to whether or not games that are high on integration lead to greater persuasion. Hence, this question remains an empirical one that needs further investigation.

Finally, the third element in the typology deals with goal overlap. Smith and Just (2009) explain that video games can vary in terms of their persuasiveness with regards to the way the goal of the game (persuasive intent) is connected to performance and progress throughout the game. In a nutshell, this refers to the requirements for advancing from one level to another in a video game. A game with a high goal overlap pushes the player to learn the persuasive message (comprehension) as a means to advancing from the first level to the second. These are a couple of general explanations for the process through which advergames may be effective. We now move specifically to discussing evidence suggesting the effectiveness of advergames.

Are Advergames Effective?

The research evidence suggests that advergames tend to enhance short-term memory for and attitudes toward brands, products, and issues (e.g., Grigorovici and Constantin 2004; Winkler and Deal 2005; Buckner 2006; Glass 2007; Mallinck-rodt and Mizerski 2007; Wise et al. 2008; Cauberghe and De Pelsmacker 2010; Gross 2010; Hernandez and Chapa 2010; Hussein et al. 2010; Jeong et al. 2011; Peng et al. 2010; van Reijmersdal et al. 2010, 2012). Many of these studies are experiments in which advergames (or different features of advergames) are compared to traditional methods of advertising that rely on "push" strategies and lack interactivity between the message and the user. It is important to acknowledge that we don't know far more than we know about the effectiveness of advergames. Some important questions that researchers are currently addressing include: How effective are advergames? In what product areas are they most effective? Is the advergame a cost-effective advertising tactic? What are the important features of the advergame that make it effective? While the answers to these questions remain to be revealed, the current evidence supports the statement that advergames can positively affect both attitudes toward and memory for products and brands.

There is also a growing body of research exploring the effectiveness of games in promoting health-related attitudes and behaviors. This research also generally suggests that health-oriented video games have positive effects on food choices, in-game physical activity, and changing health attitudes and behaviors (Mallinck-rodt and Mizerski 2007; Peng 2008; Peng and Liu 2008; Jin 2009, 2010a, 2010b, 2011; Jin and Park 2009; Pempek and Calvert 2009; Peng et al. 2012). Mallinck-rodt and Mizerski (2007) found that while playing an advergame resulted in greater preference for the healthier cereal brand, participants did not signifi-cantly differ in judging the health value of the brand as a function of playing the advergame compared to the control group that did not play the advergame. In a series of studies, Jin and colleagues found that playing exergames resulted in greater immersion, interactivity, and in-game performance as a function of the avatars' mirroring players' actual selves or projecting their idealized self images (Jin 2009, 2010a, 2010b, 2011; Jin and Park 2009). Peng (2008) found that playing a video game resulted in greater self-efficacy to engage in healthy diet choices compared to passively observing another person's video game play. Peng and colleagues (2012) found that need satisfaction was an important factor in pre-dicting in-game performance and actual physical activity measured by energy expenditure and other measures.

Persuasive games have also been used in relation to social and political causes and issues. Our research dealing with PeaceMaker, a video game simula-tion of the Palestinian–Israeli conflict, showed that the role participants played affected their attitudes toward the larger national group (Alhabash and Wise 2012). Bogost (2006) illustrated that voters who were engaged in playing the *Howard Dean for Iowa Campaign* had more favorable views of the candidate. Overall, this evidence supports the idea that video games can cause changes in attitudes, memory, and behavior across a wide range of domains.

Why Are They Effective?

What makes advergames uniquely effective relative to other ways of advertising? We offer longer exposure period and greater brand interaction as two primary reasons for their effectiveness.

Longer Exposure Period

Most television ads last 30 seconds. Product placements are short. But an adver-game can elicit exposure that, at a minimum, is likely substantially longer than most other advertising tactics. We did a study several years ago in which participants spent five minutes playing an advergame for Orbitz. There was no indication of any sort of fatigue effect in this particular study. So one simple defense of the advergame as an effective advertising strategy is simply that it allows for greater exposure than traditional forms of advertising. Greater exposure generally leads to better brand recognition, and, assuming the exposure is viewed pleasantly, enhanced brand attitude. The importance of exposure can be seen by the use of metrics such as brand exposure duration among media planners.

Greater Brand Interaction

The basis of modern advertising is building a relationship between a message and a brand or product that resonates with a particular audience. That relationship need not always be pleasant – a great deal of advertising (e.g., health, politics) is effective by inspiring fear or anger in viewers. Regardless of the affective outcome, the ability of an advertisement to elicit a compelling mental response is imperative. Advergames facilitate the building of that relationship by providing the consumer with greater interaction with the brand. General proponents of video gaming characterize this interaction as vital. McGonigal (2011), for example, who presented some of the ideas in her book in a popular TED talk (McGonigal 2010), argues that video games can create a better world. She explains that people become the best versions of themselves when they play video games. They become more collaborative, better problem-solvers, and dedicated team players. These benefits are attributed to the high interactivity, immersion, and constant motivations to win that games offer. Video games that induce excitement, give psychological reward, and evoke cognitive and emotional experiences are bound to prepare a consumer for accepting the persuasive message disseminated in an advergame.

What Features Moderate Advergames' Effectiveness?

As we mentioned earlier, a growing body of research has tested specific features of advergames, usually in a controlled experiment, to assess how these features affect desirable outcomes like enhanced brand attitude or recognition. Some features that have emerged from this research include visual prominence of the brand (D'Andrade 2007; Peters 2008; Cauberghe and De Pelsmacker 2010), involvement of the consumer with the brand (Cauberghe and De Pelsmacker 2010), thematic congruity between the game and the brand (Wise et al 2008; Gross 2010; Okazaki and Yagüe 2012). Brand interactivity, loosely defined as the degree of brand interaction, has also been shown to effect positive outcomes (Lee et al. 2010; van Reijmersdal et al. 2010; Sukoco and Wu 2011). Somewhat related to interactivity, avatar customization has also been shown to enhance affective responses (Bailey et al. 2009). These are all conceptually simple features that would appear to be easily modified by advergame developers.

Are Advergames Safe?

The counterpoint to this article is going to focus on this position so we will not spend a great deal of time on it. We tend to take an agnostic approach and leave the normative judgments to others. Clearly, to the extent that they are effective, advergames can be used to promote unhealthy behavior. And, in fact, this is largely what they are used for, as recent reviews (Lee and Youn 2008; Lee et al. 2009) suggest that (1) food-related brands are the most common creators of advergames and (2) these games tend to promote candy/gum, breakfast cereal, soft drinks, and salty snacks–common fodder for people concerned with what kids are eating. To the extent that advergames continue to facilitate brand recognition and positive brand attitudes, they will continue to be used in this regard just as other infamous executions have (e.g., Joe Camel). On the positive side, there's no reason why advergames (and persuasive games in general) cannot be used for more positive benefits. Throughout this essay we've mentioned several examples of such games, and the research to date indicates that effect strength doesn't seem to be moderated by the positivity of the goal. In other words, early evidence suggests that gaming can be an effective platform for behaviors that most consider positive as well as negative.

To summarize: The current evidence suggests that advergames can enhance people's short-term attitudes toward and memory for products and brands. Deeper brand interaction and longer brand exposure are two elements of the advergame that may contribute to its effectiveness. As is the case with all persuasive messaging, the advergame is a tactic that can be used for good or for ill. While the advergame may help persuade children to consume more junk food, it can also be used to persuade them to eat more fruits and vegetables and to exercise. As those who develop persuasive messages continue to refine how the advergame is executed, it is up to those of us in the research community to explore how this tactic affects those who are exposed to it.

References

Alhabash, S. and Wise, K. (2012). PeaceMaker: Changing students' attitudes toward Palestinians and Israelis through videogame play. *International Journal of Communication* 6: 356–380.

Bailey, R., Wise, K., and Bolls, P. (2009). How avatar customizability affects children's arousal and subjective presence during junk food-sponsored online video games. *CyberPsychology & Behavior* 12(3): 277–283.

Bogost, I. (2006). Playing politics: Videogames for politics, activism, and advocacy. In "Command lines: The emergence of governance in global cyberspace," special issue no. 7, *First Monday* 11(9). At http://www.uic.edu/htbin/cgiwrap/bin/ojs/index.php/fm/article/view/1617/1532, accessed Mar. 27, 2013.

Bogost, I. (2007). *Persuasive games: The expressive power of videogames.* Cambridge, MA: MIT Press.

Cauberghe, V. and De Pelsmacker, P. (2010). Advergames: The impact of brand prominence and game repetition on brand responses. *Journal of Advertising* 39(1): 5–18.

D'Andrade, N. (2007). The effects of varying levels of object change on explicit and implicit memory for brand messages within advergames. Master's thesis, University of Missouri, Columbia, MO.

Deal, D. (2005). The ability of online branded games to build brand equity: An exploratory study. Paper presented at DIGRA, June 2005. Downloadable at http://summit.sfu.ca/item/194 http://summit.sfu.ca/item/194, accessed Mar. 27, 2013.

Egenfeldt-Nielsen, S., Smith, J. H., and Tosca, S. P. (2008). *Understanding video games: The essential introduction.* New York: Routledge.

Glass, Z. (2007). The effectiveness of product placement in video games. *Journal of Interactive Advertising* 8(1): 23–32.

Grigorovici, D. M. and Constantin, C. D. (2004). Experiencing interactive advertising beyond rich media: Impacts of ad type and presence on brand effectiveness in 3D gaming immersive virtual environments. *Journal of Interactive Advertising* 5(1): 22–36.

Gross, M. L. (2010). Advergames and the effects of game-product congruity. *Computers in Human Behavior* 26: 1259–1265.

Harrison, J. L., Speers, S. E., Schwartz, M. B., and Brownell, K. D. (2011). US food company branded advergames on the Internet: Children's exposure and effects on snack consumption. *Journal of Children and Media* 6(1): 51–68.

Hernandez, M. D. and Chapa, S. (2010). Adolescents, advergames and snack foods: Effects of positive affect and experience on memory and choice. *Journal of Marketing Communications* 16: 59–68.

Hussein, Z., Wahid, N. Z., and Saad, N. (2010). Evaluating telepresence experience and game players' intention to purchase product advertised in Advergame. *World Academy of Science, Engineering and Technology* 66: 1625–1630.

Jeong, E. J., Bohil, C. J., and Biocca, F. (2011). Brand logo placements in violent games: Effects of violence cues on memory and attitude through arousal and presence. *Journal of Advertising* 40(3): 59–72.

Jin, S. A. (2009). Modality effects in Second Life: The mediating role of social presence and the moderating role of product involvement. *CyberPsychology & Behavior* 12(6): 717–721.

Jin, S. A. (2010a). Does imposing a goal always improve exercise intentions in avatar-based exergames? The moderating role of interdependent self-construal on exercise intentions and self-presence. *CyberPsychology, Behavior, & Social Networking* 13(3): 335–339.

Jin, S. A. (2010b). Effects of 3D virtual haptics force feedback on brand personality perception: The mediating role of physical presence in advergames. *CyberPsychology, Behavior, & Social Networking* 13(3): 307–311.

Jin, S. A. (2011). I feel present. Therefore, I experience flow: A structural equation modeling approach flow and presence in videogames. *Journal of Broadcasting & Electronic Media* 55(1): 114–136.

Jin, S. A. and Park, N. (2009). Para social interaction with my avatar: Effects of interdependent self-construal and the mediating role of self-presence in avatar-based console game, Wii. *CyberPsychology & Behavior* 12(6): 723–727.

Lee, J., Park, H., and Wise, K. (2010). Brand interactivity and its effects on the outcomes of advergame play. Paper presented to the Advertising Division of the 94th Annual Conference of the Association for Education in Journalism and Mass Communication, Denver, CO, Aug.

Lee, M. and Youn, S. (2008). Leading national advertisers' uses of advergames. *Journal of Current Issues and Research in Advertising* 30(2): 1–13.

Lee, K. M., Peng, W., and Park, N. (2009). Effects of computer/video games and beyond. In J. Bryant and M. B. Oliver (eds.), *Media effects: Advances in theory and research.* New York: Routledge, pp. 551–566.

Lenhart, A., Kahne, J., Middaught, E., Macgill, A. R., Evans, C., and Vitak, J. (2008). *Teens, video games, and civics: Teens' gaming experiences are diverse and include significant social interaction and civic engagement.* Washington, DC: Pew Internet and American Life Project. At http://www.pewinternet.org/~/media//Files/Reports/2008/PIP_Teens_Games_and_Civics_Report_FINAL.pdf.pdf, accessed Mar. 27, 2013.

Mallinckrodt, V. and Mizerski, D. (2007). The effects of playing an advergame on young children's perceptions, preferences, and requests. *Journal of Advertising* 36(2): 87–100.

McGonigal, J. (2010). Gaming can make a better world. *TED.* At http://www.ted.com/talks/lang/en/jane_mcgonigal_gaming_can_make_a_better_world.html, accessed Mar. 27, 2013.

McGonigal, J. (2011). *Reality is broken: Why games make us better and how they can change the world.* New York: Penguin.

Okazaki, S. and Yagüe, M. J. (2012). Responses to an advergaming campaign on a mobile social networking site: An initial research report. *Computers in Human Behavior* 28: 78–86.

Pempek, T. A. and Calvert, S. L. (2009). Tipping the balance: Use of advergames to promote consumption of nutritious foods and beverages by low-income African American children. *Archives of Pediatrics & Adolescent Medicine* 163(7): 633–637.

Peng, W. (2008). The mediational role of identification in the relationship between experience mode and self-efficacy: Enactive role-playing versus passive observation. *CyberPsychology & Behavior* 11: 649–652.

Peng, W. and Liu, M. (2008). An overview of using electronic games for health purposes. In R. Ferdig (ed.), *Handbook of research on effective electronic gaming in education.* Hershey, PA: IGI Global, pp. 388–401.

Peng, W., Lee, M., and Heeter, C. (2010). The effects of a serious game on role-taking and willingness to help. *Journal of Communication* 60(4): 723–742.

Peng, W., Lin, J.-H., Pfeiffer, K., and Winn, B. (2012). Need satisfaction supportive game features as motivational determinants: An experimental study of a self-determination theory guided exergame. *Media Psychology* 15: 175–196.

Peters, S. J. (2008). Get in the game: The effects of game-product congruity and product placement proximity on game players' processing of brands embedded in advergames. Master's thesis, University of Missouri, Columbia, MO.

Reeves, B. and Read, J. L. (2009). *Total engagement: Using games and virtual worlds to change the way people work and businesses compete.* Boston: Harvard Business Press.

Remondini, C. (2010). Mafia victim families fight increasing violent, brutality in video games. *Bloomberg* (Dec. 17). At http://www.bloomberg.com/news/2010-12-16/

mafia-victim-families-complain-as-violent-video-games-increase.html, accessed Mar. 27, 2013.

Smith, J. H. and Just, S. N. (2009). Playful persuasion: The rhetorical potential of adver-games. *Nordicom Review* 30: 53–68.

Sukoco, B. M. and Wu, W.-H. (2011). The effects of advergames on consumer telepresence and attitudes: A comparison of products with search and experience attributes. *Expert Systems with Applications* 38: 7396–7406.

van Reijmersdal, E., Jansz, J., Peters, O., and Van Noort, G. (2010). The effects of interactive brand placements in online games on children's cognitive, affective, and conative brand responses. *Computers in Human Behavior* 26: 1787–1794.

van Reijmersdal, E. A., Rozendaal, E., and Buijzen, M. (2012). Effects of prominence, involvement, and persuasion knowledge on children's cognitive and affective responses to advergames. *Journal of Interactive Marketing* 26(1): 33–42.

Williams, D. (2003). The video game lightning rod: Constructions of a new media technology, 1970–2000. *Information, Communication & Society* 6(4): 523–550.

Williams, D., Yee, N., and Caplan, S. E. (2008). Who plays, how much, and why? Debunking the stereotypical gamer profile. *Journal of Computer-Mediated Communication* 13: 993–1018.

Winkler, T. and Buckner, K. (2006). Receptiveness of gamers to embedded brand messages in advergames: Attitudes towards product placement. *Journal of Interactive Advertising* 7(1): 37–46.

Wise, K., Bolls, P., Kim, H., Venkataraman, A., and Meyer, R. (2008). Enjoyment of advergames and brand attitudes: The impact of thematic relevance. *Journal of Interactive Advertising* 9(1): 27–36.

14

Advertising and Sporting Events

> *I'm tired of hearing about money, money, money, money, money. I just want to play the game, drink Pepsi, wear Reebok.*
>
> Shaquille O'Neal

Sports are more than events. The idea of "sport" permeates our everyday lives. Whether or not we consider ourselves athletic, it is clear that our society celebrates the sporting metaphor. When the pressure of work or school becomes overwhelming, our friends tell us to hang in there or get "back in the game." Many professional fields have adopted "coach" (as in "life coach") as a way to keep us competitive. Even the Bible talks sports! (e.g., "I have finished the race," 2 Timothy 4:7). Considering the prevalence of sporting references in our everyday lives, it should come as no surprise that sporting events and advertising would be closely tied together. Advertisers want to put themselves into environments that make sense to a mass audience. Sporting events fit this bill nicely. But, just as with most (if not all) aspects of advertising, the pairing of advertising and sports is loaded with all sorts of potential controversies.

The first Super Bowl game was played in 1967. The 1960s is known by most advertising historians as the golden age for advertising. Ad budgets exploded,

Advertising and Society: An Introduction, Second Edition. Edited by Carol J. Pardun.
© 2014 John Wiley & Sons, Inc. Published 2014 by John Wiley & Sons, Inc.

advertising executives were regaled as creative geniuses (think *Mad Men*), consumers had a seemingly insatiable appetite for gadgets (all of which needed creative advertising to explain the need to consumers), and the mass media were booming and on the hunt for advertisers.

Is it any surprise that the Super Bowl began in this environment? At the time of the first Super Bowl, there were only three major networks available, so there was little risk with airing the first Super Bowl game. Americans loved football and they loved television. The first game garnered an average rating of only 18.5 (which meant that close to 18.5 percent of television households were watching at least some of the game). In the 1960s, that was not spectacular. (To compare, *I Love Lucy* consistently garnered a rating of over 50 during its heyday.) However, it didn't take long for the Super Bowl to transform into a ratings bonanza. Within a few years the mass audience and football came together and the ratings skyrocketed into the 40s where they've stayed ever since. Very few opportunities exist for such a mass television audience today. For example, *The Big Bang Theory*, CBS's top-rated comedy, has a rating that typically hits around 9.5. It's no wonder, then, that advertisers have maintained such a keen interest in the Super Bowl.

But what about other sporting events? Primetime viewing of the London 2012 Summer Olympics averaged 31 million US viewers for an average rating of about 21. The 2012 Final Four basketball game scored a rating of about 12.1. While not as large as the Super Bowl, both of these sporting events are considered rating hits for their respective networks. Clearly, sporting events draw an audience. And advertisers are looking for an audience. So capitalizing on the pairing of sports and advertising seems a perfect match.

Except not everyone can be an elite athlete like those we see on TV. In fact, just about everyone will fall short of the athletic ideal we see on television. We buy Air Jordans because we think they just might help us jump a wee bit higher. If we love basketball, we love Michael Jordan (okay, I love Michael Jordan; you might love Kobe Bryant). It's that simple. Most likely we don't spend a lot of time thinking about his calorie to carb ratio.

It would be difficult for an elite tennis player to achieve success while being addicted to tobacco. It would be impossible (or nearly impossible) to maintain the necessary cardiovascular fitness while filling your lungs with smoke. Looking back 40 years, it's easy to criticize a professional women's tennis group for courting a tobacco company. Yet Virginia Slims was a welcomed sponsor to the women's tennis circuit in the 1970s. It was Virginia Slims that paved the way to bring some financial parity to women's tennis. So even a harmful advertiser ended up doing an important thing. Which is the greater good?

While the Olympics feature many professional athletes, one of the joys of the event is that it is a high-level event in which amateur athletes have the chance to shine. In colleges, nonrevenue sports are typically called "Olympic Sports" for a reason. Student athletes who participate in the Olympic Sports programs usually are not the high-profile athletes we see on football field and basketball courts. Instead, they are elite athletes who spend their lives training, often holding down jobs. Sports like rowing, cross-country running, and soccer (to name just a few) require tremendous amounts of aerobic capacity – and healthy eating is a basic starting point to this disciplined lifestyle. Yet Coca-Cola and McDonald's were two of the "mega" sponsors of the 2012 Olympic Games – neither of which promotes a healthy lifestyle.

While on the surface it might seem easy to decide which side is correct in this controversy, on a second look it quickly becomes more challenging. Neither Marie Hardin nor Erin Whiteside shies away from the controversy. Instead, they each attack it head on – and while they argue from different perspectives, together they present a larger picture of the relationship between sports and advertising. Who makes the stronger argument? *You decide.*

Ideas to Get You Thinking . . .

1   Watch two different sporting events on television. For example, you might watch golf for an hour and then switch to a football game. Make a list of all the food advertising that is included during the timeframe you watched. What did you observe? Are there differences between the sports? If so, why do you think that is?

2   Watch an hour of NASCAR and try to list all the logos you see on the race cars. Go through your list and see if there is any particular conflict in the product being associated with a car. What are your observations?

3   Look at a sporting magazine. Don't limit yourself to *Sports Illustrated*. Make a list of all the food advertising in the magazine. What patterns do you see? How many healthy foods are advertised? What conclusions can you draw?

Other Topics to Debate

1   Certain kinds of advertising may be appropriate for one kind of sporting event but not another.

2   Sports that cater to an older audience have less of a responsibility to make sure the products are appropriate to that audience.

3   Global sporting events (such as the Olympics and the Super Bowl) should have higher regulations for its advertising because of the potential stronger influence these venues can have on their audiences.

If You'd Like to Know More . . .

Bee, C. C. and Madrigal, R. (2012). It's not whether you win or lose: It's how the game is played. *Journal of Advertising* 41(1): 47–58.

Jones, S. C., Phillipson, L., and Barrie, L. (2010). "Most men drink . . . especially like when they play sports": Alcohol advertising during sporting broadcasts and the potential impact on child audiences. *Journal of Public Affairs* 10(1–2): 59–73. doi:10.1002/pa.340

Sandberg, H. (2011). Tiger talk and candy king: Marketing of unhealthy food and beverages to Swedish children. *Communications: The European Journal of Communication Research* 36(2): 217–244. doi:10.1515/COMM.2011.011

Smolianov, P. and Aiyeku, J. F. (2009). Corporate marketing objectives and evaluation measures for integrated television advertising and sports event sponsorships. *Journal of Promotion Management* 15(1–2): 74–89. doi:10.1080/10496490902901977

Taylor, C. R. (2012). The London Olympics 2012: What advertisers should watch. *International Journal of Advertising* 31(3): 459–464. doi:10.2501/IJA-31-3-459-464.

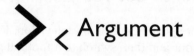 Argument

Advertising unhealthy products during sporting events makes sense as an advertising strategy

Erin Whiteside

University of Tennessee, USA

During the 2011 telecast of the Super Bowl, TiVo tracked a sample of users to examine the commercials viewers engaged most with; spots by Doritos, Snickers, and Pepsi ranked in the top five (van Riper 2011). It is not uncommon to see food and drink brands connected with sports. For instance, McDonald's has been a major corporate sponsor in the Olympic Games since 1972 and some of the most omnipresent brands during American collegiate football bowl games are related to beer – despite the fact that many of the players on the field are not of legal drinking age. The commonality among these trends is the high visibility of products associated with unhealthy habits in a venue where otherwise healthy activities (sports) are taking place.

Amateur athletics reformists have long opposed the visibility of alcohol with collegiate sports, with some success; many collegiate sports venues forbid the sale of alcohol during school-sponsored events, for instance. Recently, health advocates have raised similar concerns about the prevalence of "unhealthy" food brands in association with sporting events, arguing that the ubiquity of these ads imply that one can eat poorly and still succeed as an athlete (Barrand 2004; Cornwell 2008; Clarkson 2010). Given the rise of obesity in developed countries, health advocates are concerned that unhealthy food advertisements send the wrong message amid this growing health crisis. Addressing a health concern like obesity is a worthwhile goal, but banning companies that sell "unhealthy" products like fast food, soda, alcohol, or tobacco may do little to curb the problem at which such a ban is targeted. Assumptions underpinning these bans imply that sports are unequivocally healthy and that related diseases such as obesity or alcoholism are solely the function of faulty individual choices that reflect one's weak self control. Further, by classifying brands into "healthy" and "unhealthy" categories, sports organizations would be offering lucrative sponsorship and advertising opportunities to companies that may offer "healthy" products, but fail society in other ways that may be more far reaching. In this essay I review these arguments, and then conclude by suggesting a more complex measure for assessing a company's social worth.

Questioning the Assumptions Underpinning an "Unhealthy" Products Ban

There is no question that the United States and other Western developed countries are facing an obesity crisis. In the United States alone, a 2011 report from the Trust for America's Health and the Robert Wood Johnson Foundation showed that obesity rates in 16 states has risen in the previous year and not fallen in any one state, despite ongoing efforts from government and private sector groups to curb this epidemic. In response, health advocates have suggested banning advertising and sponsorship related to unhealthy food products in sports venues (Barrand 2004; Cornwell 2008; Clarkson, J. 2010); the efforts follow similar proposed bans in response to smoking and alcohol abuse. Advocates of the ban say that children who see those advertisements are particularly susceptible to developing unhealthy habits through the association of, say, fast food with football.

The logic of banning sponsorship and other forms of advertising from fast food, soda, and other "unhealthy" products in forums where "healthy" activities (sports) take place is grounded in two main assumptions: (1) the implication that obesity is an individual condition stemming from individual choices about food consumption, and (2) the notion that sports and its related practices are always healthy. These two assumptions are flawed and their uncritical acceptance may in fact exacerbate the very problem a proposed ban hopes to eliminate.

Explaining the Obesity Epidemic

Defining the source of the obesity epidemic is more complex than blaming the widespread availability of unhealthy food and the individual choice to consume it. Surely it is an individual decision to eat a hamburger versus a salad, given both options, but all reputable medical research shows that obesity is mitigated by myriad factors, including gender, race, geography, and socioeconomic status. For example, a review of leading research on the obesity epidemic in the United States showed that non-Hispanic blacks have the highest prevalence of obesity, and all racial minorities have a higher combined prevalence of obesity by almost 10 percentage points over whites. In addition, many studies show that individuals who have lower levels of education and socioeconomic status are associated with higher levels of obesity, as is living in the southeastern United States (Wang and Beydoun 2007). Research also shows that there are fewer supermarkets in black neighborhoods compared to white neighborhoods and that they are farther in distance, creating a disproportionate level of access to healthy food (Morland et al. 2002). These "food deserts," as they are often called, contribute to the maintenance of social hierarchies and are an example of a kind of invisible privilege enjoyed by wealthier (and often white) Americans. Thus, in addressing something like the obesity epidemic, efforts must be focused at the societal rather than at the individual level. After all, if following a long day at school you had the choice to drive 10 miles to a supermarket or one mile to a fast food restaurant (where the food is also cheaper), you might choose the latter – despite knowing it is the weaker option from a nutritional standpoint.

Noting the cultural and environmental factors at play in relation to any widespread social problem is important when addressing possible solutions. In continuing with the theme of obesity, if we engage in practices that invite us to see it as an individual rather than a societal condition, we can justify the assertion that a person – or group's – obesity problem is the function of their own lack of motivation and self-control. Ultimately, viewing any social condition as a solely individual one excuses us from confronting systemic inequities that contribute to the problem. In relation to obesity, access to healthier and better-quality food is critical to the adoption of a healthy lifestyle. The disproportionate rate at which these options are available to certain groups is one way in which social hierarchies are maintained. Thus, it is important to avoid discourse – such as a ban on unhealthy products – that invites us to see these kinds of social problems as a result of individual shortcomings.

Questioning the Idea of Sports as Always Healthy

The proposed ban on unhealthy products in relation to sports is also underpinned by an assumption that sports – especially those at the elite level where a ban on unhealthy brands would be most relevant – are in fact, always healthy and good for the body. This may seem like a strange assumption to question; after all, physical activity is, presumably, good for the body and the very antithesis of something such as smoking or unhealthy eating. Yet elite level sports are in many ways *unhealthy*. Sure, professional athletes are in prime physical shape, but recent high-profile scandals have challenged the illusion that their abilities are solely the function of long hours in the gym. Some of Major League Baseball's biggest stars have admitted to ingesting harmful drugs in order to become stronger and to recover from injuries more quickly. In another example, recent medical research has uncovered frightening data about the effect playing football has on the brain; one study commissioned by the National Football League found that its former players were diagnosed with Alzheimer's or other memory-related diseases at higher rates than the general population (Weir et al. 2009).

This is not to say that we should regard sports as unequivocally unhealthy per se, but rather to point out the faulty premise underpinning the ban of "unhealthy" products with a "healthy" activity like sports. Doing so may obscure the ways in which the pursuit of elite-level competition may invite athletes to engage in very unhealthy practices that may in turn send messages to kids that are equally as problematic as the notion that one can achieve elite-level skills on a steady diet of French fries. Already these messages are filtering down to youths; for instance, research has shown that male high school athletes are more likely to use anabolic steroids than nonathletes (Dodge and Jaccard 2006). Certainly engaging in physical activity is part of a healthy lifestyle, but by always uncritically regarding sports as "healthy," we may implicitly ignore the many ways in which it is not, at the expense of youth emulating their favorite stars.

"Healthy" and "Not Healthy" Brands Is too Simplistic

Classifying brands as "healthy" and "not healthy" also creates a problematic distinction that rewards certain companies for their choice to produce a product that is not necessarily unhealthy to the individual body upon its consumption, but destructive in other ways to wider society. There is a tremendous benefit when companies associate themselves with sporting events, and providing that opportunity only to those entities that meet an overly simplistic definition of "healthy" privileges companies who still engage in other problematic practices, including those that violate basic human rights.

The Benefit of Sports Sponsorship

The opportunity for companies to sponsor or advertise at sporting events is often an expensive marketing strategy. For example, estimates show that Fox charged about $100,000 per second to advertisers during its 2011 Super Bowl telecast (Smith 2011). McDonald's entered into an agreement with the Olympics to sponsor the 2002 Winter Games in Salt Lake City and the 2004 Summer Games in Athens in a deal valued at between $50 and $60 million (Cebrzynski 2000). McDonald's has been a steady presence in the Olympics; in fact before the International Olympic Committee even named London as the 2012 Summer Games host, the city's organizational committee had secured a £1 million sponsorship commitment from the fast food giant to support the bidding process alone (Solley 2004). Although these capital outlays are staggering, the payoff, however, is lucrative. Procter & Gamble has stated that, following its sponsorship of the 2010 Vancouver Olympic Games, it experienced a $100 million rise in incremental sales in the United States (Whitehead and Reynolds 2010). And at a recent meeting of the International Advertising Association, top company personnel discussed the benefits of sports sponsorship for their organizations; one Visa executive told his fellow conference members that his company's biggest problem was not the cost of sports sponsorship, but "finding enough sporting events of sufficient stature to sponsor" (Buchan 2006).

There is a reason companies funnel so many resources into sports; association with a well-liked sporting event leads to higher rates of interest and favor toward the brand from individuals who view that event (Speed and Thompson 2000). Take the Olympics, for example. The Games are considered "one of the most promising sponsorship opportunities in sport" in part because of how the event connotes positive feelings such as global unity, friendship, and triumph (Apostolopoulou and Papadimitriou 2004: 181). Aligning themselves with such feel-good narratives represents a golden opportunity for many brands, justifying the high cost. A longitudinal study examining the impact on brand awareness stemming from Olympics sponsorship found that each of the brands reviewed was effectively able to use its sponsorship as a way to remain in the public consciousness (Tripodi and Hirons 2009) More specifically, in the hyper-competitive footwear category, Nike entered the Olympics with about 75 percent of the adults sampled recognizing the brand's association with the Olympics. Following the event, Nike maintained its level of association with the Games, while fellow competitors Adidas and Reebok experienced a serious decline on the same measure. In an intense era of global capitalism, this kind of competitive advantage is critical to a brand's success. Thus, any decisions granting the ability to engage in sports sponsorship and advertising must be taken with the utmost care, as denying this opportunity to, say, a fast food company would come at a serious cost. Conversely, the decision to reward, say, a sports apparel company with this same opportunity would come at a great benefit.

Examining a Company's Social Worth

In making choices about who may sponsor or advertise in sporting events, we are making a judgment about a company's social worth. Yet many companies that do not sell alcohol, tobacco, or fatty foods and soda engage in practices that are destructive in other ways. It was hard to see the news coverage of the BP oil spill in 2010 and not question the harmful effects of offshore drilling on fragile ocean ecosystems as nearly five million barrels of oil spewed into the Gulf of Mexico following an oil rig explosion that killed 11 workers. Other industry practices have also resulted in human costs. The sporting goods and apparel industry has undergone intense scrutiny over the last 20 years for questionable labor practices that include child labor and unsanitary and harsh working conditions. Although a number of companies have worked to publicly repair their image and address the problem, recent reports show that the official 2010 World Cup soccer ball called "Jubilani" (which translates to "rejoice" in Zulu) was made in four countries that routinely use child labor (Hawthorne 2010). Such practices reproduce global class divisions and ultimately help maintain Western superiority at the expense of individuals in developing countries. Yet because their related products do not fall into the "unhealthy" category, these companies would be free to continue advertising at athletic events under a proposed ban. While ending the obesity epidemic and curbing alcohol and tobacco abuse are certainly worthwhile goals, we must question why these problems of developed nations are privileged over making sure laborers in developing world countries are granted basic human rights in factories or that a corporate entity minimize its effect on the environment.

Conclusion: A Better Measure

Instead of making an overly simplistic "healthy" versus "not healthy" distinction between brands, perhaps a more useful measure to use in assessing acceptable sporting sponsorship and advertising would include a consideration of a company's corporate social responsibility (CSR) efforts. According to Carroll (1991), who is often called the most widely cited authority on this topic, a company's engagement in CSR efforts are evaluated on four measures: (1) successfully pursuing maximum profitability; (2) complying with all laws and regulations; (3) operating in a way that reflects the values of society at large; and (4) supporting social welfare and charitable endeavors. David et al. (2005) further divide CSR activities into three categories they call (1) moral/ethical, for example, treating employees fairly, acting responsibly toward the environment; (2) discretionary, for example, raising awareness of social problems; and (3) relational, such as demonstrating a willingness to listen to stakeholders. These examples point to a more sophisticated way of measuring a company's benefit to society (or its harmful effect in the case of a lack of CSR efforts).

Each year, the Boston College Center for Corporate Citizenship and Reputation Institute produces a list that ranks companies by their CSR efforts. In 2011 that list included several companies not always known for healthy food offerings, including Coca-Cola at the number 13 spot. While it is true that no athlete will reach elite levels by consuming excessive amounts of soda, through its CSR efforts, the Coca-Cola company has supported healthy habits and lifestyles in other ways. For example, in the Netherlands it created "Mission Olympic," the largest secondary school platform in that country, with more than 150,000 participants and a goal to encourage Dutch youth to participate in competitions in 16 different sports. In the United States the company sponsored a series of sports clinics for youths where they had the opportunity to learn sporting *and* nutrition skills.

The goal here is not to tout Coca-Cola as much as to point to the necessary complexity in measuring a company's social value or harm. In the examples stated above Coca-Cola is engaging in a discretionary form of CSR and thus finding a way to contribute positively to the community. This assessment raises an interesting question, then: What is better, a company that sells sporting apparel using harmful labor tactics or a company that sells soda while also creating opportunities for youths to exercise and engage in sporting activity? If sports will continue to be held to a moral standard in relation to the brands associated with it, then using a CSR measure as opposed to a "healthy" versus "unhealthy" distinction would allow for a more sophisticated assessment to account for how a company's practices and strategies affect society at large.

References

Apostolopoulou, A. and Papadimitriou, D. (2004). "Welcome home": Motivations and objectives of the 2004 Grand National Olympic Sponsors. *Sport Marketing Quarterly* 13: 180–192.

Barrand, D. (2004). Sport's biggest sponsors fight their corner. *Marketing* (Mar. 18), 15.

Buchan, N. (2006). Sports sponsorship – still giving enough bang for the buck? *B&T Weekly* 56(2567): 5.

Carroll, A. B. (1991). The pyramid of corporate social responsibility: Toward the moral management of organizational stakeholders – Balancing economic, legal, and social responsibilities. *Business Horizons* 34(July–August): 39–48.

Cebrzynski, G. (2000). McDonald's extends Olympics sponsorship. *Nation's Restaurant News* 34(25): 6.

Clarkson, J. (2010). Editorial: Time to get tough on unhealthy sponsorships. *Health Promotion Journal of Australia* 21(3): 164–165.

Cornwell, T. B. (2008). State of the art and science in sponsorship-linked marketing. *Journal of Advertising* 37(3): 41–55.

David, P., Kline, S., and Dai, Y. (2005). Corporate social responsibility practices, corporate identity, and purchase intention: A dual process model. *Journal of Public Relations Research* 17(3): 291–313.

Dodge, T. L. and Jaccard, J. J. (2006). The effect of high school sports participation on the use of performance-enhancing substances in young adulthood. *Journal of Adolescent Health* 39(3): 367–373.

Hawthorne, M. (2010). No rejoicing for those stitched up by World Cup merchandise. *Age* (June 14), Business, 2.

Morland, K., Wing, S., Diez Roux, A., and Poole, C. (2002). Neighborhood characteristics associated with the location of food stores and food service places. *American Journal of Preventative Medicine* 22(1): 23–29.

Smith, A. (2011). Superbowl ad: Is $3 million worth it? *CNN Money* (Feb. 3). At http://money.cnn.com/2011/02/03/news/companies/super_bowl_ads/index.htm, accessed Mar. 27, 2013.

Solley, S. (2004). London 2012 bid aims for £12m sponsor fees. *Marketing* (Feb. 26), 1.

Speed, R. and Thompson, P. (2000). Determinants of sports sponsorship response. *Journal of the Academy of Marketing Science* 28(2): 226–238.

Tripodi, J. A. and Hirons, M. (2009). Sponsorship leveraging case studies – Sydney 2000 Olympic Games. *Journal of Promotion Management* 15: 118–136.

van Riper, T. (2011). The most watched Super Bowl ads. *Forbes* (Feb. 7). At http://www.forbes.com/sites/tomvanriper/2011/02/07/the-most-watched-super-bowl-ads/, accessed Mar. 27, 2013.

Wang, Y. and Beydoun, M. A. (2007). The obesity epidemic in the United States – gender, age, socioeconomic, racial/ethnic, and geographical characteristics: A systemic review and meta-regression analysis. *Epidemiologic Reviews* 29: 6–28.

Weir, D. R., Jackson, J. S., and Sonnega, A. (2009). *Study of retired NFL players*. Ann Arbor, MI: National Football League Player Care Foundation and University of Michigan Institute for Social Research.

Whitehead, J. and Reynolds, J. (2010). P&G to partner Coke for Olympic Games activities. *Marketing* (Aug. 4), 4.

Counterargument ＞◀

Sporting events and advertising products are contrary to athletes' lifestyles: The consequences of mixed messages

Marie Hardin

Penn State University, USA

Of the 111 million viewers who tuned into the Super Bowl in February 2011, many likely paid as much attention to the commercials as to the game (the Green Bay Packers beat the Pittsburgh Steelers). After all, the commercials were high-stakes investments, as advertisers paid an estimated $3 million for a 30-second spot (Elliott 2011a; Smith 2011).

The number of viewers for that single sitting in front of the television – and the Super Bowl's reputation as a cultural "must see" each year – make it the single most powerful TV event for advertising recall by consumers. The game has become "the preferred venue for introducing new corporate constellations, launching new products, and more routinely, building brand awareness" (Wenner 2008: 135).

What products and brands will consumers recall as a result of the 2011 Super Bowl? Although there were plenty of commercials for automobiles – Audi, BMW, Chrysler, Hyundai, Volkswagen, and Kia – and dot-com brands, such as E*Trade, GoDaddy.com, or Cars.com, almost one-quarter of commercial time was devoted to fast food and alcohol.

It's regrettable that a spectacle designed to celebrate some of the finest-tuned athletes on the planet is also a platform for products that are an anathema to healthy, fit bodies: Doritos, Pepsi, Coca-Cola, Snickers, Wendy's fast food, and beer.

The Super Bowl isn't the only place where we find such stark contradictions between promotional messages and what happens between them. Take the Olympics – a global showcase of fit, healthy, ideal bodies in a variety of athletic events. McDonald's – home of junk-food meals where a single burger, fries, and drink can account for more than half of the recommended calories and three-quarters of the recommended daily fat allowance for an adult – touts itself as a "balanced eating" sponsor (Elliott 2011b: para. 3). More than 550 health experts would characterize McDonald's menu differently – as one that promotes chronic health problems (McIntyre 2011).

The restaurant chain's junk-food fare is certainly not the stuff of athletic training tables. Case in point: Dara Torres, an Olympic swimmer and "global ambassador" for McDonald's, is well known for her careful attention to a strict diet plan – one that eschews the saturated fat found in a McDonald's French fry – and instead concentrates on lean protein, vegetables, grains and fruit (Crouse 2007; ABC News 2010; Childers 2010; Elliott 2011b; Hum, n.d.). Her own fast food meals come from "Whole Foods or Fresh Market to keep meals on the healthy side," she told an interviewer (Hum, n.d.: para. 19).

Promoting unhealthy products during the Super Bowl or Olympics – or the broadcast of any other elite-level sporting event, for that matter – should be understood as a form of "false advertising." These promotions associate healthy, active lifestyles with alcohol and junk food. The dire, long-term effects are perhaps most pronounced for children, who are most vulnerable to harmful marketing messages and to the socially beneficial messages that can be carried in elite sporting competitions.

The "Dirt" on Sports-Related Sponsorships

Of the tens of millions of viewers who push sports programming to the top of the Nielsen ratings each year, a healthy percentage are youths (Nicholson and Hoye 2009; Gregory 2010). Nine in 10 children ages 8 to 17 report that they consume sports through the media, mostly through television. More than half of youths surveyed reported watching sports content at least once a week (AAF/ESPN 2001).

Watching sports can be valuable for children because "there are important lessons to be learned, including the importance of good sporting behavior, cooperating with a team, handling disappointment and learning to focus," according to the Association for Applied Sports Psychology (AASP, n.d.: para. 2). The idea that consuming sports can be socially beneficial for children is well accepted, as sports are associated with ideals such as success, self-discipline, and hard work (Frank 2003; Eitzen and Sage 2008). Finally, watching televised sports also promotes participation in physical activity by youths – leading to healthy habits that could last a lifetime (Coakley 2004). In other words, watching sports has the potential to lead to a healthier and happier life.

It should be no surprise that an increasing number of products and brands have sought – through advertising and sponsorships – to associate with activities related to the highest levels of health and fitness. Analyses of sports-related broadcasts, for instance, have found that viewers are subject to corporate logos, plastered on uniforms, throughout stadia and in on-screen graphics, during at least half of viewing time (Sherriff et al. 2009). An analysis of literature and marketing reports shows that much of viewers' exposure is to food and beverage companies (Kelly et al. 2011a). Slightly more than half of all television beer ads appear on sports programming; they are most often seen on broadcasts of professional football, basketball, NASCAR, and college football and basketball – where many of the players themselves are not of legal drinking age (Collins et al. 2007).

Wenner (2008: 136) calls the power of sports programming "dirt" that "rubs off" from the televised event to the commercial or sponsorship message adjacent to it. Because fans identify so strongly with the positive ideologies surrounding sports, the association – the "rub" – is especially powerful. Products such as Coca-Cola, Bud Light, or Snickers, then, benefit from the logic of sports. Wenner writes that sports dirt "has long been strategically employed by advertisers looking for benefit in the mediated sports marketplace" (2008: 149).

An example is in the relationship between the promotion of alcohol (beer, most often) and displays of athleticism. A content analysis of advertising during popular televised sports events found that alcohol-related messages contained features that could be interpreted as associating the consumption of beer with social and athletic success (Jones et al. 2010).

The benefit of sports dirt for companies that market unhealthy products such as fast food and alcohol is obvious – the dirt obscures a relationship that is patently illogical. Investing in a commercial relationship with sports teams and programming may be seen as an attempt to improve the image of companies that have no business associating with fitness-related activities and lifestyles (Sherriff et al. 2009). Unfortunately, research shows that most of the food and beverage connected to spectator sports through advertising and sponsorships is unhealthy, contributing to a variety of chronic diseases and obesity (Clarkson 2010; Kelly et al. 2011a).

Promoting an Unhealthy Relationship

The investment of corporations like McDonald's and Coca-Cola in sports-affiliated sponsorships and advertising has paid strong dividends; research shows that getting "dirty" by sidling up to the world's most fit athletes with food and drink that certainly isn't part of their everyday diets produces results. For instance, sports sponsorship alone positively impacts product recall, especially if the sponsorship has been consistent over time. In fact, sponsorship brands reap strong product recall without running the same number of advertisements as competitors might run (Hastings et al. 2006). Overall, many studies have confirmed that promotion of food – unhealthy or healthy – influences individual consumption and diet-related behaviors. A report for the World Health Organization summarized the influence of food-related promotion as "significant, independent of other influences" and observes that it operates at both the category (junk food) and brand (Snickers) level (Hastings et al. 2006: 3).

The way in which sponsorships and marketing messages have been able to link unhealthy products with sports has been an effective advertising and marketing strategy (Clarkson 2010). The bottom line is that "consumption is increased" (Rehm and Kanteres 2008: 1967).

Research shows that children are especially vulnerable to this false relationship, as their attitudes toward and consumption of junk food and alcohol are influenced by marketing messages (Clarkson 2010). The World Health Organization report published in 2006 outlines a litany of studies showing that youths have "extensive recall" of food advertising in general; they are "interested in trying advertised foods and often ask their parents to buy them" (Hastings et al. 2006).

Studies have demonstrated the susceptibility of young viewers to sports dirt in alcohol advertising. In one study, interviews with children who watched alcohol advertising during sports events found that they associated a preference for alcohol with youth, athleticism, and humor (Phillipson and Jones 2007). Middle school students had a high awareness of alcohol sponsors and brands, "and associate these products with sports and with positive personal characteristics and outcomes" (Jones et al. 2010).

Research also demonstrates that young people who are exposed to messages that promote alcohol don't wait to try it. Simply put, promotion increases the probability that adolescents will drink (Nicholson and Hoye 2009). Meanwhile, the pledge by US trade associations for alcohol suppliers to restrict advertising only to programming aimed mostly at adults has generally been judged to be a hollow one. And – not surprisingly, given the allure of sports dirt – there is special concern among medical experts about the infiltration of sports programming by alcohol promotions. According to research published in the *Journal of the American Medical Association*, even in the face of increasing evidence of links between "alcohol advertising through sports and alcohol consumption by adolescents," such advertising on sports broadcasts has climbed in recent years (Nicholson and Hoye 2009: 1481). Public health experts have characterized the levels of such advertising as "unacceptable" (Sherriff et al. 2009: 19).

The Consequences of (Sports) Dirty Advertising

The societal price tag for promoting alcohol and unhealthy (junk) food to every age level – but especially to children – through sports programming is high. According to the World Health Organization, alcohol overconsumption at every age level has led to higher death rates and an increase in chronic health problems. Alcohol use has been deemed the leading public health problem among youths in the United States (Nicholson and Hoye 2009).

The consequences of promoting the myth of healthy, fit bodies fueled with Big Macs and French fries and washed down with Pepsi or Bud Light – then finished with a Snickers bar – may be even more far-reaching. Obesity and the many health ailments that come with it (such as type 2 diabetes, for instance) is becoming a global health problem. The number of obese people on the planet has doubled since 1980, and 65 percent of the world's population live in countries where the problem of being overweight kills more people than that of being underweight (WHO 2011). One-third of Americans are classified as obese (Parker-Pope 2011). And research indicates that obesity often begins in childhood (Boyse 2010).

Of course, obesity and its health-related spin offs cannot be traced to a single source, such as individual food preferences. It is the result of an interrelated web of factors involving individual choices, environmental influences, and socioeconomic factors (FSA 2004). However, there is no disputing that time in front of a television and exposure to thousands of commercials that push fattening, non-nutritional food is not a minor factor (FSA 2004; Hastings et al. 2006; Boyse 2010).

For that reason, it could be argued that all advertising of junk food should be subject to scrutiny. Public health experts, however, have reserved special criticism for the dirtiest of unhealthy marketing ploys: the attempt to pair images of healthy, fit bodies with their greasy, sugary, fattening antithesis. Logically, these experts have proposed a ban on advertising in sports-related venues as a "starting point" in helping consumers – young and old alike – better understand the true relationship between alcohol, junk food, and health (Nicholson and Hoye 2009; Clarkson 2010).

In the meantime, research also shows that the promotion of *healthy* food choices through sponsorships and advertising can net positive behavioral change among consumers (Donovan et al. 1999). So, what about advertisements for low-fat yogurt, lean protein, whole grains, and a heaping portion of fruits and vegetables during the next Super Bowl? That would be truth in advertising.

References

AAF (Amateur Athletic Foundation)/ESPN (2001). *Children & Sports Media Study*. Statistical Research Inc. At http://www.la84foundation.org/9arr/ResearchReports/AAF-ESPNCSMR2001.pdf, accessed Mar. 27, 2013.

AASP (Association for Applied Sports Psychology) (n.d.) AASP learning guides help teach kids life lessons while watching sports. At http://appliedsportpsych.org/files/learningguideintro.pdf, accessed Mar. 27, 2013.

ABC News (2010). Dara Torres' "Gold Medal Fitness Plan." *ABC News Videos* (May 12). At http://abcnews.go.com/Health/video/dara-torres-gold-medal-fitness-plan-10629491, accessed Mar. 27, 2013.

Boyse, K. (2010). Television and Children. *YourChild Development & Behavior Resources, University of Michigan*. At http://www.med.umich.edu/yourchild/topics/tv.htm, accessed Mar. 27, 2013.

Childers, L. (2010) Dara Torres' fitness tips for beating arthritis pain. *Arthritis Today*. At http://www.arthritistoday.org/community/people-profiles/dara-torres.php, accessed Mar. 27, 2013.

Clarkson, J. (2010) Time to get tough on unhealthy sponsorships. *Health Promotion Journal of Australia* 21(3): 164–165.

Coakley, J. (2004). *Sports in society: Issues and controversies*, 8th edn. New York: McGraw-Hill.

Collins, R. L., Ellickson, P. L., McCaffrey, D., and Hambarsoomians, M. S. (2007). Early adolescent exposure to alcohol advertising and its relationship to underage drinking. *Journal of Adolescent Health* 40: 527–534.

Cornwell, T. B. (2008). State of the art and science in sponsorship-linked marketing. *Journal of Advertising* 37(3): 41–55.

Crouse, K. (2007). Torres is getting older, but swimming faster. *New York Times* (Nov. 18). At http://www.nytimes.com/2007/11/18/sports/othersports/18torres.html?pagewanted=all, accessed Mar. 27, 2013.

Donovan, R. J., Jalleh, G., Clarkson, J., and Giles-Corti, B. (1999). Evidence for the effectiveness of sponsorship as a health promotion tool. *Australian Journal of Primary Health* 5(4): 81–91.

Eitzen, D. S., and Sage, G. H. (2008). *Sociology of North American sport*, 8th edn. Boulder, CO: Paradigm Publishers.

Elliott, S. (2011a). Super Bowl ads assessed, from A to Z. *New York Times* (Feb. 9). At http://mediadecoder.blogs.nytimes.com/2011/02/09/super-bowl-ads-assessed-from-a-to-z/, accessed Mar. 27, 2013.

Elliott, S. (2011b). McDonald's uses Olympics for its own balancing act. *New York Times* (July 20). At http://mediadecoder.blogs.nytimes.com/2011/07/20/mcdonalds-uses-olympics-for-its-own-balancing-act/, accessed Mar. 27, 2013.

Frank, A. M. (2003). *Sports and education: A reference handbook*. Santa Barbara, CA: ABC-CLIO.

FSA (Food Standards Agency) (2004). Defusing the diet timebomb. *Food Standards Agency News* 35(Feb.): i.

Gregory, S. (2010). Why sports ratings are surging on TV. *Time Business & Money* (Aug. 14). At http://www.time.com/time/business/article/0,8599,2010746,00.html, accessed Mar. 27, 2013.

Hastings, G., McDermott, L., Angus, K., Stead, M., and Thomson, S. (2006). *The extent, nature and effects of food promotion to children: A review of the evidence*. Geneva: World Health Organization. At http://www.who.int/dietphysicalactivity/publications/Hastings_paper_marketing.pdf, accessed Mar. 27, 2013.

Hum, M. E. (n.d.) A Day in the Life of . . . an Olympic swimmer: Five-time Olympian, Dara Torres, talks food, fitness, and family fun. *WeightWatchers*. At http://www.weightwatchers.com/util/art/index_art.aspx?tabnum=1&art_id=111291, accessed Mar. 27, 2013.

Jones, S. C., Phillipson, L., and Barrie, L. R. (2010). "Most men drink . . . especially like when they play sports" – alcohol advertising during sporting broadcasts and the potential impact on child audiences. *Journal of Public Affairs* 10(1–2): 59–73.

Kelly, B., Baur, L. A., Bauman, A. E., Smith, B. J., Saleh, S., et al. (2011a). Role modelling unhealthy behaviours: Food and drink sponsorship of peak sporting organizations. *Health Promotion Journal of Australia* 22(1): 72–75.

Kelly, B., Baur, L. A., Bauman, A. E., and King, L. (2011b). Tobacco and alcohol sponsorship of sporting events provide insights about how food and beverage sponsorship may affect children's health. *Health Promotion Journal of Australia* 22(2): 91–96.

McIntyre, D. (2011). Health experts attack McDonald's, but can they bite into its bottom line? *Daily Finance* (May 18). At http://www.dailyfinance.com/2011/05/18/health-experts-attack-mcdonalds-but-can-they-bite-into-its-bot/, accessed Mar. 27, 2013.

Nicholson, M. and Hoye, R. (2009). Reducing adolescents' exposure to advertising and promotion during televised sports. *Journal of the American Medical Association* 301(14): 1479–1482.

Parker-Pope, T. (2011). The fat trap. *New York Times Magazine* (Dec. 28). At http://www.nytimes.com/2012/01/01/magazine/tara-parker-pope-fat-trap.html?pagewanted=1&_r=1, accessed Mar. 27, 2013.

Phillipson, L. and Jones, S. C. (2007). *Awareness of alcohol advertising among children who watch televised sports*. Conference paper. *University of Wollongong Research Online*. At http://ro.uow.edu.au/cgi/viewcontent.cgi?article=1064&context=hbspapers, accessed Mar. 27, 2013.

Rehm, J. and Kanteres, F. (2008). Alcohol and sponsorship in sport: Some much-needed evidence in an ideological discussion. *Addiction* 103: 1967–1968.

Sherriff, J., Griffiths, D., and Daube, M. (2009). Cricket: Notching up runs for food and alcohol companies? *Australian and New Zealand Journal of Public Health* 34(1): 19–23.

Smith, A. (2011). Super Bowl ad: Is $3 million worth it? *CNN Money* (Feb. 3). At http://money.cnn.com/2011/02/03/news/companies/super_bowl_ads/index.htm, accessed Mar. 27, 2013.

Wenner, L. (2008). Super-cooled sports dirt: Moral contagion and Super Bowl commercials in the shadows of Janet Jackson. *Television & New Media* 9(2): 131–154.

WHO (World Health Organization) (2011). Obesity and overweight. *World Health Organization*. At http://www.who.int/mediacentre/factsheets/fs311/en/index.html, accessed Mar. 27, 2013.

15

Advertising to Captive Audiences

> *It will work. I am a*
> *marketing genius.*
>
> Paris Hilton

No matter how optimistic (and opportunistic) you might be about advertising, it's possible that you have limits on where you think ads should be shown. Is a bathroom stall okay? What about the tray-tables on airplanes? What about in a jail – where someone is arrested and waiting for bail and doesn't have a lawyer? Or how about on students' exam papers? (History brought to you by Tony's Pizza!) All of these examples actually exist.

If people don't have much of a choice about seeing the advertising – if they really are a captive audience – does that make a difference to how you feel about the issue? When the airplane captain tells you to fasten your seat belt because you're about to hit turbulence and you're illogically straining your brain, looking toward the cockpit, trying to will the plane into smooth sailing skies, do you really need to see an advertisement for Advil at that moment? And, if you had seen the ad, would you be more inclined to buy a bottle once you have landed safely? The following essays argue maybe, and then again maybe not!

Advertising and Society: An Introduction, Second Edition. Edited by Carol J. Pardun.
© 2014 John Wiley & Sons, Inc. Published 2014 by John Wiley & Sons, Inc.

Both authors discuss the validity of the concept of "captive audiences" because advertising is ubiquitous and so, in a sense, we're all captive to all advertising all the time. But, still, it seems that in certain situations the appropriateness of advertising is questionable. This issue has been debated for years in the context of school. Some estimate that about a third of middle and high school students have access to Channel One – a short news show that is geared toward teens – and, subsequently, advertising in the school. Since Channel One's introduction over 20 years ago, the concept has been embroiled in controversy – mostly because of the embedded advertising. Some research has indicated that the students watching the program in school remember the ads more than they remember the news segment. (If you're interested in learning more, check out the website at www.channelone.com.)

It's easy to say that the commercialization of schools is a bad thing, but as school budgets shrink, it might be harder to persuade a teacher. If a math teacher has a choice to pay for the paper himself or herself in order to print out an exam, or let Gatorade cover the cost, what's the harm? Maybe school buses wrapped in messages from Starbucks would provide additional funds to hire bus monitors to make a student's bus ride to school safer.

Just about every captive place where advertising occurs (or has the potential to occur) creates a controversy that eventually can be boiled down to the issue of whether the funds generated by the ad are worth the hassle (if there is one) of being exposed to the ad. Which argument wins the day? *You decide.*

Ideas to Get You Thinking . . .

1   Next time you go to the airport, take note of all the advertisements you see. What are the products being advertised? Do you think the advertisers have pushed the envelope too far? Why, or why not?

2   Think of a place that you regard as totally off-limits to advertisers (e.g., a funeral home, a church nursery). Describe the place and explain why you think it would be inappropriate. Now do some research and see if what the advertisers think. You might make a visit, talk to someone who works at the "off-limits" location, or see what you can find by doing some online research. What did you discover?

3   Go to a public place and set a timer (one hour would be appropriate). Make a list of all the advertising you can see without moving. What have you observed?

Other Topics to Debate

1   We can all agree on areas that should be totally off-limits to advertisers.

2   Advertising should be limited in places where a person feels stress (such as airplanes, dentist offices, and tax auditors' offices).

3   While advertising should not be off-limits anywhere, certain *kinds* of adver-
     tising should be (such as humorous ads in cemeteries, for example).
4   The only way to cut down on advertising clutter is to require advertisers to
     limit their advertising budgets.

If You'd Like to Know More . . .

Blank, C. (2007). The newest ad frontier: airport security lines. *Advertising Age* 78(10):
     4–39.
Phillips, J. and Noble, S. M. (2007). Simple captivating. *Journal of Advertising* 36(1):
     81–94.
Worsham, A. G. (2009). Presidential elections in the public schools: A frame analysis of
     the coverage of presidential campaign seasons on Channel One TV. Paper presented
     at the Annual Meeting of the International Communication Association, Chicago,
     May 20.

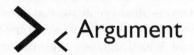 Argument

Why advertising is acceptable (almost) everywhere

Angeline G. Close

University of Texas, USA

Without doubt, marketing and advertising can overstep its bounds. Some bad
apples can ruin the bunch; however, the majority of marketing communications
do add value to peoples' lives. Advertising and marketing are increasingly out
of the home (OOH) because consumers are spending less time at home. Consumers are mobile, on the go, on social media, connected, and often unwilling to
take the time to slow down to absorb traditional advertising. Hence, by reaching
consumers – and perhaps in the process educating or entertaining them – while
they are out living life, advertisers are adapting to changes in modern consumer
behavior. Event marketing and sponsorships are an example of newer forms of
marketing communication that not only get this point, but embrace it. Advertisers are not holding consumers hostage; they are entertaining, educating, and
providing a social backdrop to modern consumer lifestyles.

While some may argue that advertising takes advantage of unknowing, trapped consumers, I hope to convince you that advertising is a good thing. The macro effects to local and global economies alone could be enough evidence to support the value of advertising. Throughout the past century, the advertising business model has been an engine of creativity for consumers and success for business markets. Achievements in television and radio programming are mainly financed by ad revenue. The same is true for the wide variety of corporate websites, social media sites, events, consumer blogs, apps, and magazines/e-zines that circulate worldwide. In the twenty-first century, modern marketers are desperately seeking ways to seamlessly integrate advertising, events, and sponsorships into consumer lifestyles, in order to reach a fragmenting audience that is increasingly out of the home.

As an author, researcher, and marketing/advertising educator, my goal is usually to present a balanced, nonbiased view of both the pros and cons of advertising, event marketing, and their impacts on consumer behavior both online and on the ground. Thus, I appreciate the premise of this book, as the counterargument provides an important side to the acceptability of advertising – when it oversteps its bounds or ventures to "the dark side" of advertising.

Here, I provide evidence for the argument that "Advertising is acceptable – anywhere," within the context of the United States. Advertising is beyond acceptable – it is necessary, and it enhances the business market. The most compelling argument for why advertising is necessary is its economic benefits. Advertising is a smart business component and sparks global awareness because it *promotes capitalism, enhances the economy, and provides jobs*. Aside from macro benefits, consumers can learn, laugh, and reinforce ego, status-seeking, and even extend the self (Belk and Pollay 1985).

It is imperative to note that advertising has both intended (often positive) and unintended (both positive and negative) effects on consumers and society. It is often these unintended effects or misuse of advertising that lend to advertising resistance. So we must be careful to separate the issue of advertising's acceptability from the broader market's acceptability. That is, if you believe that cigarette advertising is unacceptable, consider if the broader issue is that the product (cigarettes) or the surrounding market is what is actually resisted.

Hence, in this essay, I first discuss advertising's economic benefit, because that is the most macro benefit, and one that may trickle down to individual households and consumers. Second, I discuss advertising and its benefit to consumers. After addressing both the macro and consumer benefits, I then explain how advertising is a social backdrop. Although advertising is acceptable – it brings business, consumer, and societal benefits – advertising is, and should be, subject to consumer resistance. Thus, I note two areas of risk to the field of advertising – privacy concerns and attitudes of resistance. Some consumers resist markets or too much advertising – especially when they perceive it to be invasive or a threat to their privacy (understandably so). Thus, I add to the discussion of the counterargument (why advertising is not necessary) by including a plausible explanation of why consumers do not see its value and resist advertising in its entirety.

Advertising anywhere: Economic Benefits

Advertising and Competition

Advertising Promotes Competition

Why limit advertising opportunities to traditional media, when consumers spend and consume virtually anywhere these days thanks to technology? Advertising helps the economy by reinforcing competition. One of the beauties of capitalism is the notion that competition can drive up quality in the market. This applies to both goods and services. The competition between Coca-Cola and Pepsi is an excellent example of this. Since the 1950s, Coke and Pepsi have dominated the cola market by continuing to be in competition with each other. Since Coke and Pepsi can easily duplicate each other when it comes to packaging, placement, and even ingredients, the main focus of their differentiation in the market is their advertisements – and where they market. Pepsi started with their advertisement campaign on the "Pepsi Generation" while Coke used advertisements that claim to be superior in taste. Pepsi then responded with the "Pepsi Challenge" campaign – a guerilla marketing campaign that asked cola drinkers to take a blind taste test of Coke and Pepsi and choose which one tasted better – and so the cycle continues. Each company continues to improve its product line, packaging, and advertising because of its competition with the other (Yoffie 2007). And both companies realize the value of taking their marketing to the streets. No one was forcing consumers to take the Pepsi Challenge – it was fun, interesting, and an experience people lined up for.

Advertising and the Economy

Economic Contributions

The more places to advertise (e.g., in cabs, subways, even toilets), the better, when you consider the economic benefit. Advertising enhances the economy. Since 2000, advertising has continuously stayed at approximately 2 percent of the nation's GDP, which was approximately $15 trillion at the time of writing (Galbi 2008; US Department of Commerce 2011). That means $300 billion of the nation's GDP is a direct result of advertising. With this in mind, do you still find the ad in the airplane really bothersome?

Further, advertising revenues can predict economic trends. The argument is that advertising revenue increases when the US GDP increases. Although the current GDP and advertising revenue are on the rise, it is important to note that the media outlets of advertising are changing (Kantar Media 2013).

Advertising Provides Jobs

In conjunction with enhancing the economy, advertising stimulates demand and provides employment to thousands in the media, creative, and accounting fields.

Today, about 30 percent of the global job market belongs to the marketing and advertising industries (Christ 2012). This trend most likely will continue, as advertising and marketing remain popular majors. These students, like you, will help shape the future of the field as you progress in your careers.

For careers, it is crucial to understand the necessity of advertising – almost anywhere, both locally and globally, and the globalization of jobs due to virtual agencies. Virtual ad agencies are teams of industry experts that collaborate virtually, rather than having a physical bricks-and-mortars traditional ad agency with overheads (Finney and Close 2008). Virtual agencies will allow the field to provide employment regardless of physical location, thus opening up the playing field. Advertising, in sum, helps the economy by hedging capitalism and opening job markets. These benefits of ubiquitous marketing trickle down to individual households and consumers.

Advertising anywhere: Benefit to Consumers

In addition to its aforementioned macro benefits to the economy and job creation, advertising also helps us as consumers in both utilitarian and hedonic ways. It provides information to enhance our awareness of new products, services, and brands, not to mention providing us with entertainment and escape.

Advertising Is Accepted in "Captive" Spaces

Note that captive spaces do not include corporate sponsored events (these events will be addressed later). Although these audiences are also in a captive space, the audiences at these events are there for the actual event and therefore are not focused on reading text or actual advertising. In contrast, captive space advertisements appear in transit places, where people are normally waiting for or traveling to a destination.

Others may critique the field for taking advantage of consumers who are on the go – say in a cab or airplane, at an event, or waiting in line. Yet, this is just smart exposure. Advertising in captive spaces and transit media is accepted in such places as airplanes, subways, buses, and taxicabs. According to Euro RSCG 4D (a digital marketing agency), "consumers seamlessly navigate from awareness to purchase to advocacy at their (often quick) pace, and they expect their brands to do the same" (Springer 2009). Advertising in captive areas has become standard and is not only accepted by consumers, but convenient and helpful. Most recently, digital advertisements were placed in New York City's subways to keep consumers interested and to customize advertisements to the location and times of the subway (Donohue 2012). This is helpful, and the consumer can always tune it out, as some rightfully choose to do at times.

Consider these success stories of advertising in a captive area. The first example is a successful campaign from Volkswagen in a subway station. The campaign goals were to show the economic side of Volkswagen. So their agency turned the stairs that led to a subway station into a keyboard in order to promote the use of stairs over escalators. The staged event was recorded and became extremely successful online (Taylor 2009). The campaign, referred to as "The Fun Theory," went viral and is available to watch at YouTube (Fun Theory 2009).

A second success story involves taxi advertising in general. For taxi advertising, research has found that most people see taxi advertising often or very often, and more people tend to like it than dislike it. They also help reinforce brand recall and recognition (Veloutsou and O'Donnell 2005). This includes external taxi advertising (taxi tents and autowrapping), and ads in the back of the cab for travelers to see. These work especially well for destination-related products and services. In Las Vegas, these cab ads can let tourists coming from the airport know what shows are in town, where the dinner hotspots are, and other tourist attractions. Again, the ads are not holding consumers hostage – just informing them about opportunities they may be interested in.

Advertising as Product and Brand Information

Advertising Educates

Advertising, in its informative state, can educate. Advertising "educates buyers about the quality of matches" and about "relevant technologies" that help them make informed choices about their purchases and their environment (Meurer and Stahl 1994). Further, advertising also educates the government about company products, business plans, and personnel (Meurer and Stahl 1994). In addition, advertising also can enhance brand image.

Advertising Enhances Brands

Advertising provides information, and "plays a pivotal role in increasing brand awareness as well as creating strong brand association" (Yoo et al. 2000). On being exposed to such advertising, consumers begin to learn about what they may later demand. As an example, consider the last time you saw a prescription medicine advertised. Has it ever sparked you or a loved one to seek medical attention or more information on symptoms noted in an ad? Direct-to-consumer (DTC) advertising (i.e., ads for prescription-only medicines going directly to the consumer) may inform consumers of an unknown health issue. With the advent of DTC advertising, even the pharmaceutical industry plans integrated communication strategies around creating awareness of disease or health conditions. DTC advertising may raise doubt about unintended consequences (e.g., self-diagnosing, doctor–patient conflict), but these may be outweighed by its alerting someone to seek medical care for a health problem.

Of course, DTC ads often tout branded solutions. Branding is a helpful way for consumers to identify and process service and product information. Product knowledge allows the consumer to distinguish between competing brands (Roy and Cornwell 2004). For a consumer to consider purchasing a product, he or she must possess some product knowledge – and often this stems from advertising. Advertising can activate product knowledge. Consumers interpret product information based on knowledge they activated during comprehension (Lee and Olshavsky 1994). Furthermore, advertising and coexisting product knowledge influence consumer behavior (e.g., Brucks 1985; Alba and Hutchinson 1987; Kim et al. 2008). These studies find that a consumer's level of product knowledge and involvement influences his or her information-processing (from the ad or the product experience). Consumers often evaluate the value of high-involvement products by concrete attributes that satisfy utilitarian needs (Park and Moon 2003). A basic informational ad can help communicate the attributes that satisfy the consumer's utilitarian needs.

An informational ad can also enhance consumer attitudes towards a brand. Consumer research indicates a mere exposure effect; that is, as a consumer becomes aware of a product (e.g., via advertising), his or her attitude toward that product becomes more positive (Zajonc and Markus 1982). Advertising, sponsorship, and event marketing may better equip target consumers with relevant information, feelings, and experiences that can increase their knowledge about a sponsor's brands in an experiential fashion (Pine and Gilmore 1998).

Advertising Entertains

Advertising as Entertainment

Entertainment refers to the extent that experiences (e.g., watching a sports program) are enjoyable. Entertainment is important, because a consumer's perceived entertainment level may transfer to his or her assessments of the ad or brand advertised during the program. Outside of the home, entertainment favorably influences attendee attitudes toward an event, which may transfer to the sponsor (Close et al. 2006). It is a good idea to expose consumers to ads under favorable conditions where there is enthusiasm, excitement, and enjoyment, so that arousal and awareness are heightened.

Advertising as Humor

Humor in advertising persuades consumers to have positive attitudes toward advertisements, which can often transfer to the brand (Zhang 1996). Humor in advertising also increases consumer attention and comprehension of ads (Weinberger and Gulas 1992). This belief has grown popular over the years and it may be hard to find an advertisement that does not use humor. Think of your favorite television commercial. Does it have a talking shark in a focus group? Or Betty White getting tackled? Or a baby trading stocks on his iPad? Likely, the ad that you call your favorite is memorable because of a humorous element.

Advertising anywhere as a Social Backdrop

Again, the main reasons that advertising is acceptable – almost anywhere – are that it enhances capitalism and that it informs consumers while heightening awareness. Ultimately, there is a more aesthetic reason that advertising is acceptable. Advertising is a social backdrop to our everyday lives. At the same time, advertising leverages live events in society via sponsorship investments and event marketing investments.

Advertising serves as eye candy, for brand logos and models showing the latest fashions and designers are alluring images. Perhaps the next question is to what extent these images beautify an otherwise dull space, juxtaposed against the way in which they overshadow natural beauty and produce excess waste in the environment. Advertising may bring some aesthetic value to an area, or offer a place to provide information to someone outside the home. In this way, when it is done tastefully and in accordance with industry and community standards, advertising serves as an artistic backdrop to our lives.

In modern US society, advertising is acceptable – even expected – almost anywhere. From advertising in toilets (yes, toilets), on grocery carts, or on parking spaces, advertisers are constantly thinking up new ways to reach consumers with brand messages outside of the home. Today, the sky is literally the limit for OOH advertising and continues to increase in popularity and in advertising spending.

There are few limits to where advertising is acceptable in the United States and other Westernized, brand-oriented cultures. This is partly because of advertising's emerging role as a backdrop for our society. Advertising provides art and information, and it can even spark creativity in one's mind and soul. Advertising sparks ideas and dreams, and encourages us to take the next step (e.g., toward education, learning, listening to music, computing, etc.).

Event Sponsorships

Reaching consumers through event sponsorships is an accepted means of advertising, and consumers tend to appreciate that a corporate sponsor is helping host their experience (Close et al. 2006). If a corporate sponsor is successful at pulling off a great event, then the sponsorship will most likely be accepted. These days most people expect that companies sponsor major sporting, cultural, or charitable events. They see event sponsorship as a positive because it decreases the cost to the participants (Murphy et al. 2011). Again, this is smart marketing. People who attend an event are invested in the actual event. The sponsor makes the event possible for this invested audience and, therefore, has a low risk of being perceived negatively by the audience (Close et al. 2006). For a sponsorship to be successful, the brand touch points need to be articulated throughout the entire event – and this can be virtually anywhere from a cab to the event to a mobile site to recap the event.

Whether advertising is acceptable is worthy of debate because of its evolving roles in contemporary society, culture, and interpersonal and family relationships. Advertising can reinforce socially and culturally accepted norms. Advertising sparks consumption, which is an active force in the construction of culture (Wallendorf and Arnould 1991). In special events and gift markets, advertising plays an extremely important function. In the United States, gift-giving is a common ritual, accounting for much of holiday spending. Corporate America appears to play an increasing role in the consumer culture that is associated with advertised brands and fashions. Furthermore, advertising can help consumers learn about politicians (if they can see through the attack ads). Some forms of advertising, such as political advertising, are a source of resistance to consumers (Holt 2002).

Advertising Resistance and Market Resistance

Despite the macro and micro benefits of advertising, there are some unintended potential effects of advertising anywhere. While my objective here is to point out why advertising is acceptable almost anywhere, I do have some concerns regarding unethical advertising. Exploitive ads or ads that speak to vulnerable populations (e.g., children, the elderly, the poor) are the most notable. Other times, advertising is blamed for a materialistic society or even one that is too fat (as in the movie *Super Size Me* (2004)) or too thin. Of course, my premise is that responsible advertising, which abides by industry standards, is acceptable almost anywhere and is necessary in the capitalistic market system in the United States. However, resistance to advertising and marketing is a concern to the field, as the field depends on consumer attitudes and behaviors toward advertised goods and services.

Market Resistance

While advertising provides us with the many benefits mentioned earlier, some consumers resist advertising in more captive places or OOH. More specifically, resistance occurs after too much or poor advertising, because of a lack of perceived need (Rumbo 2002). This key challenge to advertising (and privacy concerns) is the notion of market resistance. I suggest that the field exacerbates the resistance by focusing on behavioral rather than attitudinal resistance. Market resistance, as I see it, entails *a behavioral opposition to stereotyped status quo behaviors and rituals.*

Voluntary Simplicity and Advertising

Sometimes consumers do not want to see ads – they want to use their time in a cab time or on a flight for some peace and quiet. Voluntary simplicity, introduced in 1936, has remained a topic of interest to advertisers (Leonard-Barton 1981; Belk 2001; Craig-Lees and Hill 2002; Shaw and Newholm 2002; Zavestoski

2002; Close and Zinkhan 2009). Voluntary simplicity manifests itself in a set of behaviors indicative of a self-sufficient, low-consumption, and economically neutral lifestyle (Leonard-Barton 1981). It entails self-determination, material simplicity, human scale, personal growth, and ecological awareness (Elgin 1981). With this trend, consumers resist the dominant markets (i.e., advertised markets) for a simpler, often more intimate solution (e.g., trading, making a product) (Close and Zinkhan 2009). Market resistance may be associated with a shift in the sphere of exchange and consumption from the traditional marketplace to the virtual marketplace and the home.

This is important to explore as it relates to advertising. It would make sense that those seeking voluntary simplicity would avoid and resist traditional advertising efforts as well as OOH or captive approaches. Traditional advertising is not acceptable to everyone; however, most consumers do not seem to mind sponsorships, promotions, or other less invasive approaches. Invasion and privacy associated with some traditional or online advertising are legitimate concerns for consumers.

Privacy Concerns and Advertising

Further, technology can fuel resistance toward advertising, as some online consumers feel that mobile advertising is too invasive and violates privacy. For instance, some free apps on Facebook and other social media sites sell information to advertisers. This is usually set out in the terms and conditions, but of course most consumers do not read these lengthy legal disclaimers. Thus online consumers are exposed to privacy issues in a previously unknown way through applications embedded with emerging marketplace technologies. Since the mobile phone network is still a relatively new advertising medium, the effects of purportedly invasive applications remains inconclusive, and more research is required (Labrecque et al. 2011; Markos et al. 2012).

Advertising as a field evolves constantly with developments in technology. This is good for the field, and eventually for consumers; however, resistant attitudes and behaviors have been noted as a result of privacy and security concerns related to Internet and mobile advertising and cyber-identity theft (Close and Zinkhan 2006). For resistance to diminish, consumer trust must be regained at the intersection of business, advertising, and technology. Changing from doing things on paper to doing them online is a huge change for businesses and consumers alike, and consumers are resistant to change. So, some may claim that advertising, or more accurately over-advertising, is not particularly necessary. As macro marketing expert W. L. Wilkie (2012) has said, "It can also overstep its bounds, but in general brings wonder and real improvements to peoples' daily lives." Hence it is important.

Advertising (almost) anywhere Is Important

In conclusion, despite resisted aspects of advertising and marketing, I reinforce the point that advertising (almost) anywhere is important, to the economy and to you as the consumer. Meanwhile, it serves as a social backdrop that can be aesthetically pleasing and informative. If consumers resist traditional advertising because it is disruptive for programming, consider incorporating event marketing and sponsorship into a communications strategy. This is especially effective when the event attracts enthusiastic and active people in a domain that is synergistic with the sponsor (Close et al. 2006). Advertising and live event sponsorship presents a synergistic way to engage the consumer, especially when the sponsors create value for the consumer's benefit.

However, consumers can be especially sensitive to any sense of corporate invasion of privacy or security. Advertisers face key challenges regarding privacy (e.g., how to maintain security while publishing GPS-based ads) and consumers' advertising and market resistance. With advancements in technology and in the field, advertising may strengthen its status not only as an economic stimulus, but as something that helps bring live events to an audience, improves our lives, and makes us laugh – and laughter is always necessary.

Acknowledgment

Thank you to Melissa Flath, undergraduate research assistant.

References

Alba, J. W. and Hutchinson, U. W. (1987). Dimensions of consumer expertise. *Journal of Consumer Research* 13(Mar.): 411–454.

Belk, R. (2001). Materialism and you. *Journal of Research for Consumers* 1(May): 1–7.

Belk, R. and Pollay, R. (1985). Images of ourselves: The good life in twentieth century advertising. *Journal of Consumer Research* 11(4): 887–897.

Brucks, M. (1985). The effects of product class knowledge on information search behavior. *Journal of Consumer Research* (June 12), 1–16.

Christ, P. (2012). *KnowThis: Marketing basics*, 2nd edn. Blue Bell, PA: KnowThis Media.

Close, A. G. and Zinkhan, G. M. (2006). Cyber-identity theft. In K. Khosrow-Pour (ed.), *Encyclopedia of e-commerce, e-government, and mobile commerce*. IGI Global, pp. 1158–1162. doi:10.4018/978-1-59140-799-7

Close, A. G. and Zinkhan, G. M. (2009). Market resistance and Valentine's day events. *Journal of Business Research* 62(2): 200–207.

Close, A. G., Finney, R. Z, Lacey, R., and Sneath, J. (2006). Engaging the consumer through event marketing: Linking attendees with the sponsor, community, and brand. *Journal of Advertising Research* 46(4): 420–433.

Craig-Lees, M. and Hill, C. (2002). Understanding voluntary simplifiers. *Psychology & marketing* 19(2): 187–210.

Donohue, P. (2012). "TV" guides on subway MTA plan would have "virtual" assistants. *New York Daily News* (Mar. 6), 2.

Elgin, D. (1981). *Voluntary simplicity: Toward a way of life that is outwardly simple, inwardly rich*. New York: William Morrow.

Finney, R. Z. and Close, A. G. (2008). The virtual agency as a new force in the promotions industry. In S. Ann Becker (ed.), *Electronic commerce: Concepts, methodologies, tools and applications*. Hershey, PA: Information Science Reference, pp. 2240–2246.

Fun Theory (2009). Piano stairs – TheFunTheory.com– Rolighetsteorin.se. *YouTube*. At http://www.youtube.com/watch?v=2lXh2n0aPyw, accessed Mar. 28, 2013.

Galbi, D. (2008). U.S. annual advertising spending since 1919. At http://www.galbithink.org/ad-spending.htm, accessed Mar. 28, 2013.

Holt, D. B. (2002). Why do brands cause trouble? A dialectical theory of consumer culture and branding. *Journal of Consumer Research* 29(June): 70–90.

Kantar Media (2013). Kantar Media reports U.S. advertising expenditures increased 3 percent in 2012. *Kantar Media* (Mar. 11). At http://kantarmediana.com/intelligence/press/us-advertising-expenditures-increased-3-percent-2012, accessed Apr. 4, 2013.

Kim, S., Haley, E., and Lee, Y. J. (2008). Does consumers' product-related involvement matter when it comes to corporate ads? *Journal of Current Issues and Research in Advertising* 30(2): 37–48.

Markos, E., Labrecque, L. I., and Milne, G. R. (2011). Online personal branding: Processes, challenges, and implications. *Journal of Interactive Marketing* 25(1): 37–50.

Labrecque, L. I., Markos, E., and Milne, G. R. (2012). Web 2.0 and consumers' digital footprint: Managing privacy and disclosure choices in social media. In A. G. Close (ed.), *Online consumer behavior: Theory and research in social media, advertising, and e-tail*. New York: Routledge, pp. 157–184.

Lee, D. H. and Olshavsky, R. W. (1994). Toward a predictive model of the consumer inference process: The role of expertise. *Psychology & Marketing* 11(Mar.–Apr.): 109–127.

Leonard-Barton, D. (1981). Voluntary simplicity lifestyles and energy conservation. *Journal of Consumer Research* 8(Dec.): 243–252.

Meurer, M. and Stahl, D. O., II (1994). Informative advertising and product match. *International Journal of Industrial Organization* 12(1): 1–19.

Murphy, J. H., Cunningham, I. C. M., and Stavchansky de Lewis, L. (2011). *Integrated brand promotion management: Text, cases, and exercises*. Dubuque, IA: Kendall Hunt.

Park, C. W. and Moon, B. J. (2003). The relationship between product involvement and product knowledge: Moderating roles of product type and product knowledge type. *Psychology & Marketing* 20(11): 977–997.

Pine, B. J., II and Gilmore, J. H. (1998). Welcome to the experience economy. *Harvard Business Review* 76(July–Aug.): 97–105.

Roy, D. P. and Cornwell, T. B. (2004). The effects of consumer knowledge on responses to event sponsorships. *Psychology & Marketing* 21(Mar.): 185–207.

Rumbo, J. D. (2002). Consumer resistance in a world of advertising clutter: The case of adbusters. *Psychology & Marketing* 19(2): 127–148.

Shaw, D. and Newholm, T. (2002). Voluntary simplicity and the ethics of consumption. *Psychology & Marketing* 19(2): 167–185.

Springer, P. (2009). Introduction. In *Ads to icons: How advertising succeeds in a multimedia age*, 2nd edn. London: Kogan Page, pp. 1–22.

Taylor, L. C. (2009). Swedes do the piano two-step: Subway riders ignore escalator to make music on stairway with keyboard in online ad campaign. *Toronto Star* (Oct. 22), A04.

US Department of Commerce, Bureau of Economic Analysis (2011). Table 1.1.5: Gross domestic product. National Income and Product Accounts Tables. At http://bea.gov/iTable/iTable.cfm?ReqID=9&step=1, accessed Mar. 28, 2013.

Veloutsou, C. and O'Donnell, C. (2005). Exploring the effectiveness of taxis as an advertising medium. *International Journal of Advertising* 24(2): 217–239.

Wallendorf, M. and Arnould, E. (1991). "We gather together": Consumption rituals of Thanksgiving Day. *Journal of Consumer Research* 18(June): 13–31.

Weinberger, M. C. and Gulas, C. S. (1992). The impact of humor in advertising: A review. *Journal of Advertising* 21(4): 35–59.

Wilkie, W. L. (2012). Seeing marketing through emerging theoretical lenses: A focus on marketing's organization and societal roles. Paper presented at the Winter Marketing Educators' Conference, St Petersburg, Feb. 17.

Yoffie, D. (2007). Cola wars continue: Coke and Pepsi in 2006. HBS Case 9-706-47, Harvard Business School, Boston. At http://cvonline.uaeh.edu.mx/Cursos/Lic_virt/Mercadotecnia/DMKT008/Unidad%203/36_lec_Cola_Wars_Continue_coke_and_Pepsi_2006.pdf, accessed Mar. 28, 2013.

Yoo, B., Donthu, N., and Lee, S. (2000). An examination of selected marketing mix elements and brand equity. *Journal of the Academy of Marketing Science* 28(2): 195–211.

Zajonc, R. B. and Markus, H. B. (1982). Affective and cognitive factors in preferences. *Journal of Consumer Research* 9(Sept.): 122–131.

Zavestoski, S. (2002). The social-psychological bases of anticonsumption attitudes. *Psychology & Marketing* 19(2): 149–165.

Zhang, Y. (1996). The effect of humor in advertising: An individual-difference perspective. *Psychology & Marketing* 13(6): 531–545.

Counterargument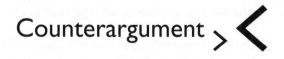

Who wants to be held captive by advertisers? Not me!

Charles Pearce

Kansas State University, USA

At the end of a short but wearying family trip, I was in a very long line going through airport security at 5.30 in the morning at the Nashville airport. The four of us – all in separate lines – got to the metal detectors, the conveyer belt, and the stern-looking uniformed staff, and I picked up one of those plastic tubs in which to empty my pockets, place my belt, my iPhone, and my shoes. It wasn't until I had cleared the conveyer belt, the metal detector, and the body scanner and was putting things back in my pockets that I noticed the ad at the bottom of the tub. The ad was printed on the paper sanitary protection placed in every tub. Sitting down at a row of chairs to put my shoes on, I looked up, and there across the wall opposite me was a row of poster ads, aimed directly at people trying to get their shoes back on.

There were four people in our party, and no one except me remembers even seeing the ads. I remember seeing them because I was livid at having an ad forced on me in a high-stress situation when I was trying to make sure that I was reunited with my possessions and no longer had to walk through the airport in my socks. Here's the thing: I remember there being ads, *but I can't remember what they were for*.

The question being debated is whether or not it is appropriate to bombard people with advertising in environments where they don't have the freedom to ignore the advertising. Three words jump out at me from that question: "appropriate," "bombard," and "freedom."

Is it appropriate? Or, to ask it the other way around: Is it *inappropriate* to bombard people? Any measure of what is or isn't appropriate shifts and changes such that what is inappropriate at one time is, if not appropriate, acceptable at other times. This is especially true in advertising where, for instance, at one time it was considered inappropriate to use the word "period" in feminine hygiene ads, and models for underwear and foundation garments in TV ads wore them on top of leotards because it was considered inappropriate to show them next to the skin. When it comes to showing skin and lace, advertising has long been held to a different standard than, say, the daytime television programs that carried the ads. And the debate over the appropriateness of advertising sugar-laden breakfast cereals, fast foods, and toys to children has yet to be resolved.

"Bombard" is a word that can easily be applied to all advertising. Ads are so much with us these days that, for the most part, we hardly even notice them. I've always been amused at statements by textbook writers and pundits who say that Americans are exposed to some 600, 3,000, or 10,000 (or whatever number has the most shock value) advertising messages a day. I'm amused because I don't think anyone has a way of really knowing. Try counting the ads that you see in a day, and you'll probably grow tired of the exercise after a few minutes, or simply forget. There's little doubt that advertising is pervasive, but much of it goes unseen or unregistered by people.

Clutter in advertising is not only a problem for consumers as they are bombarded with sheer tonnage of advertising; it is a huge problem for advertisers. The conventional wisdom says that the more ads an advertiser has out there, the more likely the ads will be seen by a good proportion of the target audience, at the least cost. That's the double punch of reach and frequency. But, as Advertiser A ratchets up reach and frequency in order to rise above the clutter, Advertisers B, C, and D are ratcheting up their reach and frequency to rise above the increased level of clutter, which causes Advertiser A to escalate, which leads to more clutter. In other words, advertisers fight clutter with more advertising, which, of course, increases the clutter.

Given this barrage of advertising, people are simply awash in it and it has become background – a continuous white noise, as it were. People have learned to tune much of it out – unless, that is, it is intrusive to the degree that it stands out from the background noise of competing messages or media content.

The intrusive nature of advertising has been complained about, probably for as long as there's been advertising. Advertising interrupts our television programs – even on channels that are subscribed to, such as on cable or satellite TV. For every page of editorial material in most consumer magazines there are at least two pages of advertising. Commercial radio interrupts a steady stream of music or talk. Even music delivered through the Internet through services like Pandora, are interrupted occasionally by commercial messages – unless the listener pays to upgrade from free access to the subscription version. Highways may be less cluttered with billboards than before the Highway Beautification Act, but outdoor boards are still very much with us. Early adopters of the World Wide Web decried the day that the web went commercial, and it didn't take long before the Web was packed with ads. And so it goes. Anytime a new medium arises, advertisers are among the first to try to exploit it.

Commercial message avoidance has become routine with television viewers. The remote control was the first device that allowed viewers to conveniently skip channels when the commercials came on. Viewers used the remote to cycle through the channels during the commercial, and it became a game (at least for me) to judge how long to pause on each channel to get back to the original channel just when the program returned. With DVRs becoming more common, people find that skipping commercials is easier than ever, either by fast-forwarding, or skipping over them. Some advertisers have attempted to defeat the fast-forwarding by keeping the logo stationary on the screen through the commercial. Even if the viewer skims the commercial by fast-forwarding, at least the logo gets seen. There is some speculation that viewers' attention to skimmed messages may be heightened as they watch for the commercials to end.

One key to understanding audience members' avoidance response to intrusive advertising on television is in the name of the device that they have adopted to counter it – the remote control. The operant word is "control." It is the networks and advertisers that control when commercials interrupt our television programs. People don't like intrusions, and they want control. The power of control over the media being consumed is often manifested in who controls the remote control. Many televisions these days can't even be operated without the remote, thus giving the one who controls the remote the power to control the medium. Take that, advertisers!

But we all know that this control doesn't give us the power to control all of the advertising coming at us. After a while, trying to skip the commercials becomes like work: it takes constant vigilance and ready access to the remote, so most folks give in and let the commercials simply wash over them again. Advertisers know that, and know that while consumers may be able to duck some messages, they can't duck them all – if, that is, there are enough messages out there.

The so-called new media have become advertising-laden, as iPod and iPad apps carry ads to keep the apps low-cost or even free. When Apple launched the App Store, it announced that the apps could carry advertising, called iAds. Apple sells the ads and keeps 40 percent of the revenue, the remaining 60 percent going to the developers. At the time, Apple was looking beyond simple banners toward "totally immersive and interactive" ads within the apps.

Computer game developers include ads to generate revenue, but also because they think the ads give the games more of a sense of realism. Or, to look at it another way, advertising is so present in our world that a computer or video game wouldn't look realistic unless there are ads in the background. A new category of advertising has been created called "advergames." These are games that are offered free online, especially on social media sites, such as Facebook, which generally revolve around a product or service being advertised. Before one can play a popular game like "Farmville" on Facebook, for instance, the player has to agree to give up all of the information in his or her personal profile, including profile picture, gender, networks, user ID, list of friends, and any other information they have made public. Ads for products or services targeted at people with certain kinds of interests shown in their profile will soon appear on their user page.

Ads have even been placed above and inside urinals in public restrooms. Los Angeles County has proposed selling space at the public beach, such as lifeguard stands, trash cans, and volleyball nets – even allowing (paying) companies to stamp their logo in the sands. And, of course, nearly every professional sporting event is sponsored by advertising, and ads surround the fields of play – some are inserted electronically so that people watching the event at home will see ads directed at them, while the people in the stands see others.

The Internet is certainly not free of ads. Banners, interstitials, pop-ups, pop-unders, overlays, audio on web pages that starts when the page opens, adware, cookies, and so on are prevalent on the Web. Pop-up blockers come built in to most web browsers these days, but advertisers quickly found a way around that with pop-unders – ads that appear below the browser window and are seen only when the user closes the window. Banner ads are animated so that they are hard to ignore while they insistently bounce or flash or jiggle. The search engine Google makes most of its money with advertising and tracks users to check their browsing history and gather information that may be useful to advertisers.

And it wasn't long after email went public (as opposed to being channels used only by universities and government agencies) that email inboxes began filling up with unwanted email advertising, otherwise known as "spam." Compounding people's aggravation with spam is the dubious nature of many of the products or services being offered. Almost as soon as one's spam-blocker or filter is trained to look for certain patterns of language or certain keywords, the "spammers" find other ways to sneak through.

In short, instead of trying to count all the places and ways that advertising is aimed at us, we would find it easier to think of places where ads are *not*. Few places come to mind where one is not confronted with advertising. What about churches, you ask? Some churches have found that they can offset the cost of printing the service bulletin by including "safe" and "noncontroversial" ads. What about schools? Schools have become prime targets for advertisers. Some even offer free educational programming to the schools in return for allowing advertising into the classroom. Kids are so brand-conscious that even if ads in schools were banned, logos would show up anyway on apparel, backpacks, lunch boxes, notebooks, and so on.

Universities are not above selling ad space inside student unions, on information boards, kiosks, and other high-traffic areas. Ads are sold on concert and theater programs, museum guides, and anywhere a logo or message can be printed. Sporting teams are often sponsored by athletic apparel and footwear companies, such as Nike and Reebok to the extent that many teams have agreements to use the goods of one company only. Many universities are "Coke campuses," while others are "Pepsi campuses," as universities enter into exclusive agreements to allow only one brand or the other to sell and vend on campus.

To ask the question again: Where can one go to completely escape advertising? The only places that come to mind are deep wilderness, or the middle of an ocean (not on a cruise ship, of course). The bombardment is so continuous and so ubiquitous that one finds it challenging, if not impossible, to imagine a world devoid of advertising. So, whether it is appropriate for advertisers to bombard people with messages is a moot point, because we're already continually being bombarded and it isn't likely to slow down, much less stop.

But what about my freedom, or lack of it, to avoid intrusive messages? Proponents of unfettered advertising will say that no one has a gun to the public's collective heads, no one is making people watch, listen to, or read ads. And, while that's true, what it ignores is the advertisers' growing adeptness at putting messages precisely where it is difficult, if not impossible, to ignore them. As we stated above, advertisers fight advertising clutter with more advertising, which leads to more clutter, which is fought with more advertising, and on it goes.

However, consumers are also becoming adept at advertising avoidance. The DVR, the remote control, the page flip, the mouse click, give consumers the freedom to duck many, if not most, ads. But, even these methods require some work by consumers and can't eliminate all advertising. Some of it is going to get through whatever barriers consumers put up. And the fact that advertising is so much with us means that it is inevitable that ads are going to reach us in environments and spaces that make avoiding them impossible.

It can be argued that most intrusive advertising is unwanted advertising; it has little or no value to the consumers who don't want it, and didn't ask for it. For instance, anyone above the age of, say, three has seen commercials for Viagra and Cialis, but only a tiny portion of the audience find those ads of any value. And the same can be said of nearly all the prescription drug advertising that uses mass advertising to reach a small number of people. Those advertisers use a shotgun where a rifle would be more effective.

Those who don't find value in some advertisements are likely to consider the ads annoying interruptions, intrusive, and wasteful. But people who find some value in some ads don't find those ads intrusive, wasteful, or annoying. People often seek out advertising when faced with making a purchase decision that has some risk to it, when they feel that the information they possess is limited or outdated, or when new products enter the marketplace (in order to learn about them). People seek out, or are receptive to, advertising that has entertainment value.

Ads have gone viral on YouTube, leading to these ads being seen by millions of sets of eyes – eyes that *want* to see the ads. Many people watch the Super Bowl as much for the ads as for the game – especially if their team isn't one of the two playing. People like talking about ads they've encountered that they enjoy, that entertain or inform them. In short, people tend to hate advertising, but love ads.

Even ads that are enjoyed by people may work against the advertiser. The advertiser runs the risk of making the ad too entertaining, so that people remember the ad, but forget the advertiser. Or, what entertains some people – even in the target audience – may annoy others, even if they're all in the same target audience. And ads that initially entertain people may quickly wear out, once people know the premise and the punch line. No one likes to hear the same joke over and over, so even entertaining ads that run too long run the risk of wearing thin and annoying people.

Thus, my argument is that most ads, almost by definition, are intrusive. Second, ads are inescapable. And, third, while people may have some freedom to avoid ads, avoiding all of them is nearly impossible. This makes nearly all of us audiences, captive audiences.

It is not *inappropriate*. Out of necessity, advertisers find themselves in an environment where everyone is shouting at the same time, and the advertiser that shouts the loudest and longest just might get noticed. It could be argued that every advertising budget for nationally advertised consumer products or service could be cut in half, or more, and the cacophony may quieten down by half. But it would take every advertiser to cut their budgets simultaneously, and that is not likely ever to happen.

As a consumer, I may become annoyed when I am bombarded with advertising in an environment where I don't have the freedom to ignore it, but that's about the worst thing that will happen. If anything is remembered from this unpleasant encounter, it probably will be the annoyance and not the advertiser. Even if the advertiser is remembered, I have now associated a negative feeling toward the brand and may go out of my way to avoid not only future advertising for it, but the brand altogether. Finally, while it may not be inappropriate for these advertisers to target a captive audience, it might work, it might not work, or it just might boomerang. So, why do it?

16

Advertising and Social Responsibility

> *There are always protests,*
> *whether you do something good*
> *or bad. Even if you do*
> *something beneficial, people say*
> *you do it because it's*
> *advertising.*
>
> Giorgio Armani

We have tackled a number of advertising issues in this book. By now, you have probably figured out that no matter how one-sided a controversial issue might appear to be, there is always more than one way to think about it, at least when it comes to advertising.

Advertising and social responsibility, cause-related marketing, socially conscious advertising campaigns, or any of the other names you might attach to it – this is an issue that at first glance seems like a winning strategy for the advertiser and the consumer. How can it be otherwise?

The other night, while driving to a meeting, I heard a story on the radio about a diaper company planning to donate millions of brand-name diapers to a diaper center that would then distribute them to low-income families who would not otherwise be able to afford them. What could possibility be wrong with that? The news report highlighted the strategy of the company. At the forefront was

Advertising and Society: An Introduction, Second Edition. Edited by Carol J. Pardun.
© 2014 John Wiley & Sons, Inc. Published 2014 by John Wiley & Sons, Inc.

the notion that getting the brand into the hands of parents and the tiniest consumers was a sure way to build brand loyalty over the long haul. Much later in the story came the idea that the company wanted to help struggling families.

In this "leaner, meaner" corporate environment, when a company devotes part of its profits to socially responsible causes, we tend to be appreciative and, perhaps, even a little star struck. But is it compassion, or is it consumerism? Debra Merskin and Peggy Kreshel each have their opinion and make their arguments thoroughly and thoughtfully. Who makes the strongest case? *You decide.*

Ideas to Get You Thinking . . .

1   Pick a magazine that has a lot of ads (you might try a weekly news magazine like *Time*). Look at each ad and see if there is something in it that indicates "social responsibility." Make a list of all the ones you find. What's the proportion of socially responsible ads compared to other ones? Is there any kind of pattern as to the kinds of companies that tend to use social responsibility as a strategy?

2   Find an ad that uses social responsibility as its creative strategy. Identify what "social good" the company is selling and then do some research and see if you can verify what the company is claiming. To get started, you might go online and look at the company's homepage, read the annual report, or do a newspaper search with LexisNexis. Does the message on the corporate website match the message in the ad? How significant is the contribution that the company is providing?

3   Should all companies practice social responsibility? If so, should they advertise the good they are doing? Think of some companies that are often thought of negatively (you might start with oil companies). Think of a socially responsible act this company could engage in. Try to write an ad about it.

Other Topics to Debate

1   Companies should be required to reveal how much money is being spent in an effort to be "socially responsible."

2   A labeling system should be developed that would indicate how deeply committed a company is to social responsibility (perhaps like fair trade labels on coffee). These labels should be required on every advertisement that a company prints if it wants to use social responsibility as an advertising strategy.

3   Only companies that pass a certain level of "social caring" should be allowed to use social responsibility as a creative advertising strategy. For example, tobacco companies might not be allowed to use social responsibility as a strategy because the Surgeon General has determined that smoking is not a social good.

If You'd Like to Know More . . .

Du, S. and Bhattacharya, C. B. (2010). Maximizing business returns to corporate social responsibility (CSR): The role of CSR communication. *International Journal of Management Reviews* 12(1): 8–19.

Fernandez, D. and Santalo, J. (2010). When necessity becomes a virtue: The effect of product market competition on corporate responsibility. *Journal of Economics and Management Strategy* 19(2): 453–487.

Kotler, D. and Lee, N. (2004). *Corporate social responsibility: Doing the most for your company and your cause.* Hoboken, NJ: Wiley.

Luo, X. and Bhattacharya, C. B. (2009). The debate over doing good: Corporate social performance, strategic marketing levers, and firm-idiosyncratic risk. *Journal of Marketing* 73: 198–213.

Michelli, J. A. (2006). *The Starbucks experience: Five principles for turning ordinary into extraordinary.* New York: McGraw-Hill.

Sangle, S. (2009). Critical success factors for corporate social responsibility: A public sector perspective. *Corporate Social Responsibility and Environmental Management* 17: 205–214.

Sisodia, R., Wolfe, D., and Sheth, J. (2007). *Firms of endearment: How world-class companies profit from passion and purpose.* Upper Saddle River, NJ: Pearson.

Argument

Companies are wise – and ethical – to use "social responsibility" as a creative strategy

Debra Merskin

University of Oregon, USA

"We see a dream of the sea," says the headline for a recent Microsoft ad touting its teaming up with Boys & Girls Clubs of America to connect kids with technology. The copy tells readers the company has established more than 2,700 computer learning centers, which help more than one million children. The double-page, four-color ad shows a happy African American girl sitting at her computer gazing out the window, upon which an aquarium scene is painted. The white drawing on the window makes it look as if she is wearing a deep-sea diving helmet. Another "brown" child walks by, toting his backpack, looking longingly in. Above the logo is the statement, "Your potential. Our passion." Microsoft Corporation and founder Bill Gates give millions of dollars every year to causes. They also spend millions of dollars each year telling consumers about their generosity.

In this essay, I briefly describe the foundations of social responsibility (SR) as a corporate and creative strategy, provide examples of this approach, discuss the benefits to advertisers and to consumers, and finally articulate three reasons why SR is a smart, ethical, and effective creative strategy for advertisers to use. I argue that SR is smart and ethical if three conditions are met: (1) the advertiser is truthfully and actively engaged in the cause or concern represented; (2) there is a clear and associative relationship between said cause and the advertised product; and (3) the ads educate and inform consumer citizens about social issues, concerns, and needs. Presenting the SR position of the company therefore rises above motivation for purely economic gain, and avoids the charge that it is "the maximization of personal wealth or other forms of self interest" (Clark 1993: 307).

What Is Social Responsibility?

What you stand for is even more important than what you stand in.

Kenneth Cole, 2003

Organizations, be they governmental, corporate, religious or educational, are obligated to act in an ethical manner when it comes to performing responsibilities. States, for example, have a responsibility to insure the democratic rights of citizens. Corporations are responsible for the well-being not only of employees, but also of the society that supports them. SR is a "multidimensional" concept that goes beyond respecting people, places, and things, to recognizing and appreciating the "interdependence and connectedness with others and our environment" (Berman and La Farge 1993: 7). Defined as "the alignment of business operations with social values," SR involves "integrating the interests of stakeholders, all of those affected by a company's conduct, into the company's business policies and actions" (Coors and Winegarden 2005: 10). However, not everyone agrees with this approach.

In 1962 the influential libertarian economist Milton Friedman (2002 [1962]) said that if good is done in the interest of generating a profit, fine, but that businesses have no obligations to society, only to stockholders. While Friedman did not approve of fraudulent or deceptive practices, he felt that corporations were generating goodwill by providing jobs for communities, and as a result more profits. Today, however, consumers are increasingly following the money corporations make and are increasingly aware of the impact these companies have on their environments and on local economies.

SR as a creative strategy made its official foray into advertising in the 1980s. In 1983 American Express launched a campaign to help restore the decaying Statue of Liberty and pledged money every time a consumer signed up and was given a new card, bought traveler's checks, or purchased an Express travel package worth $500 or more. Cardholder charges rose 30 percent and the company donated $1.7 million to the Statue of Liberty–Ellis Island Foundation. The company spent $4 million advertising its involvement and pledge (Wiegner 1985: 248).

Jerry Welsh, marketing executive at American Express Travel Related Services, declared, in 1985, "social responsibility is a good marketing hook" (quoted in Wiegner 1985: 248). Welsh was not referring to philanthropy, nor to public service advertising, but instead to a growing consumer consciousness about the importance of doing business with corporations that do good in terms of employee well-being, impact on the environment, and concerns with social issues. He found social consciousness a surprising survivor of the 1970s "me generation's" narcissism and hyper-individuality. Similar efforts came from General Foods, which, in partnership with Pacific Bell, launched a "Pop into a Park" campaign to encourage year-round state park use. The same year, General Foods' Tang sponsored a "March Across America" for Mothers Against Drunk Drivers, donating 10-cent coupons and guaranteeing a contribution of not less than $100,000.

Kenneth Cole (2003), in his autobiography *Footnotes*, states that the atmosphere in the United States was changing with the economic downturn and high unemployment and people responded. "A pervasive consciousness, a sense of activism was sweeping the United States. The idea that we could collectively impact these tragedies was mobilizing everyone" (2003: 142). Cole and other corporations joined the growing commercial consciousness by aligning with social causes and activism, and made this apparent in their advertising.

Social Responsibility as a Creative Strategy

At first glance, SR and advertising creative strategy might seem mutually exclusive. However, if it is applied clearly and honestly, it can be employed to their advantage by companies whose products have a perceived relationship with quality-of-life issues and the concerns of consumers to reinforce corporate image, to establish "reason to buy" for a particular product or service, and to give back to the world from which they earn their profits. Tinic (1997: 4) posits that advertising can be regarded as a "significant site of cultural production" and thereby become a location for public discourse around meaning, social values, and corporate goals. More simply put, "advertising which typically aims to sell a product by associating it with a resonant image, identity, lifestyle or ethos, is a form of persuasive communication that can be effectively harnessed for explicitly prosocial purposes" (Stadler 2004: 592). Thus, the brand becomes an active agent in the process.

Sometimes a company's involvement with social issues and the promotion of these activities in advertising are obviously linked. Companies such as women's clothier J. Jill's Compassion Fund (www.jjill.com), established in June 2002, has given out more than $700,000 in grants, and donated more than $3 million to "help women in need regain their self-sufficiency and independence." The Massachusetts-based national women's clothing retailer targets organizations that help poor and homeless women.

An example of an unsuccessful use of the SR strategy was the $100 million advertising campaign by the Philip Morris Companies (now the Altria Group) publicizing their charitable giving. The company "patted itself on the back for donating to, among others, flood victims and battered women" (Elliott 2005: 9). Several companies who wanted to show concern for the south Asian tsunami victims steered clear: the thinking was that anything but philanthropy would be "perceived as exploiting a tragedy," according to Cliff Sloan, former president and CCO of the Sloan Group – "It's just not appropriate to plant your flag in a fresh wound" (quoted in Elliott 2005: 9).

The Spectrum of SR

Does the "do good," or at least "do no harm," approach work when combined with advertising? Obviously, the objective of any advertising campaign is to increase something: sales, awareness, market share, or brand image. Many corporations have used social responsibility as a creative strategy, particularly corporate social responsibility (CSR). CSR campaigns fall along a continuum from institutionalized programs at one end to promotional programs at the other (Pirsch et al. 2007). Institutionalized programs, using company-wide programs, integrate the aim of decreasing consumer skepticism with diversity, human rights, and environmental programs and enhance loyalty (e.g., Stony-field Yogurt), whereas promotional programs use SR as a sales tool to focus on increasing sales and pleasing stockholders (e.g., Bombay Co.). Some of the more effective and ethical companies that tend toward the institutional-ized end of the spectrum include Kenneth Cole, Tom's of Maine, Ben & Jerry's, and Starbucks, all of whom use a variety of media and methods in their advertising tactics. These and other companies have often eschewed the use of traditional or conventional advertising, instead relying on word of mouth, collateral materials (on recycled paper), and product placement to present a consistent message built around corporate images as a socially responsible agent.

Kenneth Cole

Kenneth Cole, the founder and the corporation, is known for attention to social issues and concern for AIDS awareness. As Cole writes, "Advertising is an opportunity to introduce your point of view, as well as to define the nature of the relationship you'd like to have with the customer. And it can even be a chance to say something important" (2003: 121). Cole's company, Kenneth Cole Productions, has often focused on AIDS awareness and prevention. In 1986 Cole's first ad promoting AIDS awareness was "For the Future of Our Children." Photographed by Annie Leibovitz, it featured supermodels Christie Brinkley, Beverly Johnson, Andie MacDowell, and Kelly Emberg, among others, holding children and babies. In 1992 another Cole ad only had the copy, "If we told you a shoe could help find a cure for AIDS, would you buy it?" This ad announced a month-long campaign in which 15 percent of every shoe purchase price would go to AIDS research. The Kenneth Cole Foundation established Awearness (www.awearness.com), a nonprofit initiative that uses blogs, events, products, and partnerships to encourage awareness and reward activism. All proceeds from related events and sales go to the fund (Liodice 2010).

Reebok

Athletic shoe and apparel maker Reebok stepped up to the corporate responsibility plate in May 2007 when it launched the Reebok Global Corporate Citizenship Program. Reebok employees, retailers, consumers, artists, and athletes participate in this extension of the company's Reebok's Global Corporate Citizenship platform. For example, "Reebok 4 Real" is a program designed to empower by recognizing and rewarding individual achievement among global youth with scholarships. According to the corporate website, the program is "the catalyst for realising the brand purpose: empowering global youth to fulfill its potential." The program has two components: the Human Rights Student Advocate Program and the Community and Education Program. The Human Rights Student Advocate Program pairs Reebok employees with high school students, offers grant opportunities to schools, and encourages mentorships with employees and students in community relations work. The Community and Education Program connects athletes and artists with committed students. Reebok donates supplies and equipment to high-achieving students and their schools.

Tom's of Maine

Founded in 1970 in Kennebunk, Maine, by Tom and Kate Chappel, Tom's of Maine, a natural personal and home care company, makes "products without artificial preservatives, sweeteners, or dyes and without animal testing or animal ingredients." Close identification with consumers is part of their corporate philosophy: "Tom's of Maine will become the trusted partner in natural care among consumers with whom we share common values."

Tom's of Maine's advertising promotes all-natural ingredients, environmentally sensitive packaging, and, with clean, clear graphics and exaggerated image proportions of fruit, herb, or mineral, the ads focus on messages of purity and trust. Advertising for Tom's appears in publications such as *Yoga Journal*, *Prevention*, and *Natural Health Magazine*, the latter of which provided complementary copy touting the ingredients and benefits of Tom's mouthwash:

> Tom's of Maine's Natural Anticavity Fluoride Mouthwash is alcohol free and contains the antioxidant green tea along with aloe vera juice and chamomile to soothe the mouth all of which makes it ideal for sensitive sorts. (Natural Health Magazine 2006)

The company website states the credo: "We believe our company can be profitable and successful while acting in a socially and environmentally responsible manner."

Ben & Jerry's

Ben Cohen and Jerry Greenfield went into business together in Burlington, Vermont, in 1978. Their ice cream business was built on an SR premise, including in their products "only fresh Vermont cream & milk, & the best & biggest chunks of nuts, fruits, candies & cookies." Distinctive products with names such as Chunky Monkey, Cherry Garcia, Sorbet Volcano, and Phish Food, connect with consumers' sense of the past and the present. This style is reinforced by graphics and designs on product containers. In 1992 Ben & Jerry's made the following public statement upholding its values:

> Affirming our belief that business has a responsibility to the environment and should uphold a set of aspirational principles. Whether it is in sourcing ingredients, supporting non-profit organizations, or using our ice cream to help better the environment, we think it's important to lead with our values.

The company's strong graphic identity consistently presents a happy, black-and-white bovine standing in a green field, with white, fluffy clouds frolicking above. The company has used advertising not only to promote products, but also to speak out on issues. The website includes links to the mission statement (which addresses social product and economic missions), the Occupy Movement (supporting it), an "Environmental" page about their greener, cleaner freezers, nongenetically modified beings, and a Peace and Justice page. There are links to pages about the environment, waste, and global warming. For more than 20 years the company has produced a "Social and Environmental Assessment Report." The 2010 report emphasizes fair trade towns and universities and the Ben & Jerry's Foundation, which provides grants to grassroots community organizations.

Ben & Jerry's ice cream cartons are also used to carry the company message of commitment to SR. A container of "Fossil Fuel" ice cream, for example, carries the statement: "We oppose recombinant Bovine Growth Hormones," and a pledge from family farmers who supply milk and cream to the corporation. Outdoor advertising, cinema ads, and free taste-testing promotions are also a part of the creative strategy that effectively links the brand with environmental

SR. The company was listed among "10 companies with social responsibility at the core" by *Advertising Age* magazine in 2010 (Liodice 2010).

Starbucks

Also listed among *Advertising Age*'s 10 companies is Starbucks. Founded in 1971, Seattle-based Starbucks identified early and often the importance of promoting its products in a way that highlighted the importance of the process of procurement. Each year, Starbucks produces "Beyond the Cup," an annual report of the company's social responsibility, which describes the company's social, "environmental and economic impacts in the communities" in which it does business. Its "Guiding Principles" include building community, a commitment to youth, a supplier diversity plan, and sustaining coffee communities.

Howard Schultz, Starbucks founder and chair, established the Starbucks Foundation in 1997. The "Make Your Mark" campaign matches volunteer hours with cash contributions to designated nonprofit organizations ($10 per hour, up to $1,000 per project). In 2005 the company contributed more than $1.4 million to such organizations.

A full-page, two-color ad in the *New York Times* describes Starbucks' commitment to fair trade coffee beans. The headline for the all-text ad, "Small coffee farms don't grow small coffee," appears over a background of an exterior, pale green wall, and a cornice featuring the Starbucks logo. Notably, the copy about the company's commitment appears above the logo as a way of visually demonstrating purpose over profits. The ad invites readers to visit Starbucks' website, "To learn more about what we value," at www.whatmakescoffeegood.com, where viewers can "follow the bean" from picking to grinding, accompanied by the ambient sounds of a busy Starbucks store. Its "Ethos Water" campaign brings clean drinking water to more than one billion people. Starbucks has committed more than $6.2 million in grants to the program (Liodice 2010).

Conclusion

How do corporations benefit by taking the SR approach in their advertising? Certainly, having employees who are committed to corporate causes is good for morale and corporate image. Sherry Southern, a vice president at Starbucks, said she targeted the company in her job search because "I really wanted to work at a company that treats its employees with respect and as part of the solution instead of the opposite" (quoted in Weber 2005: para. 7). A 2003 study by Stanford University and the University of California, Santa Barbara, of 800 MBA students at 11 top North American and European business schools found that 94 percent would accept as much as a 14 percent lower salary to work for environmentally friendly, employee-concerned, socially responsible corporations (Weber 2005).

Out of respect for people who purchase their products, I argue, corporations, particularly those that avow socially responsible practices and use this position as an advertising creative strategy, must acknowledge their debt to the people who work for them, to the people who support them, and follow through with participation and performance – that is, walk the walk of the talk they profess.

Despite protests by ice cream lovers, investors, lagging stock prices, and slowed sales led to Ben & Jerry's sale to Unilever in 2000. The ice cream company with a corporate conscience became another unit in Unilever's port-folio. Odwalla, who was picked up by Coca-Cola, picked up Fresh Samantha. Nike bought Converse. Stonyfield Farms sold to Danone. Estée Lauder bought Aveda, and L'Oreal picked up Body Shop. Tom's of Maine became a subsidiary of Colgate-Palmolive. Will it make a difference in philosophy and advertising strategy and ethics that these once alternative, natural companies are now part of multinational conglomerates? If, as Tom's of Maine founder Tom Chappell says, 25 percent of Americans are interested in buying their products from SR companies, and it was the growth that made them attractive to the big compa-nies, that is a good thing. Coors and Winegarden (2005: 11) remind us, "Just because the advertising comes in the form of social responsibility does not make it any less like advertising." Yet SR, grounded in ethical fundamentals, is a crea-tive strategy from which we can all benefit. SR as a creative strategy is ethical if the company legitimately supports the causes for which it clamors, has a con-nection to the product, and is truthful in its statements. Consumers benefit by receiving complete information and can spend their dollars with companies who share their opinions, beliefs, and ideals.

References

Berman, S. and La Farge, P. (1993). *Promising practices in teaching social responsibil-ity*. New York: SUNY Press.

Clark, C. R. (1993). Social responsibility ethics: Doing right, doing good, doing well. *Ethics & Behavior* 3(3–4): 303–327.

Cole, K. (2003). *Footnotes*. New York: Simon & Schuster.

Coors, A. C. and Winegarden, W. (2005). Corporate responsibility or good advertising? *Regulation* (Spring), 10–11.

Elliott, S. (2005). The delicate task of showing corporate concern for the tsunami victims, without seeming promotional. *New York Times* (Jan. 4), 9.

Friedman, M. (2002 [1962]). *Capitalism and freedom*. Chicago: University of Chicago Press.

Liodice, B. (2010). 10 companies with social responsibility at the core. *Advertising Age* (Apr. 19). At http://adage.com/article/cmo-strategy/10-companies-social-responsibility-core/143323/, accessed Mar. 29, 2013.

Natural Health Magazine (2006). A sweeter smile. *Natural Health Magazine* (Mar.), 28.

Pirsch, J., Gupta, S., and Grau, S. L. (2007). A framework for understanding corporate social responsibility programs as a continuum: An exploratory study. *Journal of Business Ethics* 70(2): 125–140.

Stadler, J. (2004). AIDS ads: Make a commercial, make a difference? Corporate social responsibility and the media. *Continuum: Journal of Media & Cultural Studies* 18: 591–610.

Tinic, S. (1997). United colors and untied meanings: Benetton and the commodification of social issues. *Journal of Communication* 47: 3–25.

Weber, G. (2005). The recruiting payoff of social responsibility. *Workforce Management* (Jan.). At http://www.workforce.com/section/06/article/23/93/45.html, accessed Mar. 29, 2013.

Wiegner, K. K. (1985). A cause on every carton? *Forbes* (Nov. 18), 248–249.

Websites

Ben & Jerry's: www.benjerry.com/
Kenneth Cole: www.kennethcole.com
Starbucks: www.starbucks.com/
Tom's of Maine: www.tomsofmaine.com

Counterargument ❯❮

Cause-related marketing as a business strategy is ethically flawed

Peggy Kreshel

University of Georgia, USA

> *Philanthropy is like hippy music, holding hands. RED is more like punk rock, hip hop; this should feel like hard commerce. People see a world out of whack. and they want to do the right thing, but they're not sure what that is. RED is about doing what you enjoy and doing good at the same time.*
>
> Bono at World Economic Forum, 2006

In January 2006, rock star and activist Bono introduced the global brand Red to benefit the Global Fund to Fight AIDS, Tuberculosis and Malaria at the World

Economic Forum in Davos, Switzerland. Red campaign partner corporations (at the time of the launch, GAP, American Express, Armani, and Converse) produce and market Red-themed specialty products, and a portion of the revenue from the sale of these products goes to the Global Fund. Today, choosing from "hundreds of products in more than 70 countries," shoppers contribute by buying items ranging from GAP Empowe(Red) T-shirts, Red iPod Nanos, and Nike Red shoelaces to Starbucks beverages, Hallmark greeting cards, and Belvedere Vodka in a special edition bottle.[1]

Bono emphasized at the outset that Red was a *commercial* venture, *not* philanthropy. Bringing together a globally recognized cause, corporate "partners" with highly marketable brands, high-profile celebrities, and consumers already immersed in a highly commercialized culture, who rarely question how buying "stuff" translates into the alleviation of human suffering on "faraway" continents, Red was the first cause-marketing effort to allow brands as well as the cause to make a profit. This commercial imperative, Bono explained, was essential to maintaining a revenue stream for the Global Fund.

The Red campaign helped people understand a new fundraising model (Kingston 2007), so perhaps it is not surprising that the campaign has been surrounded by controversy. One of the most recognized critics is a San Francisco-based organization, Buy(LESS), whose mission is "on an individual level to provide a means for people to donate directly to charity, to remind them that this is the most efficient way to support a cause, and to inspire less consumption over all." On the site, in an open letter to Bobby Shriver, Red's CEO, Ben Davis, a San Francisco marketing executive and co-creator of the site, lauds the Red campaign as "an extraordinary and innovative endeavor [with] the potential to do amazing good"; however, echoing a common criticism, he urges Shriver to provide more administrative transparency and make it easy to donate to the fund without purchase. The Buy(LESS) site provides information about and direct "donate" links to a number of charities including the Global Fund.[2]

The rapidity with which the Red campaign has become a highly visible, widely recognized component of American culture, and indeed, global culture, is noteworthy. Today, in a practice critics label "celebrity colonialism," a stable of celebrities among them, Oprah Winfrey, Steven Spielberg, Christy Turlington, Penelope Cruz, and Mary J. Bilge support Red and help sell products, enhancing the brand's "cool quotient" and credibility. As of December 2011, Red had contributed $180 million to the Global Fund.[3]

Still, controversy surrounds the campaign. A 2011 book, *Brand aid: Shopping well to save the world*, offers a stinging critique of what it calls Red's "compassionate consumption," arguing that "problems are created and understood only in the ways that allow them to be solved by these [corporate] interventions. Thus, in the Red example, AIDS can be thought of in no other way outside of the primacy of drugs" (Richey and Ponte 2011: 15). Individuals have an opportunity to become involved through "heroic shopping."

The Red campaign and a constellation of related efforts have emerged in the context of changes (perhaps appropriately identified as transformations) in culture, and more particularly in business culture. Amid corporate scandal, financial uncertainty, government bail outs, and increasing recognition of both the necessity for and the fragility of global relationships, consumer expectations of corporations have changed fairly dramatically. The public has shifted from merely accepting the corporation as a plausible solution to social problems to "demanding that corporations become 'full-fledged' global citizens" (Benett et al. 2009: 5).

In response to this demand, corporations have increasingly adopted a corporate social norm to do good (Kotler and Lee 2005; Benett et al. 2009; Littler 2009), undertaking a variety of initiatives in the name of corporate social responsibility and good corporate citizenship; cause-related marketing is but one. The coupling of product marketing and cause fund-raising has transformed corporate philanthropy. Once viewed as an obligation, corporate giving is increasingly viewed as a strategy to attain corporate objectives while simultaneously signaling corporate social responsibility (Smith 1994; Kotler and Lee 2005; White 2007).

In this essay, I will argue that the use of cause-related marketing as a business strategy is ethically flawed. In making my argument, I begin with a brief history of the evolution of corporate social responsibility and the emergence and evolution of cause-related marketing as a business strategy. As a part of that account, I highlight early, widely recognized, influential critiques of the concept of social responsibility as it applies to business. These critiques, clearly products of particular historical circumstances, nonetheless provide a valuable starting point from which I develop my argument: widely publicized celebrations of the successes of cause-related initiatives camouflage a number of troubling ethical issues which should be considered, and indeed which might have emerged upon a more critical examination of the often touted "win–win–win" cause-marketing scenario. Interspersed throughout that discussion are snapshots drawn from a health or disease-related cause, breast cancer, illustrating the bases of my argument as well as providing evidence of its veracity. In a concluding section, I provide a brief summary and pose a series of questions to bring to the forefront precisely that which has gone unexamined in "a nation that shops to save the world."

The trend toward increased recognition and adoption of corporate social responsibility as a philosophy and a set of practices, as well as the controversies, comforts, and discomforts surrounding it are best understood in the context of an evolving social contract. In this section, I first clarify the concept and then overview the evolution of corporate social responsibility in the "cycle of definition and redefinition" of that contract.

A complex philosophical theory about how groups of people maintain social order, the social contract in a *vastly oversimplified* sense, is about how society is structured so that we "get along." White writes that the social contract was a precursor to the ideas of democracy wherein ultimate power resides with citizens who willingly delegate certain authority to the state so that individuals might fruitfully participate in a social arrangement that enhances the shared prospects among all prospects in a shared community. (2007: 4)

Early formulations of the social contract didn't include corporations, but were about the relationships between individuals and between individuals and the government. Public health, education, welfare, and safety were just that – *public* goods; providing those goods was a government function. Corporate intervention was rare.

Corporations became actors in this contract only as they expanded in scope and complexity. In the late nineteenth century, corporations came to be granted many of the privileges and protections of "natural persons." In *Good for business: The rise of the conscious corporation* (2009), Benett and colleagues note that this change in legal status had a profound impact on corporations' behavior:

> Had corporations shown a "human face" in ensuing decades, the world would look very different today. Instead, many companies accepted all the rights and privileges of being "human" without adopting most of the positive traits that arguably constitute such, including empathy, respect, fairness, and generosity. Once freed from the charters that had long bound them, these businesses sought to maximize profit and growth at any cost.

As the social contract evolved to include the relationship between *business*, government, and society: the responsibility of business became the creation of shareholder profits.

> According to an unspoken ethic, society was well served when each of its three sectors, business, government, and nonprofit was permitted to do what it did best without intruding in the affairs of the others. (Smith 1994)

When government began to issue rules directed at corporate behavior (e.g., limits on resource use, pollution, etc.) in the second half of the twentieth century, corporations were forced to divert a part of their economic resources to compliance and away from shareholder profit. This "signaled at least a temporary weakening in the grip of shareholder primacy as the paramount principle in defining the boundaries in the social contract between business and society" (White 2007: 8). The expectations of these corporate social obligations deeply divided the business community.

Adam Smith, a Scottish economist and philosopher, writing in *The Wealth of Nations* (1776), argued that free market economies are both more productive and more beneficial to society: "By pursuing his own interest [an individual] frequently promotes that of the society more effectually than when he really intends to promote it. I have never known much good done by those who affected to trade for the public good." In other words, private gain would yield public good.

Theodore Levitt, an economist and later a professor at the Harvard Business School, echoed Adams in a *Harvard Business Review* article, "The dangers of social responsibility": "The governing rule in industry should be that *something is good only if it pays*. This is the rule of capitalism" (1958: 48). And, Nobel Prize-winning economist Milton Friedman (1970), made precisely that argument in a *New York Times* article titled "The social responsibility of Business is to increase its profits."

Friedman, like Levitt, believed in Adam Smith's notion that "the invisible hand" would guide the marketplace, and that social good would come from the pursuit of profit. A corporate executive who assumes a "social responsibility" in his capacity as a businessman, acts in a way other than in the best interests of his employers.[4] Friedman explained:

> Insofar as his actions in accord with his "social responsibility" reduce returns to stock-holders, he is spending their money. Insofar as his actions raise the price to customers, he is spending the customers' money. Insofar as his actions lower the wages of some employees, he is spending their money. (Friedman 1970: SM17)

Identifying social responsibility as both unethical in the sense that "the corporate executive would be spending someone else's money for a general social interest," and "fundamentally subversive" in a free society, Friedman concluded with what has become recognized as "the Friedman doctrine":

> there is one and only one social responsibility of business to use its resources and engage in activities designed to increase its profits so long as it stays within the rules of the game, which is to say, engages in open and free competition without deception and fraud. (SM17)

The cycle of definition and redefinition of the social contract, the relationships between business, government, and society have been the result of changes in norms and expectations. The contract continues to evolve. The stark position advocated by Levitt and Friedman decades ago seems no longer defensible. Yet, as recently as 2010, Aneel Karnani, a University of Michigan professor, made a similar case against corporate social responsibility in the *Wall Street Journal*. Corporate social responsibility, he argued, is both irrelevant and ineffective. Companies that boost profits will end up increasing social welfare, so social responsibility efforts are irrelevant. In situations where social welfare and profit are in opposition, corporations will take profit over social welfare, so social responsibility is ineffective. But unlike Levitt and Friedman, Karnani added another element to the discussion:

> The danger is that a focus on social responsibility will delay or discourage more effective measures to enhance social welfare in those cases where profits and the public good are at odds. As society looks to companies to address these problems, the real solutions may be ignored. (2010: R4)

Over the last two decades, concerns about global economic stability; the escalation of unresolved social perils: poverty, disease, climate change, health care; corporate scandals and stories suggesting a business culture of excess and greed; and perceptions that the "safety nets provided by governments around the world have grown increasingly tattered" (Benett et al. 2009: 5) have contributed to an obvious discomfort with the way "we get along." Relationships between business, government and society have changed dramatically. According to the 2011 Edelman trust barometer findings, fewer than half of US consumers trust business to make the right ethical decisions (Edelman 2011). Somewhat ironically, perhaps, consumers are nonetheless looking to business to tackle global challenges; the 2012 Edelman goodpurpose global study found that 87 percent of Americans believe business "needs to place at least equal weight on society's interests as on those of business" (Edelman 2012). Norms and expectations of corporate involvement in social welfare have taken on a new complexity:

> Rather than simply assume the rights of "natural persons" under the legal systems in which they operate, corporations now also are expected to accept the responsibilities that come with being part of the human family. (Benett et al. 2009: 5)

In the section which follows, I briefly introduce cause-related marketing, outlining the dimensions it has assumed in our culture and in our business culture.

Cause-Related Marketing: Getting Consumers (Citizens?) Involved

Once, corporations were somewhat reluctant to link themselves with a cause, concerned that consumers would view corporate involvement as exploiting that cause for commercial gain. However, as noted, over the past 20 years, societal expectations about businesses' role in society have changed dramatically; consumers appear not only to expect corporate involvement in social concerns, but to reward it, and, indeed, to demand it. According to the 2010 Cone cause evolution survey, 88 percent of Americans say "it is acceptable for companies to involve a cause or issue in their marketing," and 90 percent indicate they want companies to tell them the ways they are supporting causes (Cone 2010). Additionally, the results of the survey indicate that consumers will reward companies they view to be good citizens in a number of ways including switching brands, trying a new or unfamiliar brand, purchasing a more expensive brand, deciding which companies they want doing business in their communities, choosing where to work, holding a positive image of the company, and recommending products or services to others.

One of a stable of corporate initiatives undertaken by corporations in response to consumer demands for greater social responsibility, cause-related marketing refers to those corporate initiatives that depend upon consumer participation. It first appeared on the scene nearly 30 years ago (1983), when American Express undertook to help in the restoration of the Statue of Liberty for its centenary in 1986. American Express donated 1 cent for each dollar cardholders charged to their card, plus made an additional donation for each new card application. At the conclusion of the effort, American Express donated $1.7 million to the Statue of Liberty–Ellis Island Foundation, and saw a 27 percent increase in card usage, and a 10 percent increase in new card applications (Kotler and Lee 2005; Schoenberg 2007).

Cause-related marketing initiatives today are diverse; the degree and nature of consumer involvement varies; the relationships developed in the process are often both intricate and complex. In some instances, consumers simply are asked to purchase a product; a percentage of sales (in many cases the percentage remains unspecified) goes to the cause. One of the best known of these purchase-triggered initiatives is Yoplait Yogurt's "Save Lids to Save Lives" program. Yoplait Yogurt promises to donate 10 cents for each pink foil lid redeemed via mail or online to Susan G. Komen for the Cure.[5] In other cases, companies create items particularly to raise money for a cause. In 2011 Coca-Cola introduced a limited edition white can in an "Arctic Home" holiday promotion benefitting the WWF (World Wildlife Fund). A code prompting consumers to text $1 donations to the WWF's efforts to protect polar bear habitats appeared on each can or white bottle cap; Coke matched consumer donations.[6]

In something of a hybrid of these two approaches to cause-related marketing, actor Paul Newman developed Newman's Own, a line of all-natural food products ranging from popcorn to salad dressing to lemonade. According to its website, Newman's Own "donates all profits and royalties after taxes for educational and charitable purposes." Another company, TOMS Shoes identifies itself as a "for profit with giving at its core," and promises "with every pair [of shoes] you purchase, TOMS will give a pair of new shoes to a child in need." Although TOMS is not without its naysayers, the company has become something of a movement among the college-age set.

In other instances, consumers are asked to buy a symbol of their support of a cause breast cancer's looped pink ribbon, a red dress pin for heart disease, a royal blue bracelet for prostrate cancer, "wearable proof," a visible declaration of concern" (Walker 2004). The Nike/Lance Armstrong "Live Strong" yellow silicone bracelets introduced in 2004 quickly became a widely recognized "charitable must-have" (Walker 2004). Extreme, fitness-based, fund-raising events such as the Leukemia and Lymphoma Society's Team-in-Training, the Susan G. Komen Race for a Cure, and Avon's 2-Day Walk for Breast Cancer have also become commonplace. In these events, charitable foundations link with corporate sponsors to provide endurance training programs for individuals who participate in long-distance bike rides, walks, marathons, and so on to raise money for a cause.

The Dangers of Cause-Related Marketing:
Underlying Ethical Problems

> *Cause related marketing's case*
> *has never been clearer or more*
> *compelling. More people are*
> *becoming increasingly*
> *civic-minded; supporting causes*
> *by purchasing products that*
> *promote them is a simple way to*
> *express this disposition.*
> *Simplicity is the key. That's why*
> *cause related marketing provides*
> *so much money for charitable*
> *causes; it's simply more*
> *convenient for consumers than*
> *other forms of fundraising.*
>
> Glenn 2003: 18

There is little doubt that corporate cause-related marketing fits almost seam-lessly, perhaps even comfortably, into America's consumer culture. Individuals routinely create their identities and announce their allegiances (as well as their generosity): buying, charging, even cooking for a cause; sporting yellow brace-lets, pink ribbons, Red iPods, and rough diamond and malachite bracelets; walking, running, and cycling for a cause. Indeed, cause-related marketing initiatives are so much a part of the business and cultural landscape that they proceed virtually unnoticed. Nearly 10 years ago, a writer in the UK trade press predicted:

> One day soon marketers will drop the prefix "cause-related" and see campaigns that stir the consumer's conscience as plain, simple marketing, unremarkable and barely worthy of comment. (Glenn 2003: 18)

His words now seem prescient. Rachel Chong (2010), CEO and founder of Catchafire ("Give What You're Good At"), wrote in the *Huffington Post*: "As a member of the Millennial Generation, cause-related marketing seems like plain ol' marketing to me."

The "good deeds" achieved through cause-related marketing are touted regu-larly in the media and public relations releases; there is no doubt that efforts depending on the "kindness of shoppers" raise considerable sums of money for "good causes." But, *are* cause-related marketing campaigns "unremarkable and barely worthy of comment"? It is precisely the normalization, the almost unconscious participation in an increasingly commodified philanthropy that underlies my belief that cause-related marketing as a business strategy is ethically flawed.

Cause-related marketing has been constructed as a "win–win–win, [providing] consumers an opportunity to contribute for free to their favorite charities" (Kotler and Lee 2005: 23). Yet, such celebratory assessments are simply snapshots of isolated campaigns, essentially micro-sites of success. At the risk of sounding clichéd – in looking at the trees we fail to recognize the forest of which they are a part. Such assessments naturalize the perception of consumption as a route to social benevolence, camouflage demands placed upon causes and transformations which occur as causes construct themselves to better fit the commercial logic inherent in cause-related marketing, and leave critical dimensions of the emerging social contract unexamined.

My argument is grounded in two characteristics inherent in the cause-related marketing enterprise:

- The injection of market-driven, profit-motivated strategic considerations into what might be identified as the "public sphere," that is, arenas never intended to be part of a market-based model.
- The blatant appeal to conspicuous consumption as an avenue to "building a better world," and the subsequent reconstruction of activism from a political act to an act of "buying more stuff."

The corporate adoption of cause-related marketing as a business strategy, and the resultant transformation of "causes" to "marketable products" has numerous far-reaching, and I believe, undemocratic, repercussions.

Injection of Profit-Motivated Strategic Considerations

My concern with regard to profit-motivated strategies entering into the realm of social issues is by no means a new one. Levitt (1958), writing more than half a century ago, voiced a concern similar to mine in his essay "The dangers of social responsibility." He noted there that

> at bottom [a corporation's] outlook will always remain narrowly materialistic. What we have, then, is the frightening spectacle of a powerful economic functional group whose future and perception are shaped in a tight materialistic context of money and things but which imposes its narrow ideas about a broad spectrum of unrelated noneconomic subjects on the mass of man and society. Even if its outlook were the purest kind of good will, that would not recommend the corporation as an arbiter of our lives. (Levitt 1958: 44)

In short, responding to calls for corporate social responsibility, he was pointing out the danger of corporate logic, with its "tight materialistic context of money and things," overwhelming the public sphere.

Several critics have pointed out, correctly I believe, that cause-related marketing is unsuited to create real social change (Schwartz 2003; Stole 2006; Eikenberry 2009). Vital social issues, by their very nature are controversial, and perhaps best addressed by "edgy" groups or through the use of controversial tactics (Stole 2006). Yet, focused on corporate and shareholder goals, corporations choose "safe" – noncontroversial, universally accepted, and popular causes. As such, corporations, critics argue, focus on symptoms more than on core problems. "The problem isn't shoelessness," wrote Kelsey Timmerman (2011), author of *Where Am I Wearing?* "The problem is poverty." "Consumption philanthropy," another critic noted, "distracts our attention and resources away from the neediest causes, the most effective interventions, and the act of critical questioning itself" (Eikenberry 2009: 52).

> Because CRM is driven by the need to increase a business's return on its investment, causes are selected not on the basis of the potential good that can be achieved but, rather, on the free publicity and increased sales a particular affiliation might bring to the business. (Stole 2006)

Today, frequently camouflaged in headlines of dollars raised and annual reports on corporate social responsibility is the simple fact that corporate decision-makers, motivated primarily by the needs and objectives of the *corporation* rather than by social welfare, regularly make decisions about the relative importance of the social needs in achieving or maintaining public welfare. What's a more vital concern? Environmental sustainability? Education? Or health care? Where should resources be allocated? To AIDS? To providing clean drinking water to the rural villages of Guatemala? Or to the preservation of the rainforest?

The "danger" of this decision-making is compounded by the fact that corporate decision-makers may have little or no competence or expertise of note upon which to make decisions, which in themselves may have far-reaching and long-term implications. Again, decisions regarding resource allocation in some of the most vital arenas of public welfare health, environment, and education are made by *marketing* professionals and *corporate executives* who are focused on corporate needs and objectives, rather than by professionals in the relevant areas. The lack of expertise is amplified by the fact that a decision to "partner" with a particular group involved in a cause is, at the same time, a decision to advocate a *particular* solution to the problem over other possible solutions. What is the best way to approach a health-related problem? Awareness? Early detection? Treatment availability? Research to find a cure? Research to find the cause? Do corporate decision-makers have the knowledge base and experience to weigh the efficacy of these approaches to solving the social problem?

In *Corporate social responsibility: Doing the most good for your company and your cause*, Kotler and Lee (2005) provided insight into how these decisions

---

Box 16.1   The Case of Breast Cancer Philanthropy

Samantha King has written that "breast cancer research and education remains a, if not *the*, favorite issue for corporations seeking to attract female consumers" (2004: 476). This suggests that corporations have made strategic decisions to "partner" with the cause. Why might this be so?

- In *Pink ribbon blues: How breast cancer culture undermines women's health*, Gayle Sulik notes: "Breast cancer has been transformed from an important social issue to a lifestyle choice that is now available to anyone who displays the brand . . . [A corporate sponsor] does not have to modify its own brand associations . . . Even without mention of awareness or research, pink symbolism and lifestyle are sufficient to convey the breast cancer brand and provide proper associations" (2011: 133, 144–145).
- Another reason might be name recognition and the pink ribbon. Barlette (2007) wrote: "The pink ribbon is the poster child for corporate cause-related marketing: it boosts the public image of the company and increases profits." And then, there's pink, which has "commandeered an entire month of pink ribbons, pink-clad NFL teams, Bank of America pink checking accounts, pink armbands, pink lunchboxes, pink Kitchen Aid food processors" (Horwell 2011).

---

are made when they identified "tough questions" corporations need to ask when choosing a social issue. These questions are:

- How does this support our business goals?
- How big a social problem is this?
- Isn't the government or someone else handling this?
- What will our stockholders think of our involvement in this issue?
- Is this something our employees can get excited about?
- Won't this encourage others involved in this cause to approach us (bug us) for funds?
- How do we know this isn't the *cause du jour*?
- Will this cause backfire on us and create a scandal?
- Is this something our competitors are involved in and own already? (Kotler and Lee 2005: 19)

Is this an ethical process of making decisions with regard to public welfare?

Box 16.2   Susan G. Komen for the Cure

Nancy Brinker, founder of Susan G. Komen for the Cure is "widely credited with turning [breast cancer] into a marketable product with which consumers, corporations and politicians are eager to associate" (King 2004: 475).

"The Komen Foundation's focus on early detection and cure-oriented science has helped it win generous sponsorship from pharmaceutical companies and mammography equipment and film manufacturers" (King 2006: 37).

Certainly everyone wants to find a cure, but "feminists even more ardently demand to know the cause or causes of the disease." The fact that the disease is increasing in industrialized nations suggests the possibility of environmental factors. But "[feminist] emphasis on ecological factors is not shared by groups such as Komen and the American Cancer Society. Breast cancer would hardly be the darling of corporate America if its complexion changed from pink to green." (Ehrenreich 2001: 47–48)

The ramifications of the commercial imperative become visible in other troubling ways. In the midst of what one author (Panepento 2007) writing in the *Chronicle of Philanthropy* identifies as "cause clutter," relationships between nonprofits and corporations become increasingly complex. Corporations seek associations with "well-known" causes and negotiate to establish initiatives that will "stand out." This is typically accomplished through some spectacular event, being "the first," or creating a particularly newsworthy initiative.

In the cause-related marketing scenario, nonprofits might view corporate involvement as "an opportunity to leverage big business to address complex social issues. What advertisers see is an ability to leverage desired demographics," and through the use of advertising, an opportunity to promote their corporate generosity (Koulish 2007). "More than a few cause campaigns are promoted in self-congratulatory advertising with larger budgets than the actual contributions the sponsors make" (Elliott 2009).

Box 16.3   The Breast Cancer "Audience"

"It is the very blandness of breast cancer, at least in mainstream perceptions, that make it an attractive object of corporate charity and a way for companies to brand themselves friends of the middle-aged female market" (Ehrenreich 2001: 48)

"The audience of breast cancer survivors, women at risk and supporters is the most highly valued product in the political economy of breast cancer, and corporations within and beyond the breast cancer industry pay large sums of money for access." (Sulik 2011: 112)

In aligning themselves with particular causes, and with particular participants in that cause, corporations are actively attempting to shape their own public image. At the same time, through their alliance with the cause and the promotion of that alliance, corporations shape public perceptions of the cause, its "definition," its characteristics, its scope, and its relative importance. Increasingly, celebrities are enlisted as "public faces" of the cause or effort. These celebrities, who frequently possess no particular expertise beyond their celebrity status, nonetheless contribute to the cause or brand's credibility. In *Brand aid: Shopping well to save the world*, Richey and Ponte note:

> Thus, it becomes not simply acceptable, but expected to find a photograph of Bono accompanying any major piece of news on African development in the media. The popular assumption that international development is a field populated by experts who tour exotic places in the company of supermodels helping grateful masses is a powerful virtualism. (2011: 13)

Then too, cause-related marketing provides corporations a way to "do good" and to enhance their social responsibility profile in a manner unrelated to what they do. This opens the possibility that behind a mask of benevolence, a corporation may be creating some of the very problems its cause-related marketing efforts are attempting to overcome. This scenario has become so commonplace as to have acquired a moniker: green-washing, once linked to the environmental movement, has given way to cause-washing and even pink-washing, "when a company or organization that claims to care about breast cancer by promoting a pink ribbon product at the same time produces, manufacturers, and/or sells products that are linked to the disease" (Breast Cancer Action 2011).

Box 16.4   Pink-Washing

A company or organization that claims to care about breast cancer by promoting a pink ribbon product, but at the same time produces, manufactures, and/or sells products that are linked to the disease is said to be pink-washing. Pink-washing also implicates the breast cancer organizations that are willing to accept donations and form partnerships. Breast Cancer Action has initiated a "Think Before You Pink" campaign to alert consumers to the practice.

The Story of AstraZeneca

National Breast Cancer Awareness Month (NBCAM) was founded in 1985 by Zeneca (now AstraZeneca), a multinational pharmaceutical corporation and then subsidiary of Imperial Chemical Industries. AstraZeneca is the manufacturer of tamoxifen, the best-selling breast cancer drug, and until corporate reorganization in 2000 was under the auspices of Imperial

Chemical, a leading producer of the carcinogenic herbicide acetochlor, as well as numerous chlorine and petroleum-based products that have been linked to breast cancer.

AstraZeneca's interest in promoting mammography and thereby raising detection rates and increasing sales of tamoxifen is a story widely circulated in activist circles and progressive media but almost entirely ignored in mainstream discourse. And, not surprisingly, AstraZeneca and its allies in National Breast Cancer Awareness Month, such as the American Cancer Society, continue to carefully avoid environmental issues, or indeed reference to prevention in general. (King 2006: xx–xxi)

In sum, the realization that a decision to support one cause over another, one solution over another, may be the result of no greater urgency than the corporate need to appear beneficent to a particular target market certainly gives one pause. Is this an ethical decision-making process?

To be sure, charities receive funding, sometimes substantial funding, from these partnerships, but again, in the corporate decision-making process, name recognition of the charity is likely to trump any social welfare criteria. What, one might ask, becomes of those worthy nonprofits doing vital work that don't fit the corporate profile or appeal to a "desirable" customer group?

In this "marketplace," charities are put in the unfortunate situation of having to construct their cause as a commodity in order to enhance their promotional attractiveness to potential "corporate partners." This is no easy task; the necessary research and negotiation take time and resources, both of which are frequently in short supply. "Suddenly," McAllister points out, "the supposedly noncommercialized not-for-profit organization becomes in essence a commercial entity" (1996: 214).

Philanthropy and Consumption: Who Knew Striving for Social Justice Was so Easy?

- Is the rise of philanthropic fashionistas decked out in Red T-shirts and iPods really the best way to save a child dying of AIDS in Africa? (Frazier 2007)
- Do you have to suffer and sacrifice to make the world a better place? Or can you just buy more cool stuff? (Schoenberg 2007)
- One problem with relying on consumers to right the world's wrongs is that most consumers are not very interested in or capable of righting the world's wrongs. The primary goal of people in marketplaces is to make choices that fulfill their self-interested, individual material needs and desires. In this capacity, they generally have little impetus to consider "the public" or "the public good." (Eikenberry 2009)

The Red campaign, grounded in the blatant appeal to conspicuous consumption, reignited a critical conversation about the linkage between consumption and charity inherent in cause-related marketing. Amid already virulent concerns about the ramifications of overconsumption exploitation and depletion of resources, environmental degradation, growing social inequities, intractable global poverty, concern of sustainability, escalating energy consumption, lack of clean drinking water, air pollution "the mix of conspicuous consumption and messianic benevolence" is indefensible to many (Marketing Week 2007).

This conversation is important insofar as it calls our attention to the often unnoticed, and hence unquestioned, commercialization of everyday life. I will not elaborate on that issue here. Instead, I'd like to suggest that in focusing narrowly upon the obvious issue of consumption another equally troubling dimension has been left out of this discourse: the redefinition of activism, the relinquishment of political voice.

Box 16.5   Pink Ribbon Culture: Is It Working?

- Pink ribbon culture has not succeeded in preventing and eradicating breast cancer, providing access to quality treatment and care, offering adequate and inclusive support or representations for the diagnosed, or managing conflicts of interest between advocacy, care and profit. (Sulik 2011: 23)
- Barbara Ehrenreich told an NPR interviewer that awareness created by the breast cancer culture is not getting at the real problem. "I'm not afraid of dying. But I'm terrified of dying with a pink teddy bear tucked under my arm. This is ugly. This is nasty. I want to know why it happens and I want to stop it" (Ehrenreich 2011).

Activism is typically viewed as an intentional action to bring about social or political change. Activism can take any number of forms: well-organized movements, boycotts, demonstrations, protests and marches, civil disobedience, letter writing. In the historical sense, activism incorporates dimensions of dissent, critical questioning, and demand for change. That is, it is a *political act* pursued by individuals and groups in their role as *citizens*. Increasingly, buying more stuff has replaced political activity: we are addressed as consumers rather than as citizens; we are invited to participate as individuals rather than as a collective; we are asked to buy to "make a difference," rather than to question or carefully consider the solution offered or even the beneficiaries of our largess. Unfortunately, immersed as we are in a consumption culture, we too rarely notice:

A person who uses a charity-licensed credit card to pay for an expensive meal, and thereby sends a percentage of his purchase to a cause that fights hunger, may no longer feel obligated to find out who is hungry or why they are hungry. Without this knowledge, he may feel less empathy for poor people, and therefore less compelled to change the conditions that cause their plight. (Eikenberry 2009: 54)

Conclusion

In this essay, I have argued that cause-related marketing as a business strategy is ethically flawed. At the heart of my argument is Levitt's observation: even if the corporation's "outlook were the purest kind of good will, that would not recommend the corporation as an arbiter of our lives" (1958: 44). The injection of profit-motivated corporate strategies into the public sphere has created a marketplace in which social causes are constructed as commodities, in which social causes are essentially "bought and sold" primarily to meet corporate objectives rather to advance public welfare. This is not ethical. This is not democratic.

- Should corporations, which by definition in our capitalist economy are profit-motivated enterprises, be primary decision-makers in identifying what is important, what is *most* important, for our social welfare?
- Are corporate decisions in the public arena informed by knowledge, expertise, and competence beyond that of marketing? Upon what criteria are those decisions being made?
- Are corporations interested in public welfare, or only the welfare of those (as experts in the field tell us) who have resources to spend and are willing to spend them?
- Should social causes be constructed, marketed, and sold like dishwashing detergent, breakfast cereal, and automobiles?
- Despite possible short-term benefits, are cause-related marketing efforts a suitable avenue to creating real, long-term social change?

Finally, in the midst of silicone bracelets of every hue; pink ribbons; red iPods; charging, running, riding, and cooking for a cause, what has become of activism? What does it mean to be politically active?

What we have witnessed over the past two decades is the emergence of a corporatized public sphere in which political sentiments and critical energies are largely expressed through the purchase of products, the donation of money to "good" causes or participation in volunteer activities. And, as the belief that America's survival depends on publicly celebrated, personal, consumer-based acts of generosity has attained hegemonic status, it becomes ever more difficult to think critically about such philanthropy and volunteerism and their place in US culture. (King 2004: 489–490)

Still, we must think critically. For in the midst of celebratory success stories, cultural spectaculars, and a buoyant trade press, any suggestion that cause-related marketing as a business strategy is ethically flawed may seem rather extraordinary. And yet, if we examine what goes on behind the curtain of the seeming normality of consuming for a cause, and if we ask and answer the difficult questions, perhaps it doesn't seem so extraordinary after all.

Epilogue

"Cause-related marketing, as we know it, is dead. It's not about slapping a ribbon on a product any longer." That assessment came from Carol Cone, nationally recognized as the "mother of cause marketing," late in 2010. Indeed, there are indications that corporate involvement in causes and cause-related marketing is changing, perhaps in very fundamental ways. By way of example, the Internet has provided a platform through which corporations "empower" consumers to "vote" on charitable causes to receive corporate funding. The Pepsi Refresh Project, for examples, gives millions to charities and good ideas submitted and subsequently selected by Americans across the country. Celebrity Kim Kardashian, acknowledging her status as a "brand," promoted her decision to stop posting on her social media accounts, to return only after she had raised $1 million for "Keep a Child Alive." An article in the Atlantic, "This is not charity" (Rauch 2007), discusses Bill Clinton and Ira Magaziner's creation of a foundation (with the help of a team of management consultants) to organize demand for public goods globally (in this case AIDS drugs) so that businesses are drawn to produce those goods. Essentially, they offered a business proposition if we get you the demand, can you get us the supply? Clinton noted: "I believe that in the years ahead, the organization and expansion of public-goods markets will become one of the most important areas of philanthropy, and will be an area where philanthropy sometimes blurs into strict private enterprise."

Do these efforts "recommend corporations as arbiters of our lives"? (Levitt 1958: 44). In this historical moment fraught with social and economic perils and uncertainty, efforts to link commercial interests strategically to charitable, social welfare initiatives should not be dismissed out of hand as ethically flawed, nor should they go unexamined.

Notes

1 See "The (Red) Manifesto" at http://www.joinred.com/aboutred.
2 Davis is credited with coining the term "causumer" for those who shop for a better world, trying to effect change through the marketplace."
3 See http://www.joinred.com/red/#impact. According to an Associated Press release dated January 23, 2011, the Global Fund reported that at least two-thirds of some grants were "eaten up by corruption" – donated drugs had been resold on black or commercial markets; funds had been lost, unaccounted for, pocketed, or misspent. The Fund

announced it was suspending grants from nations in which corruption had been discovered. The inspector general argued that the fact that the Fund was serious about uncovering corruption should be viewed as a "comparative advantage" to anyone thinking about supporting it.

4 I use the masculine pronoun here only because Friedman did so in his article.

5 Yoplait donations are capped at $2 million.

6 Donations were capped at $1 million.

References

Barlette, D. R. (2007) Pink ribbons or green dollar signs? *Arkansas Traveler* (Apr.). At http://www.uatrav.com/2007/04/19/pinkribbonsorgreendollarsigns/, accessed Apr. 8, 2013.

Benett, A., Gobhai, C., O'Reilly, A., and Welch, G. (2009). *Good for business: The rise of the conscious corporation*. Basingstoke: Palgrave Macmillan.

Breast Cancer Action (2011). Pledge to prevent pinkwashing. At http://bcaction.org/wp-content/uploads/2011/09/Pledge-to-Prevent-Pinkwashing.pdf, accessed Apr. 8, 2013.

Chong, R. (2010). Cause-related marketing: Just plain ol' marketing? *Huffington Post* (Jan. 4). At http://www.huffingtonpost.com/rachael-chong/cause-related-marketing-j_b_409633.html, accessed Mar. 29, 2013.

Cone (2010). Cone cause evolution study. Boston: Cone. At http://www.slideshare.net/EdelmanDigital/edelman-trust-barometer-executive-findings-6689233, accessed Apr. 8, 2013.

Edelman (2011). 2011 Edelman trust barometer findings. *Edelman Digital* (Jan. 24). At http://www.slideshare.net/EdelmanDigital/edelman-trust-barometer-executive-findings-6689233, accessed Apr. 8, 2013.

Edelman (2012). Edelman goodpurpose 2012 global consumer survey. *Edelman Insights* (Apr. 20). At http://www.slideshare.net/EdelmanInsights/global-deck-2012-edelman-goodpurpose-study, accessed Apr. 8, 2013.

Ehrenreich, B. (2001). Welcome to Cancerland: A mammogram leads to a cult of pink kitsch. *Harper's Magazine* (Nov.), 43–53.

Ehrenreich, B. (2011). Amid Breast Cancer Month, is there pink fatigue? (Audio interview). *NPR All Things Considered* (Oct. 16). At http://www.npr.org/2011/10/16/141402115/breast-cancer-when-awareness-simply-isnt-enough, accessed Mar. 29, 2013.

Eikenberry, A. M. (2009). The hidden costs of cause marketing. *Stanford Social Innovation Review* (Summer), 51–55.

Elliott, S. (2009). For causes, it's a tougher sell. *New York Times* (Nov. 12). At http://www.nytimes.com/2009/11/12/giving/12BUY.html?pagewanted=all&_r=0, accessed Apr. 8, 2013.

Frazier, M. (2007). Costly Red Campaign reaps meager $18M: Bono & Co. spend up to $100 million on marketing, incur watchdogs' wrath. *Advertising Age* 78(1): 1. At http://adage.com/article/news/costly-red-campaign-reaps-meager-18-million/115287/, accessed Mar. 29, 2013.

Friedman, M. (1970). The social responsibility of business is to increase its profits. *New York Times Magazine* (Sept. 13). At http://www.colorado.edu/studentgroups/libertarians/issues/friedman-soc-resp-business.html, accessed Mar. 29, 2013.

Glenn, M. (2003). There's a simple rationale behind ties with causes. *Marketing* (UK) (Mar. 20), 18.

Horwell, V. (2011). Singing the blues for pink. MediaPost News (Oct. 25). At http://www.mediapost.com/publications/article/161046/singing-the-blues-for-pink.html?e#axzz2Pehi8bhF, accessed Apr. 8, 2013.

Karnani, A. (2010). The case against corporate social responsibility. *Wall Street Journal* (Aug. 23), R1, R4.

King, S. (2004). Pink Ribbons Inc: Breast cancer activism and the politics of philanthropy. *International Journal of Qualitative Studies in Education* 17(4): 473–492.

King, S. (2006). *Pink Ribbons, Inc.: Breast cancer and the politics of philanthropy.* Minneapolis: University of Minnesota Press.

Kingston, A. (2007) The trouble with buying for a cause. *Maclean's* (Mar. 26), 40.

Kotler, P. and Lee, N. (2005). *Corporate social responsibility: Doing the most good for your company and your cause.* Hoboken, NJ: Wiley.

Koulish, R. (2007). Turning to corporate America to save the world. *Baltimore Sun* (July 22), 19A.

Levitt, T. (1958). The dangers of social responsibility. *Harvard Business Review* (Sept.–Oct.), 41–50.

Littler, J. (2009). *Radical consumption: Shopping for change in contemporary culture.* Maidenhead: Open University Press.

Marketing Week (2007). Charity: Paved with good intentions. *Marketing Week* (Mar. 15), 24.

McAllister, M. P. (1996). *The commercialization of American culture: New advertising, control and democracy.* Thousand Oaks, CA: Sage.

Panepento, P. (2007), Courting consumer dollars. *Chronicle of Philanthropy* 19(19): 21.

Rauch, J. (2007). "This is not charity." *Atlantic* (Oct.). At http://www.theatlantic.com/magazine/archive/2007/10/-ldquo-this-is-not-charity-rdquo/6197/, accessed Mar. 29, 2013.

Richey, L. A. and Ponte, S. (2011). *Brand aid: Shopping well to save the world.* Minneapolis: University of Minnesota Press.

Schoenberg, N. (2007). Buy(Less) targets cause-related marketing. *Chicago Tribune* (Mar. 23). At http://articles.chicagotribune.com/2007-03-23/features/0703220486_1_cause-related-marketing-charity-global-fund, accessed Mar. 29, 2013.

Schwartz, J. (2003). Socially responsible advertising: Altruism or exploitation? At http://www.judithstudio.com/acrobat/jschwartzessay.pdf, accessed Apr. 8, 2013.

Smith, C. (1994). The new corporate philanthropy. *Harvard Business Review* (May–June), 105–116.

Stole, I. (2006). Cause-related marketing: Why social change and corporate profits don't mix. *PR Watch* (July 14). At http://www.prwatch.org/node/4965, accessed Mar. 29, 2013.

Sulik, G. (2011). *Pink ribbon blues: How breast cancer culture undermines women's health.* New York: Oxford University Press.

Timmerman, K. (2011). The problem with TOMS shoes & its critics. At http://whereami-wearing.com/2011/04/toms-shoes/, accessed Apr. 8, 2013.

Walker, R. (2004). Live Strong bracelet. *New York Times Magazine* (Aug. 29).

White, A. L. (2007). *Is it time to rewrite the social contract?* Business for Social Responsibility. At http://www.tellus.org/publications/files/BSR_AW_Social-Contract.pdf, accessed Mar. 29, 2013.

Websites

Breast Cancer Action: www.bcaction.org
Business for Social Responsibility: www.bsr.org
Buy (Less): www.buylesscrap.org
Cause Marketing Forum: www.causemarketingforum.com
Cone Communications: www.conecomm.com
Edelman: www.edelman.com
Good Purpose: http://purpose.edelman.com/
Newman's Own: www.newmansown.com
Red campaign: www.redcampaign.org
Susan G. Komen: http://ww5.komen.org
Toms Shoes: http://tomsshoestoms.com/
Whereamiwearing: http://whereamiwearing.com/
WWF (World Wildlife Fund): http://worldwildlife.org/
Yoplait: http://yoplait.com/yoplait-in-action

Index
